Private/Public in 18th-Century Scandinavia

Cultures of Early Modern Europe

Series Editors:

Beat Kümin, Professor of Early Modern European History, University of Warwick, and Brian Cowan, Associate Professor and Canada Research Chair in Early Modern British History, McGill University

Editorial Board:

Adam Fox, University of Edinburgh, UK
Robert Frost, University of Aberdeen, UK
Molly Greene, University of Princeton, USA
Ben Schmidt, University of Washington, USA
Gerd Schwerhoff, University of Dresden, Germany
Francsesca Trivellato, University of Yale, USA
Francisca Loetz, University of Zurich, Switzerland

The 'cultural turn' in the humanities has generated a wealth of new research topics and approaches. Focusing on the ways in which representations, perceptions and negotiations shaped people's lived experiences, the books in this series provide fascinating insights into the past. The series covers early modern culture in its broadest sense, inclusive of (but not restricted to) themes such as gender, identity, communities, mentalities, emotions, communication, ritual, space, food and drink, and material culture.

Published:

Food and Identity in England, 1540–1640, Paul S. Lloyd (2014)
The Birth of the English Kitchen, 1600–1850, Sara Pennell (2016)
Vagrancy in English Culture and Society, 1650–1750, David Hitchcock (2016)
Angelica's Book and the World of Reading in Late Renaissance Italy,
Brendan Dooley (2016)
Gender, Culture and Politics in England, 1560–1640, Susan D. Amussen and
David E. Underdown (2017)

Food, Religion, and Communities in Early Modern Europe,
Christopher Kissane (2018)
Religion and Society at the Dawn of Modern Europe,
Rudolf Schlögl (2020)
Power and Ceremony in European History: Rituals, Practices and Representative Bodies since the Late Middle Ages, Anna Kalinowska and
Jonathan Spangler (eds.)
Private/Public in 18th-Century Scandinavia, Sari Nauman and
Helle Vogt (eds.)

Private/Public in 18th-Century Scandinavia

Edited by
Sari Nauman and Helle Vogt

BLOOMSBURY ACADEMIC
LONDON • NEW YORK • OXFORD • NEW DELHI • SYDNEY

BLOOMSBURY ACADEMIC
Bloomsbury Publishing Plc
50 Bedford Square, London, WC1B 3DP, UK
1385 Broadway, New York, NY 10018, USA
29 Earlsfort Terrace, Dublin 2, Ireland

BLOOMSBURY, BLOOMSBURY ACADEMIC and the Diana logo are
trademarks of Bloomsbury Publishing Plc

First published in Great Britain 2021

A catalogue record for this book is available from the British Library.

A catalog record for this book is available from the Library of Congress.

ISBN: HB: 978-1-3502-2489-6
         ePDF: 978-1-3502-2490-2
         eBook: 978-1-3502-2491-9

Typeset by Integra Software Services Pvt. Ltd.
Printed and bound in Great Britain

To find out more about our authors and books visit www.bloomsbury.com
and sign up for our newsletters.

Contents

Figures

Tables

Contributors

Charlotte Christensen-Nugues is Associate Professor in History of Ideas and Sciences at Lund University. Her research focuses on marriage and family in medieval and early modern legal, religious and political thought. She has published on tensions between individual and society, private and public, and their historical evolvement. Among recent publications is 'Parental Authority and Freedom of Choice: The Debate on Clandestinity and Parental Consent at the Council of Trent' (2014).

Jesper Jakobsen is Postdoc in History at the Centre for Privacy Studies, University of Copenhagen. His research interests focus on urban history, print culture and police regulation in eighteenth-century Scandinavia and northern Germany. He has published on censorship in eighteenth-century Copenhagen and Denmark-Norway.

Pernille Ulla Knudsen is Associate Professor in Legal History at the Faculty of Law, University of Copenhagen. Her research interests focus on legal history in early modern period with emphasis on the legal source material. She has researched and published on criminal law, administrative law, social history, procedural law, case law and legal methodology.

Ulrik Langen is Professor in History at the Saxo Institute, University of Copenhagen. His research focuses on urban and cultural history 1650–1850 and he has published several monographs within the fields of social history of communication including studies on ritualization, rumours, public disturbances, print culture and historical narrativity.

Dag Lindström is Professor in History at the Department of History, Uppsala University. His research interests focus on houses, households and cohabitation patterns in Early Modern towns, history of violence, craft guilds and unmarried adults in pre-industrial society.

Johannes Ljungberg is Postdoc in History at the Centre for Privacy Studies, University of Copenhagen. His publications focus on limits of toleration, notions of privacy, and entanglements of Enlightenment ideas and confessional culture in the Nordic countries and the German lands during the long eighteenth century. He is the editor-in-chief of *1700-tal: Nordic Journal for Eighteenth-Century Studies*.

Jørgen Mührmann-Lund is Associate Professor in History at the Western Norway University of Applied Sciences. He holds a PhD in early modern police history and has published a number of publications on this subject in Danish and English. In 2019, he published a monograph in Danish based on his PhD dissertation on police regulation in provincial towns and the countryside during Danish absolutism.

Sari Nauman is Postdoc in History at the Centre for Privacy Studies, University of Copenhagen, and the University of Gothenburg. Her research concerns early modern political culture, focusing on issues of uncertainty, such as communication, security, trust and control. Among her recent publications are the award-winning monograph *Ordens kraft: Politiska eder i Sverige, 1520–1718* (Lund: Nordic Academic Press, 2017) and '"You Cannot Pass": The Reception and Rejection of a Stranger in Helsingborg 1744', in *Migrants and the Making of the Urban-Maritime World* (ed. Christina Reimann and Martin Öhman).

Camilla Schjerning is Curator at Odense City Museums, where she is currently working on imagined geographies and urban identities in Odense 1800–2020. Her primary research interest lies within early modern urban cultural history, with a particular focus on the history of bodies, emotions and gender. She holds a PhD from the University of Copenhagen on the subject of violence, authority and emotional communities in eighteenth-century Copenhagen.

Göran Tagesson is Associate Professor in Historical Archaeology, and researcher at Department of History, Uppsala University. His main research interest is urban and buildings archaeology. 2016–2019 he was working with the research project *House and Household in Swedish Towns 1600–1850*, and from 2021 with the project *Houses and Social Practices in Swedish Towns 1600–1850*. His latest books are G. Tagesson & P. Carelli (eds.) (2016), *Kalmar mellan dröm och verklighet: Konstruktionen av den tidigmoderna staden,* and G. Tagesson et al. (eds.) (2020), *'For My Descendants and Myself, a Nice and Pleasant Abode': Agency, Micro-history and Built Environment: Buildings in Society International BISI III*, Stockholm 2017 (Archaeopress).

Helle Vogt is Professor of Legal History at the Faculty of Law, University of Copenhagen, Denmark. Her research has focused on comparative studies of Nordic law and legal practice especially in the middle ages and the early modern period focusing on penal law, kinship, inheritance, family, marriage, and the interaction with religious norms and learned law. She has published five monographs and edited eighteen books.

Acknowledgements

Private/Public in 18th-Century Scandinavia has generously been made Open Access by the Centre for Privacy Studies, University of Copenhagen (DNRF 138).

The private in the public: Scandinavia in the eighteenth century

Sari Nauman and Helle Vogt

The private is elusive.[1] Try to impose a definition upon it, and the concept will slowly seep through its margins, forcing the scholar to add qualifications and conditions until the definition is so cumbersome and circumscribed that it neither stimulates nor provokes. Try to focus on the phenomenon of the private, and it either fades or transforms into something else: something open, something public, something probed. Still, this should not lead us to despair. This volume understands elusiveness not as an impediment to study, but as an opportunity. The vague contours of the private, both as a term and as a concept, enable us to study it situated, as it always is, in its context. We seek to study the private not in contrast to the public, but in relation to it: in short, we explore the private in the public.

Most of the scholarly research on the private aspects of history has concentrated on the largest cities of Western Europe, chiefly London, Paris and Rome. It was in London that private life was born in the late seventeenth century, Philippe Ariès famously asserted, and during the next century or two it spread throughout Europe and to the rest of the world.[2] Even so, we suggest that focusing on the centre of the change only tells part of the story. A periphery does not passively absorb change; it adapts and acts on it as well. These actions may reverberate back to the centre, in an ongoing dialectical motion where cause and effect will be hard to differentiate. Thus, if we only keep our eyes on the centre, we risk overlooking the significant contributions to the narrative made by actors from the periphery. We seek to address this deficit by presenting research on the private in eighteenth-century Scandinavia. Research on the Scandinavian reception and adaptation of the private during this century is crucial, not only to remedy the narrow gaze of previous research, but also on its own terms. During this century, the two states of early modern Scandinavia – Denmark-Norway, and Sweden with Finland – experienced the same structural transformations that have been given explanatory value in the history of privacy in Western Europe: they witnessed state-formation, urbanization, globalization, the advances of print culture, confessionalization and commercialization. Furthermore, the aristocracy of both states frequently looked towards the major states of Europe for inspiration, modelling their homes and themselves after Parisian fashions. They welcomed foreign diplomats as their guests and travelled abroad for both business and pleasure. It seems as if the conditions for an easy spread of ideas concerning the private were ideal, making Scandinavia a model case study for the diffusion of such ideas.[3]

Then again, other conditions indicate a not-so-smooth transfer of ideas. As we will show in this introduction, the political culture in the Scandinavian countries differed considerably from its European counterparts, but it also differed markedly between the two Scandinavian states. In both states, the aristocracy had taken a step back during the eighteenth century, though this was due to very different reasons. In Denmark-Norway, absolutism remained strong throughout the period, forcing the aristocracy to compete internally for favour and position. In Sweden, peasants had had representation in the *riksdag* (the estates assembly) since the sixteenth century, and this estate continually gained influence. Additionally, members of the burgher estate grew increasingly prominent, and during this century their wealth often surpassed that of the aristocracy. When it comes to religion, Sweden was a confessional Lutheran state throughout the century, with minimal concessions allowed for other religious movements. In contrast, the Pietistic movement had gained considerable ground in Denmark-Norway during the first half of the eighteenth century. The significance of these political, economic, cultural and religious differences in shaping the reception of ideas about the private in the public still needs to be addressed. Yet research on the early history of the private in the Scandinavian countries remains scant, and often inaccessible to scholars working outside of the region.[4]

A major impediment to research on the private in Scandinavia is a linguistic one. As we shall discuss below, there is no word for privacy in Danish, Norwegian or Swedish. The absence of any direct translation of privacy into the Scandinavian languages not only hampers an etymological investigation, but it may also indicate a significant difference in approach to the concept of privacy, as well as to its implementation, in comparison to elsewhere in Europe. For this volume, we have therefore chosen to focus on 'the private' rather than on 'privacy' to come to terms with this difficulty. Whereas some of the contributions address the history of the term 'private' and how it was used in public life, others focus on how present-day notions of the private worked in the early modern setting. A joint conclusion from our investigations is that the private had a significant economic undertone in the Scandinavian languages during the eighteenth century, which influenced how people talked about and acted upon the private in the public.

In the following, we shall present the analytical tools of our endeavour – the props, if you will. We start with an investigation of the terms privacy, private and public in the Scandinavian languages, followed by an overview of research into the relationship between the private and the public. The volume starts from the assumption that the private and public neither were, nor are, fully separated, but instead constantly operate in relation to each other. In order to study the private, we thus have to pay special attention to the public, and to how the two interact. The section ends by identifying three key challenges facing those who seek to understand the private in the public during the early modern period: linguistics, the spatiality and temporality of the concepts, and the hitherto narrow geographical focus of existing research. After introducing our props, we then set the stage itself, presenting an overview of Scandinavia during the eighteenth century. Finally, we present our programme and open the curtains to our ten chapters on the subject.

Why the private instead of privacy?

On 27 April 2016, the European Parliament passed the General Data Protection Regulation (GDPR), and on 15 May 2018, the law came into force. The law is based on the principle of protecting the personal information of EU citizens. It was the culmination of a long tug-of-war between the European Parliament and private internet operators over the use of sensitive personal data on the internet. During this lengthy debate, one of the key issues under discussion (among other things) was the individual's right to self-determination and his or her control over the circumstances in which internet providers may use such information. With the adoption of this law, a new word familiar to all internet users entered into the Scandinavian languages: *privacy*.

Privacy belongs to the family of ideas centred on a citizen's rights in relation to the state and to his or her fellow citizens. The conceptual ancestry of privacy lies in the discourse of natural law that resurfaced in eighteenth-century Europe. The right to privacy is attached to the individual and to his or her needs, but it is difficult to define unambiguously what the concept of privacy covers. Often, it is simply defined as the right to have no one interfere in one's personal matters or as 'the right to be let alone'.[5] In this sense, privacy is often understood as the right to be one's self with regard to sexuality, attire, home or body. This right is to be enjoyed free from the infringement or interference of third parties, though it of course also operates within the restrictions set by the state's regulatory frameworks, both for the protection of the privacy of others and for criminal law.[6] However, it is only with the constitutional rights of the nineteenth century that the element of protection can first be seen, although it does not appear as an absolute right.[7] The protection of privacy as a legal right depends on the law, and not on the individual's personal understanding of when his or her privacy is violated.[8] Before it became a legal right, however, privacy had different connotations, which the word still evokes today. It belongs to the sphere of the individual, that which is close to home – both literally and figuratively.

Despite the difficulty in defining privacy, Scandinavians use the English term and talk about 'privacy policy', simply because there is no Scandinavian noun for this phenomenon. In Danish, it has recently been translated into *privathed*, a word that in its origin simply means something that is private and is now almost exclusively used in a legal context. Sweden still lacks an authorized translation of 'privacy'.

'Private', on the other hand, was a word imported into the Scandinavian languages much earlier, coming from the Latin *privatus*. In the second half of the eighteenth century, it became a regular word, spelled as *privat*. To investigate how *privat* was defined in the eighteenth century, we have consulted contemporary dictionaries. In the beginning of the eighteenth century, the Danish-Norwegian word *privat* had a very limited meaning. *Moth's Dictionary*, written by Matthias Moth (1649–1719) around 1700, is the first real Danish dictionary. It was a novelty internationally; not only did Moth register the language of the elite, but he also included slang and specialist terms.[9] Moth defined *privat* as civil – in the meaning of non-noble – or single.[10] In addition, *privat* was used adjectivally as an element with three compounds: private case, private school and private estate, the latter again meaning non-noble.[11] For Moth, *privat* was thus not defined as the antonym of public; this latter, that is, *publik* (public), was defined as 'common' or 'obviously'.

About hundred years later, in 1798, Christian Fredrik Bay published the first Danish-English Dictionary, and here we can observe quite a change in the definition of the word. Bay translated the Danish word *privat* as 'private' or 'particular',[12] but he also noted that *privat* was often used as an adverb, translated as 'privately'. Interestingly, if one looks up 'privately' in modern English-Danish dictionaries, all examples are from the economic sphere (e.g. to sell or own *privately*).[13] In the hundred years that had passed between the two dictionaries, the understanding of 'public' had also changed: the word *publik,* from the French *publique,* had been replaced by the German-inspired *offentlig (öffentlich).* This term unfortunately lacks English translations other than 'public', although it also has connotations of openness and of falling within the responsibility of the state. More importantly, Bay translated *offentlig* as belonging to the state or public, and thus as the antonym of 'private'.

Two early Swedish dictionaries, Archbishop Haquin Spegel's *Glossarium – Sveo-gothicum* (1712) and Jesper Swedberg's *Swensk ordabok* (1714), include neither *privat* nor *publik.* In Abraham Sahlstedt's Swedish-Latin dictionary, *Dictionarium Svecicum* (1773), *privat* was firstly defined as that which is not public, and secondly as personal or separate, *enskild.*[14] *Publik,* on the other hand, was defined by Sahlstedt as communal *(allmän)* and *offentlig.*[15] According to Sahlstedt, *offentlig* meant *solemnis* in Latin, that is solemn or established.[16] Spegel and Swedberg both gave *offentlig* the Latin definition of *apertus* (open) and *manifestus* (manifest, evident), and Spegel suggested an English translation of 'openly'.[17]

More information on the private is given in *Svenska Akademiens ordbok* (SAOB) (1954), which includes a report on how the term has been used since it first occurred in the Swedish language in the middle of the sixteenth century. According to SAOB, during the sixteenth and seventeenth centuries, *privat* was mainly used as an adjective, modifying nouns in such a way as to mark that they did not pertain to the state or the public: for example, a private gathering, private business, private house. During the eighteenth century, *privat* also developed connotations of 'non-noble'. Mainly, though, *privat* kept its place as a term signifying that which did not pertain to the state, to the public, or to the common good of the people – this during a period when public debate was limited to discussing issues of the state. The private was thus something potentially harmful, signalling (economic) resources that did not contribute to the public goods.[18]

The dictionaries provide a good indication of eighteenth-century developments in the meaning of *private* within a Danish and Swedish linguistic context. Our investigation indicates that the word private – in the meaning of 'not public' – came into the Swedish language much earlier than the Danish, although it was not defined in early dictionaries. For this reason, this volume includes a contribution by Charlotte Christensen-Nugues investigating how the word *privat* was used in the public discourse in Sweden during the period 1521–1730. Christensen-Nugues focuses on the debates within the Swedish *riksdag,* and her chapter provides an in-depth analysis of how *privat* entered the Swedish language. Her findings are followed up by Pernille Ulla Knudsen in a chapter investigating the use of the word *privat* in eighteenth-century

Danish newspapers; together, these two chapters provide an indispensable foundation for the other investigations in this volume.

The private and the public intertwined

Street life in the major cities in Europe began to stir during the late seventeenth and eighteenth centuries, stimulating public debate about political issues – a process that Jürgen Habermas famously described as the emergence of a public sphere.[19] As men moved into the public to debate politics, women moved to a secluded indoors, with an increasing responsibility for and devotion to domestic life. Whereas, before, opportunities for privacy had been sorely lacking and perhaps not even missed, Victorian homes now closed their doors to the public and focused on private family life. Or so the story goes.

Although it subsequently became envisioned as such, for Habermas, the public sphere was not a spatial concept at all. According to Brian Cowan, such an interpretation resulted from the untranslatability of a central Habermassian concept: Habermas wrote about *Öffentlichkeit*, which in English and French became spatialized as the 'public sphere', or *l'espace public*.[20] The English and French translation of the German term *Öffentlichkeit* effectively changed Habermas' meaning – and with it, his theoretical framework. Nevertheless, it proved to be quite a fruitful change; as Cowan puts it, 'as much was gained as was lost'.[21] The idea of separate spheres initially inspired researchers to spatialize public and private life, locating the public in outdoor spaces, where men met to discuss and make their influence known on politics and development. In reaction to this, early feminist scholars turned their gaze inwards, investigating indoor spaces, especially the homes, which were identified as the private spaces to which women were confined. The Victorian household was especially scrutinized, since it was viewed as the centre from which the idea of separate spheres slowly spread across Europe.[22]

The last three decades of research have been devoted to the deconstruction of this traditional narrative. Major contributions have been made, primarily from the field of gender history, that expose how the boundaries between the two spheres were neither factual nor absolute. There are some excellent research overviews of these developments, so there is no need to enter into historiographical detail here.[23] To keep it short, we will limit ourselves to highlighting two main findings. First, the home was never quite as private as previously imagined. Small living spaces were shared by the majority of the people, and subletting apartments to travellers and newcomers ensured a steady flow of outsiders within the boundaries of the home. Private homes continued to act as public spaces that were open for guests and were arenas for both political debate and commercial activities.[24]

Second, public spaces were not all male, and neither were they altogether public. Although there might have been an ideal for some women to stay at home from the late eighteenth century onwards, such enclosure was very seldom practical. First of all, the ideal was not common to all – it might have been present for upper- and middle-upper-class women, but common people were dependent on movement between spaces. Secondly, wives and daughters, not to mention servants, frequently strayed outside, conducting businesses, shopping, travelling, gossiping and arguing. Private business could be resolved in the streets, and open spaces were accessible to more groups than has previously been acknowledged – although some spaces were of course more accessible than others.[25]

The current line of research thus supports what Dena Goodman had already concluded in 1992: the private and the public were never strictly opposed, nor were they even essentially separated, and they were not restricted to practices conducted indoors or outdoors.[26] Lately, this recognition has directed the scholarly gaze towards the previously assumed boundaries between spaces; concepts such as liminality and thresholds have generated new, exciting results on how public and private could spill over into each other.[27] For example, Amanda Vickery has shown that the steady stream of lodgers in the houses of eighteenth-century London led to constant renegotiations of private space. 'Access to privacy was an index of power', she concludes, but even the lowliest servant usually had access at least to the private space of a small box.[28] Other scholars have focused on street life, and how private and public intermingled in these open spaces. Based on an investigation of violence in the streets of Bologna, Sanne Muurling and Marion Pluskota have shown how peoples' actions need to be taken into account when defining spaces, and they argue for the addition of 'spaces of sociability' into our framework of early modern urban life. The ability to stop and exchange private information in public spaces certainly shows just how complex it is to see the private and the public as separate entities.[29]

Together, the evidence suggests that whether a space was private or public is not merely a product of its spatial location, but it must also be seen as temporally contingent. A space could be private, or public, or even both simultaneously, depending on what happened there at that particular moment. Thus, concepts that speak to the spatiality of these concepts – liminality, porosity – need to be complemented by concepts that address its temporality, such as simultaneity, coincidentally or subsequentality. As Danielle van den Heuvel has suggested, for example, focusing on movement and how the meaning of spaces was constantly being negotiated might be a way forward.[30] We also need to acknowledge the many different publics available, both on various levels of society – the family, the neighbourhood, the state – and for different aspects of public life – morality, sociability, economic aspects. The different kinds of public become clear in the contributions to this volume by Camilla Schjerning and Ulrik Langen, who show that while the state, through legislation and court practice, tried to protect the home and the 'private life' of its inhabitants, the public morality of the neighbourhood challenged both the state's public polities and the peace and order of public spaces.

Another way forward has been suggested by Daniel Jütte and Laura Gowing respectively. In his studies of early modern thresholds, doors and windows, Jütte has highlighted how material innovations have influenced not only peoples' capability to promote privacy within their homes, but also their perceptions of home and the private in general.[31] In a recent study of bedposts, Gowing has further highlighted the potential rewards of placing materiality into focus. By investigating what kinds of action could take place at a space that is, to us, so clearly marked as private, she thus demonstrates empirically some of the abstract points that Erica Longfellow has argued for: if we start by assuming that our notions of private match those of earlier times, we may miss out on highly thought-provoking results.[32]

What also adds to the difficulties in defining a shift in the role of private and public life during the seventeenth to nineteenth centuries is the fact that as soon as we zoom in on particular cities, neighbourhoods, households or individuals, it becomes harder and harder to define an exact moment for this shift. Different regions, different periods and different scholarly approaches generate considerably different results; while some researchers place the shift earlier in history, others push its commencement towards later periods, or deny that it happened altogether.[33] The historian's endeavours to avoid simplification and to stress the complexity of change further accentuate the need to draw attention to these differences. Separate spheres rose as an ideal, influencing the everyday life of – at least – townspeople in European cities during the eighteenth century; but how individuals handled day-to-day challenges in this respect is a different story.

Several researchers of late have therefore started to make comparisons between case studies in order to determine which factors influenced variations in the configuration of the public and private. Manon van der Heijden and Sanne Muurling, for example, have shown that men and women living in eighteenth-century Bologna and Rotterdam had the same experiences of violence in the streets. But legal and socio-economic positions of women in the two cities meant that women from Rotterdam were more likely to stand up against violent husbands, as well as to take part in violent acts far away from their homes.[34] In a comparison between St Petersburg and Helsinki, Marjatta Rahikainen argues that the materiality of cities must be taken into account, as buildings bear traces of past power structures: 'the physicality of urban space is conservative in essence.'[35] These findings should encourage us further to compare different regions, in order to understand the range of possibilities that existed in the early modern world. For example, comparisons between urban and rural areas are perturbingly few, and the tale of urban private and public spheres has been set as the standard for the eighteenth century. Still, a clear majority of people in all European countries dwelled in rural settings at the beginning of the nineteenth century. Moreover, Western Europe – and mainly England and France – have been given a dominant position in the historiography, and the findings from these countries are assumed to be applicable for less researched areas and taken as a truth, without regard for possible differences. In recent years, the international research community has started to amend this troubling deficiency, and cities in the Netherlands, the Holy Roman Empire, Spain and Italy have been incorporated into the general narrative. Still, a wider gaze is sorely needed.

The three challenges identified above can be summarized as follows:

1. Whereas linguistic definitions of the private and the public tend to separate the two terms, those who investigate them in practice increasingly argue for a conceptual amalgamation of the two, or at least awareness of the possibility of such.
2. The private and the public have spatial connotations, but cannot be spatially contained. To investigate them, we need to add a temporal perspective, focusing on movement and materiality.
3. A strong geographical focus on the major cities of Western Europe has resulted in a one-dimensional narrative, neglecting the potential insights to be gained by looking at the periphery.

This volume presents research on the private in early modern Scandinavia, a region in the periphery of Western Europe. While some of the chapters investigate the term private – how it was used and what it meant in different settings – other chapters explore what the private meant in practice. All start from the assumption that the private cannot be clearly separated from the public. Our research concerns that which is defined as private, either by historical actors or by our own understanding, but is discussed and scrutinized in the public. In fact, when looking for the private, all investigations herein make almost exclusive use of public source material: legislation, newspapers, court practice, records, insurance policies, wills, etc. Hence, we study the private from a public point of view, which also means that the closer we come to the private, the more blurred the line between private and public becomes.

Our joint endeavour is thus to investigate the private *in* the public. To do so, it is vital to recognize different kinds of private and public. Both concepts need to be treated as spatially and temporally contingent, meaning that what was private in one setting was not necessarily defined as such in another. In this volume, we adhere to this claim by not proposing an overall definition of the private, choosing instead to stay open to the particularities of each case study. The privateness of a conversation between individuals may not be readily comparable with the private business of a bailiff taking bribes, but it is our contention that the sheer range of possible connotations says something essential about the private. It demonstrates the elusiveness of the concept, and the need for a broad perspective if we are to understand it more fully.

The Scandinavian setting

When comparing Scandinavia to other countries in or outside of Europe, it is easy to point to all the similarities within the Scandinavian region. Five centuries ago, Denmark, Norway and Sweden (with Finland) were tied together in a personal union under a joint ruler. Today, the countries share a common social politics, with a relatively high tax load to provide social securities for its populations. Cooperation is extensive, passports are not needed for travel within the region, and there is even talk about a common 'Scandinavian culture', blurring the borders between the states. However, the idea of Scandinavia as a homogeneous region is a twentieth-century phenomenon.

Political life

In the early modern period, Scandinavia was composed of two kingdoms: Denmark-Norway, a unified realm over the period 1537–1814, and Sweden, which also incorporated Finland until 1809, when Finland became part of the Russian Empire. Norway and Finland only received independence in 1905 and 1917 respectively. At the beginning of the eighteenth century, Denmark-Norway and Sweden had been at war on and off for more than two centuries. In 1721, a peace treaty ended the Great Northern War. Previously, Sweden had been a major player in European politics, and it enjoyed a firm hold of the Baltic region; but according to the peace treaty, many of its territories were to be ceded to, among others, Russia and Brandenburg-Prussia. As the eighteenth century progressed, both Denmark-Norway and Sweden were forced to accept their fate as small states. Yet, despite their shared prospects, differences in political life were considerable.

In Denmark-Norway, a far-reaching absolutism was imposed in 1660, and the system proved to be very stable: it was only replaced by a constitutional monarchy in 1848.[36] With the introduction of absolutism, the old Danish nobility lost much of its power and its privilege.[37] In a combined effort to raise money for the state and to create an influential group loyal to the king, a new nobility with purchasable noble ranks was introduced in 1671.[38] The interests of this new nobility and the bourgeoisie often overlapped, but conflicted with those of the landowning and conservative nobility. Peasants were excluded from political influence; even freeholders were dependent on their landlord or the king, legally and economically.[39]

In Sweden, on the other hand, absolutism never gained a strong hold. It was introduced in 1682 but abolished in 1719. Reinstated for a short period in 1772, it was finally abolished for good in 1809. The years between the two absolutist periods have been labelled 'The Age of Liberty' in Swedish history, which is renowned as a period during which the *riksdag* experienced its heyday. The *riksdag* included representatives from all four estates – nobles, priests, burghers and peasants – and took part in internal and foreign affairs, taxation and legislation. Because of its strong negotiating position vis-à-vis the king and government during these years, the *riksdag* effectively ran the country.[40] The peasant estate thus played a significant political role in the seventeenth and eighteenth centuries. It had undeniable rights that royal and governmental authority had to respect, even in wartime, or risk rebellion.[41] Sari Nauman's contribution to this volume attests to the readiness of the Swedish peasant population to protest against wayward public servants and use the undertones of the public and private to argue their case.

Economic life

Sweden and Denmark-Norway both mainly stayed neutral in the relentless wars between the great European powers.[42] Neutrality made it possible for Scandinavian ships to enter ports across Europe and the colonies, and to trade with all.[43] This 'blossoming trade period', as it was known in Denmark-Norway, differentiates the Scandinavian countries from those where continuous wars drained national treasuries.[44] The flow of money to Bergen, Copenhagen and Stockholm increased during the century, and only came to a halt when Denmark-Norway entered the Napoleonic Wars.

The material culture of the aristocracy shared many common features across Europe at this time, although slight regional variations were of course also the case.[45] Consequently, life in Scandinavian towns seems to have differed in degree rather than in kind from that of other European towns. Goods were brought in from around the world to satisfy the desires of families of means, and port cities were frequented by sailors, travellers, diplomats and spies.[46] In eighteenth-century Stockholm and Copenhagen, coffee and alehouses enabled people (almost exclusively men) to meet and discuss the economy and politics on a daily basis – though, similar to other

European cities, some women also had access to these spaces. These localities enabled meetings that bridged political, economic and gender barriers, among others.[47]

Not only men, but women too participated in commercial and public life in early modern Scandinavia, including trade, credit and vending markets.[48] Scandinavian society during this period was built upon a two-supporter system; even though a man nominally stood as the owner of a business, he depended on his wife and, most often, his servants to operate it – and furthermore, this was recognized and taken for granted by both state and society. If a man passed away, his widow could get permission to take over his business and run it on her own or with the help of servants for several years, sometimes for the rest of her life.[49] In addition, as shown in this volume by Pernille Ulla Knudsen in her article about Margrethe Stampe, women could run businesses in their own right – without the interference of a husband – if the couple had made private arrangements before they married. A husband's right to control the property of his wife could thus be circumvented.

During the eighteenth century, the question of whether businesses relating to public life and spending – such as tax revenues, street lighting and waste management – should be under the state's organization or handled by private persons was a recurring subject of debate. The same types of argument resurfaced over the years: private companies could do a more effective job, but were prone to corruption and sought profit at the expense of the common man.[50] A significant difference in the Swedish debate on the one hand, and the Danish-Norwegian one on the other, was that the *riksdag* in Sweden was an important arena for discussions on the private economy and taxes, and state regulated trade as opposed to free trade. In Denmark-Norway, this discussion tended to take place instead within patriotic societies, journals and newspapers.[51]

Religious life

Both states embraced the Lutheran reformations from an early date. In Sweden, the process started in 1527, but, because of a later dynastic connection with Catholic Poland, a full transformation was slow. It did not fully take hold until the seventeenth century and was marked by the strong observance of Lutheran orthodoxy.[52] In Denmark-Norway, the reformation was introduced in 1536–1537, and the state's control over the church and religious behaviour was strong from early on.[53] To avoid religious conflicts, both Scandinavian kingdoms developed mono-religious cultures, making it increasingly difficult for non-Lutherans to settle; even if they were allowed, they were subject to severe restrictions. Immigration therefore primarily came from other parts of Scandinavia, or from Lutheran Germany and the Baltic region, and centred on labour migration.

One of the foundational building blocks in Lutheran states was the idea of the household, both as an analogy for the state and as a family ideology. Whereas the king was responsible for upholding the Christian faith and for controlling the behaviour of his subjects, it was the obligation of the householder and housewife to uphold morality and Christian behaviour within their household, and to instruct and correct those who violated Christian norms. To perform this task, the head of the household was to read aloud to his subordinates from the Bible and from other moral literature, such as the many books of sermons.[54] The Lutheran ideal of the housefather was most instrumental to the high literacy rates of both Sweden and Denmark-Norway from an early date. Confirmation, which included lessons in reading, was made mandatory in Denmark-Norway in 1734, and in Sweden in 1811. Even earlier, the Swedish Church law of 1686 made it obligatory to know Luther's *Small Catechism* by heart before receiving first communion. Even children of the lower classes were to acquire elementary reading skills, and most children received some education in reading and religion.[55]

With the emergence of Pietism in Denmark in the eighteenth century, increased focus was placed on the education of the common people, one of the consequences of which was that the Danish Poor Laws of 1708 gave poor children the right to receive a free education.[56] The Pietistic movement came to the Nordic countries from Germany and represented a new way to embrace the Protestant faith. It focused on the individual's relationship with Jesus, challenging both state institutions – that is, the parish priest and the church – and the housefather's central function. The official approach to Pietism differed markedly between Denmark-Norway and Sweden. In Denmark-Norway, a state Pietism developed in the 1720s; the state adopted Pietistic religious ideas and controlled the movement. In Sweden, on the other hand, Pietism never gained public recognition, and Pietistic ideas were seen as heresy. Johannes Ljungberg's article in this volume investigates how the Swedish state tried to deal with private, Pietistic expressions.

Social life

Increased literacy rates were combined with liberal legislation on censorship in the late eighteenth century, in both Scandinavian countries. In 1766, Sweden became the first country in the world to introduce legally guaranteed freedom-of-print, with exceptions only applying to religious and state matters. Denmark followed with an unrestricted bill in 1770, although it was gradually curtailed in subsequent amendments from 1771 and 1773.[57] The legislation was effective: several print publications began to circulate, disseminating news from around the world. Moreover, a considerable amount of the printed texts – such as books, newspapers, leaflets etc. – that circulated came at such low prices that even the lower classes could afford them. In his contribution to this volume, Jørgen Mührmann-Lund shows that the texts were often formatted to look like letters, both signed and addressed, giving them the trustworthiness of private communication. The publications opened up a completely new world of fiction, as well as providing knowledge about foreign places and customs, serving as a forum for gossip, etc., thereby giving readers food for thought. As Jesper Jakobsen demonstrates in his chapter, the Danish market was used to expose private information to further the publisher's or writer's interests, forcing the government to deal with the right to privacy before this right was ever formulated.[58]

Still, there was not much private physical or mental space within most individual households. In rural and urban communities alike, most people lived in small houses of one or two rooms, sharing sleeping quarters with family and guests.[59] Scandinavia was – and is – less densely populated than the rest of Western Europe, and it was also less urbanized. At the beginning of the nineteenth century, Sweden's largest city, Stockholm, had about 75,000 inhabitants, and its second largest city, Gothenburg, only 15,000. Ninety per cent of Sweden's total population still lived in rural areas.[60] During the same period, Denmark was only slightly ahead with 100,000 living in the capital of Copenhagen, and about 80 per cent living in rural areas.[61] Urbanization was definitely not a generalized Scandinavian phenomenon; rather, it was concentrated to the two capitals of Copenhagen and Stockholm, and the Norwegian trade town of Bergen. Other Scandinavian towns were quite small compared to their European counterparts.

Scandinavian households during this period are, like many others in Europe, best described as open: residents, friends and family constantly crossed its thresholds.[62] Spatially focused studies of Scandinavia thus support the wider research trends concerning European privacy, concluding that private and public spaces were neither clearly separated nor exclusively gendered, but should instead be understood as porous and permeable. However, even in the provincial towns, household patterns and the structure of living quarters experienced significant change over the eighteenth century. Increased urbanization in this period led to other kinds of households that had just one or two members, challenging the traditional idea of the household as one of the core building blocks of society. As Dag Lindström and Göran Tagesson demonstrate in their chapter, even in a small provincial town such as Linköping, larger town houses were built during this century with a greater number of clearly differentiated rooms. Although their sources do not permit conclusions as to the actual usage of the rooms, the transformation certainly increased the potential for an indoor private life. Stockholm witnessed a similar development, largely due to the growing importance of the parliament during this century.[63] During the first two decades of the eighteenth century, the city received large numbers of refugees from Finland and the Baltic provinces due to the Great Northern War, which put a strain on the economy of the city and its inhabitants; but overall, the eighteenth century was a period of economic growth.[64]

The same transformations are noticeable in Copenhagen. It was the most important city in the twin-monarchy of Denmark-Norway, both politically, economically and intellectually; it was the residential city of the monarchy, the trade centre of the state and Denmark's only university was found here. The city witnessed significant changes during the second half of the eighteenth century: the poor areas became even more overpopulated, and, in the wealthier parts of the city, new grand town houses and domiciles cropped up.[65] In this volume, Camilla Schjerning and Ulrik Langen both demonstrate that as Copenhagen became increasingly crowded, private matters were taken as public evidence for the degradation of homes and people, forcing residents to defend themselves with words and deeds.

Structure of the book

All chapters in this volume address the private in the public. They investigate this issue by using public records and sources in which the private is addressed either linguistically or conceptually. A first section, 'Situating the Private', comprises two chapters that use a terminological approach to examine the use of the word private in contemporary sources. In the first chapter, Charlotte Christensen-Nugues studies occurrences of the word *privat* in the Swedish *riksdag* records from 1521 to 1730. Not only was *privat* an antonym to *publik* but it was also used to signal a direct threat to the public interest. In contrast, eighteenth-century Danish newspapers primarily used *privat* in an economic context, as shown by Pernille Ulla Knudsen. Here, citizens emerge as private economic actors in the framework of civil society. The legal theory of private property as formulated within natural law by Samuel Pufendorf contributes to a general understanding of the development of the private economy in early modern times.

The following section, 'Communication', collects four chapters that deal with private communication in a public context. Chapters 3 and 4 concentrate on communications explicitly labelled as private. Johannes Ljungberg uses protocols from commissions sent out to investigate reports on Pietistic activities in 1720s Sweden as his main sources. He argues that the judicial processes rested on older notions of privacy, but also triggered new ideas on how communication could be classified and evaluated, as well as protected from external control by being described as private. Jørgen Mührmann-Lund examines the imitation of private letters in Danish printed news articles on foreign events. Drawing on the traditional letter genre, Mührmann-Lund shows that the letters' style conveyed authenticity and immediacy to the reader and was therefore considered to be more reliable than official news. Early modern readers thus used a form of source criticism, leading them to prefer personal to official communication. Both Ljungberg and Mührmann-Lund are able to demonstrate that the private could have positive connotations to an eighteenth-century audience.

Chapters 5 and 6 make use of present-day notions of the private and investigate how the authorities and individuals came to terms with private affairs being vented publicly. Jesper Jakobsen examines the work of the censors in late eighteenth-century Copenhagen. While we know from previous research that early modern states were keen on suppressing discomforting information regarding foreign and internal affairs, Jakobsen reveals how they also suppressed defamatory announcements in what can be described as early interventions for the right to privacy. Camilla Schjerning makes use of court records from Copenhagen, focusing on the phenomenon of house-scorning. She argues that exposures of the hidden body and secrets of the household became strategic means for negotiating both the physical and moral boundaries of the household. The body and emotional practices such as shaming emerge as vehicles for both producing and understanding privacy in the early modern world.

The section on communication clearly shows that private communication was a public event. Even though the specifics of what was said were not to be communicated further, the ability to have private conversations, and to have them protected from external interference, was discussed and defended publicly. Furthermore, making others' private lives public knowledge was used to further one's own position in the public, both by demonstrating one's knowledge of other peoples' business and by degrading and shaming others.

The third section, 'Spaces', takes the reader indoors into private homes, courthouses, brothels and communal buildings, and outdoors to the streets, squares and courtyards.

The chapters in this section investigate how people interacted with space and place, and how the private was performed within the public. Chapters 7 and 8 examine the town houses of merchants and the elite, respectively. Combining archaeological, architectural and historical sources, Dag Lindström and Göran Tagesson uncover profound modifications to the town houses of Linköping in Sweden during the eighteenth century. While population density and the number of tenants and lodgers increased, the average number of people living in a household declined. New building elements were introduced, which enhanced indoor comfort and promoted possible seclusion. A new house type thus developed among the merchants, separating a potentially semi-public indoor space from more private indoor spaces. Pernille Ulla Knudsen probes a specific elite town house in Copenhagen further, namely that of Margrethe Elisabeth, the widow of the Prime Minister Henrik Stampe. By going through executor records and fire insurance policies, Knudsen creates a holistic picture of the private life inside the walls of this town house and gives a 'reconstruction' of the physical rooms of the Stampe mansion.

The ninth chapter takes us to the Struensee regime in Copenhagen 1770–1772. Ulrik Langen investigates the spatial references in a specific bill to houses as places fundamentally off-limits to city authorities. He discusses the imagined social consequences of protecting the spatial privacy of city dwellers even for the short duration of the Struensee regime, during which it was illegal for the police to enter peoples' private homes. By studying both the ordinance of Struensee and the countermeasures taken after his fall, Langen exposes the controversial qualities that were ascribed to private life by the public.

The tenth and final chapter leaves the city altogether and examines a peasant rebellion in rural Sweden. Using court records, Sari Nauman investigates accusations made against a bailiff who had taken payments for private gain when conducting his public affairs. Nauman shows how the peasants adapted their actions to different public spaces, using the courthouse to present their argument, the courtyard to perform their punishment, and the open road to dispose of the body. Together, the actions speak to the peasants' spatial awareness and to the importance of publicly performing accusations, even those that concerned private business.

From the chapters in the second section, we conclude that private and public spheres were especially malleable because people moved into and out of them – and people used this malleability to their own advantage. Private actions and private lives took place within public actions and public lives, not in isolation from them. By looking at the interaction between private and public, rather than treating the two notions as distinct and antagonistic, the studies collected here let us see how early modern people navigated the private aspects of life, along with all the potential dangers and benefits that accompanied those private aspects.

Notes

1   This project has received generous support by the Centre for Privacy Studies, University of Copenhagen, funded by the Danish National Research Foundation, and the Centre for Interdisciplinary Studies of Law, Faculty of Law, University of

Copenhagen. Sari Nauman's research for this chapter has been funded by a grant from *Vetenskapsrådet* (*The Swedish Research Council*), no. 2018–06596.

2　Ariès 1986.

3　Regarding the conditions for the rise of the idea of the private, see, among others, Ariès 1986; Crowley 1999; Gowing 2000; Harvey 2001; Stobart 1998; Vickery 2008.

4　For a notable exception, see Laitinen 2017a. Scandinavian research on the private is discussed further below.

5　Warrend and Brandeis 1890, 195.

6　With the technological developments in the 1950s and 1960s, privacy began to enjoy more general interest in the Anglo-American world, culminating in Alan Westin's 1967 book *Privacy and Freedom*. See Holvast 2009, 15.

7　Koops et al. 2017.

8　Thomson 1984, 272–89.

9　For further information see: https://mothsordbog.dk/kort-om-moth-og-hans-ordbog

10　http://static.ordnet.dk/moth/faksimiler/Moth_P/P_154.jpg, 'privat: borgerlig enlig'.

11　http://static.ordnet.dk/moth/faksimiler/Moth_P/P_154.jpg, 'privatstand, privat sag, privat-skole'.

12　Bay 1798, 705.

13　Nielsen 2000, 'privately'.

14　Sahlstedt 1773, 422.

15　Ibid., 425. On *offentlig*, see SAOB, Spalt O 265 band 18, 1949.

16　Ibid., 381.

17　Spegel 1712, 327; Swedberg [1714] 2009, 468. See also the discussion on *privat* in early modern Swedish dictionaries in Charlotte Christensen-Nugues' chapter in this volume.

18　SAOB, Spalt P 1896 band 20, 1954.

19　Habermas [1962] 2001 (English translation: Habermas 1989). See also Koselleck [1959] 1973 (English translation: Koselleck 1988).

20　Cowan 2013, 42.

21　Ibid.

22　See, for example, Cott 1977; Ryan 1981.

23　See in particular the two introductions in Davidoff and Hall [1987] 2019. See also van den Heuvel 2019.

24　Eibach 2011; Orlin 2007; Vickery 2008.

25　Barker and Chalus 1995; Cohen 2008; Gowing 2000; van der Heijden 2013; Longfellow 2006; Whyman 2009; Vickery 1993.

26　Goodman 1992, 13–20. For recent takes on this, see the excellent overview in van den Heuvel 2019. See also Crane 2009; Laitinen 2017b; Muurling and Pluskota 2017; Williamson 2015.

27　Besides the examples below, see Justitz 2002; Williamson 2015.

28　Vickery 2008, 167.

29　Muurling and Pluskota 2017.

30　van den Heuvel 2019.

31　Jütte 2015, 2016. On the material aspects of privacy, see also Crowley 1999.

32　Gowing 2014; Longfellow 2006.

33　Gowing 2000; Hall 2019.

34　van der Heijden and Muurling 2018.

35　Rahikainen 2019, 106–7.

36　For an English introduction to the Danish-Norwegian political history, see, for instance, Munck 1998.

37 The Norwegian nobility had been non-existent since the Middle Ages.
38 'Forordningen om grevernes og friherrernes privilegier 25. maj 1671', in Schou 1777, 69–90.
39 On the peasantry see Christiansen 1995; Munck 1979.
40 For an English introduction to the Swedish political system, see Nilsson 2017, 115–29.
41 Glete 2002, 174–212; Hallenberg, Holm and Johansson 2008.
42 Sweden was in war with Russia 1741–3 and 1788–90, but in the long run, this did not affect Sweden's status as neutral.
43 Müller 2013, 2019.
44 Feldbæk 1997.
45 Ilmakunnas 2019; Lyngby 2015.
46 On commerce in early modern Scandinavia, see, for example, Ågren 2016; Feldbæk 1993, 1997; Runefelt 2015; Simonton 2019. On port cities, see Lawton and Lee 2002; Reimann and Öhman 2021.
47 Sennefelt 2011, 2014. On the Copenhagen coffeehouses, see Hoff 2015.
48 See, for example, Ågren 2013, 2018.
49 Ågren 2017, 140–7. See also Norrhem 2007; Taussi Sjöberg 2009.
50 Hallenberg 2008; Linnarsson 2017, 2018.
51 Engelhardt 2006, 33–63; Horstbøll 1989, 26–50.
52 Brilkman 2016.
53 For the Scandinavian Reformations and their political and legal impact, see, for instance, Korpiola and Pihlajamäki 2021.
54 Nina Javette Koefoed has written extensively on the subject. For an English introduction, see Koefoed 2018. See also Pleijel 1970.
55 Johansson 2002, 258; Villstrand 2011, 342–5. On the impact of literacy on Swedish society, see Nauman 2017, 151–3.
56 On Pietism, see Larsen 1984. For the Danish Poor Laws, see *Forordning om Betlere i Danmark af 24 September 1708*, art. 7 and 20, in Schou 1722, vol. 2, 178: 20.
57 For a comparison between the Danish and Swedish approaches to the freedom of the press, see Nordin and Laursen 2020, 217–37.
58 Ulrik Langen's and Frederik Stjernfelt's research project: *Trykkefriheden og en ny offentligheds tilblivelse*, Investigate the Danish prints 1770–1773, https://www.carlsbergfondet.dk/da/Nyheder/Nyt-fra-fondet/Nyheder/Trykkefrihed-og-tilblivelsen-af-en-ny-offentlighed; Skuncke and Tandefelt 2003; Bodensten 2016, 123–53.
59 See, for example, Laitinen 2017a, 153; Ulväng 2004, 205–10; Skuncke and Tandefelt 2003; Bodensten 2016, 123–53.
60 https://www.scb.se/hitta-statistik/artiklar/2015/Urbanisering–fran-land-till-stad/
61 https://danmarkshistorien.dk/leksikon-og-kilder/vis/materiale/danmarks-befolkningsudvikling/
62 Ågren 2017; Hassan Jansson 2017; Laitinen 2017b. On open households, see Eibach 2011.
63 Ilmakunnas 2019; Linnarsson 2014; Sennefelt 2011.
64 On the reception of these refugees, see Aminoff-Winberg 2007; Nauman 2019.
65 See, for example, Schjerning 2019.

Part One

Situating the private

1

'Only to the benefit of some private persons': The concept of 'private' in records from the Swedish estates assembly, 1521–1731

Charlotte Christensen-Nugues

The early modern era sees critical changes in the relations between individual and society, home and community, self and other. A notion of the private, both as a potential threat against communal welfare and stability, and as something worthy of protection, is gradually emerging and can be traced in politics, religious practices, ideas on family and personal relations, as well as in architecture and spatial organization. This development is also reflected in terminology and can be traced through the increased use of words with the root priv-, such as *privy, privauté* or *privat*.

In this chapter, I explore different uses and meanings of the word *privat* in records from the Swedish *riksdag* (estates assembly) from the sixteenth century to the beginning of the eighteenth. I investigate how the word was used in different contexts, such as questions concerning, for example, private and public religious practices, relations between individuals and communities, and relations between households and the common good. More specifically, I analyse the concept of 'private' in relation to and, as was often the case, in opposition to public welfare and the common good; 'private' in relation to secrecy; and, finally, the often ambiguous use of the word *privat* in religious contexts, where it could be used both to describe dangerous and potentially heretic practices, and as something desirable, and even necessary, for a good Christian.

The aim of this study is not to address all issues that we would now describe with words like 'private' or its cognates, but rather to explore different uses and meanings of the word *privat* (in its different forms) and how they changed and evolved during the period. Questions, spheres or preoccupations that we would now define as private were not necessarily so described in the early modern era. Words such as *enskild* (individual), *avskild* (separate) or *hemlig* (secret) were in Sweden often used to describe acts, relations or situations that we would now describe in terms of private or related concepts. However, the modern concept of private did not appear out of nowhere sometime in the nineteenth century without any connection to how the word was used before. A study of the historical uses of a word like *privat* can hopefully be of some help to disentangle the different layers of meaning that have contributed to our modern understanding of the private.

Historiographical accounts of private and public in the early modern world have long been dominated by two different perspectives: the first, represented by scholars such as Jürgen Habermas and Reinhart Koselleck, takes politics and the public as its points of departure, while the second, represented by, for example, Philippe Ariès and Roger Chartier, focuses on the history of private life and how it was manifested in family and other forms for sociability.[1] However, these two perspectives necessarily depend on each other, as it is impossible to imagine private without public and vice versa. As Chartier expresses it: '[T]he limits of the private sphere depend primarily on the way public authority is constituted both in doctrine and in fact.'[2] However, the boundaries between private and public were not fixed, but constantly shifting. In early modern society, private was 'the not public' and thus depended on definitions of public: civil society could be private in relation to state, families in relation to the greater community, individuals in relation to family and so on.[3] The distinction between private and public was articulated both descriptively and, perhaps more importantly, axiologically: private and public expressed not only different spheres but also different values.

The primary source material for this study consists of Swedish state records from the period 1521 to 1731. They include records from early state assemblies and similar meetings for the period 1521 to 1617, as well as records from the *riksdag* of the estates for the period 1627–1731. Already in the sixteenth and seventeenth century, some of these records were printed, both to conserve them and to assure better publicity for some of the more important decisions. In the first half of the eighteenth century, Anders Anton von Stiernman published a more systematic collection of governmental decisions and statutes for the period 1521 to 1731.[4] Finally, in the second half of the nineteenth century, the Swedish State Archives decided to publish all surviving early records, and from 1855 and onwards, records of the estates for the seventeenth and eighteenth century have also been made available in modern editions.[5] This material was recently digitized by the Swedish Royal Library, making an investigation of specific words and concepts such as *privat* possible in the huge body of source material.[6] I principally rely on this digitized version for this study, in some instances supplemented by earlier printed editions, such as von Stiernman, *Alla riksdagars och mötens besluth* (1728–1731) or early modern dictionaries, such as Jonas Petri's Latin-Swedish-German dictionary from 1640.

Debates at the *riksdag* were an important part of, and a driving force behind, societal changes in early modern Sweden.[7] During the period 1527 to 1660, the estates were established as the political centre of the realm, and from the 1630s and onwards, the *riksdag* of the estates decided in questions concerning legislation, the finances of the realm and warfare. Apart from a period of monarchical absolutism under Charles XI and Charles XII (1682–1718), the crown could never sidestep the *riksdag* for important decisions.[8]

The records of the *riksdag* constitute an important source for the political, economic and social history of early modern Sweden and have been used in several studies.[9] I am particularly indebted to the works of Swedish historian of ideas Bo Lindberg and his analysis of central political concepts in early modern Sweden and how Swedish gradually developed as a political language.[10] Other works of relevance for the present study include Martin Melkersson's investigation of changing perceptions of the state in early modern Sweden and the emergence of concepts such as *frihet* (freedom), *individ* (individual) and *medborgare* (citizen) in the late eighteenth century; Magnus Linnarsson's study of debates concerning public or private administration of public services from the 1620s and onwards and Leif Runefelt's study of virtues (and vices) in relation to husbandry and economic thought in early modern Sweden.[11]

The timeframe of the study, from the beginning of the sixteenth century to the beginning of the eighteenth century, covers the development of the Swedish state under the Vasa monarchy (*Vasatiden*), the period of consolidation and expansion during the age of great power (*stormaktstiden*), monarchical absolutism under Charles XI and Charles XII, and the first decade of the so-called Age of Liberty (*frihetstiden*). The timeframe corresponds to an early history of the concept of private, before it began to take on meanings more similar to our own.[12] This was also a period when Swedish gradually developed as a political language. The two principal languages for politics in early modern Sweden were Swedish and Latin. They existed side by side but were not necessarily used in the same contexts or with the same aims. Scholarly literature on political theory was written in Latin, but those directly engaged in the politics of the realm expressed themselves in Swedish. Swedish was at the time a poorly developed language, and the Swedish political vocabulary was to a large extent dependent on Latin.[13] However, classical Latin terminology was not always translatable to the political realities of early modern Sweden (hence the discrepancy that Lindberg describes as 'den antika skevheten', 'the ancient skewness'). This also holds for the word *privat* (*privatus*). Even if *privat* was used with Swedish spelling and grammatical forms, it was essentially perceived of as a foreign, Latin word. In Jesper Swedberg's dictionary, *Swensk ordabok*, from 1716, there is only one entry for a word with the root priv-, and that is *privet*, meaning 'toilet/latrine'.[14] In another early modern Swedish dictionary, Haquin Spegel's *Glossarium-Sveo-Gothicum eller Swensk-Ordabook*, there is no entry for any word with the root priv- at all.[15] To find early modern definitions of private in Swedish, one must rely on dictionaries from Latin. In Jonas Petri's Latin-Swedish-German dictionary from 1640, *privatus* is translated as 'Synnerlig/egen/thet enom i synnerheet tilkommer' (own, particular, what particularly befalls one person) and 'The som inthet öfwerhetz kall bekläda/Priwatz personer' ('those who do not hold an office of authority, private persons').[16] This definition corresponds roughly to how the word was used in the records of the *riksdag*, or at least the ambitions for its use. As we shall see, the political and social realities made the use of *privat* less clear-cut and also contributed to a more ideologically charged use of the word.

Frequency and collocations

This first section concerns frequency and collocations – how often the word *privat* appears in the sources, how this changed over time, and with what other words *privat* was most commonly used. I have only included terms formed by the word *privat*. Some very common terms with the root priv- that I have excluded include *privatione officii et beneficii* (ecclesiastical privation) and *privilegium*, specific privileges held by certain groups or individuals. These terms hold a relatively stable definition, even if their precise content (what kind of privation or privilege) or the persons typically concerned could change over time. I have also excluded occurrences of *privat* within texts written wholly in Latin or other non-Swedish languages such as German. I have, however, included Latin forms of *privat* (*privatus, privati, in privato, privatorum*, etc.) in texts otherwise written in Swedish.

My material covers the period from 1521 to 1731, but I have very few examples from the sixteenth century. One reason is that there are simply very little written documents left from this period. But even within the existing material there is a much greater prevalence of the word *privat* in material from the seventeenth and early eighteenth century than from the sixteenth. To just take some examples: the material from 1521 to 1560 covers about 800 pages in the printed editions and there are altogether eight occurrences of the word *privat*, including three in Latin texts and two in German.[17] The word appears more frequently from 1600 and onwards: in the material from 1617, that covers approximately 300 pages, it appears fourteen times, and in the records from the noble estate for 1664, *privat* appears no less than thirty-one times.

Table 1.1 shows all occurrences of the word *privat* in my material. I have divided the material into double decades (except for the last period, 1720–1731) and compared the occurrences of *privat* with the total number of words for each double decade. It should be noted that there are no records at all for the period 1598–1611 in my material (only a few pages from Stiernman) and the records from 1611 to 1632 are also somewhat decimated due to a great fire that destroyed most of the royal archive in the castle of Stockholm in 1697.

The first thing to observe is that *privat* was not a common word. In the sixteenth century, there are only a handful of occurrences, and the frequency is less than 0.5

Table 1.1 *Occurrences of the word* privat *by double decade for the period 1521 to 1731, as compared to the total numbers of words.*

Decades	Total number of occurrences	Occurrences per 10.000 words
1521–1539	5	0.20
1540–1559	2	0.18
1560–1579	11	0.34
1580–1599	31	0.28
1600–1619	22	0.57
1620–1639	21	0.58
1640–1659	103	1.04
1660–1679	157	1.63
1680–1699	152	2.66
1700–1719	147	1.13
1720–1731	366	1.1

in 10,000 words. The total number of occurrences augments significantly in the seventeenth century, especially after the 1640s. This is mostly due to a much larger source material from this period but also to a more frequent use of *privat* in the records. In 1640 to 1660, the frequency of the word *privat* is 1.04 in 10,000 words, and this rises to 2.66 in 1680–1700. In the early eighteenth century, the frequency drops to a little more than one occurrence in 10,000 words.[18] One possible explanation for the increased use of *privat* during the late seventeenth century is the rise of monarchical absolutism that made arguments opposing private benefit to the good of the state particularly useful. The reductions during the same period also generated a significant number of occurrences of *privat*, especially in the collocation *privatorum händer*, to designate estates fallen into 'private hands' that ought to be returned to the crown. What the numbers tell us more generally is that the word *privat*, from having been nearly inexistent in the sixteenth century, gradually enters the political language, albeit at a modest level, in the seventeenth century.[19] The number of occurrences can seem quite limited, but private is not a very common word in more recent times either, at least not in state records. If we look at corresponding sources from the 1970s, we get substantially the same results. In records from the Swedish *riksdag* from 1970, occurrences of *privat* oscillate between 1.1 and 1.8 in 10,000 words.[20] This does not mean that the word 'private' was used as frequently in the seventeenth century as in the twentieth in general – only that it occurs about as often in the specific political context covered by the records.

The first occurrence of the word *privat* in my material is in the context of the forced resignation of Archbishop Gustaf Trolle in 1523. According to the *Rigesens Rådh* (Council of the Realm), the bishop had, through his crimes against his fatherland, forfeited both life and estate. However, they decided to let mercy precede law 'so that he must resign the archbishopric, give himself over to the pope, and then lead a quiet private life'.[21] This is also the first occurrence of the word *privat* (and any combination thereof) recorded in the *Swedish Academy Dictionary*, SAOB, which records historical usages of Swedish terms. 'Private life' is otherwise not a common collocation in the records, and other collocations such as *priwatz person* (private person), *privatorum händer* (private hands) or *privat nytthe* (private gain) figures much more prominently.

Table 1.2 shows the most common collocations with the word 'private' in my material. I have only included collocations that appear at least five times.

The collocations in the table were obtained using a window of five words, that is, within five words to either side of *privat*. I then excluded so-called empty words, such as *och, den, också, för* (and, the, also, for), etc. The most common collocation is with 'person' (e.g. *privats person, private persohner, privatpersoner*). This group becomes even more important when we consider Latin forms corresponding to private person(s) such as *privatus* and *privati*. The prevalence of collocations with the word 'person' is not astonishing. Most entries concern what people do and can do, and/or what they have the right to do. During the early modern era, with a growing state administration staffed by state officials, it became increasingly important to distinguish both between private and public persons and between what an office holder did as part of his official duties and what he did as a private person.[22]

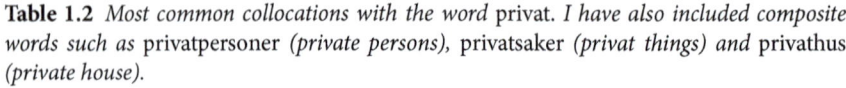

Table 1.2 *Most common collocations with the word* privat. *I have also included composite words such as* privatpersoner *(private persons),* privatsaker *(privat things) and* privathus *(private house).*

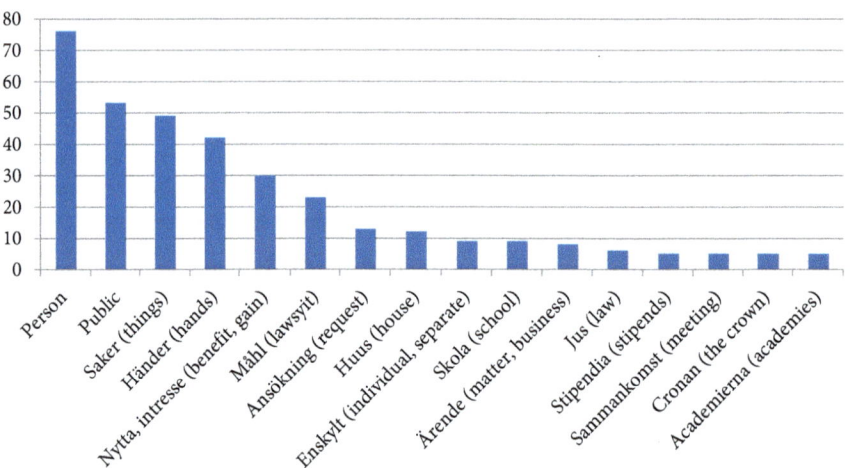

The second most common collocation is with 'public' (*publik, publicus, publique*). This collocation often intersects with persons but also with things and, to some extent, with all other collocations. This does not mean that private was opposed to a fixed idea of the public. As mentioned above, the boundaries were constantly shifting and something that was private in one context could be public in another. Even if the word 'public' is not pronounced, 'private' is in general defined in opposition to, or as an absence of, something larger and/or more official such as the common good,[23] state or crown. The collocation 'private things' typically refers to matters, concerns or businesses that are not public or official and do not pertain to the state or a greater community but to a person (or a household) as a separate entity. Sometimes the adjective *enskylt* (separate, individual) is appended to further underscore the non-public, non-official character of the matter in question.[24]

Collocations with words such as *nytta* (benefit) or *interesse* (interest) are relatively common and would be more common still if less frequent words with similar meaning, such as *vinning* (gain) or *fördehl* (advantage), also were included in the table. These collocations are nearly always used in a pejorative sense, in opposition to the common good or the interest of the crown. In the very few cases when 'private' was used with words such as *iniuria* (injury) or *skadhe* (damage) it was, on the contrary, either to defend private interests/persons or to demonstrate virtuous willingness to suffer private injury for the common good.

As mentioned above, the collocations in the table were obtained using a window of five words, but if we only count words directly adjacent to *privat* we get substantially the same results: the most common collocation is still 'private person(s)' with sixty-four occurrences, followed by 'private things' (forty-four occurrences), 'private hands' (thirty-six occurrences) and 'private benefit/interest' (twenty occurrences).[25] The most important difference is the complete absence of collocations with the word 'public' when only counting directly adjacent words. This is simply because there is always a word (*och, eller, et, vel, aut,* etc.) between 'private' and 'public' in my material – hence the necessity of using a wider window than simply adjacent words.

Textual statistics concerning frequency and collocations can give some interesting indications, but it does not say very much about *how* the word *privat* was actually used; in what contexts it proved useful; with what aims it was used; and its positive, or, as was mostly the case, negative connotations. There are also a number of 'blind spots', notably religion. Notions of the private had particular significance in some religious contexts, such as questions concerning religious practices of non-Lutherans or prohibitions of private religious gatherings for Lutherans. Yet there are very few collocations with identifiable 'religious terms'. However, some collocations that at a first glance seem to have nothing to do with religion, such as *privat huus* (private house) or *private sammankomster* (private gatherings), are mostly found within religious contexts.[26] The same holds for words such as *enskylt* (individual/separate) or *afskylt* (secluded). A significant number of collocations with 'public' are also found in the religious realm, for example, when debating the religious practices of non-Lutherans.

Another problem is that words or concepts used in opposition to private often do not appear even when using a relatively large window. In a phrase such as 'exhorted them all to disregard what could be disadvantageous for their private interest but rather with zeal and sacrifice regard the common good', the important distinction is between private interest and common good, but that cannot be observed unless using an extremely wide window.[27] In the following sections, I will turn to the texts themselves and investigate more closely some specific contexts when the word *privat* was typically used.

Public need and private interests

In early modern society, the terms 'public' and 'private' were considered 'relational', that is, they each depended on the other.[28] However, the boundaries were not fixed, but constantly shifting and often ambiguous. The notion of *privatus* (private person) as opposed to persons holding a public office was relatively clearly defined in classical Roman law, but was not always easy to apply in early modern society and politics.[29] In early modern monarchies, it could be difficult to distinguish between public power and the personal power of the king. It was also often unclear when an office holder was acting within his office or as a private person.[30]

Even though the boundaries between private and public were often blurred, there was, as Bo Lindberg has pointed out, an ambition to make a clear distinction.[31] Several entries, especially from the seventeenth century, attest to this drive to define and separate public from private: the *riksdag* should consider 'that there is great difference between public and private',[32] 'public law should be distinguished from private',[33] 'one must distinguish between private and public persons',[34] and, concerning royal authority, 'distinguish and separate between a private person and a king'.[35] Other entries describe what can (or cannot) be done or said both publicly and privately. So, for example, are non-Lutherans forbidden to practise their religion both publicly and privately,[36] the people are exhorted to pray for the King and all authority both privately and publicly,[37] and, in 1686, the estate of clergy states that harmful novelties, and especially the Cartesian philosophy, should not be propagated either publicly or privately.[38]

The distinction between private and public could also be used as an argument to hinder or further the actions of certain persons. During the debate concerning the contested will of Charles X Gustaf (1622–1660, r. 1654–1660), the notion of private was used as an argument to exclude the king from making a legally binding testament: 'Wills pertain to private law and not to public law [...] As long as a king is a king, there is nothing domestic or private to take into consideration in him, all is public'.[39] The question of whether a person is considered to be private or public, what she can do in either case, and how she can do it was also an important argument in the debate concerning the religious practices of Queen Christina (1626–1689, r. 1632–1654) when she returned to Sweden in 1660 and 1667. Queen Christina had abdicated the throne in 1654 and officially converted to Catholicism shortly thereafter, and the question of whether she should be allowed to practise her 'papist' religion when in Sweden became a contentious issue. The queen, writes the estate of clergy, should not be considered *ut privata* (as a private person) and therefore her religious practices, whether she exercised them publicly or privately, were of utmost importance for the whole realm.[40]

The strong relation between public and private should not lead us to the anachronistic conclusion that private and public were perceived of as complementary, equally legitimate spheres. In some instances, especially in terms derived from Roman law, 'private' denoted a clearly defined sphere or division (e.g. *jus privatum*, 'civil law'). Otherwise, 'private' was before 1700 essentially a negative term, used to describe 'whatever did not pertain to the nation and community'.[41] 'Public' was, as Conal Condren has pointed out, strongly associated with moral, legitimate office holding, not only within spheres that we would now consider as 'public', but also in relation to, for example, parenthood or husbandry.[42] 'Private', on the other hand, connoted absence of legitimate, moral office holding and is in my material very often presented in direct opposition to public interest, the good of the community or the needs of the crown.

This opposition appears in phrases such as: 'not to the Crown, but to the benefit of private persons'[43]; 'for the private benefit of a few, the public is overthrown'[44] or 'to the detriment of all, for the private benefit of a few'.[45] The word *privat* frequently appears in the context of corruption or abuse, often in collocations such as *privat nytthe* (private benefit) or *privat interesse* (private interest). Means dedicated to the defence of the realm or to appease troubles and misery were *förryckiadt* (stolen), *wändt* (turned) or simply *nyttiadt* (used) for private benefit or interest. In 1617, Gustaf II Adolph (1594–1632, r. 1611–1632) addressed the estates concerning taxes levied for the war. He emphasized that taxes imposed to defend 'our Christian faith and blessedness, our Fatherlands freedom' should go directly to the king and not, as unfortunately had often been the case before, 'be taken away and used for private benefit'.[46] Private use of public means was frequently denounced, and in 1686 the estates are reminded that such means have been accorded 'by *allmogen* (the common people) for the *allgehmene* (common) welfare and not for any-one's private benefit'.[47] Private benefit was moreover often described as the benefit of some few private persons against not only the crown or the public good, but also against people in general: 'to the detriment of all for the private benefit of a few'.[48] At times the term 'private person' was used in direct opposition to people. When the estate of clergy criticized how Palmstruck had governed the newly established banking office, they stated 'that mostly some private persons have had benefit thereof, to the detriment of so many *menniskior* (people)'.[49]

Growing notions of 'patriotic solidarity' and the requirement to subordinate personal gain to the benefit of the state contributed to a moralizing use of private in opposition to the common good.[50] In times of danger or need, the rights and freedoms that private people could normally enjoy must be subordinated to the common good. This argument was notably used during the period of monarchical absolutism to legitimate extraordinary powers of the crown: 'civil laws must rest and the rights of private persons in many cases fall, when the public is in danger'.[51] In 1682, the king, wishing to curb insubordination against rules and measures taken by the crown, urged the noble estate 'that they, as upright patriots, now as before, put all private interest away and seek to promote the public'.[52]

The public (state, crown or common good) was associated with duty and sacrifice, while the private was associated with absence of such commitments. In 1614, the king declared that he understood his subject's wish for peace, comfort and the possibility to devote themselves to their private and own affairs. However, he continued, nobody suffered as much as the king, who even in times of peace always, through his high royal office, had to care for the welfare of the realm.[53] For less exalted persons, it was a sign of virtuous, patriotic behaviour to sacrifice one's own private affairs for the good of the state. In 1627, the noble estate humbly accepted conscription of their peasants to strengthen the army and thereby 'defend the realm and our own welfare' even if it, as they pointed out, 'did great damage to them in private'.[54]

The representations of private and public were not wholly black or white. Private enterprise was at times necessary and could also be considered as beneficial for society as a whole. During the seventeenth century, the Swedish state outsourced parts of the public services (e.g. within the post service, tax collection and certain custom duties) to private entrepreneurs.[55] These private entrepreneurs were often criticized for selfishness and short-sighted profiteering, but the state still needed them. Other enterprises, institutions or assets could be presented as beneficial both to the public and to private persons. Sweden's first bank, *Stockholms Banco* founded in 1656, was described in 1660 as 'such a useful institution, for the public as well as for private persons'[56]; the office of justice in 1664 as 'such a beneficial institution, both for the public and for all the inhabitants of the realm in private'[57]; and, at the *riksdag* of Stockholm in 1668, the exploitation of Sweden's natural resources was described as fundamental 'both to the common good as well as to each and every-one's private needs'.[58] In the beginning of the Age of Liberty, there are several entries that describe both public and private benefices of newly founded companies or institutions and warn for measures that could impede private enterprise.[59] There are even, from the beginning of the 1730s, statements that explicitly question the opposition between private and public benefit: '[it is] an infallible sign of a badly ordered state, when the *allmänna* (public) should be obtained through the want or poverty of *privatorum* (private persons).'[60] However, even when considering this later period, associations between 'public' and 'private' good remain quite rare compared to the much more common opposition between what is good for society as a whole and the interests of private persons. The overwhelming impression is that of a perceived conflict between the common good and private interests, the latter often associated with corruption or at least self-serving behaviour.

Secrecy, discretion and the private

The word 'private' was not only used in relation to something more 'public' (be it the Crown, people or the common good) but also, more specifically, in connection to secrecy and discretion.[61] Jonas Petri's Latin-Swedish-German dictionary gives two definitions of *privatus*: the first as bereft of public functions, and the second as 'Synnerlig/egen/ thet som enom i synnerhet tilkommer' (specific, own, what particularly belongs to one person). The related, and frequently used adverb *privatim*, is translated into Swedish as *hemlig* (secret). In my material, the word 'private' is often associated with words such as *eenshylt, för sigh siälfw* (separate, apart) or *afshylt* (secluded). 'Private' was sometimes used nearly synonymously with 'secret' (*privat confession / heml. bekännelse*), and often in a derogatory sense, for example, to describe secret and underhand dealings (*privateske handel*). The adverb *privatim* appears in expressions and phrases such as *communicera privatim* (communicate privately/secretly), to *privatim afhielpa* (privately/secretly remedy) or to make use of unofficial/secret ways to obtain political aims: 'through intrigues *privatim* bring an estate to this or that opinion'.[62]

We are used to a society where the state is expected to act openly and publicly while ordinary citizens should be accorded a private sphere separated from the public realm. In the early modern era, the situation was rather the opposite: secrecy was potentially dangerous when practised by private persons, but the state was expected to act in secret. Early modern regimes tended to view secrecy as a legitimate part of governance, and the term *arcana imperii* (originally from Tacitus's *Annals*) became a key concept for the theory of rational and efficient government.[63] Discretion and secrecy were necessary to sustain and expand political power, and crucial political knowledge was best restricted to the smallest possible group. When Gustaf II Adolph founded the *Secreta utskottet* (Secret Committee) in 1627, it was well understood that this committee should deliberate questions that demanded particular discretion: 'saak som icke allmen bör vetas' (things that should not be generally known).[64] The workings of the committee should be kept secret and only a restricted number of persons were allowed to participate. *Secreta utskottet* should deliberate questions of particular interest to the public realm, while questions concerning private persons or interests could be deliberated more openly. The instructions for the committee from 1727 state that questions of whether treaties and alliances had been executed with regards to the public realm were to be handled by *Secreta utskottet*, while questions concerning private persons who could have pretensions through the peace treatises could be communicated and investigated *in pleno*.[65]

Words such as 'private' or 'secret' were also used more generally when there was reason to keep a matter or a conversation unofficial. Some things were better said privately and secretly than with the authority of formal office. When representatives from the estate of clergy interrogated the *riksdrots* (chancellor of the realm) about the religious practices of Queen Christina in 1660, he answered that he did not want to speak of these matters as a *Regeringzperson* (person of government) but could say something in *privat familiar diskurs* (private familiar discourse) that he wanted to be kept secret.[66] Economic matters could also be considered delicate enough to require special discretion. In 1650, members of the estates demanded that economic difficulties should be handled by a particular committee because people did not want to show their poverty publicly but rather treat it privately with the king,[67] and during the establishment of the state treasury in 1664, the noble estate warned that 'a private person does not much like to have his economic situation made public'.[68] In some situations, a private admonition was deemed more appropriate than a public or formal warning: swearing servants should first be admonished by the housefather, then privately by the parish priest,[69] and priest, who in their sermons deviated from Lutheran orthodoxy, should, if possible, be admonished privately to avoid disturbances in the congregation.[70] More generally, *inbördes admonitio privata* (mutual private admonitions) were part of a Christian's duty towards his fellow Christians.[71] The notion of 'private admonition' had, as Johannes Ljungberg's contribution indicates, particular significance during the Pietism controversy in the early eighteenth century.

The private and Lutheran orthodoxy

The notion of 'private' had important implications in the context of religion, particularly concerning the religious practices of foreign, non-Lutheran diplomats, workers or manufacturers, and the religious practices and gatherings of Lutherans in places other than the Church (the latter finally leading up to the prohibition of such gatherings in 1726).[72]

In the case of religious practices of non-Lutherans, the notion of 'private' was used to distinguish and describe the only possible way for them to legitimately practise their religion. Religious unity was considered essential for national unity, and non-Lutherans were generally denied the right to practise their religion. However, Sweden was also much in need of foreign competence, for example, in the ironworks and textile industry, and exemptions could be granted for religious immigrant groups. In his *konungaförsäkran* (royal declaration) from 1611, King Gustaf II Adolph emphasized Lutheran orthodoxy and promised that no one of another religion ('Papist', Calvinist, Anabaptist or anyone else) would have the right to hold any office in Sweden. However, if any foreign *privatz-personer* (private persons) needed to be in the country for trade or military reasons, they could be allowed to practise their religion in private, as long as they kept 'silent and calm and did not spread their heresy'.[73] Very much the same formulation was used in the project for a royal declaration some hundred years later: foreign merchants or artisans could have the right to practise their religion 'för sig sielfwe i sine huus' (among them-selves in their houses) as long as they did it 'in privato stilla ock utan förargelse' (in private, calmly and without disturbances).[74] Moreover, the right to privately practise a non-Lutheran religion was something that according to the noble estate should be accorded privately to certain groups and not publicly through an open placard.[75] *Privat* is in this context often associated with words such as *stilla* or *roolig* (calm), *afshylt, för sig sielfw* (secluded, among them-selves), *utan förargelse* (without disturbance).

In the case of religious practices of Lutherans, the word *privat* was often used to describe the dangers of a practice that was disorderly, undisciplined and potentially heretic. If non-Lutherans ought to practise privately in secluded places, Lutherans, on the other hand, ought to practise openly and publicly. The first remarks on religious practices that include the word *privat* in my material date from the end of the sixteenth century and concern private confessions (as opposed to *almennelige skriftermål*, public confessions).[76] The word *privat* appears more and more frequently in this context from the middle of the seventeenth century and onwards, especially in the collocation 'private house'.[77] At the *riksdag* in Stockholm 1660, the clergy warned that the Church's public ministry risked being despised because of the frequent preaching and use of the sacraments in *privat huus* (private houses).[78] Four years later, they declared that the *Gudztienst* (worship) should be held in churches and not in private houses.[79] Over time, such complaints became more pressing and private house preaching and religious ceremonies outside of church were denounced for creating great disorder and making the people 'säkert och sielffswördigt' (self-assured and undisciplined).[80]

However, the meaning of 'privata och enskylta sammankomster' (private and separate gatherings) as well as the status of private religious practices was, as the clergy admitted, 'a very difficult question'.[81] Why should one complain about private meetings among fellow Christians, when all, according to the Lutheran faith, were *andelige präster* (spiritual priests) who could and should instruct each other?[82] The *konventikelplakat* of 1726 explicitly accepted private religious devotion in the household, but what if a father, for example, held a *privat husandacht* (private house devotion) and someone incidentally came by and then stayed on for his own edification?[83] Was there not a Christian value in private worship and edification among fellow Christians? There was an ambiguity in how 'private' should be understood, and the risks, as well as values, that it represented in this context. On the one hand, private gatherings and practices could foster disorderly, undisciplined behaviour and in the worst case lead to heresy, but on the other hand, private religious practices, as well as private mutual instruction and admonition, were also something desirable, and even necessary, for a good Christian.

Concluding remarks

It is impossible to conclusively define early modern understandings of the term 'private', even within such a relatively restricted source material as records from the Swedish *riksdag*. 'Private' was essentially a negative term and was defined as an absence of, or in opposition to, something larger and/or more official. This could be the public, the state or the crown but also the people, inhabitants of the realm, or any larger community in general. The institutions, communities or persons, against which private was defined, could change according to context and the boundaries were constantly shifting.

'Private' was not only negative in the sense of absence or opposition, but also in terms of value. 'Private' denoted absence of legitimate office, indifference to the common good, and unwillingness to sacrifice one's own comfort for a higher purpose. At times, the word *privat* seems more like a rhetorical device to denounce self-serving, egoistical and unpatriotic behaviour than as a meaningful description of different spheres or preoccupations. It is difficult, for example, to understand the meaning of an opposition between 'private persons' and 'people' (see the example on Palmstruck and the banking office above), except as a way to denounce a certain behaviour or a certain set of persons.

We are used to a society where the private, or privacy, is viewed as a positive value and as something worthy of protection. This was not the case in early modern society. Private gain and enterprise could be viewed as something positive as long as they served the interests of the state or the greater community, but this is not the same thing as regarding the private as a value in itself. The private, in the sense of secret, could be useful, and even necessary for political reasons, but the private was not viewed as a protected, or even desirable, sphere for ordinary persons. The only context where there was at least an opening, or an ambiguous space, for a positive definition of private was in the religious realm. Even if the word *privat* in the religious context was mostly used to denounce secret, secluded acts or gatherings, it could also express a desirable, and even necessary part of a Christian's life and faith.

Notes

1   Key texts are Habermas 1962, Koselleck 1973 and Ariès, Duby and Chartier 1986. For an overview and analysis of the historiography, see Goodman 1992, 1–20.
2   Chartier 1986, 15.
3   Brewer 1995, 9–10.
4   Stiernman 1728–33 and 1743.
5   *Svenska riksdagsakter,* 1. 1, vol. 1–4 (1521–1611); Ibid., 1. 2, vol. 1–2 (1611–1617); Ibid., 2, vol. 1–3 (1719–1734); *Sveriges ridderskaps och adels riksdagsprotokoll,* vol. 1–17 (1627–1697); *Sveriges ridderskaps och adels riksdagsprotokoll från och med 1719,* vol. 1–32 (1719–1779); *Prästeståndets riksdagsprotokoll,* vol. 1–13 (1642–1752); *Borgarståndets riksdagsprotokoll före frihetstiden; Borgarståndets riksdagsprotokoll från frihetstidens början,* vol. 1–10 (1719–1752); *Bondeståndets riksdagsprotokoll,* vol. 1–13 (1720–79). For this material, see also Förhammar 2011, 19–46 and Lindström 2011, 61–80.
6   The digitized material was made available in March 2018 at https://riksdagstryck. kb.se.
7   Linnarsson 2017, 14.
8   Ibid. See also Schück 1992, 11–66 and Rystad 1992, 67–123.

9   For the relevance of parliamentary sources in conceptual history, see Ihalainen and Palonen 2009.
10   Lindberg 2006, 2014.
11   Linnarsson 2017; Melkersson 1997; Runefelt 2001.
12   Cf. the concept of *Sattelzeit* (ca. 1750–1850), when, according to Koselleck 1972, central political concepts gained meanings that approach the present day.
13   Lindberg 2006, 25–6.
14   Swedberg 2009 [1716], 501.
15   Spegel 1712.
16   Petri 1640.
17   The German text *Memoriall etzlicher anderen beyhantel, dar ahn geleghen* was included in the records from the meeting in Arboga in 1544 and include references to 'privaten sachen' and 'Dennemarkische privaten fur sich und unns nit angehendt handelunge', *Svenska riksdagsakter* 1. 1, vol. 1, 424.
18   The code, developed by Pierre Nugues, as well as generated statistics is available at https://github.com/pnugues/stats_textuelles/tree/master/débats du riksdag.
19   The political counterpart of 'private' – 'public' - is used used about two times more frequently (mostly in its Latin forms) and reaches three to four occurrences in 10,000 words by the end of the seventeenth – beginning of the eighteenth century. As with *privat,* there are very few occurrences of *publi[k/c/que]* for the period 1521 to 1640. From the 1640s and onwards, the relative frequency ranges from 2.7 to 3.9/10,000. Exact numbers are available at https://github.com/pnugues/stats_textuelles/tree/master/débats du riksdag.
20   *Riksdagens protokoll. Första kammaren* 1970, A01, vol. 1; *Riksdagens protokoll. Andra kammaren* 1970, B01, vol. 1. See exact numbers at https://github.com/pnugues/stats_textuelles/tree/master/débats du riksdag.
21   'Således at han Erchiebiskopzdömet resignera motte/och uthi Påwens wåld och händer öffuergiffua/och sedan ett roligit Priwatz leffuerne föra', Stiernman vol. 1, 1728, 5.
22   See Lindberg 2006, 121–2.
23   The notion of 'common good' was very important in early modern society and the distinction between 'private' and 'public' can often be more adequately approached using this term instead of 'public'. See Linnarson 2017, esp. 12 and 41.
24   So, for example, was the phrase *som een privat och eenschylt saak anlangar* (that concerns a private and individual matter), used in 1617 to distinguish between political and private correspondence with the enemy (both should be punished, but the latter a bit less harshly than the former). *Svenska riksdagsakter* 1. 2, vol. 2, (1617), 157. *Enskylt*, as well as *afskylt*, was otherwise mostly used in the sense of secret, hidden, secluded.
25   The less frequent collocations are also approximately the same: 'lawsuits' (18), 'house' (11), 'requests' (9) and 'matter' and 'business' (5 each). Exact numbers are available at: https://github.com/pnugues/stats_textuelles/tree/master/débats du riksdag.
26   The notion of 'private conversation' (as opposed to formal or public conversation) had particular significance in conflicts over Pietism in 1720s Sweden. See Johannes Ljungberg's chapter in this volume.
27   'Förmaante dem alle ifrå något, som af privat interesse kunde wara der emot, uthan heller med nijt och ofwer till de allgemene bästa', *Sveriges ridderskaps och adels riksdagsprotokoll,* 5 (1655), 47.
28   Condren 2009, 21.

29   For the definition of *privatus* in classical Roman law, see Berger 1953, 651.
30   On the confusion between public and private actions of an office holder, as well as
     the problem of corruption, see Sari Nauman's contribution in this volume.
31   Lindberg 2006, 121–2.
32   'Att stohr åtskildnat är emellan publicum och privatum', *Sveriges ridderskaps och adels
     riksdagsprotokoll*, 10 (1668), 317.
33   'Att publicum jus distingveras ifrån privato', ibid., 328.
34   'Distinguendum inter personas privatas et publicas', ibid., 9 (1664), 79.
35   'Distingveras och åthskillias imellan een privat person och een konung', ibid., 11
     (1672), 74.
36   *Prästeståndets riksdagsprotokoll*, 2 (1660–1664), 406.
37   Ibid., 474.
38   Ibid., 4 (1680–1714), 304.
39   'See wij till materiam testamenti, så är then juris privati och icke publici […] Så widha
     en Konungh är Konung, så kommer inthet domesticum eller privatum hos honom i
     consideration, uthan alt publicum', *Sveriges ridderskaps och adels riksdagsprotokoll*, 7
     (1660), 64. For the debate concerning the will of Charles X Gustaf, and especially the
     importance of oaths in this context, see Nauman 2017, 115–16.
40   *Prästeståndets riksdagsprotokoll*, 2 (1660–1664), 434.
41   Longfellow 2006, 31.
42   Condren 2009, 21.
43   'Kom icke så Cronan, uthan mehr privat personer till nytta', *Sveriges ridderskaps och
     adels riksdagsprotokoll*, 5.1 (1652–1654), 41.
44   'För någre privats nytta måtte publicum everteras', ibid., 5.2 (1655), 23.
45   'Allom ett förfångh för någres privat nytrta', ibid., 24.
46   'Wår christelige troo och saligheet, wårt Fädherneslandz frijheet', 'förryckias och
     wändas till privat nytther', *Svenska riksdagsakter*, 1. 2, vol. 2 (1617), 148.
47   'Af allmogen till det allgehmene bästa och ingens privat nytta bevilliade', *Sveriges
     ridderskaps och adels riksdagsprotokoll*, 15 (1686, 1689), 382.
48   'Allom ett förfångh för någres privat nytta', ibid., 5.1 (1652–1654), 24.
49   *Prästeståndets riksdagsprotokoll*, 2 (1660–1664), 485.
50   Lindberg 2006, 121–2.
51   'Leges civiles måste hvijla och privatorum rätt i många stycken falla, när publicum
     löper fahra', *Sveriges ridderskaps och adels riksdagsprotokoll*, 15 (1686), 199.
52   'Att dhe som redelige patrioter, nu som förr, sättia alt privat interesse effter och sökia
     främia dät publique' ibid., 14 (1682), 229.
53   *Svenska riksdagsakter* 1. 2, vol. 1–2 (1614), 382.
54   'Rijket och vårt egett välståndh dermed att defendere', 'oansedt ded [*sic*] dem in
     privato till stoor skada länder', *Sveriges ridderskaps och adels riksdagsprotokoll*, 1
     (1627), 81.
55   Linnarsson 2017, 39–59.
56   'Itt så publico som privatis här till nyttigt wärk', *Sveriges ridderskaps och adels
     riksdagsprotokoll*, 7 (1660), 281.
57   'Itt så publico som alle richsens inbyggiare in privat[o] helsosampt värck', ibid., 9
     (1664), 355.
58   'Både till thet allmenne bästa så vähl som hvars och ens privat tarfvor', ibid.,10
     (1668), 547.
59   See, for example, the delegation for economy and commerce (*ekonomi- och
     kommersdeputationen*) in 1726. *Borgarståndets riksdagsprotokoll*, 3 (1726–1727), 738.

60 'Ett ofehlbart tecken till en illa bestält republique, när det allmänna ska ricktas igenom privatorum afsaknad eller fattigdom', *Sveriges ridderskaps och adels riksdagsprotokoll från och med 1719*, 7 (1734), 581.

61 For connections between private and secret see Camilla Schjerning's chapter in this volume

62 'Genom intrigues privatim bringa något ståndh på een eller annan mening', *Sveriges ridderskaps och adels riksdagsprotokoll*, 9 (1664), 159.

63 Horn 2011, 103–22.

64 *Sveriges ridderskaps och adels riksdagsprotokoll*, 1 (1627–1632), 58.

65 *Sveriges ridderskaps och adels riksdagsprotokoll från och med 1719*, 4 (1727), 52.

66 *Prästeståndets riksdagsprotokoll*, 2 (1660–1664), 119.

67 *Sveriges ridderskaps och adels riksdagsprotokoll*, 4 (1645–1649), 326.

68 'En privat vill inthet gärna sin stat låtha publicera', ibid., 9 (1664), 98.

69 Ibid., 10 (1668), 502.

70 *Prästeståndets riksdagsprotokoll*, 4 (1680–1714), 74.

71 Ibid., 6 (1723), 27.

72 For the Pietist controversy see Ljungberg 2017 and Nordbäck 2004.

73 'Sigh stille och rooligen förholle, sin wilfarelse icke utsprijde', Stiernman, vol. 1 (1728), 653.

74 *Prästeståndets riksdagsprotokoll*, 5 (1719–1720), 391–2.

75 *Sveriges riddeskaps och adels riksdagsprotokoll*, 11 (1672), 323.

76 *Svenska riksdagsakter*, 1. 1, vol. 2. 1 (1561–1574), 437.

77 For early modern notions of 'private house', see Ulrik Langen's chapter in this volume.

78 *Prästeståndets riksdagsprotokoll*, 2 (1660–1664), 270–1.

79 Ibid., 662 and ibid., 4 (1680–1714), 503.

80 Ibid., 5 (1719–1720), 160.

81 'Mechta granlaga quaestion', ibid., 7 (1726–1731), 268.

82 Ibid., 6 (1723), 509.

83 Ibid., 7 (1726–1731), 339.

Private as an economic concept: Natural law and economic agency

Pernille Ulla Knudsen

Private property is the basic precondition for the free movement of goods and services, and as such, it is considered to be the foundation of the modern economic system. Accordingly, property rights enjoy special protections at law. The legal definition of private property can be traced back to the rise of modern natural law in the seventeenth century, when, for the first time, private property was defined as a right that attached to the person. Private property can thus be considered as the starting point for the notion of fundamental legal rights, a notion that much later would be codified in the free constitutions and the international declarations of human rights.

Despite this obvious connection between the private economy, private property and legal rights, the *private economy* has received little attention from researchers interested in exploring the dichotomy between the private and the public in the early modern period.[1] It should be noted, however, that private economic development in the eighteenth century was considered to be the basic foundation for the emergence of Jürgen Habermas' both famous and controversial 'political public sphere'. According to Habermas, 'In the meantime, the public very much assumed its specific form; it was the bourgeois reading public in the world of letters even as it assumed political functions; education was one criterion for admission – property ownership the other'.[2] As Habermas continued to explain,

> On the contrary, only property owners were in a position to form a public that could legislatively protect the foundations of the existing property order; only they had private interests – each his own? – which automatically converged into the common interest in the preservation of a civil society as a private sphere. Only from them, therefore, was an effective representation of the general interest to be expected, since it was not necessary for them in any way to leave their private existence behind to exercise their public role.[3]

I owe thanks to Prof Helle Vogt, who helped me with the word mining of 'private' in the Copenhagen newspapers, and who helped in writing the report upon which many of the observations in this article are based; she has also provided many stimulating discussions, and helped ruthlessly cut the text down. I also owe a big thank you to Dr Matthew McHaffie for his excellent help with proofreading and copyediting.

Habermas here articulated the emergence of a civil society that changed the traditional understanding of the private and public, and transformed it into what we may term the private *in* the public.[4]

The private economy and private law form the subjects of this present article. Its starting point is a major terminological study of the occurrence of the word 'private' in the Copenhagen newspapers during the period 1673–1800.[5] The study showed that two-thirds of the occurrences of the word 'private' were linked to economic concepts. It is hardly surprising that newspapers, which at the time served as an important medium for commerce and trade, situated the concept of 'the private' within an economic framework. However, a study of 'the private' in relation to the private economy and, consequently, to private property allows us to see perspectives of the private that would normally be hidden by an excessively rigid theoretical division of the private and public in early modern history.

Private property is a personal right connected to human beings in their capacity as economic agents. By attaching the private to *people* instead of to *places*, we get an opportunity to recognize the private as an element of social interaction. An agent-centred perspective[6] usefully shifts our focus away from a place-bound framework for understanding the private and the public. A place-bound framework rests on the sharp demarcation traditionally thought to separate the private household from an indefinable public space, where the doorstep of the private home serves as the threshold at which everything else (i.e. the public) is kept out. However, with an agent-centred approach, we see that women and men moved in, out and across those thresholds in complex social and economic patterns that could only unfold because the same agents engaged in social and private economic interactions. During the eighteenth century, the private market economy was expanding all over Europe, including in Copenhagen.[7] A focus on agency takes us away from a spatially determined definition of private and public by which historians end up paralyzing the people of the past.[8] Some agents had goods for sale while others were buyers: but both were necessary for private enterprise. The private market was conceptually linked to private property, which itself was an individual legal right that existed independently of the state and which was perceived as inviolable.

Within the Copenhagen newspapers, citizens emerge as private economic agents operating in the framework of a Habermassian 'civil society'. The newspapers allow us to focus on a conceptual understanding of classic economic ideas about private property and the private economy. The interpretation of the relationship between private economy, private property rights and legal rights requires an understanding of how modern secular natural jurisprudence during the seventeenth century came to set entirely new legal standards that remain the basic principles that inform present-day public and private law. A new legal framework was formed for this natural jurisprudence that was based on the systematic reinterpretation of the concepts of duty and right, drawn from the general law of obligations. Habermas also recognized the importance of the law of obligations in driving economic development, but he discussed it only briefly:

> The concept of the legal transaction as involving a contract based on a free declaration of will was modelled in the exchange transaction of freely competing owners of commodities. At the same time, a system of private law that in principle

reduced the relationships of private people with one another to private contracts operated with the assumption that the exchange relationships that came about in accordance with the laws of the free market had model character. Of course, parties to a contract were not in every case also exchange partners, but the relationship of the latter, which was central to civil society, supplied the model for all contractual relationships.[9]

A recent study by the economist Arild Sæther has examined how natural law influenced the origins of politico-economic thought in the seventeenth and eighteenth centuries. Sæther's study is based on the German-born natural law jurist Samuel Pufendorf (1632–1694), who played a key role in the development of a new natural law theory in the late seventeenth century. In 1672, he published his legal masterpiece, *De jure naturae et gentium liber octo* (*On the Law of Nature and Nations in Eight Books*). However, it was the shorter, summary compendium of *De officio hominis et civis juxta legem naturalem libri duo* (*On the Duty of Man and Citizen According to Natural Law in Two Books*), published in 1673, that made him the most influential *legal* (as opposed to political) philosopher for more than a century. This work was translated into English, French, Swedish, German and Danish, among others, and reached a wide readership across Europe.[10] Sæther's reinterpretation of one of the most significant theoretical lawyers in legal history provides an opportunity to take Pufendorf's natural law theory as a starting point to explain how his natural law doctrine of duty came to form the legal basis for the private market economy, as described in the above quotation from Habermas.

My interpretation will be based on Pufendorf's compendium, which will provide a legal framework into which the results of the terminological study of 'private' as found in the newspapers and the private economic market can be placed. The theory of natural law, as illustrated through private property law, will broaden our general understanding of law's influence on the development of the notion of 'the private' in the eighteenth century.

Searching for *private* in the Copenhagen newspapers 1673–1800

In recent years, the digitization of historical newspapers has been carried out across Europe, under the auspices of national libraries, and allows researchers to conduct systematic searches in an otherwise large and inaccessible body of material. In Denmark, the digitization of the *National Newspaper Collection* was completed in 2017.[11] As part of an interdisciplinary terminological project, we have therefore been able to use the Copenhagen newspapers from the period 1673 to 1800 to carry out a systematic registration of the word 'private', as it occurred both textually and contextually.

In 1634, the first weekly newspaper was founded in Copenhagen by royal privilege. It was not until 1749, however, when the publisher E.H. Berling reformed the newspaper market with his publication *Kiøbenhavnske Danske Posttidender* (1749–1762) that newspapers became common. With a mixture of local advertising, international newsletters[12] and monthly official information, Berling's newspaper became the model for other political newspapers in the eighteenth century. Even so, there was no political newspaper in the modern sense of the term because the newspapers were subject to censorship during most of this period.[13]

Local news acquired an entirely new dimension in Copenhagen from 1759, when the publisher Hans Holck introduced his advertisement-based newspaper, *Adresseavisen* (1759–1854).[14] The main content of *Adresseavisen* was advertisements, classifieds, commercials, lost and found property, local news and all kinds of other useful public information. Holck opened the newspaper medium to a wider audience, and because of this, *Adresseavisen* opens a privileged window on to the agents' perspective within their social context.

According to modern estimates, in 1766, just under 10 per cent of households in Copenhagen had access to newspapers at home. In addition to household circulation, individuals could also access newspapers at public coffeehouses, clubs and bars. Compared to the 1720s, it has been estimated that newspaper circulation in Copenhagen had tripled in volume by the 1760s.[15] In the early nineteenth century, the Copenhagen newspapers had between 7,000 and 9,000 daily subscribers, yet a significant portion of the city's households still did not have access to them. People with low or unstable incomes could not afford to buy a newspaper,[16] although they did still have access to advertisements and the job market at *Adresseavisen*'s office. During the second half of the eighteenth century, newspapers became the most widely distributed media in Copenhagen. When adopting a terminological approach to the concept of private in the eighteenth century, the newspapers therefore unquestionably had the widest impact, the most readers and the broadest reach of any media across all social strata in Denmark at the time.[17]

Looking at the occurrences of the word 'private' in the newspapers allows for some main conclusions, of which the three main conclusions will be summarized briefly as follows:

1. *Private was not a frequently used word.* The registration of occurrences of the word 'private' in newspapers over the years 1673–1800 shows that it only appeared 4,069 times out of roughly 167,000 digitized newspaper pages that have been digitized in the database, *Mediestream.dk*. The overall conclusion must be that the word 'private' was seldom used in the newspapers during this period – although a small increase in usage can be observed for the second half of the eighteenth century. On the other hand, it should also be emphasized that the newspapers probably also constitute the only type of Danish material where the word 'private' occurred in such large numbers at all during this period.

2. *Private was not a homogeneous concept.* 'Private', when used as an adjective, appeared alongside a surprisingly heterogeneous range of words that had both material and conceptual meanings. A total of 381 different words were used in connection with private – 180 of which occurred only once in the material. In addition, it is noticeable that usage of the word 'private' was much more varied in the past, compared to nowadays. The dichotomy between the private and public, which is otherwise traditionally associated with the concept of the private in historical theory, cannot be applied to the 4,069 occurrences of the word 'private' in the newspapers.[18]

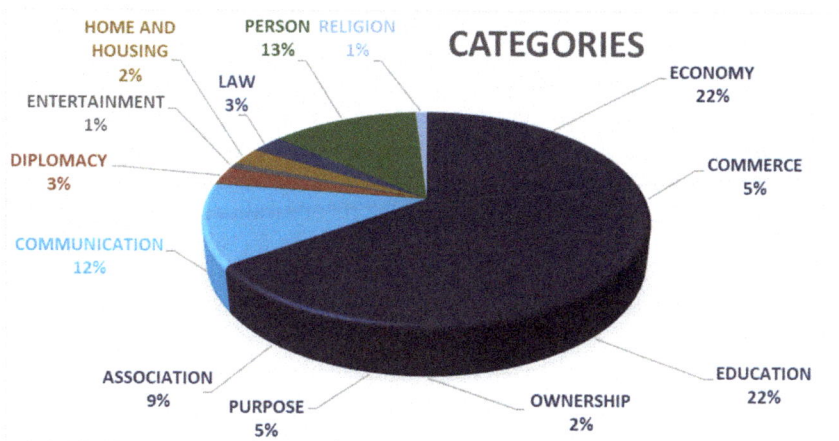

Figure 2.1 The overall result. The 4069 instances of the word private are systematized according to content in thirteen different categories. Of these, six categories comprise themes that can be considered as economic in the broad sense, which corresponds to 65.2 % of the total number of occurrences recorded (here all marked in the same dark blue colour). Knudsen 2020.

3. *Private was primarily an economic notion.* When 'private' appeared in the newspapers, it was typically found in connection to different economic concepts, such as business, commerce, proclamations, private education, private associations and ownership. More than 65 per cent of instances of 'the private' occurred in combination with words related to the economy, either based on the immediate context in which the word was used, or on its direct linguistic meaning. This observation is important in helping us understand how the modern understanding of 'private' as an individual protected legal right came into being.

It is not so much the occurrences of the word 'private' *per se* that is of interest when seeking to understand the term, but rather the context in which 'private' occurs – what we have named 'private+' (i.e. private plus something more). The collected data showed that the word private was normally used as an adjective modifying nouns and, to a much lesser extent, as an adverb modifying verbs. The research process then moved from quantitative data-collection and registration to a more traditional qualitative historical source analysis, where we identified thirteen different categories that can account for various usages of the word 'private'.[19]

Economy

The six categories named economy, commerce, education, ownership, purpose and association comprise together more than 65 per cent of the occurrences of the word private. These six categories all comprise themes that can be directly connected to *private economy* in a broad understanding of the term *economy*. The result represents such a large proportion of the results that there can be no doubt that the connection between the word private and various economic concepts constitutes the central understanding of the word's practical use in the newspapers, during the period 1673–1800.

A few words should be attached to the six categories that are included in the collective term, economy. Mentions of private 'commerce' referred to both local and international trade. Instances of local private trade are typically found in advertisements; for example, the private stock exchanges regularly advertised auctions for all kinds of good, ranging from kitchen utensils to dining room furniture. When considering international trade, the phrase 'private expeditions' calls for special attention. This phrase appeared in advertisements encouraging investors to finance private foreign-trade expeditions. This does not mean, however, that all other international trade was *publicly* funded. The real distinction here was between investors who were external and those who were internal to the established trading companies.[20] Therefore, the absence of the word 'private' in connection to trade does not signify that trade was a public economic matter. The trading companies with a monopoly and other associations were, despite their royal privileges, primarily financed by private shareholders.

The fuzziness of the word 'private' and its usage emerges clearly in the category of 'associations', taking as an illustrative example the advertisements for *Det Private Livrente-Societet* (the Private Annuity Society) – a private pension company founded in 1775. The society's name itself amounted to more than half of all occurrences of the word 'private' in this category. As the company's name shows, this was a private company, even though it was established by law and the state provided a guarantee for its members' deposits in the event of the company's dissolution.[21]

The second largest category, 'education', consists of different types of privately offered teaching, ranging from children's basic education to private university courses. In total, 886 occurrences of 'private' fall within this category. This largely reflects the fact that teaching was offered as a private commodity during the eighteenth century. With very few exceptions, education could just as easily have been included in the category 'commerce'. Usage of 'private' in the realm of education did not indicate any qualitative difference from public teaching; 'private' only speaks to the way in which the teaching in question was provided.[22]

Closely associated with the category of 'private commerce' is that of 'private economy'. This accounts for the largest category, with 918 occurrences of the word 'private'. This category also encompasses the greatest diversity of words found in connection to 'private'. Such words include cost, creditor, account, business, service, tax, subscription, due, money, loan, fine, work and commission, to name just a few. In sum, 'private' appears in combination with eighty-eight different words within this category.

Within the category of 'private economy', one type of notice dominates: advertisements made for the benefit of creditors (*proclama*: proclamation) following a succession, bankruptcy or the occasion when a public official left office. Prior to the newspapers, the public notification of private changes in economic circumstances – thereby informing potential creditors of such changes – had taken place at the local court of justice.[23]

While advertisements or notifications for creditors meant that the newspapers regularly made use of the category 'private economy', the same cannot be said for the category of 'private ownership'. Indeed, in only eighty-five instances was private used in connection to the words ownership or possession.

Nevertheless, private property formed the basis of the private market and of the private economic activities that were mentioned in the newspapers. Once again, we must appreciate that the absence of the word 'private' does not indicate that the newspapers did not address private property – far from it. As we have seen above, the newspapers during this period were principally an advertising media. Their primary purpose was to facilitate contact between buyers and sellers. Thus, it is hardly surprising that the economic notion of the private that emerges from a survey of the newspapers cannot be linked to the traditional private sphere of household and family, but instead referred to actions that took place in a public 'marketplace'. As such, the private economy, based on how it appears in the newspapers, cannot be tied down to a physical place or sphere. The 'private' is instead a conceptualizing term: what matters is not the private itself, but what the 'private' helps qualify, namely the room for manoeuvre available to economic agents, which again was based on the private ownership of goods on the private market.

The 'business plan' of *Adresseavisen* was laid out in a royal letter of privilege dating from 14 April 1759. The letter of privilege divided the information that the newspaper had a duty to publish into sections, which together provide a good indication of the newspaper's private economic purposes: (1) all travellers who arrived or left the city; (2) the price of all food; (3) weekly lists of the dead, born and married; (4) the exchange rate; (5) the arrival of ships and their cargo; (6) employment services for jobseekers; (7) merchants or others in the provinces with stockpiled goods for trade; (8) wholesale goods; (9) all other goods, either movable or immovable property, which someone wanted to sell or requested to buy, rent or auction; (10) transport from Copenhagen; (11) proclamations on death; and (12) provisions of capital for loans.[24] This listing clearly shows that regardless of whether the word 'private' had been included in the newspapers, the primary purpose of the newspaper was to facilitate private economic activity.

Private purpose and the utility of society

It is in this context that we encounter another set of distinctions, this time between the individual (and private) economic agent and the interests of the state, as well as between the individual citizen and so-called civil society. The category of 'private purpose' encompasses ideas such as private matter, private best, private virtue, private advantage, private freedom, private benefit, private deed, private intention, private interest, private passion, private bliss, private manner, private utility and private prosperity. These concepts all brought together disparate political, legal and economic discourses during the eighteenth century. The category of 'private purpose' is not large – there are only 204 occurrences, with seventy-three different words appearing in combination with 'private' – but the category of 'purpose' differs markedly from the others. It is in this category, for instance, that we find what can best be described as value-laden expressions by which 'private' acquires either a positive or a negative character.

The four words used most frequently in this category are happiness (20), interest (16), purpose (20) and utility (30), and they were used throughout the period 1751–1800. This is the only category for which the word 'private' can be identified as a marker of value. In the other twelve categories, the word 'private' was used as a neutral description. However, the few instances of 'private' in the 'private purpose' category do not allow for any conclusions as to the wider significance of these occurrences when thinking more generally about the potential 'moral' values attached to the word private in this period.[25]

The idea that economic policy could improve society was the first political topic to become the subject of general public discourse under the Danish-Norwegian monarchy. In part, the spread of such a discourse can be linked to what Habermas identified as the rise of bourgeois 'public opinion'. Yet conversely, it does not make much sense to talk about free public debate within an absolute state that practised censorship. Nevertheless, because of a top-down governmental interest in strengthening the theoretical basis for economic policies, a controlled public debate on economic improvements was introduced and permitted. Here, Denmark-Norway was no different from wider European developments, but the way in which the economic debate was launched in Denmark remains remarkable. A state appeal was issued on 31 March 1755, urging all righteous patriots to come up with 'all the insights that serve to maintain the country's prosperity, reduce spending, multiply incomes and, in general, the needs of the people'. This call for patriotism led to the creation of a new state-controlled and state-financed economic magazine, *Danmarks og Norges Økonomisk Magasin* (Denmark and Norway's Economic Magazine) in 1757–1764, with the university's pro-chancellor as editor, and with contributions from priests, civil servants, merchants and landowners.[26]

Henrik Horstbøll has examined the significance of this journal and similar such publications in the second half of the eighteenth century. He identifies how the theoretical economic policy changed from what had previously been an orientation to microeconomic practice towards, instead, a macroeconomic societal perspective. As Horstbøll puts it, 'Instead of the traditional discourse on good management of the household and estate, we now find discussions concerning progress, improvement, growth and profitability'.[27] This debate can also be traced in the newspapers, especially after the abolition of censorship in 1770. During the 1770s, the newspapers present a lively discussion about the merits of the old economic system, consisting primarily of large trading companies with royal privileges (e.g. the West Indian Company), or whether free trade was in fact more beneficial to the state and its citizens.

The second half of the eighteenth century witnessed the establishment of private or semi-private associations, each pursuing different social or economic goals. One of the more successful of these was the *Det Kongelige Danske Landhusholdningsselskab* (*Royal Danish Society for Agricultural Housekeeping*), an association established in 1769 (modelled on a foreign example) that still exists today.[28]

Legal professor Peder Kofod Ancher (1710–1788) wrote a lengthy preface to the Danish translation of a French economic dissertation in 1759. In the following excerpt, we gain a sense of the character of the Danish economic debate:

Moreover, there are such innocent deeds, which have no connection with the state: these should be voluntary and left to everyone's own will. Something must be left over where everyone remains his own master. This is yet another remnant of the first and original state, of which the subjects engaged in civil trade should not be deprived. Such activity requires by nature a peculiar diligence and devotion, and is conducted solely by the conception of self-interest. It is necessary that everyone be allowed the freedom to pursue his use and his sustenance in any way that seems best and most advantageous to him. For in promoting his own happiness, every man desires to act according to his own will.[29]

Ancher's statement demonstrates a clear conceptual relationship between free trade and the citizenry's autonomy to pursue their own economic activity without direct interference from the state. This freedom and right was a consequence of natural law, and self-interest was understood to be a necessary precondition for such a right. This was exactly the same idea that Adam Smith would, seventeen years later, describe in his 1776 manifesto on capitalism, *The Wealth of Nations*. That Ancher and Smith reached the same conclusions shows that they were each directly inspired by and applied the jurisprudence of Pufendorf's modern natural law to their economic theories.[30] It is in this capacity that Pufendorf becomes relevant when we come to interpret the association between the word 'private', and the more general economic matters that we have observed in the newspapers during the second half of the eighteenth century. Pufendorf's legal doctrine provides a general framework for understanding the concept of the private in both legal and economic contexts, and it helps us to understand how 'private' and 'privacy' became legal rights.

The second part of this article therefore takes a closer look at Pufendorf's legal principles in order to explain how they formed the legal basis for private economic development. Here, private property came to play a crucial role. As Ancher put it: 'Everyone must be sure that they can always keep what they once legally acquired. It is this certainty that encourages a trader to venture so much, and without it, he seems to put all his diligence and effort at stake.'[31] Rights arising from private property connect the economic developments of the eighteenth century to the modern understanding of the notion of the private as an individual legal right. Private property came to form the spearhead of the legal guarantees that would later be codified as constitutional civil liberties and international human rights.

Samuel Pufendorf and the natural law

Pufendorf created a new paradigm for modern natural law, and his work contributed to the development of an independent legal science that was detached from both moral theology and political philosophy.[32] Pufendorf obtained the first professorship in natural law at the University in Heidelberg in 1661. By this point, he was already a well-known, albeit controversial figure in German academia. He accepted another professorship in natural law in 1668, at the University of Lund, in Sweden. Then, in 1677 he was appointed as the royal Swedish historiographer and counsellor at the Royal Court in Stockholm, before being called to Berlin in 1688 to serve as royal historiographer and legal counsellor. Pufendorf died in Berlin in 1694. Pufendorf's legacy as an innovator of a modern universal jurisprudence extended far beyond Scandinavia and Germany.

Throughout the eighteenth century, Pufendorf's legal theories enjoyed enormous influence in France, England and the North American colonies. His 'duty doctrine' served as a common ground for jurisprudence across both civil and common law, and its influence continues to be felt today, not least since it constitutes a basic principle in both private and international law.[33]

A secular natural law

Pufendorf's *De jure naturae et gentium* offered a comprehensive presentation of modern natural law, along with the basic principles of private and public law. Pufendorf was, of course, indebted to the works of other legal writers – especially those of Hugo Grotius (1583–1645) and Thomas Hobbes (1588–1679) – but in *De jure naturae*, he managed to create a new, coherent legal system for a modern European jurisprudence. He detached modern natural law from the Christian models that had hitherto provided the basis for it, whether that be the Catholic version based on Thomas Aquinas (1225–1274), or the Lutheran version based on Augustine (354–430) and Philipp Melanchthon (1497–1560).

Pufendorf did not try to challenge the idea of God's creation, nor to deny the fundamental social importance of moral theology. He simply insisted that religious dogmas were not a part of either natural or human jurisprudence. Pufendorf explained this legal secularization by referring to the division between 'external' and 'internal' human 'actions'. Human law and natural law were only concerned with the external actions of human beings: 'For moral theology however, it is not enough to mold men's external conduct to propriety. Its chief task is to conform the mind and its internal motions to the will of God.'[34] It is hardly surprising that this part of Pufendorf's new legal philosophy was particularly controversial – opposition from protestant theologians was especially fierce.[35] It was not until 1687, however, that Pufendorf addressed the question of 'religious tolerance'. His discussion of this issue fell within his work *De habitu religionis christianae ad vitam civilem* (*Of the Nature and Qualification of Religion in Reference to Civil Society*).[36] Pufendorf constructed his doctrine of religious tolerance upon conceptual foundations that juxtaposed the public and private: 'For, if these [religious standpoints] are kept within the compass of peoples thoughts, without breaking out into public or outward actions, they are not punishable by the law, neither can any human power take cognizance of what is contained only, and hidden in the heart.'[37]

On the Duty of Man and Citizen

In 1673, Pufendorf published a summary of his *De jure naturae* in two small books entitled *De officio hominis et civis juxta legem naturalem libri duo* (*On the Duty of Man and Citizen*).[38] In the preface, he wrote that the purpose of this 'compendium' was 'to expound to beginners the principal topics of natural law in short'.[39] His compendium introduced new standards for legal textbooks in central and northern Europe for more than a hundred years. Although it is only 177 pages in the modern English translation, *De officio* nevertheless provides an introduction to all the general legal principles upon which both private and public law are built. *De officio* was translated into the main

European languages, and countless legal students, civil servants and lawyers across eighteenth-century Europe studied this work, ensuring that Pufendorf's legal principles enjoyed a deep influence and were applied in the daily legal practices of those who had studied his work.[40] The significance of this textbook for the dissemination of a modern European jurisprudence in the eighteenth century cannot be overstated. *De officio* was first translated into Danish in 1742,[41] with the stated intention that it be used as part of the legal curriculum at the University in Copenhagen, which had been reformed in 1736.[42]

The doctrine of duty

It is easy to overlook the fact that Pufendorf was neither a political nor a moral philosopher. He has the distinction of being the first pure philosopher of law. This is important when seeking to understand his work and influence. Pufendorf based his legal synthesis on the law of obligations, that is, on his 'doctrine of duty'. The first volume of *De officio* dealt with the principles of natural law and with their consequences for private law. The second volume covered public law, including Pufendorf's interpretation of the 'social contract' as a common model for the foundation of the state within his vision of modern natural law.

The law of obligations was based on the general assumption that obligations must be kept – that is, the maxim *pacta sunt servanda*.[43] Pufendorf employed this axiom when outlining his doctrine of duty: 'The general duty imposed by natural law in this matter is, that every man must keep his faith given, or fulfil his promises and agreements. For without this, we would lose most of the possible advantage of mutual exchange of services and things' (I.9.3). In the first two chapters of Book I, Pufendorf defined the legal basis for a modern law of obligations through a few general legal principles, placed within a framework of natural law. Bilateral agreements made between two parties had, by their own merit, a legally binding effect, and thus existed independently from any stately intervention – at least in principle. Pufendorf further substantiated the separation between private and public law by pointing out that natural law, on a theoretical level at least, antedated the first processes of state-formation: that is, natural law comes from the time before humans decided to renounce their natural liberty and, through the social contract, submit to a state's sovereignty. In this way, Pufendorf very cleverly established a connection between private law and individual liberty that existed in the state of nature. Pufendorf thus stated that this original natural freedom remained in force in the private law of obligations. It is not surprising then that Ancher thought that trade 'should be voluntary and left to everyone's own will'.

The principles of contract

A contract or agreement is a 'legally binding' promise made between two parties. Hence, a promise is an undertaking by one person to do something (or to refrain from doing something) if another person does something in return. In order for an agreement or contract to be legally binding, the parties must exchange both an offer and an acceptance.[44] Both parties, moreover, must agree to the contract with their own free will. A party's genuine consent is an essential element in the creation of a legal obligation.[45] There must therefore also be mutual acceptance (*consensus*) among the parties of the agreement or contract. Free will represents the alpha and the omega in the law of obligations: every legal agreement imposes a restriction on human freedom, whereby one person assumes a duty towards another. If one person has a duty, the other, conversely, has acquired a right. A right in the law of obligations is, accordingly, a reflection of a duty. Duty, understood in this context, is something completely different from a moral or religious duty.

The newspapers were full of (private) offers. Newspaper advertisements were, in fact, nothing more than the first step in the creation of a contract – they were the offer, so to speak. Prior to that, the advertiser had entered into a contract with the newspaper in order to publish the advertisement in the first place. Another contract had put the advertiser in possession of the product that he now wanted to sell. A single newspaper was thus composed of a myriad of contracts with their underlying duties and rights, free will, offer and acceptance, and consensus.

The constitutive legal principles of mutual duties and rights formed, according to Pufendorf, the core of all human coexistence, both in the original state of nature as a principle of natural law, and as the legal basis for public law and state regulation.[46] As Reinhard Zimmermann states: 'Thus, to the natural lawyers, contract was the essential tool for the regulation of human affairs, the cornerstone of all the institutions of the positive law.'[47] The first principle of private law is that agreements entail both duties and rights. In *De officio*, Pufendorf systematized his duty-doctrine into three principal types, each of which was imposed upon humans by the law of nature itself, even in the absence of a human-made law or regulation that could force individuals to adhere to them or prosecute individuals when they failed in these duties. The three divisions were (1) duty to God, (2) duty to oneself and (3) duty to others.[48]

In Chapter 4 about duties to God, Pufendorf, on the basis of natural law, identified that man (as an individual) was obliged to recognize the existence of God (I.4.1).[49] Here, Pufendorf reviewed a long list of obligations that one has towards God. The trained lawyer, however, would immediately realize that duties towards God were not *absolute legal* duties. One cannot make a mutual agreement with God, which would be unenforceable, because one cannot summon God for breach of contract. The prerequisites that are necessary for an agreement to qualify as a legal contract are therefore not applicable in the case of God. Thus, one's duties to God are not legal agreements. As for duty to oneself, Pufendorf argued that 'self-love' compelled man to have a careful concern for himself 'and to get all the good he can in every way' (I.5.1). Man thus had a duty to self-preservation and, arising from this, he also had a right to self-defence. In the state of natural liberty, this right was more far-reaching than it would be under a civil government (I.5.8–9). Pufendorf explained the principles of self-defence in relation to attempts 'on life, limbs, virtue, and property' (I.5.10–16), and he thus defined the fundamental objects of human rights (I.6.3 and 5). For Ancher and Adam Smith, this meant that the citizen, in principle, also had the same duty to act in his benefit when it came to his own private economy.

Absolute duties and private law

In relation to duties to others, Pufendorf introduced two other legal concepts: absolute duties and perfect rights. By using the words 'absolute' and 'perfect', Pufendorf emphasized the point that duties to life, limbs, virtue and property were *legally* binding by merit of the law of nature itself, thereby allowing for the pursuit of self-help outside of any direct intervention from the state.

The first absolute duty was as follows: not to harm others with respect to their life, limbs, chastity, liberty and property (I.6.3). The second absolute duty obligated each man to value and treat the other as a natural equal in the state of nature. This natural equality disappeared, of course, when humans formed societies, but natural equality nevertheless remained the legal basis upon which agreements were formed in the law of obligations. Legal agreements required, as we have seen, the use of free will, consensus and the recognition of a mutual obligation, meaning that both parties were equally obligated (I.7.3–4).

The third absolute duty was an extension of the second. As Pufendorf put it: 'The duty owed by every man to every man, to be performed for the sake of common sociality, is: Everyone should be useful to others, so far as he conveniently can' (I.8.1). It is thus not enough to refrain from harming others; one must also be obliged to care for others. These three absolute duties summarized the basic legal principles of obligations – and still today provide the binding standards of legal responsibility.[50] Here we meet the key distinction in the economic discourse of the eighteenth century that emerges from the Copenhagen newspapers and the state-controlled debate on the economy. The dynamic between the duty to oneself and the duty to others has, since the time of Pufendorf's duty-doctrine, constituted the fundamental legal understanding of social interaction between the individual and the community. What Pufendorf described was not a dichotomy between private and public interests. Pufendorf instead explained that before the states were formed, and before man-made regulations had been imposed upon people, the state of nature itself had required that every human being discharge their absolute duty to each other. Therefore, one can argue that Pufendorf in reality created a notion of 'a civil society', as a legal concept, that existed *before* the state was founded.

Private law was (and is) not subject to the same degree of regulation as public law. Private agreements and contracts thus constitute the binding 'rules' in private law. The interpretation of such contracts is based on general legal axioms and principles, and takes place in the civil courts.[51] Pufendorf detached the principles of natural law from its hitherto metaphysical and moral-theological framework, and instead established close relationship between it and private law. Accordingly, he also drew a close relationship between individual liberty as it had once been possessed in the state of nature, and the continued individual freedom to enter into private agreements after the formation of states and into the present. This is why, for Pufendorf, the state should refrain from interfering in the private market.

Ownership and property law

In the second half of Book I of *De officio*, Pufendorf discussed the principles of the two major branches of private law: the law of obligations and property law. In the field of property law, Pufendorf's theory formed a new legal understanding of private property rights and of their origins:

'It follows [from ownership] that we may dispose as we will of things which belong to us as property and bar all others from using them, except insofar as they may acquire a particular right from us by agreement' (I.12.3). The right to property is a consequence of the first absolute duty not to harm others with regards to their life, limbs, chastity, liberty *and property* (I.6.3). Treating the right to property as an extension of the duty not to harm others, however, does not explain how private property first came into being. Pufendorf thus explained that God had made all things available to all men. As he put it:

To avoid conflicts and to institute good order at this stage, [the humans] took the step of dividing the actual bodies of things amongst themselves, and each was assigned his own proper portion … In this way, property in things [*proprietas rerum*] or ownership [*dominium*] was introduced by the will of God, with consent [*consensus*] among men right from the beginning and with at least a tacit agreement [*pactum*]

(I.12.2).

Pufendorf claimed that property antedated the formation of states, and that it was founded upon mutual agreement. The protection of property was therefore an *a priori* 'right' that man had already acquired in the state of nature. The original allocation of property within the state of nature, as such, created a fundamental legal principle that implied the inviolability of private property.[52] This legal definition of a proprietary right to 'things' also formed the basis of a 'private right'. We return to the two lines quoted above: 'We may dispose as we will … and we may bar all others from using them.' Herein lies the essence of 'private' property – and probably also of the right to privacy. We can elaborate this further by referring to the legal division of *positive* and *negative* rights in property. Positive rights include the rights that the owner of a 'thing' has to sell, give away, destroy, abandon and otherwise use his property as he sees fit. Negative rights, in contrast, refer to the basic idea that others do *not* enjoy these same (positive) rights to the 'thing' in question. In addition to the list of positive rights that derive from property, this negative right of property thus also conveys an (implicit) right of privacy.[53]

In this light, the private economic perspective as it appears in the newspapers suddenly becomes an expression of something that was protected by a special legal right. This idea makes it particularly relevant to investigate the relation between the expansion of a private economic market in the second half of the eighteenth century, and modern legal concepts of property.[54] The question now is how Pufendorf applied his duty-doctrine, articulated for the state of natural liberty, to the foundation of states.

The foundation of states and the social contract

In Book II of *De officio*, Pufendorf presented what can, in general terms, be described as public law. He reviewed the basic principles of criminal law, family law and inheritance law, and he derived from them the legal framework for what we today call constitutional law: that is, the legal framework for state formation and state governance based on the natural law principle of the social contract. The social contract represented the transition from the state of nature whereby people voluntarily surrendered their natural freedom and submitted to a state in order to obtain security against the abuse of others. Here, Pufendorf applied the doctrine of duty to the legal principle of a binding contract through which the subjects surrendered their sovereignty to state government and obligated themselves to obey and remain faithful to the sovereign. In return, the government undertook to ensure the security and safety of its subjects.

Hugo Grotius (1625) and Thomas Hobbes (1651) had already introduced the idea of the social contract into the framework of modern natural law. Hobbes saw the state of nature as one of constant war between humans, and he argued for a theory of total submission in which individual self-preservation was the only motive behind state formation.[55] In Grotius's social contract, humans formed states because of their innate sociability, which helped motivate them to construct states.[56] Pufendorf sought to harmonize these two contrasting models of self-preservation and sociability.[57] According to him, humans did *not* have an innate predisposition for sociability; they instead had to learn social skills, not only for their own survival but also for the sake of the common good. Pufendorf considered such sociability as a survival strategy. The willingness for mutual commitment was, of course, a necessity in Pufendorf's duty-doctrine, and it formed the basis of human coexistence. It must be noted, however, that mutual commitment would be meaningless if the protective considerations that followed from the absolute duties to life, body, virtue and property in the state of nature had formally disappeared following the development of states.[58]

Duties and rights of the sovereign

In full accordance with Pufendorf's duty-doctrine, the power of the sovereign was also described in the dyadic terms of duties and rights. Pufendorf explained that duties to oneself in the state of natural liberty amounted to the principle of self-defence with respect to attempts on one's life, limbs, virtue and property (I.5.10–16). In the state (in the political sense), this list was translated into the sovereign's right to and monopoly over the infliction of punishments on subjects who had committed action defined by the state as crimes. According to Pufendorf, 'With the introduction of government among men, the security of societies requires that rulers too have the capacity to suppress the wickedness of their subjects, so that most men may live securely with one another (II.13.5)'. The right to punish criminal behaviour stemmed from the very rationale underlying state formation: namely, the creation of security. Punishment could be imposed on life, limbs, virtue and property, whether through the death penalty, corporal punishment, deprivation of honour or the confiscation of property. In this connection, one should briefly note that virtue or reputation, for Pufendorf, was seen to be as a value (price) of a person 'in common life': 'Reputation in general is the value of persons in common life [*vita communis*] by which they may be measured against others or compared with them and either preferred or put after them' (II.14.1).

Honour and reputation – or the lack thereof – played a fundamental role in social interactions in the early modern period. Pufendorf placed reputation within a proprietary context because it was a concept linked to an individual's opportunities to act as a private agent. Because of the importance attached to one's capacity to enter into agreements with other economic and social agents, it is little wonder that Pufendorf argued that reputation could have a direct influence on social and economic relationships. Pufendorf explained the seriousness of reputation:

> It is a still greater wrong to give signs of contempt for others by deeds, words, looks, laughter or slighting gesture. This sin is to be regarded as worse, in that it vigorously excites the hearts of others to violent anger and desire for revenge. In fact, there are many men who would prefer to expose their lives to instant danger, to say nothing of disturbing the public peace, rather than let an insult go unavenged. The reason is that fame and reputation are sullied by insult; and to keep their reputation intact and unsullied is very dear to men's hearts.
>
> (I.7.6)

The importance of reputation is echoed in Camilla Schjerning's chapter in this volume about the phenomenon of house-scorning and the readiness felt by individuals to defend any perceived attack on their personal reputations, as well as in Ulrik Langen's chapter about the consequences of a public moral uprising against some Copenhagen homeowners and their businesses. However, Pufendorf's concept of reputation in a legal and economic context provides an additional dimension to discussions of early modern honour.

On the power of the sovereign over property within the state

The rights of the ruler did not, however, come without limitations. In fact, these limitations were particularly relevant when considering the protection of private property, along with its accompanying and incipient legal definition of individual private rights. Pufendorf limited the sovereign's right to interfere in the citizen's use of private property to three specific situations that arose from the social contract: 'Property of which citizens have obtained full ownership by their own industry or in any other way is subject to three principal rights, which, by the nature of states and as necessary to their purpose, belong to sovereigns' (II.15.1). Two of these rights are today regulated in constitutional law: the right to expropriate private property and the right to collect taxes. Just like in modern constitutions, Pufendorf emphasized that there must be exceptional circumstances before the state could exercise expropriation, and the owner required compensation for his loss.[59]

The right to collect taxes, on the other hand, was more complicated. Rights of taxation allowed 'the sovereign to collect a fraction of the citizens' property as tribute or tax'. But how much was 'a fraction'? Pufendorf used this discussion to provide guidance to rulers: 'Prudent rulers would be wise to take into consideration the resentment felt by ordinary people, and to make an effort to give as little offence as possible in collecting taxes' (II.15.3). The role played by taxation in mediating the relationship between the state and its citizen in relation to private property should not be underestimated. By the time that Pufendorf wrote his work, war and war-funding dating back to the Reformation had long-burdened large parts of Europe.[60]

Sari Nauman shows in her contribution to this volume the consequences that could follow when a tense relationship between subjects and the local representatives of the state led to direct rebellion.[61]

The use of private property

Far more interesting than expropriation and taxation, however, was the ongoing regulation in the early modern period of the private economic market, which led to restrictions being placed on the individual's right to dispose of private property. In Pufendorf's words, 'The sovereigns may make laws obliging the citizens to accommodate their use of their property to the interest of the state; or defining the extent and nature of possessions, and the method of transferring property to others, and other matters of this kind' (II.15.2). It is especially the words *may* and *laws* that give pause for reflection. If sovereigns wished to restrict their citizens' right to dispose of their own property however they wished, then this was only possible *by law*. Today, we would call this principle the 'rule of law'. The sovereign was therefore not allowed to act for his private benefit; it was only the utility of the state that could legitimize state interference in an individual's property. The modern English translation renders Pufendorf's original Latin text of *ad utilitatem civitatis* (1673) as 'the interest of the state'.[62] It is actually possible to get a little closer to Pufendorf's understanding of the relationship between state and citizen, for example, when he writes: 'Nevertheless, sovereigns must not merely collect from the citizens' property the funds necessary for the preservation of the state. … For the strength of the state consists also in the virtue and wealth of the citizens, and therefore the sovereign must take whatever measures he can to ensure the growth of the citizens' personal prosperity' (II.11.11).

The regulation of private property to which Pufendorf referred was an element in the ongoing legislative processes during the early modern period that articulated the so-called good policy, a set of initiatives which aimed at creating a new kind of welfare-promoting legislation, not least in the field of economic trade. This regulation had significant effects for the framework in which private economic activities were conducted, in the same way that trade and consumer regulations do today. This regulation helps shed light on the relationship between the private interests of individual citizens and the needs of the state – and thus also on 'civil society'.[63] Here one must keep in mind that in classical economics, there are two traditional perspectives: that of the merchant and that of the consumer. These two roles, however, can easily exist within the same person, and thus which role one emphasizes when adopting an agent-centred perspective will always depend on the specific situation.

It is important to stress that state regulation of the private economy and the market is not in itself considered to be a one-sided state intervention that can lead to a fixed and definite understanding of the private, as opposed to the public. The dividing line here is not a clean cut between the state and the citizens, but is in fact a multi-faceted nexus of contact between different agents and interests. The private market worked insofar as no regulation or conflict took place in complete independence from state interference. The conflicts over private economic space did not take place between the state and the citizen, but rather between citizens as private economic agents.

Once again, the idea that the individual citizen's personal prosperity brought actual benefits to the state helps us conceptually differentiate the economy of citizens and the economy of the state: the private economic market is left to 'a civil society', that is, to the sum of all citizens.

Social and economic agents

The newspapers contain countless examples of this 'good policy' regulation, which was officially enforced by a myriad of different types of local officials. Copenhagen was physically enclosed by a massive military-defence system that was shut to outsiders every night; the city thus had the opportunity and the means to control all incoming and outgoing activity. Censuses from the second half of the eighteenth century recorded and registered the city's population of approximately 100,000 people. Citizens' lives were monitored by quartermasters, appointed taxation citizens, overseers of the poor and the corps of watchmen.

The police chief, his officers, the magistrate and the parish priests all supervised the citizenry's affairs and livelihood, while the royal court and civil servants devoted an especial attention to citizens' lives in the city. Although the state had a unique opportunity for extensive control and surveillance of its population, the newspapers nevertheless leave us with a picture of a private economic market that, in the midst of price regulation, trade restrictions and market control, existed and developed in the best possible way because of the accretion of interactions between private agents from across all social strata. The newspapers, day-by-day, week-by-week and year-by-year document continuous economic enterprise throughout the second half of the eighteenth century. Newspapers such as *Posttidende* and *Adresseavisen* well attest to this reality.

An assessment of the level of economic activity as presented in the local newspapers – though of course knowing that there were many other economic transactions besides those recorded in the newspapers, some of which were undoubtedly both shady and criminal – leaves the impression that measures of public control, along with litigation in the civil courts, were surprisingly inactive. What does this tell us about the private economy in Copenhagen during this period? Perhaps this indicates that the market actually was far more autonomous than the many regulations would lead us to believe. Private agents acted on market terms, and the state and local authorities seem to have given private economic enterprises the leeway that was called for in the economic debates of the time. This was a debate in which modern natural law helped to create a legal understanding of the private economy, with obligation and property law lying at its foundation. The level of activity reflected in the newspapers suggests that the Danish-Norwegian state had recognized the private market, even though it would take more than fifty years before the formal liberalization of traditional mercantile economic policy was abolished, with the Freedom of Trade Act, dated to 29 December 1857. How was the market able to evolve despite this outdated economic regulatory tradition? It seems that private law compensated for its shortcomings. Large segments of public 'good policy' regulation could easily be circumvented if the private agents agreed to do so. This applied, for example, to pricing, working conditions and to privileges.

Private agreements on marriage, inheritance and family matters could also be agreed upon bilaterally if arrangements other than those stipulated in public regulations were to apply; indeed, as a last resort, one could always apply for a dispensation from the rules. The long lines of closely written protocols surviving from petitions presented to the central administration of the Danish-Norwegian monarchy provide excellent examples of some creative solutions.[64]

Concluding reflections

The result of the newspaper survey invites reflection on whether the methodology of word-mining for the term 'private' will lead to anything other than scattered examples of usage of the word within early modern sources, as well as observations as to how that usage is influenced by the scholar's choice of source material upon which to conduct the study in the first place. Let us take an example of another source. We have examined a very popular legal textbook, Lauritz Nørregaard's *Forelæsninger over den Danske og Norske Privat Ret* (*Lectures on Danish and Norwegian Private Law*), published in seven volumes in 1784. In the 2,770 pages about private law, only 315 occurrences of the word 'private' can be identified, and it appears in conjunction with sixty-one different words. The words used with 'private' in Nørregaard's textbook appear to have been somewhat narrower in terminological scope than were those found in the newspapers. No surprise there. More thought provoking, however, is the observation that the word 'private' does not appear to have been used to a significantly greater extent than it was in the papers. Similarly, Pufendorf's *De officio* in the original Latin used the word 'private' on only a handful of occasions, and the rendering of 'private' from the Latin varies across the different languages into which the text was translated.[65]

On the one hand, our study shows what the use of the word 'private' in the newspapers was clearly associated with private economic meanings. As soon as we started to analyse the material with a traditional source-critical approach, however, it turned out that the word 'private' appeared in the newspapers with an astonishing infrequency. Apparently, there was no need to utilize the term in order to create a legal or a private economic terminology when describing something that individuals already seem to have recognized as a basic premise. The 'private economy', as a concept, is so prevalent in the newspapers that the word 'private' itself loses its significance. This realization only became apparent after we went from the quantitative, electronic registration of the word, to the qualitative analysis of how that word was used in context.

That said, our study has nevertheless established a convincing link between notions of the private and the economy. This led us to pursue how the notion of the economic market related to and interacted with property rights and the legal protection of those rights, which Habermas had already touched on in his theory describing the transformation of the public. The category that we labelled as 'private purpose' gave us a more conceptual understanding of the word 'private', as opposed to the spatial idea of private contra public. This understanding helped shape our wider interpretation of the connection between the private economy and private property. The interpretation of modern natural law also contributes to our understanding of the link between the private economy and private property. From modern natural jurisprudence, we have seen that it is not sufficient to limit our understanding of private to the supposed dichotomy between the private and public. The protection that the social contract sought to guarantee primarily aimed at protecting citizens from whatever abuses they might suffer, either from each other or from external enemies. In this light, when looking at the private *in* the public, it is precisely in the conflicts between members of a 'civil society' that the boundaries of the private become clear, and where one finds the role of the authorities in conflict resolution.

Let us return briefly to Pufendorf's definition of duty to oneself and of duty to others. When writing about duty to oneself, Pufendorf explained the principles of self-defence when an individual was faced with attempts on life, limbs, virtue and property (I.5.10–16). Concerning duties to others, the first 'absolute duty' of the individual was to refrain from harming another's life, limbs, chastity, liberty and property (I.6.3). This is the first time in the legal tradition that we see a legal system constructed on the definition of rights. And since Pufendorf connected these fundamental rights to the sphere of private law, he also created a protectionist interest, especially with regards to 'the private'. 'Private', in his schema, became closely linked to basic legal principles; and through Pufendorf's work, these principles have achieved the importance they retain today. Therefore, Pufendorf's principles can also help bridge the gap between the past and the present when we talk about the 'private' as something to protect. In discussing the duty to oneself, Pufendorf further found his way to criminal law, via the social contract. For him, duty to oneself served as the general model for criminal law. The protection that followed from the individual's self-defence in the state of nature was handed over to the state in order to ensure that citizens did not suffer harm or loss with respect to their rights.

Judith Jarvis Thomson, in her article *The Right to Privacy*, discusses whether there are any independent protection rights in relation to privacy at all. It is Thomson's opinion that those rights that she refers to as 'the grand ones' already cover privacy: 'The right to life, the right to liberty, the right to not be hurt or harmed, and property rights.'[66] Concerning the right to privacy, she concludes that 'it is not a distinct cluster of rights but itself intersects with the cluster of rights, which the right over the person consists in [life and body] and also with the cluster of rights, which owning property consists in'.[67] There is little difference between how Pufendorf and Thomson each define rights. How we approach these basic legal principles has a profound influence on our understanding of private legal rights, in the contexts both of the early modern period and of today. Research into the private and privacy often mentions different sorts of rights – regardless of whether the discussion is about the lack of a particular right, or what should be protected by a right. However, there is often considerable uncertainty when it comes to the protection of a right to privacy. Protection of what, from whom, and by whom? These questions are nearly intractable, given that only *legal* rights can be protected.

The notion of a 'space' that is constituted by civil society – of a space between the private that is attached to the individual or the family, and the public as the 'state' or 'the absolute monarchy' – is an essential element in Habermas's theory about the structural transformations of the eighteenth century. The establishment of a 'middle ground' position created a space in which the private agents of 'civil society' could pursue their social and economic activities; this space gives us the missing link in the private-public dichotomy.[68] Pufendorf's legal doctrine of duty provides a legal basis to understand the private market as follows: it was the sum of private economic activities that unfolded as a result of the meeting of economic agents who formed private legal contracts and agreements. The material from the newspapers shows how contact between these economic actors could be facilitated.

Notes

1   Private economic perspectives on privacy are primarily dealt with in contemporary research. This is especially the case for the issue of private information as a commodity, usually in the field of information technology, on which see Posner 1984, 334–45; and Roessler and Mokrosinska 2015 on personal data and health from a market perspective. See also Lindgreen 2018, 181–207 for the economy from a cost-benefit perspective. In this handbook on privacy studies, the private economy is not mentioned at all in the historiographical article of Kuelen and Kroeze 2018, 21–5. Benn and Gaus 1983 remain a central work; see also McKeon 2006. McKeon discusses the private economy and rights in relation to the traditional theories about the distinction between the private and the public. However, the economic perspective does not constitute the main theme of the book.

2   Habermas [1962] 1991, 85.

3   Ibid., 87. Habermas's model does not rest on a dichotomy between the private and the public (political) sphere. For Habermas, incipient liberalism and trade capitalism are the real forces behind the development of a political public opinion. Interesting in Habermas's theory is 'the buffer-zone' that he created between the private and the public – what he termed 'the civil society', and which, according to him, formed the framework for the private economic market.

4   The concept of civil society in the eighteenth century is a separate topic for discussion, and is left untouched here. However, the fact that the trade economy in this period had evolved beyond a traditional economic model with the household and the family at its centre is quite obvious. According to Habermas [1962] 1991, 74: 'The social precondition for this "developed" bourgeois public sphere was a market that, tending to liberalized made affairs in the sphere of social reproduction as much as possible a matter of private people left to themselves and so finally completed the privatization of civil society. Under absolutism, the latter's establishment as a private realm was conceivable at first only in the privative sense that social relationships were stripped for their quasi-public character. The political functions, both judicial and administrative, were consolidated into public autonomy. … With the expansion and liberation of this sphere of the market, commodity owners gained private autonomy; the positive meaning of "private" emerged precisely in reference to the concept of free power to control over property that functioned in capitalist faction'. For a new interpretation of the development of liberalism, see Rosenblatt 2018.

5   The research project of mapping all the instances of the word 'private' in the Copenhagen newspapers 1673–1800 was a part of The Danish National Research Foundation Centre for Privacy Studies (PRIVACY) research program: https://teol.

ku.dk/privacy/about-privacy/. The purpose of the project was to test the centre's terminological research approach on a large body of material in order to shed light on actual usage of the word 'private'.

6   The agent-centred perspective has been well-described, and it is connected to two other concepts, interest and assess, that allow for an interesting alternative theoretical approach to the private and public; see Gaus 1983, 183–222.

7   Andersen and Johansen 2016, 454.

8   An example on the interesting use of the concept of agency in an historical perspective can be found in the collection of essays edited by Simonton and Montenach 2013.

9   Habermas [1962] 1991, 75.

10 Sæther 2017, 143.

11 An overview of the digitalized Danish newspapers and Danish newspaper history can be found at http://mediastream.dk/.

12 The international newsletters are discussed in Jørgen Mührmann-Lund's chapter, in this volume.

13 Censorship is examined in Jesper Jacobsen's chapter, in this volume.

14 For further information on *Adresseavisen*, see Jesper Jacobsen's chapter in this volume.

15 Søllinge 1987, 29.

16 Ibid., 54.

17 Reading *Adresseavisen* is like walking through the streets of eighteenth-century Copenhagen: the closest one can get to time travel. Where can you get fresh lemons this week? Have you seen that Widow Green has put the house in Easter Street up for sale – and that the king is back from the castle in Fredensborg? Details, names, locations, books for sale, linen, beef, lectures, theatre plays and Supreme Court decisions: all of these amazing impressions disappear when engaged in text mining. Fortunately, they return when the results of the actual usage of words require qualitative analysis.

18 This once again leads to the fundamental problem of using modern analytical concepts to explain the past. This issue is also addressed in Keulen and Kroeze 2018 in relation to Aristotle's (384–322 B.C.) distinction between *oikos*, the private domestic sphere of the family, and *polis*, the public sphere: 'By using these references, historical review of privacy, suggest that in over 2200 years of history privacy was mainly understood in the same way' (24). This critique is also formulated in McKeon 2006, 48–9.

19 The study's most important methodological finding consists in its variation, and this is the reason why we must agree with the general critique of the traditional theoretical dichotomy between the private and the public. From the beginning, we had planned to record every instance of this dichotomy, but we found very quickly that such a dichotomy only existed if we interpreted it directly into the material. Each of the occurrences has been analysed in its own context. The thirteen categories that we have identified contain some methodological considerations on selection and deselection. In this specific case, the intention was not to carry out an etymological analysis. Hence, in the subsequent systemization, priority was given to the historical meaning of the words rather than to their linguistic form.

20 Andersen and Johansen 2016, 504. In 1772, Indian trade was liberated and handed over to private traders. From 1772 to 1807, private expeditions surpassed the number

of company expeditions, while the East India Company retained its monopoly on Chinese trade.

21 Although the company was not fully subscribed according to its original plan, it nevertheless remained in business until the Ministry of Finance took over its leadership in 1853. The last stakeholder died in 1866.

22 The category of 'teaching' has been placed on its own to emphasize how widespread the word 'private' was in connection to advertisements for teaching in the newspapers. In the eighteenth century, most of the education at all levels was handled by private individuals. This was true both for private schools, and for teaching that took place in the home of a private teacher or in the students' own homes. Language teaching, sewing, dance lessons and accounting have also been included in this category, as have the private lessons given by university professors in their own homes.

23 With access to newspapers, the requirements for public proclamations became considerably easier to implement, and more than half (52.8%) of the occurrences of private in the category 'economy' (a total of 484) were related to advertisements for proclamations.

24 Westen 1780, 24–5.

25 A search in Mediestream.dk for *lyksalig** (happy) produces 1,880 hits and *nytte** (utility) produces 10,370 hits; this more than indicates that the addition (or not) of the word 'private' does not qualify such concepts as good or bad. Furthermore, the 204 occurrences that we have found will hardly bring us closer to a conceptual understanding of whether the idea of private was good or bad.

26 Horstbøll 1989, 42–3.

27 Horstbøll 1987, 27.

28 *The Royal Society for the Encouragement of Arts Manufacture and Commerce* was established in 1759 as the first of its kind in England, followed by the French *Société royale d'agriculture de la Généralité de Tours* in 1760. The purpose of the Danish-Norwegian association was to improve the methods of agricultural cultivation and thereby improve the economy. See Dybdahl 1968 and Hertel 1919–1921.

29 Ancher 1759, 66–7: 'Der er desuden sådanne uskyldige gerninger, som ingen sammenhæng har med staten: Samme bør være frivillige og overlades til enhvers eget behag, at der må dog være noget tilovers, hvor udi enhver er sin egen herre. Dette er endnu en levning af den første og oprindelige friheds stand, som ikke bør betages undersåtterne i den borgerlige handel, som den er af den beskaffenhed, at den udfordrer en besynderlig flid og hengivenhed, og drives alene ved forestilling af egennytte, så det er fornødent, at der tillades enhver den frihed at drive sit brug og sin næring på hvad måde han synes selv bedst og fordelagtigst. Thi i at befordre sin egen lyksalighed, ønsker ethvert menneske at gå frem efter sit eget hoved'.

30 For the influence of Pufendorf's jurisprudence on Adam Smith (1723–1790), see Sæther 2017, 228–51. It is noteworthy that Smith used Pufendorf's theories of value, money and trade (from *De officio* I, ch. 14) in his work, *The Wealth of Nations* (1776), for which see Haara and Lahdenranta 2018, 19–37. Smith was translated into Danish in 1779–1780.

31 Ancher 1759, 82: 'Enhver må være vis på, bestandig at beholde, hvad han engang lovligen har erhvervet. Det er denne vished, som opmuntrer en handlende til at vove så meget, og uden samme synes han at sætte al sin flid og møje på spil'.

32   Tully 1991, xiv–xxxvi; Modéer 2001, 11–23; Hochstrasse 2009, 40–71.

33   Today, Pufendorf's legacy has become again the subject of intensive studies, especially his influence on later writers such as John Locke (1632–1704), Christian Thomasius (1655–1728), Christian Wolff (1679–1754), Charles-Louis de Secondat Montesquieu (1689–1755), Jean-Jacques Rousseau (1712–1778), Adam Smith (1723–1790), Jeremy Bentham (1748–1832), John Stuart Mill (1806–1873) and the Founding Fathers of the United States. See Sæther 2017 and Scattola 2009, 21.

34   Pufendorf 1991, 9.

35   Darwall 2000, 987.

36   Translated by Crull 1698. This publication was a reaction to the Edict of Nantes in 1685, and was soon followed by John Locke's *Letter Concerning Toleration* (1689). For a general introduction to Pufendorf's religious standpoints, see Zuruchen 2000, 779–814.

37   It is tempting to claim that there is a connection between religious tolerance and a defined right to an inner private 'space'. For Pufendorf, however, *external* and *internal* only served as a strict legal demarcation in relation to human legislation, where the fundamental principle remained that only external actions could be subject to legal regulation and prosecution. Pufendorf 1991, II.13.11: 'If we reflect on the purposes of punishment and the condition of the human race, it becomes clear that not all offences are fit to be punished by human justice. The following are exempt from human punishment: Purely internal acts, i.e. delicious thoughts of sin, greed, desire and intention without action, even if subsequent confession reveals them to others. For no harm is done to anyone by such an internal impulse; and it is in no one's interest that anyone be punished for it.' Pufendorf returned to this division in relation to 'human speech and thought'. In the context of the law of obligations, the parties had (and have) a duty to disclose all necessary information when entering into a contract. Nondisclosure could (and can) be considered as fraud, but only in a strict contractual meaning: Pufendorf 1991, I.10.4: 'But it is not always the case that my thoughts have to be shared with another. … And so, I may rightly conceal by silence, however pressingly questioned, what the other party has no right to get from me, and which I have no obligation to reveal'. On the modern legal conditions of private information, see Schoeman 1984, 411–12.

38   The English translation from 1991 is used for quotation.

39   Pufendorf 1991, 6.

40   Sæther 2017, 136; Haakonssen and Seidler 2016, 388.

41   Pufendorf 1742.

42   For the influence of modern natural law in Denmark-Norway, see e.g. Knudsen 2001, 58–60; Vogt 2007, 590–613; Sunde 2007.

43   Zimmermann 1996, 576–7. The Roman law assumption became wedded through canon law to the moral precept of faithfulness (i.e. *fides*), on which see ibid., 568. Grotius blended this tradition into a natural law concept that placed special emphasis on natural freedom and on the obligational part of a promise (544). Grotius's contract theory and its intersection between theology and law have recently been addressed in Astorri 2020, 88–107.

44   Zimmermann 1996, 571.

45   Ibid., 569.

46 Pufendorf 1991, I.2.3: 'Obligation is commonly defined as a bond of right by which we are constrained by the necessity of making some performance. That is, obligation places a kind of bridle on our liberty'. Grotius was also concerned with the idea of rights in his *The Rights of War and Peace, vol. II,* but here the law of obligations appeared only in two chapters (ch. 11 on promises and ch. 12 on contracts).

47 Zimmermann 1996, 544; see also: Haakonssen and Seidler 2016, 386–7.

48 Pufendorf 1991, I.3.13.

49 By defining religion as a duty of the individual, Pufendorf removed all forms of theological normativity from natural law and civil law. Later, this secularization of jurisprudence would lead to the religious freedoms that are guaranteed in constitutions and in human rights declarations: see Sloot 2018, 106.

50 Duty to care remains today the legal standard of reasonable care in actions on negligence in the common law. In the civil law tradition, the legal standard for negligence is *culpa.*

51 Another characteristic of private law is that the parties themselves seek redress in a court when a dispute arises, as opposed to criminal law where the state is responsible for legal prosecution. There is, therefore, an additional, private perspective to legal dispute resolution in private law, which can have quite an influence on how we understand early modern private disputes. With private law, we thus have a large area of social interaction that operates outside of the state's immediate remit, because it is the parties themselves who decide to go to court. It is important to keep this in mind when dealing with private conflicts, especially since the criminal courts tend to dominate the historical legal material. However, for the conflicts that arose between private 'agents', one must consult the records from the civil courts.

52 Pufendorf 1991, I.13.1: 'Every man is obliged to allow everyone (except an enemy) quietly to enjoy his own property, and neither by force nor fraud attempt to spoil, steal or misappropriate it. This is why theft, robbery and similar crimes against others' property are forbidden'. John Locke is traditionally seen as the founder of the inviolability of property and of the modern political economy. Sæther 2017 shows, however, that Pufendorf was Locke's primary source (148–65). Although Locke did not always agree with Pufendorf, key elements of Locke's economic theory can be traced directly back to Pufendorf. In *Two Treatises of Government* (1690), the inspiration from Pufendorf can be found in the famous quote by Locke: 'The state of nature has a law of nature to govern it, which obliges every one: and reason, which is that law, teaches all mankind, who will but consult it, that being all equal and independent, no one ought to harm another *in his life, health, liberty or possessions',* emphasis added (II.2.6).

53 Thomson 1984, 275. Thomson argues that the right to privacy can be defined as an analogous interpretation of the negative right to property – that is, the idea of a right to privacy stems from a negative property right (278–80).

54 For a thorough legal introduction to Pufendorf's approach to property rights, see Buckle 1993, 54–124; note also Bisset 2015, 541–62; and Haakonssen and Seidler 2016, 377–401.

55 Hobbes 1651, part I, ch. 13.

56 Grotius 1625, I, VIII.

57 Pufendorf 1991, II.5.2.

58 Pufendorf gave the social contract a legal 'constitutional' shape. The first step of state-formation took place when people in the state of 'nature wish[ed] to enter into a single and perpetual union ... each and every one must consent to this agreement'

(II.6.7). Then governance was introduced by legal decree, and finally everyone made the final agreement, thereby submitting their will to the sovereign 'and devolved on him the use of their strength to the common defense' (II.6.8–9). On sociability and Pufendorf's relation to Hobbes, see Darwall 2000, 987–1025; Haakonssen and Seidler 2016, 377–401; Haara 2018; Saastamoinen 2019, 107–31; Rosello 2012, 255–79.

59   Pufendorf 1991, II.15.4: 'The third right is eminent domain, which means that in a national emergency sovereigns may seize and apply to public use the property of any subject which the crisis particularly requires, even if the property seized far exceeds the amount which had been fixed as his normal obligatory contribution to his country's expenses. For this reason, however, as much of the excess as possible should be refunded to him'.

60   Pufendorf 1991, II.11.10: 'The only ground on which citizen must bear taxes and other burdens is that these are necessary. The duty of the sovereigns in this matter is not to extract more than the necessities ... and to keep the burdens as light as possible, so that the citizens suffer as little as possible'. Not that this made much of a difference in Denmark-Norway in the seventeenth and eighteenth centuries. In the wake of absolutism, the tax-financed part of the state-budget grew significantly, and so too did military spending: see Jespersen 2016, 341–2.

61   Some 103 years after Pufendorf's *De officio* was published, taxation became a central justification for the American colonies' declaration of independence from the English crown, July 4 1776: '[I]t is their right, it is their duty, to throw off such Government, and to provide new Guards for their future security'. See https://www.archives.gov/founding-docs/declaration-transcript. For the relation between Pufendorf and The American Declaration of Independence, see Sæther 2017, 200.

62   The translation of the Latin word *civitas* to mean 'state' in early modern times has been interpreted as a clear distancing from the traditional Aristotelian division of *oikos* and *polis*, on which see Becker 2004, 146–7 and Saunders 2003, 476ff.

63   Mührmann-Lund 2019, 407. For the concept of 'good policy', see the registration project of good policy regulation in the early modern period: Härter and Stolleis 1996 (both the Danish and Swedish legislation are registered); Härter 2010, 41–65.

64   Bregnsbo 1997.

65   The English, Danish and French translations have been compared. The English follows the Latin original. The Danish follows the French tradition, where *privatus* is translated as *particulier*.

66   Thomson 1984, 280.

67   Ibid., 281.

68   For an introduction to the general concept of civil society, see Walton 1983, 249–66.

Part Two

Communication

Talking in private – and keeping it private: Protecting conversations from exposure in Swedish Pietism investigations, 1723–1728

Johannes Ljungberg

From private talk to public investigation

At a wedding reception in Stockholm, in June 1723, a clergyman and a state secretary began to argue about the translation of the recent edition of the Swedish bible, which dated from 1703.[1] A series of judicial documents about their conversation, recorded in a royal commission from the following year, provides us with more details about the issues at stake.[2] The documents also inform us as to why their conversation would be reported to and discussed within the context of a state commission. First, one of the parties, the clergyman Jonas Alroth, referred to this specific dialogue as a clear example of how the other party, the state secretary Elias von Wolker (1660–1733), had been talking 'against the pure doctrine'.[3] Secondly, Wolker accused Alroth of 'shouting out' a distorted version of their conversation 'from a public pulpit'.[4] The further investigation revealed that Alroth had indeed mentioned the conversation with Wolker in one of his sermons, citing it as an alarming example of how Pietist ideas were circulating in the Swedish capital. As one of the first townsmen in Stockholm who had opened up his home for spiritual gatherings inspired by German Pietists, Wolker stated that the clergyman, out of aversion for such spiritual practices, exaggerated what he had heard Wolker say at the wedding reception. Both accusations were examined carefully by the seven appointed committee members, comprising three public officials and four clergymen, of whom two sympathized with Pietism while the other two were openly critical of Pietism.[5]

This example illustrates how specific face-to-face conversations were raised as topics of discussion and given significance in the context of one of the three royal commissions set up to investigate so-called 'Pietist activities' in Sweden between 1723 and 1728. These commissions functioned in Swedish political culture as a tool for communication between state and subject. By talking to a commission, the people concerned had an opportunity to communicate directly to representatives of the state.[6] The first two commissions targeted Pietist activities in cities of a rather different character: urban Stockholm and Umeå, with an almost rural character. These two cities had become hotspots for Pietist activity during the first two decades of the eighteenth century. The third commission investigated the circle around a particular minister in Stockholm, Erik Tollstadius (1693–1759). Apart from these royal commissions, conflicts related to Pietism were handled in one of Stockholm's lower city courts (*Stockholms norra kämnärsrätt*), in the ecclesiastical consistories of the concerned dioceses, in the deliberations at the *riksdag* and in censorship cases at the royal chancellery. The records of these investigations amount to an extensive documentation consisting of thousands of handwritten pages, kept in the National Archive, Stockholm.[7] The investigations were not solely directed against suspected sympathizers of Pietism, but also against their fervent opponents who channelled their criticism in their sermons, literature and social interactions.[8]

In this article, sources from the Swedish Pietism investigations are used to illustrate the different ways in which private conversations were protected from public exposure and thereby expressed what we may understand as claims of privacy. 'Conversations' here are understood in a general sense, in line with the first definition provided by the Cambridge online dictionary: '[a] talk between two or more people in which thoughts, feelings, and ideas are expressed, questions are asked and answered, or news and information is exchanged'.[9] The protection of an individual's right to conduct interpersonal exchanges free from outside intervention is a key element in several contemporary laws and theories about privacy. A recurring point of reference is Alan Westin's magistral book *Privacy and Freedom* (1967), in which four types of privacy are stipulated: solitude, intimacy, anonymity and reserve. Among these types, intimacy includes the right to share confidential communication with selected others.[10] The issue of protecting communication in terms of privacy has later been developed by scholars within information science, i.e. Helen Nissenbaum, who has successfully influenced various privacy policies with her concept of 'contextual integrity', which provides a formal language for evaluating privacy matters by taking into account the parties and the principles of transmission in any specific case of information flow.[11] Such a terminology was not yet available to people of eighteenth-century Europe, at least not as a right to invoke when defending private life.[12] However, this article will demonstrate the ways in which conversations were protected by looking at how individuals used language that explicitly referred to the 'private'. Moreover, I will argue that we can detect further arguments in favour of the protection of interpersonal exchanges by observing the social and spatial demarcations in the stories told to the investigations. This approach is inspired by research on the private and the public in the early modern period, which argues that these entities can hardly be studied as different spheres, but should rather be viewed as the products of spatial practices and social interaction.[13] The examples used here consist of specific conversations that were caught up in the investigative processes of the authorities, and were subsequently at risk of public exposure. Although it is not surprising that the accused persons defended themselves, their motivations for so doing can offer us an understanding of the circumstances under which conversations would be perceived as private matters, thus pertinent to discuss as potential notions of privacy.

There are good reasons to choose the Swedish Pietism investigations as a case study by which to explore the protection of conversations as private. To begin with, these sources are rich with various terminological references to the private. Both the adjective '*privat*' (private) and the adverb '*privatim*' (privately), spelled out in a Latinized form, recur throughout the material. These terms lead us towards the consideration of three issues, the first of which comprised the gatherings held in private houses that were referred to as '*privata conventicula*'.[14] The emergence of such meetings, bringing together men and women across household hierarchies to pray, sing and discuss the Sunday sermon, constituted a new element in the religious landscape of the time. Moreover, state authorities considered such activities a matter of spatial disorder.[15] Prior to 1700, religious activities designated as 'private' comprised either private devotion, or religious services undertaken in noblemen's private chapels or non-Lutheran foreigners' houses.[16] Second, the investigations worked on the suspicion that Pietist ministers expressed something different in their 'private teaching' from what they proclaimed in their public sermons delivered from the pulpit.[17] This is, for example, illustrated by a document handed to the commission by several colleagues of Tollstadius, which demanded that he reject the 'heresies' he was accused of 'in his parish, *publice* and *privatim*, in conversations and in the company of others, especially the erring people'.[18] Third, anxieties were expressed that the gatherings would risk generating supposedly dangerous 'private interpretations' of Bible verses.[19] The background was that Lutheran orthodox theologians generally criticized Pietists for making their private piety the centre of faith, instead of the clergy's public teaching. This criticism was, for example, presented by the Gießen theologian Philip Ludwig Hanneken (1637–1706).[20] Hanneken's pamphlet against Pietism was translated into Swedish and printed in 1723, next to an authoritative text by Martin Luther about 'Winckel-Predikanten'.[21] The commissions' worries about private meetings, teaching and interpretations each articulated a threat that was clothed in the terminology of the 'private'. A significant part of the threatening aura around Pietist activities came from the fact they took place beyond the pale of public places, or outside of official channels of communication.

The wide usage of the word 'private' in the context of the Pietism investigations is especially remarkable considering that the dictionaries in the Swedish language of the time did not yet include this term. Archbishop Haquin Spegel's dictionary from 1712 contained no entries at all with the root *priv-*, while clergyman Jesper Swedberg's *Swensk ordabok* from 1716 contained only one word, and that was *privet*, meaning latrine.[22] Interestingly, both Spegel and Swedberg were by that time already significantly involved in the conflicts over Pietism – i.e. those conflicts in which the term 'private' acquired significance. Only one year after his dictionary was published, Spegel issued the pamphlet 'Short but mature thoughts about *privatis conventiculis*' (1713) in which he criticized the Pietist practice of gathering in private.[23] This pamphlet was followed by a steady stream of anti-Pietist literature condemning the concept of 'private conventicles', a smear word for the pious gatherings. Swedberg adopted a more moderate approach than Spegel. He personally visited the earlier mentioned Wolker's weekly gathering while he was attending the *riksdag* in 1723. In the deliberations of the clerical estate, he praised the participants for their piety, but complained about their lack of hierarchical order.[24] The contrast between the absence of references to the private in the dictionaries of the 1710s and the wide use of this word in the Pietism conflicts of the 1720s indicates a shift towards the explicit use of language that referred to the private. This potential linguistic shift calls for a closer examination, especially since these conflicts predate the establishment in Sweden of what international research generally points to as the catalyzing institutions and arenas for new ways of referring to the private, such as coffee houses, a periodical press and political party struggles, all of which first developed in Stockholm only in the 1730s.[25]

Besides the terminological scope, the present focus on conversations aims to add nuance to a widely adopted view whereby early modern society is thought to lack privacy in its social practices of communication. This is, for example, demonstrated by the literary historian Patricia Meyer Spacks in her monograph *Privacy: Concealing the Eighteenth-Century Self* (2003), in which it is suggested that representations of conversations in eighteenth-century literature 'constituted a mode of public display', whereas in the nineteenth century, they 'clearly belonged to the sphere of a private relationship'.[26] Indeed, this normative shift observed in fictional worlds echoes the explicit argument made for the very first introduction of legal right to privacy in Samuel D. Warren's and Louis Brandeis' paradigmatic article from 1890, which concerned the right to be protected from exposure in the boulevard press.[27] For what concerns the other side of the shift, research within cultural history has, since the 1970s and following in the wake of the *annaliste* historian Philippe Ariès, depicted early modern societies as existing in a state of permanent publicity, exemplified with how intimate episodes such as baths and deaths took place in public, in sight of others.[28] Furthermore, scholars have pointed to the fact that punishments related to speech offences were frequently delivered not only for blasphemy, swearing and cursing, but also for gossip, slander and defamation.[29] Similarly, a steady stream of Nordic research from the 1990s has depicted early modern society as one with no private spheres, nor with spaces for private actions free from possible social repercussions; instead, it has been argued that any such spaces served as a forum for the public protection of personal honour.[30] Indeed, in the course of the eighteenth century, Scandinavian courts handled more cases about defamation than cases concerning physical violence.[31] This understanding of an apparent permanent publicity has led researchers to suggest that information in this culture could hardly be defended as private once it was formulated aloud. It has been suggested in international research that 'open' and 'hidden', and other terms signifying notions of visibility or transparency, correspond to contemporary notions of the public and the private.[32] With this background, it is understandable that these social conditions acted as an impetus for the stricter codification of conversations. Often inspired by Norbert Elias's thesis on the civilizing process in early modern Europe, several studies have discussed how handbooks regarding etiquette rules, conversation topics and sophisticated formulations responded to the pitfalls of oral exchange; this development subsequently raised barriers between a staged, superficial and hypocritical public appearance, and a more relaxing and permissive private environment for social life.[33] The role played by private circles as a temporary refuge from this dangerous public scene has been widely noted by scholars.[34]

However, even though communication in early modern society in general seems to have been deeply affected by an extensive notion of publicity, this does not mean that people had no need to talk in private. The issue at stake in this article centres precisely on how it was possible to protect conversations from public exposure. Using eighteenth-century sources to localize conversations considered as private is typically a complex pursuit of subtle references. Luckily, as often is the case with Scandinavian court records of the time, the encounter between subject and authorities is relatively well preserved in the Pietism investigations, including the defence of the person accused.[35] It could rightly be questioned to what extent the stories told in judicial investigations such as these were adapted to certain models of 'forensic rhetoric'. However, this is beside the core question, which is: how were conversations of various kinds examined, classified and defended by conceptual, social and spatial demarcations?

Within the field of cultural history, stories noted in court records have often served the purpose to unveil perceptions of the social practices that were object for investigation.[36] Historians who have researched privacy in historical and contemporary societies, such as Barrington Moore Jr and David Vincent, have argued that intrusions into people's lives form an excellent starting point for researching claims of privacy, since such an intervention may typically trigger the process of explaining and protecting any given situation as a private matter.[37] Similarly, the legal scholar Daniel J. Solove has argued that 'privacy should be conceptualized from the bottom up rather than the top down, from particular contexts rather than in the abstract'.[38] With the aim to formulate a functional approach to study privacy across cultural borders, Solove has postulated that 'privacy invasion interferes with the integrity of certain activities and even destroys or inhibits some activities', encouraging researchers to map out 'specific types of disruption'.[39]

In accordance with Solove's approach, I shall present a number of examples from the various Pietism investigations in which exposure of a private conversation was at stake. The examples display three different situations, along with their respective dynamics. The first category constitutes the most formalized context: the confidential talk between clergyman and layman, as stipulated in the Church Law of 1686. The second group of examples demonstrates how the terminology of 'private' and 'public' could be used to justify the denunciation of private talks before public investigations, including objections against such denunciations in the first place.[40] Finally, in the third section, two examples serve to illustrate different ways of protecting less formal conversations from being exposed, without referring to the as yet unavailable terminology of the right to privacy. Together, these three categories provide indications about how publicly exposed conversations were discussed within judicial processes during a time in Swedish history when the terminology referring to the private was more frequently adopted. Before moving on to those examples, however, the emergence of Pietism in eighteenth-century Scandinavia needs to be more fully discussed.

Pietism and the private

What does it mean to search for notions of private conversations in the context of Pietism? The word 'Pietist' was first formulated to label participants of the so-called '*collegia pietatis*', which were arranged in private houses after churchgoing in 1670s Frankfurt by the Lutheran minister Jacob Philip Spener (1635–1705). Similar social practices were performed in England and the Netherlands, in some cases without the presence of the local clergyman. In addition to the organizational form, Spener initiated a spiritual reform programme focusing on moral improvement for individual, state and church.[41] In the 1680s, the *collegia pietatis* and the reform program spread to Saxony, particularly to the network around August Hermann Francke (1663–1727) in Halle. A first major conflict with Lutheran orthodox theologians broke out in Leipzig in 1689–1690, in which the term '*Pietisterey*' appeared as a mere accusation of heresy.[42]

Pietist ideas and practices reached Scandinavia in several ways. Recurring gatherings modelled on the Pietist concept of *collegia pietatis* emerged in Copenhagen from 1701 and in Stockholm from at least 1702. Both Danish and Swedish authorities reacted by prohibiting people from taking part in these meetings.[43] Spener's and Francke's books were widely accessible, and students staying at northern German universities forged personal bonds with Pietist sympathizers. One of these students was Nils Grubb (1681–1724), a vicar in Umeå by the time of the commission's investigation. During the Great Nordic War (1700–1721), several officers and soldiers in the Swedish army took an interest in Pietist ideas, and exchanged correspondence with Francke and his personal circle in Halle.[44] On the initiative of the superintendent in Swedish Pomerania, Johan Friedrich Mayer (1650–1712), 'secret conventicles' were forbidden by a royal letter in 1694, a prohibition that was repeated in 1713 and 1721.[45]

The scepticism towards Pietism was rooted in a combination of theology and particular visions of the proper social order. A central issue for the investigations was to discover what was taught during the sessions, by whom and to whom. Lutheran household ideology allowed for the housefather to gather his household at a *husandakt* (household prayer), but the Pietist version of this legitimate practice was considered to be a complicated matter in that both women and servants from various households tended to be present, and because they tended to have speaking roles that were normally reserved for the minister or the housefather.[46] Although Spener and Francke supported the idea of social hierarchies, their emphasis on the Lutheran doctrine of a priesthood of all believers, as well as a focus on the morals of everyday life instead of dogmatic matters, permitted a broader spectrum of people to speak up.[47] Compared to the refined conversations in noble circles, Pietist gatherings were a less formalized context. Leading Pietists condemned the focus on scholarly dispute, and called instead for a more upright and thorough exchange of ideas.[48] Furthermore, the early Swedish Pietist Olof Ekman (1639–1713), whose main book was widely disseminated and well known in Pietist circles, stressed that confession could be made to a Christian layperson, and that all Christians should admonish and instruct each other.[49] This principle practically challenged the public office of the local clergyman. As we shall see, it also affected the perception of private conversations.

In contrast to public services in church buildings, the Pietist gatherings took place in private.[50] As stated in one of the commissions, the congregation was drawn 'out of the church for explanation in private houses, in the name of brotherly love'.[51] Accordingly, the Pietist circles have often been depicted as a parallel or alternative sociability to other expanding arenas that were flourishing in a private context during the eighteenth century, such as clubs, societies and coffee houses. They have also been depicted as a parallel to other spiritualties, such as similar movements in the Netherlands and

England, or the Jansenist branch of the Catholic Church.[52] On a theoretical level, and from a perspective of modernization, Pietist gatherings have been integrated into Jürgen Habermas's famous theory about how public spheres grew out of private spaces, and thus constituted a new type of public space.[53] In addition to the forms of sociability, there are strong ties between the Pietists and the expanding book market. A large number of the new book titles in early eighteenth-century Sweden were either Pietist literature, or comprised of books typically read by Pietists.[54]

It is not, however, the spiritual dimensions, nor practices of sociability, that make conflicts over Pietism a valuable example for studying notions of private conversation as understood in this article, or at least not directly. Rather than connecting the Pietist movement to processes of modernization à la Habermas, the ambition of this article is to follow the dynamics of how private conversations were under threat by public exposure, and to try to understand the arguments individuals made in attempts to keep those conversations private, or to expose private talks to a public investigation.

Following the frameworks of the Church Law

The confidential talk between clergyman and layman was a formally defined category of conversation that should be kept private. Even though the medieval concept of private confession was not considered a sacrament according to Lutheran doctrine, and the equivalent ritual was instead performed collectively and in public (*allmänt skriftermål*), confidential conversations between a priest and a layman were nevertheless still encouraged in Sweden's Church Law of 1686, especially in cases where someone had committed an 'evident and publicly known sin' ('*uppenbar och allom witterlig synd*').[55] In such cases, the law stipulated that the clergyman should try to 'correct' the sinner 'in seclusion' (*uti ensligheet*)[56] as a first step towards reconciliation. If that did not have the desired effect, the law then prescribed that he should talk to the person 'accompanied by two or three pious and wise men of the parish'.[57] As a final step, the clergyman was required to perform a so-called 'public correction': this meant to spell out a ban from the pulpit, and thereby ritually remove the person from the congregation.[58] This process, which was rooted in the monastic tradition and formulated already in Benedict's rule (516), illustrates both the importance of keeping secluded talks private, and the act of shaming a recalcitrant individual in public.[59] While the shame punishment served as a deterrent for others, the efforts to avoid making a public scene, as long as it was not publicly known, were motivated by the desire to avoid scandal (*scandalum*) or uproar (*förargelse*), which were terms denoting the social risks involved in making knowledge of the sin public.[60] The Stockholm commission of 1723 expressed this principle, for example, when the committee member Herman Schröder (1676–1744) stated in a memorandum that the chances were far better to correct someone if the teacher 'speaks with such souls' rather than 'publicly thunders' against them.[61]

The instruction that it was preferable to talk with sinners in seclusion provided a useful tool to those clergymen who were questioned by the commissions. By referring to this instruction, some of them effectively claimed that previous conversations should be kept private. The vicar Nils Grubb, who was the main target of the Umeå commission in 1723, faced accusations of not having done enough to stop the illegitimate gatherings in his parish. Although Grubb in general defended the Pietist activities in Umeå, he nevertheless agreed that some of the gatherings could be considered as a form of misbehaviour. However, in his defence regarding those cases, he stated that he 'had not neglected to punish such things during the sermons, if the *Gradus admonitionis* [degree of admonition] is observed',[62] with explicit reference to the paragraph in the 1686 Church Law, as explained above. Later in the same interrogation, he also stressed that he had abstained from 'public correction' (*offentlig correction*) since that would have caused uproar (*förargelse*).[63] This line of reasoning was accepted by the commission, and when the affair was discussed in the Council of the Realm, it was simply declared that he had performed his pastoral duties well.[64]

A similar pattern can also be detected when critics of Pietism were questioned. No fewer than five clergymen in Stockholm were called to the commission in the autumn of 1723 to clarify why they had preached publicly against Pietism and, explicitly or implicitly, identified certain individuals as Pietists. They were each requested to present evidence to support their accusations.[65] More precisely, the commission wanted to know which specific gatherings they had referred to, and requested the names of the people involved. But all of the five clergymen focused on justifying why they could not do this, probably because giving names would have practically meant making accusations, which was very risky in a society that punished defamation severely. In this situation, the court chaplain Nils Barchius (1676–1733), who was called to justify a sermon he had delivered two years earlier, presented the most convincing explanation. He started by stating that the gatherings in question were no longer held, and were therefore not worthy of mention. Then followed his key argument: his office as a clergyman prescribed that a person who, on his instruction, had been led in on 'the right path' should not be reported, since 'such things concern the conscience'.[66] Barchius thus referred to his official duty as a minister and the secluded or confidential – i.e. non-public – character of the conversation in question. With this argument, Barchius managed to convince the commission that the situation had changed during the two intervening years between his sermon and the interrogation. An external lawyer from the Royal Court of Appeal (*Justitierevisionen*) commented on this particular case, and confirmed that those who had stopped committing sins because of Barchius's instructions should not be denounced by him. On the other hand, Wester stated that if these people had not been successfully 'corrected ... [then this fact] must not be silenced even though some years have passed'.[67] This claim corresponded to what the Church Law prescribed for 'secret confession' (*secret skriftermål*): when the sin is so 'secret' (*hemlig*) that only God and the sinner are aware of it, then it should remain secret.[68] Barchius's claim was not discussed any further, which is understandable given that clergymen possessed a certain right to judge in disciplinary matters, including in cases concerning heresy.[69] Indeed, the silence over the concrete proceedings in specific disciplinary matters has been noted by previous scholars.[70]

The strength of Barchius's reference to the privileged position of secluded talk in his capacity as a clergyman emerges clearly when one considers the fact that none of his four colleagues who were also interrogated by the commission over the same matter ended up escaping criticism, even though they presented apparently reasonable arguments in their defence. A second minister, Johannes Cröll, referred to the various letters and edicts that had warned against Pietism, and declared that it was his official duty to warn his congregation of such things.[71] A third minister, Jonas Alroth, who had the exchange with Wolker at the wedding, was defended by his vicar who stated that Alroth had not said anything that was more 'intolerable' than what other clergymen had uttered without further notice.[72] A fourth minister, Jonas Stricker, tried to convince the consistory about his knowledge of the Pietist 'heresy'; he recounted that he had devoted much time to his assiduous studies in the matter, including attending lectures as a student in Uppsala and extensive discussions with a Pietist in Königsberg.[73] However, none of these explanations were sufficient for the commission; in the concluding text of the protocol, they were all condemned by name for having 'publicly shouted out [denounced] innocent people as heretics'.[74] Barchius's name, however, was not included in the commission's condemnation. His explanation had obviously convinced the commission. To refer to secluded talk was evidentially superior to other arguments advanced to justify anti-Pietist utterings from the public pulpit.

These different examples demonstrate how clergymen, with different attitudes to Pietism, could refer successfully to the roles and responsibilities of their office to justify keeping conversations private – or to justify making them public. On the one hand, this indicates the relationship between one's ability to declare a conversation as private and one's position within a social hierarchy. To have confidential conversations formed part of the clergyman's public office, but as Charlotte Christensen-Nugues shows in her contribution to this volume, housefathers were likewise encouraged to admonish privately their servants who swore.[75] On the other hand, the sources also indicate that this privilege came with certain expectations. For example, Umeå's local judge (*häradshövding*), Marcus Bostadius (1662–1728), accused the local vicar Grubb of having told the commission that he (Bostadius) had not treated his daughter well, and had forced her into marriage. He phrased his complaint by stating that such an accusation would be difficult even to hear from 'a private person ... in a private room', but far more difficult to hear 'from one's own soul carer in front of a royal commission'.[76] This comment suggests that secluded talk not only provided a useful tool for clergymen when attempting to keep conversations private, but that they also had a responsibility to keep those conversations private in the first place.

Accessing a fluid terminology

While the references to confidential talk as stipulated in the 1686 Church Law were not questioned, all other efforts to keep private conversations from being repeated to the court elicited greater discussion and numerous counterclaims. This is, first and foremost, reflected in the disputes over whether the proceedings should be held *privatim* or *publice*. These were judicial distinctions, but they also reflected the different levels of private and public correction as mentioned in the Church Law, ranging from secluded confession to public shaming. The conflict involving the clergyman Erik Tollstadius illustrates well the issue of conflicting claims about the appropriateness of these different levels. Tollstadius was accused of heretical teaching in a series of interrogations from the 1720s onwards. His case was first handled by the consistory of Stockholm in 1722. The preserved protocol presents the situation by stating that the members of the consistory were ready to '*confer* with him as clerical brothers, in full confidentiality'. Tollstadius replied that the consistory should assure that a 'brotherly *conference*' was held '*privatim*, and not *publice in Consistorio*'.[77] The chairman of the consistory meant, however, that they could speak '*publice* as well as *privatim*'.[78] The matter came to an end, this time, when Tollstadius successfully kept his mouth shut concerning the deviant doctrines of which he was accused of teaching.

Five years later, when he was called to the commission that was now set up to investigate both him and his potential adherents, the protocol presents a series of examples in chronological order demonstrating how Tollstadius had been warned first in private, then in public. First, four 'honourable men' (mentioned by name) had 'talked with him *privatim*' against teaching deviant doctrines. A fifth person had also sent a written warning.[79] After this, Tollstadius was interrogated by the Consistory in 1722.[80] The protocol counted three public admonitions, two from the consistory and one from the Royal Court of Appeal.[81] Then came the new information: several of Tollstadius's fellow clergymen, who were also known as sympathizers of Pietism, had testified to the commission that their colleague had been teaching heresies.[82] They told the commission about how they had tried to convince Tollstadius 'private conversations', but without success.[83] What is interesting here is not so much what the colleagues perceived of as heresy – to follow up on that would be a totally different matter – but their modus operandi to 'correct' Tollstadius, which was in considerable detail by some of them.

Tollstadius's colleague Jonas Hellman offered the most extensive account. He recounted that he had visited Tollstadius several times in his home to speak with him about the deviant doctrines, but had done so for a long time without success. One evening, however, when they were sitting in Tollstadius's chamber discussing the upcoming Sunday sermon, Tollstadius had revealed his 'heretical' opinion.[84] The description of the secluded and intimate setting in the domestic context stands out when compared to the confidential talks between clergymen and laymen discussed above, where such details were left unspecified. According to Hellman, Tollstadius only reacted angrily to his efforts to discuss the issue with him.[85] Despite this failure, Hellman did not report his colleague to the consistory until many years later. His reason for so doing was that he had considered his colleague to be in '*statu tentationis*', which means he was in need of pastoral care and direction, rather than judicial procedure. Hellman's attitude had obviously changed by the time he recounted the whole story before the royal commission.[86]

Another intriguing example of how the same distinctions were at play can be found in a censorship case that gained wider notice among the higher clergy, centring on a manuscript that had been placed at the censor's desk at the royal chancellery in 1725, and thereby made public. The case involved the already mentioned ministers Barchius and Schröder. Since both were clergymen, as well as active writers, it was perfectly legitimate for them to read about and to discuss what was considered as heresy or as 'difficult' theological matters. Their different attitudes to Pietism would, however, lead to conflict. It all started with Barchius letting Schröder read a manuscript that was critical against some of the doctrines of Pietism. Displeased with the reading, Schröder left the manuscript on the censor's desk. The text was consequently criticized during the censoring process. When called upon to defend the text, Barchius claimed that he had handed over the document to Schröder '*privatim*', and not '*publico nomine*', and therefore it should not have been object of investigation in the first place.[87] Moreover, Barchius stated that it would have been preferable to handle the disagreement by 'private conference', instead of through a 'public deduction'.[88] Schröder did not object to this distinction, but pointed to the fact that he thought that the text was meant for the censorship office. The morally defensible position was clearly to claim that the other party had made the conflict public, and was therefore responsible for causing it, regardless of the content that lay beneath the conflict. For our present purposes, it is highly significant that both Barchius and Schröder made use of the distinction between private and public discussion. Even though Schröder and Barchius had completely opposite attitudes towards Pietism, both parties counted with the need to have the opportunity to discuss matters in private.[89]

Indeed, Barchius had good reason to expect tactfulness from Schröder. As research on censorship in Sweden has indicated, the person who was tasked with reading (and censoring) a manuscript was sometimes crucial for the outcome of the censorship process, and it was therefore common practice for individuals to steer the entire censorship process by searching for a potential censor.[90] The existence of this institutional practice implies that Schröder crossed an important line when, according to Barchius, he ceased acting as an informal contact who looked at the manuscript, and instead became a figure instrumental in the publication process of that manuscript. As research on early eighteenth-century printing practices has indicated, the publication process of manuscripts applied similar norms as those concerning oral messages. Therefore, it seems right to state that Schröder's launch of the censorship process constituted a transition from private to public conversation.[91]

Both of the above cases demonstrate how the application of terminology aimed at declaring a situation to be 'private' came into play. The way in which Tollstadius was handled followed the prescriptions of the Church Law, beginning with private admonitions and ending with public denunciation. In Hellman's case, this public/private terminology was associated with detailed descriptions of social and spatial demarcations. In both cases, the dividing line between a 'private' discussion and the process of making such a discussion public knowledge seems rather less clear when compared to the examples involving confidential talks as regulated by the Church Law. All persons involved were grasping after a fluid terminology. Because of Hellman, the efforts to 'correct' Tollstadius in private should be considered as warnings prior to the display of his views in public. Schröder also had reason for acting the way he did. Allegedly, he read the manuscript according to the normal publication process of manuscripts delivered for print. On the whole, in what started off as internal ecclesiastical affairs, the actors involved ended up articulating claims that sought to declare certain situations as conceptually 'private'.

Protecting informal conversations

Finally, let us have a closer look at two particularly intriguing efforts to formulate the grounds for protecting specific conversations from public exposure. In contrast to the previous examples, the following cases centre on laymen. The first of these concerns a military officer named Carl Gustaf Österling (1673–1732), one of the men from the Swedish army who had developed a preference for Pietist spirituality during the Great Nordic War. His plea to keep conversations private was formulated as an accusation against Tollstadius. Similar to Hellman, he stated that he had met Tollstadius in his own home, to which he arrived alone, and in this context witnessed him confess twice and 'from his own mouth' to the 'heresies' of which he was suspected.[92] In order to bolster his report in which he emphasized that Tollstadius should be considered a public danger, he stated that Tollstadius had wrongly divulged information concerning what people had done in private:

> [H]e [Tollstadius] must consider that the errors of weakness that one could commit in *private* under difficult temptations, which in fact do not cause public damage and impending danger, is something totally different. Such errors should not be declared in public; not by a proper Christian, and even less by a proper Teacher, and certainly not in an abominable manner.[93]

Österling's distinction reveals something important about the perception of what should rightly be kept private: a person's sinful nature. As demonstrated above, Hellman had also highlighted that the state of temptation was worthy of protection from public exposure. Österling further specified that Tollstadius denounced people who normally lived a pious life, but who had been led to temptation and committed 'errors out of weakness'.[94] Such a moralistic attitude was typical for Pietist spirituality, and something that caused irritation among people.[95] However, Österling did not criticize this attitude as such, but more precisely the fact that Tollstadius made people's sins public. Österling's criticism may also be seen as an expression of the expectations placed upon the clergy in these matters, similar to what we saw in the example of the local judge in Umeå. But most of all, the idea that Tollstadius had denounced the errors that people had committed in private reveals a key element in Christian anthropology: the sinful human nature. Consequently, some conversations ought to be kept private, especially in a society with a high sensitivity for the publicly spoken word. Interestingly, such a perspective brings the condition of the individual under consideration, and broadens our understanding that there may have been an intrinsic value to private conversations, and concerns over private conversations extended beyond the apparent danger of spreading one's words to others. It indicates some kind of interest for the protection of one's inner life. Perhaps this reference to normal weakness, dressed in the normative theological language for the time, indicates that there was a cultural understanding that conversations of a more informal kind be kept private.

This hypothesis brings us back to the conversation between Alroth and Wolker at the wedding reception, which opened this article, and which was discussed extensively in the royal commission. On the one hand, that conversation can hardly be described as one of a totally informal nature. Alroth was a clergyman, Wolker was a well-known sympathizer of Pietist spirituality, and they were speaking about theological issues at a well-attended event. On the other hand, the wedding reception seems to have been a far less formal context than the various efforts taken to admonish Tollstadius. During the commission's interrogation of Wolker, he claimed that he had not expected that his words would be scrutinized in such detail:

> Speaking of the accusations, I cannot possibly remember further what was said at the wedding after this long time, than what I have already indicated in my letter to the honorable consistory, as I have not thought much about it since then, as I could not imagine that someone unknown would be so malicious that he would distort and make use of the discussion the way he did.[96]

Wolker's comment is multilayered. As mentioned earlier, he complained both that his counterpart had distorted his words, and that he had repeated them in public. More precisely, Alroth's announcement had been made from the pulpit, i.e. the place where he performed his authority as a clergyman. Additionally, the language in the commission's protocol is far from grammatically coherent – which is perhaps more visible in the Swedish original, making it hard to translate – suggesting that Wolker struggled with formulating his claim. This struggle indicates an absence of a clear terminology that could be used to declare that the conversation had been a private one. Yet it seems that this was precisely what Wolker was trying to say by stating that he could not remember his exact words: his rationale was that he thought it so unlikely that someone would mention such a small chat at a wedding reception beyond that particular context. To be sure, he assured the commission that it did not matter what exactly he had said, since it could not possibly have differed substantially from what he had told them.

How should we interpret Wolker's statement? Was he really surprised that someone would recall his exact words when it concerned the translation of Bible verses, the holiest letters on earth to a Lutheran mind? Did he mean that the conversation was of such a nature that it should not be the object of a public investigation? Did his complaint intimate his own expectations that a clergyman like Alroth should not repeat things that he had heard in private? What we do know is that Alroth eventually lost the case. By the end of the commission's protocol, he was mentioned by name as one of the clergymen who was guilty of identifying Pietists from a public pulpit.[97]

Concluding remarks

Although early modern Scandinavia has often been described as a highly public society, this study has demonstrated various ways in which individuals attempted to protect what we may identify as the private nature of some of their conversations. Terminology that referred to the private was used in various ways, and with different implications. A first way of protecting the private nature of certain conversations was by referring to confidentiality between the parties. Clergymen enjoyed a privileged ability to declare conversations as private, according to the regulation in the Church Law, but this privilege also came with certain expectations. If a problem had been solved privately, it should be kept private. The exposure of the private conversations that took place between Erik Tollstadius and his colleagues was motivated precisely because of the assumption that the practice of correcting him in private had failed. Thus, they had crossed a conceptual dividing line whereby those conversations were no longer able to be classified and protected as private.

Contrary to contemporary definitions of privacy, the context of the private admonitions discussed here indicates that such conversations were not protected simply because they were a part of private life.[98] Instead, there were multiple factors underlying the desire to protect private conversations. These included the avoidance of spreading knowledge of sin, the avoidance of causing public shame and the maintenance of private honour. However, one reason for keeping these conversations private that came to the surface in the sources investigated here is especially noteworthy: a specific understanding of the sinful human being who is a victim of temptations. Given that this anthropological notion was widely shared in the culture, it is likely that it resonated more widely amongst people as a good reason for keeping not only disciplinary conversations, but also conversations of more informal nature, private. Indeed, both the practice of talking in private and the tendency to correct private moral were typical for Pietists.

The censorship case displays another way to protect conversations – here in the form of more informal discussions – as private. It shows how two learned clergymen each defended the legitimacy of their private discussion about a handwritten manuscript. The demarcation between private and public conversation was, in this case, clear in the censorship process itself, and in the subsequent publication of the manuscript. The situation has similarities with the case of private discussions between Tollstadius and his colleagues, which were eventually reported to the authorities. Both cases suggest that it was possible to protect conversations as private by describing the situation once the private conversation had crossed certain lines. Additionally, some of the examples discussed above indicate that not all discussions made sense to be made public. On the whole, this seems not too far from what prevails in contemporary theories about the right to have a free exchange, even though this was far from being normative or explicitly and fully articulated in early modern Scandinavia.

To conclude, these various examples demonstrate that it is possible to nuance the widely accepted view of early modern Scandinavian society as a predominantly public one. Admittedly, the examples analysed in this article all display the threat of public exposure. However, as demonstrated here, it is also a fruitful approach to start from the other end and notice various efforts to protect conversations as private. By shifting our perspective, other norms emerge concerning the regulation of confidentiality and of various moments of private exchange between people engaged in formal, informal and intimate conversations, although still related to the social roles between the men of the higher social strata that figure in these examples. Furthermore, and perhaps more importantly, this article has demonstrated the possibility to explore how people struggled to keep conversations private, as it became an object of scrutiny afterwards.

Notes

1   Research funded by the Danish National Research Foundation (DNRF 138).
2   Swedish National Archive (hereafter SNA), Äldre kommitéer (hereafter ÄK) 190, acta, 577–83.
3   'Som han menar wara stridande emot wår rena Evangeliska lära', SNA, ÄK 190, acta, 577.Alroth's years of birth and death are not to be found in the collection of biographies of the Swedish clergy (*herdaminnen*).
4   'På offentelig predikostohl', in ibid., 578.
5   The civil servants were Olof Nordenstråle (1683–1742), Johan Rosenadler (1664–1743) and David Silvius (1663–1732).The clergymen who sympathized with Pietism were Anders Båld (1679–1751) and Herman Schröder (1676–1744).The clergymen who were openly critical against Pietism were Sven Caméen (1667–1729) and Jöran Nordberg (1677–1744).
6   See Lennersand 1999, 31–7.
7   SNA, ÄK vol. 189–91.
8   Ljungberg 2021.
9   Cambridge Dictionary, A1: https://dictionary.cambridge.org/dictionary/english/conversation (visited 9 January 2020).
10 Westin 1967, 31–2. For a further discussion of this aspect of privacy, see Inness 1992, 96–112.
11 Nissenbaum 2010.
12 See the introduction to this volume by Sari Nauman and Helle Vogt.
13 Cf. Kilian 1998; Rau 2004.
14 Norberg 1982, 509.
15 Ljungberg 2017, 79–124.
16 See Charlotte Nugues-Christensen's contribution to this volume, as well as the introduction.
17 'Frågandes om Magister Tollstadius ej allenast uthi sina predikningar, uthan och som man förmoda will särdeles wid dess *privates* underwisningar sökt, att uthur Gudz Ord grundeligen förelägga dem, som af Dippels skrifter till större eller mindre dehl smitta fått', SNA, ÄK 191, acta, 108; 'Hwartill Ulander swarade, det han av prosten Grupp både *publice* och *privatim* lärt, hwad en rätt husfaders plikt är', in SNA, ÄK 190, protocol, 123.
18 'Så *publice* som *privatim* i samtal och umgänge med andra, besynnerligen med de willfarande', SNA, ÄK 191, acta, p.43. See also SNA, ÄK 189, protocol, 123: 'hwartill Ulander swarade, det han av prosten Grupp både *publice* och *privatim* lärt, hwad en rätt husfaders plikt är'.
19 'Prosten Wallerius yttrade sig att *scriptura sacra non est private interpretationis*', Ibid., 120.
20 Matthias 2015, 34–5.
21 Hanneken 1723.
22 See Charlotte Nugues-Christensen's contribution to this volume.
23 Spegel 1713.
24 Lenhammar 2000, 53–7; Swedberg 1960.
25 Forselius 2015; Ågren 2006; Nilzén 1971.
26 Meyer Spacks 2003, 115.
27 Warren and Brandeis 1890.

28   Ariès 1977, 1986.
29   Bardsley 2006; Cressy 2010; Horodowich 2012; Cohen 2012; Malmstedt 2012; Juster
     2014.
30   Sandmo 1999, 132; Collstedt 2007, 86–8.
31   Ylikangas et al. 2000, 79.
32   Freise 2004, 19.
33   Burke 1993, 95–118, 126–7; Meyer Sparks 2003, 116–23; Fauster 1991; Adam 1997;
     Horodowich 2008; Snyder 2009; Bishop 2017, 208–20; Arnold 2016, 345–7; Halsey
     and Slinn 2008. Scudéry 1682 has been a source of inspiration for many studies.
34   This distinction connects to Jürgen Habermas's concepts of 'repräsentative
     Öffentlichkeit' and 'bürgerliche Öffentlichkeit', see Habermas 1990 [1962].
35   Österberg and Sandmo 2000, 22–3.
36   Cf. Davis 1987, 7–76; Cohen and Cohen 1993, 159–87; Kermode and Walker 1994,
     4–5; Lindstedt Cronberg 1997; Hansen 2006.
37   Moore jr.1983, ix; Vincent 2016, viii. See also van der Geest 2018.
38   Solove 2008, 9.
39   Ibid.
40   This ties into Pierre Bourdieu's theory of 'officializing strategy', see Bourdieu 1990
     [1980], 109.
41   Lehmann 2017.
42   Wallmann 2005, 22; Mori 2014, 204–10.
43   Jakubowski-Tiessen 1995, 446–71; Montgomery 1995, 490–522.
44   On the importance of correspondence in Pietist networks, see Gleixner 2014, 448–51,
     458–9.
45   Lenhammar 2000, 22–31; Ljungberg 2017, 48–55.
46   Gleixner 2016, 423–5.
47   Van Horn Melton 2001, 300–01; Matthias 2015; Nordbäck 2004.
48   Claesson 2015.
49   Ibid., 88–90, 108–9.
50   Nordbäck 2006, 224.
51   'Hwar igenom menigheten skal dragas utur kyrkian in uti private hus til ordets
     förklaring, under namn af den broderliga kärleken', SNA, ÄK 190, protocol, 119.
52   Brecht 1997, 261–73; Gierl 2014, 363–5; Van Horn Melton 2001, 308–9; Van Kley
     1996.
53   Habermas 1990 [1961]; Van Horn Melton 2001, 315–27.
54   Nordstrandh 1951.
55   *1686 års kyrkolag*, Kap.10, § I–II; cf. Claesson 2015, 151–5, 224.
56   Ibid., § II.
57   Ibid.
58   Ibid.
59   Naess and Österberg 2000, 149. In the section on excommunication in Benedict's rule it
     is stipulated that disobedient brothers 'should be warned twice privately by the seniors
     in accord with our Lord's injunction […] If he does not amend, he must be rebuked
     publicly in the presence of everyone', *The Rule of St.Benedict*, § xxiii, see Fry 1865.
60   Lindberg 1992, 419–42.
61   'Om läraren istället för ett sådant publique dundrande wänligen och christeligen
     tahlte med sådana siälar', SNA, ÄK 190, protocol, 504.
62   'Refererar Pastoren det han ei underlåtit, at straffa sådant under predikningarna, om
     Gradus admonitionis derwid är observerade', SNA, ÄK 189, protocol, 70–1.

63 'Offentel.Corrrection', in ibid., 77. Concerning 'förargelse', see Lindberg 1992, 419–42.
64 SNA, K 23:1138, 8–9.
65 SNA, ÄK 190, protocol, 350–1, 360–6.
66 'Blifwit på rätta wägen ford … hälst sådant rörer samwetet', ibid., 361.
67 'Så woro det en uppenbar förargelse, some ey får ned tystas, för det, at några åhr sedermera skola förflutit', ibid., 361–2.
68 *1686 års kyrkolag*, Kap.7, § 2.
69 Claesson 2015, 151–72.
70 Oja 2000, 58–9.
71 SNA, ÄK 190, protocol, 205–6.
72 Ibid., acta, 555.
73 Ibid., protocol, 250–8.
74 'Offentligen utropat oskyldigt folck för kättare och swärmare', ibid., protocol, 821.
75 See Charlotte Nugues-Christensen's contribution to this volume.
76 'Som för svårt vore av en privat person obevisligen att höra på privat rum, fast mera av sin egen själasörjare inför en kunglig kommission', SNA, ÄK 189, acta, 105–6.
77 'Tollstadius tackade för en borderlig *conference*, men som den bör anstellas *privatim*, ock icke *publice* i *Consistorio*', SNA, ÄK 191, acta, p.7.
78 '*Publice* som *privatim*', ibid., 8.
79 '*Privatim* talt med', ibid., 30–6.
80 Ibid.
81 Ibid.
82 Ibid., 100.
83 'I private discourser', ibid., 104.
84 Ibid., 102.
85 In another publication, I have suggested that the distinction between temptation and malicious intent was considered important for discerning seditious Pietists from people who were expected to be temporarily seduced and thereby soon recover, see Ljungberg 2021.
86 'Intolerabel', SNA, ÄK 191, acta, 108.This uttering is taken from the protocol of the Royal Court of Appeal, which was attached to the commission's files.
87 SNA, E XII: 30.59, 61.
88 Ibid., 27.
89 For Schröder's comment, see SNA, E XII: 30, 66.
90 Öhrberg 2011, 112–32. A similar distinction between manuscript meant for 'private' usage versus printed book can be found in Jakobsen 2011, 29.
91 Bellingradt 2012, 237–8; Forselius 2015, 16.
92 'Vad själva huvudsaken angår, att Tollstadius varit besmittad av Dippels lära, så haver jag det själv hört av hans egen mun och bekännelse då han ensam varit hos mig, och det även två gånger', SNA, ÄK 191, acta, 153.
93 'Men han måste besinna, det wore af ganska olika beskaffenhet, hwad en privat kan begå för swaghets felachtigheter under swåra frestelser, de der i sielfwa wärket icke angå någon publici skada och förestående fara, hwilka fehl också af ingen rätt christen, mindre af någon rättsinnig Lärare kunna eller böra til hans nästas förklaring, och hälst på at allom wederstyggeligit wis, publice utgifwa', ibid., 261–2.
94 'Då han således uppenbarliga röjer och utropar de swaghets fehl, som några Personer, hwilka eljest, uti almänt, ombeflita sig om en stilla och gudelig wandel, under anfächtning warit frestade till', ibid., 261.
95 Ljungberg 2017, 139–43.

96 'Hwad nu sielfwa beskyllningarna widkommer, så ehuruwäl iag nu så långt efter
    omögeligen kan widare minnas, huru talat ock discourserne på bröloppet fallit,
    än ofwannemde mitt memoral till Ven: Consistorium wid handen gifwer, som iag
    ock sedermera så mycket mindre der uppå tänkt, som iag aldrig kunnat förmoda
    någon förewarande så illa sinnad finnas, at han hwad då *discourserna* taltes på ett så
    obeskiedeligt sätt förwända ock åtföra skulle', SNA, ÄK 190, acta, 573.
97 SNA, ÄK 190, protocol, 821.
98 Rössler 2005 [2001], 18.

Private news: Private letters as a source of news in eighteenth-century Copenhagen newspapers

Jørgen Mührmann-Lund

Shocking news

On the morning of Saturday, 1 November 1755, Lisbon was struck by an earthquake that completely destroyed the Portuguese capital. It took over a month before news of this shocking event was published in the Copenhagen newspaper, *Kiøbenhavnske Danske Post-Tidender* (Copenhagen Danish Gazette). On 14 November, the Danish and German issues of this newspaper had printed reports from anonymous correspondents in Amsterdam, Glückstadt and Lübeck about a mysterious movement of water that had hit those ports on 1 November. The cause of this tsunami was not revealed to the Copenhageners until 5 December. On that day, the newspaper contained a short notice that 'particular letters' about the earthquake in Lisbon had reached Copenhagen. It was briefly reported that 100,000 of the inhabitants had perished, but that the king had survived. The use of the definite form reveals that 'the earthquake' was already the talk of the town when the notice was written. The following issues were full of detailed accounts of the disaster. Some of these were official diplomatic reports, but the majority were 'particular' or 'private' letters and accounts that supplied the readers with first-hand and often very emotional accounts. Written in the present tense, they created a sense of contemporaneity between the time of the event and the time of reception, which is typical of the news genre even to this day. An example is a letter from an anonymous French merchant to 'his correspondent' that was published on 15 December:

> I am the only one of my household to have survived, with the cloak I wear on my body, this terrible disaster that has swallowed up Lisbon. (…) From a spot in the fields, to which I had escaped, I have seen the great and mighty city be destroyed and the largest buildings being lifted up by the earthquake and thus be thrown back and forth, as though they had been placed in a sling. This terrible sight was accompanied by the pitiful wails and laments of many thousand people who screamed towards the heavens and pleaded for the mercy of God whose harsh judgement they were experiencing.[1]

The fact that the recipient is a correspondent reveals that this account was produced for a professional news agent. Other private accounts of the earthquake published in the newspaper appeared to be genuine private letters addressed to a specific recipient and not the general public. This is the case in an excerpt from another private letter printed in the issue of 12 December. Judging from the content, this author was also a merchant:

> I am writing these few lines to you on an open field to inform you of the terrible earthquake that befell on this city on the first of this month in the morning around ten o'clock in the morning. All of the houses and the churches in the city are destroyed, and what the earthquake has spared is being ruined and laid waste because of the fire that is spreading across the rest of the city and has already destroyed the customs house and its Indian House with all of its goods. As soon as the dead, whose numbers are estimated to be many thousands, are buried, it will be clear if anything may be saved. It is assumed that the king will have the salvaged goods distributed equally among all.[2]

The content of this letter is not as emotional as the previous account, but it contains information of importance to other merchants who were the main target audience of the Copenhagen newspaper. Thus, the newspaper noted on 8 December that it was impossible to publish the rate of exchange as usual, because the earthquake had caused great confusion all over Europe.

It seems that private letters could be addressed to specific persons as well as to the general public. This is demonstrated by the letter from a group of German merchants in Lisbon to a correspondent in Hamburg that was published in *Kopenhagener Deutsche Post-Zeitungen* (Copenhagen German Gazette), which was the German equivalent of the above-mentioned newspaper. The letter was addressed to 'my most noble lord!', but it also contained a list of German survivors and a postscript requesting that the letter be read out aloud to inform the relatives of the named survivors.[3] In this way, a letter could be private and public at the same time. Publishing the letter in a Copenhagen newspaper would serve as reading it out loud while informing the general public as well.

These examples raise the question of what may then be regarded as private about these letters and accounts. One answer could be that they were written by private actors such as merchants and not by persons employed by the state such as diplomats or courtiers. However, it is notable that eighteenth-century news in general consisted of unedited, subjective accounts and in some cases had the form of private letters written to specific recipients rather than the general public. Did this mean that the newspapers sought to convey to the reader some sense of privacy, intimacy or confidentiality in a positive sense? This privacy of correspondence is the topic of the following investigation of the eighteenth-century concept of the private letter. By privacy of correspondence I mean a less formal, more confidential and personal form of communication by letter between two persons and not intended for a wider public. Although private letters ceased to be private when they were published, it is still possible to investigate whether notions of communicative privacy were associated with this type of news.

The investigation begins with a short survey of the use of private letters and accounts in Danish newspapers during the period from 1750 to 1800. Secondly, I will investigate the phenomenon of private news as a remediation, a term used by media scholars designating the tendency to incorporate older forms of media into new ones. In this case, private letters in newspapers can be said to represent the manuscript newsletter that preceded the printed newspapers, but also continued to exist alongside them. Thirdly, I examine letter privacy and secrecy in relation to mail surveillance and postal espionage. Finally, the emergence of the new eighteenth-century ideal of the private letter as an expression of subjectivity or personality will be discussed in the context of publication.

Private letters in eighteenth-century Copenhagen newspapers

In a survey of the use of the word 'private' in Copenhagen newspapers from 1749 to 1800 by Pernille Ulla Knudsen and Helle Vogt, about 10 per cent – 368 out of 3,562 occurrences – concerns private letters (*breve, skrivelser*) and accounts (*beretninger, efterretninger*) that were used as sources for foreign news. The short notices about private letters and accounts are not explicit as to what was 'private' about these, but it is possible to locate small hints from the context in which they appear. All of the examples in this analysis come from the main source of foreign news in Copenhagen in the second half of the eighteenth century: The newspaper published twice a week by the Berling family, from 1749 to 1762 called *Kiøbenhavnske Danske Post-Tidender* (Copenhagen Danish Gazette) and from 1762 to 1808 *De til Forsendelse med Posten allene privilegerede Kiøbenhavnske Tidender* (The Copenhagen Gazette reserved exclusively for Distribution by Post). From 1749 to 1767, the Berlings also published a newspaper in German, called *Kopenhagener Deutsche Post-Zeitungen* (Copenhagen German Gazette), with the same layout as *Kiøbenhavnske Danske Post-Tidender*, but with a different content.

Private letters are primarily mentioned as sources for news about wars and other disastrous events of importance to the international economy, as we saw in the case of the Lisbon earthquake. Private letters and accounts were used as sources for the major international conflicts of the period such as the Seven Years War, the American War of Independence, the Russo-Turkish and Austro-Turkish Wars and the revolutionary wars at the end of the century. Foreign news dominated the Danish newspapers of the time. In 1720, it took up 84 per cent of the content, in 1750 61 per cent and in 1800 76 per cent of the content. It has been estimated that the number of newspaper readers went from 1 per cent in 1720 to 10 per cent of the population in 1800. The great emphasis on foreign news indicates that the readers were mainly court officials and merchants from the upper strata of society, with a special interest in that kind of information.[4]

The newspapers used private letters and accounts in the absence of and as a corrective to more biased official sources during times of conflict. One such example comprises the reports by London correspondents from the American War of Independence. On 7 July 1775, the *Kiøbenhavnske Tidender* printed news about the beginning of the war under the headline 'Of Letters from London, 20 June'. The correspondent quoted private letters from Americans who were ready to defend their rights in response to the British siege of Boston. He also mentioned that the court had received an American peace offer in a dispatch from the British general Sage, but that this was contradicted by private letters from America, and concluded from the perspective of a Brit that one should expect a protracted war in 'our' colonies.[5] In another report in the same newspaper, this one from a London correspondent on the fall of Charleston in 1780, an American officer taken as prisoner of war was quoted for saying that the morale on the American side was low. Contradicting this statement, the correspondent referred to private letters stating that the Americans had fought with great resolution during the siege of the city and had only surrendered when provisions ran out.[6] Later, news of the decisive British defeat at Yorktown in 1781 also came via private letters from London addressed to a correspondent in Hamburg, before official news from London confirmed it.[7]

Quotes from private letters give the reader some sense of getting confidential information from a friend with inside knowledge. A report from the London correspondent published in the *Kiøbenhavnske Tidender* on 5 July 1776 contains an excerpt from a private letter sent from Philadelphia to what appears to be a British merchant: 'Perhaps you hope to see our trade restored to its former condition; but you may be assured that the ministry has driven the dealings with us so far that no one would ever consider a peace agreement. We are now looking for good alliances and have in particular our eyes on Spain.'[8] During a crisis between Britain and France in October 1787, the newspaper published a private letter from what appeared to be a French minister:

> At this very moment, I am returning from Versailles. The decision to go to war has been made; all members of the council, except one principal minister, have voted for it. An order has been sent to all harbours to work most eagerly on the preparation of our ships. People will wonder at our efforts, and the world will see that France is not as bereft of means as people think.[9]

This letter seems to be an example of strategic communication rather than a leak of top-secret information. However, such letters must have met a desire on the part of private citizens to know the secrets of states. During another time of international crisis, in 1785, an Austrian correspondent impatiently lamented in the newspaper that:

> The point at which most news-lovers promised to reveal to us the great secrets of cabinets has passed, without the public yet having been informed about the secret political order of Europe and about the subject of the so long and eagerly led negotiations. In a time, where according to public as well as private accounts, there can be no doubt of the amicable settlement of the Dutch cause, the movements of the Imperial Forces have, however, not ceased.[10]

The reliability of private sources was in some cases questioned. In a news report about 'letters from London' from 4 February 1777, a correspondent mockingly wrote that people 'amused themselves' with rumours from private letters, because the court had not yet received news from the Philadelphia campaign. As he explained, 'some' regarded new rumours to be truthful, because previous rumours had turned out to be true. Later that year, a London correspondent complained that, because the court had not made any announcements about the capture of Philadelphia, the newspapers do battle about whether the British troops had won the campaign or not. Their 'weapons' were 'private letters, truthful or invented'.[11]

The preference for private sources instead of official news, as well as the fear of misinformation, is also present in the reports from the Russian and Austrian wars with the Ottoman Empire. During the outbreak of the Austro-Turkish war in 1788, a Vienna correspondent complained that it was impossible to obtain 'genuine private accounts' from the front in Hungary, because a lot of them were fake news, presumably exaggerating the victories of the Austrians.[12] Another report from this war hinted at postal censorship, as the Vienna correspondent said that he was only allowed to write that the emperor as well as Russia recognized the Ottoman governor, Mahmud Bassa, as the sovereign ruler of Albania.[13] As shown by Jesper Jacobsen in his chapter about censorship, the Russian government was especially concerned with controlling information about Russian affairs in foreign newspapers. Thus, during the secret negotiations between Catherine the Great and her allies in Kiev in 1787, a correspondent wrote that the police kept a close eye on foreigners. Private residents must be careful what they wrote about the affairs of the state in their letters and even 'persons of rank' were not allowed to send dispatches without permission.[14]

These examples from an eighteenth-century newspaper show that 'private letters' were typically newsletters written by private persons such as merchants who were not in the service of states. The news from private sources would normally be regarded as more trustworthy than official statements but could also be rejected as unsubstantiated rumours. We have also seen that private news correspondence posed a threat to the control of information by states during times of international conflict. However, the use of the private letter as a news source could also be seen as a remediation of manuscript newsletter that preceded and existed alongside the printed newspapers.

Remediating the private letter

Tilda Maria Forselius has used the concept of remediation to explain why the genre of private letters was used as a way of addressing the readers of the first Swedish weekly magazines of the eighteenth century. Remediation is a term developed by media scholars David Bolter and Richard Gruisin to describe the tendency to incorporate older types of media into new ones. The goal is to create a sense of transparency by removing attention from the mediation and insisting on some contact point between the media and what it represents. Put simply, it seeks to make the content seem as real as possible.[15] Thus, the first printed newspapers could be seen as a remediation of the handwritten newsletters that emerged during the Renaissance and still existed in the eighteenth century as a more exclusive form of news service. Forselius has investigated a collection of forty-eight handwritten newsletters sent to a Swedish noblewoman in 1727 and 1728, but finds no noteworthy differences between these and contemporary printed newspapers, except for some emphasis on domestic topics that might reflect specific interests. Unlike the magazines, the author is not present in the first person and does not address the receiver personally, except in a postscript included in the last issue of the collection.[16]

This find should lead us to question the simplicity of Robert Darnton's theory that handwritten newspapers continued to exist, because they were not subject to censorship, as were the printed newspapers; there might be more to the story.[17] In an investigation of English manuscript newsletters from the eighteenth century, Rachel Scarborough has also noted that the manuscripts contained the same uncontroversial news as did printed newspapers. Both media contained unedited anonymous letters from diplomats and correspondents in order to increase the trustworthiness of the news as first-hand accounts. She therefore argues that the continued existence of the manuscript newsletter cannot be ascribed to the lack of censorship and suggests contemporary concerns about the impersonality of print as an alternative explanation.[18] Recent research on eighteenth-century manuscript culture has also emphasized the continued importance of the manuscript, because the emergence of a print culture meant that handwritten documents came to appear as more closely linked to the private body and the individual personality.[19] This indicates that the private or personal character of the communication actually increased the value of its news contents.

Heiko Droste has offered a convincing explanation why subscribers were willing to pay five to ten times the price of a printed newspaper for a manuscript newspaper. At the beginning of the early modern period, the establishment of paper mills and postal infrastructures had enabled the spread of letters as a medium of communication. To begin with, news was exchanged in letters among members of the elites as signs of mutual friendship, although such letters would also be copied and circulated to larger audiences. The first handwritten newspapers were sold as articles of commerce in the 1500s and were later supplemented with printed newsletters in 1600s. Droste finds a possible explanation for the survival of the manuscript newsletter in a tract from 1700 by the German jurist Johann Peter von Ludewig (1668–1743) on the use and abuse of newspapers. Arguing from the perspective of the prince, Ludewig thought that the value of news decreased, the more it became available to the public. Thus, a personal letter from a diplomat to the prince would contain more valuable news than those that could be read in a printed newspaper. This could explain both why the elite preferred handwritten newsletters well into the eighteenth-century and the use of private letters in the printed newspapers.[20]

Degrees of publicity

In older studies of Danish media history, it is often assumed, as Darnton does, that handwritten newspapers survived into the eighteenth century, because they were not subject to the same censorship as were the printed newspapers.[21] The earliest known handwritten newsletter is included in a letter to the Danish-Norwegian King Christian III (1503–1559; r. 1536–1559) from Philip Melanchthon (1497–1560), the Lutheran reformer at Wittenberg, in 1550. Like the later printed newspapers, this newsletter contains very brief and factual reports on war and peace in various European countries. Such newsletters can be seen as a way to secure the favour of a patron, but Christian III is also known to have paid correspondents in the German cities of Lübeck and Strasbourg. One of them was the Weimar court-preacher, Johannes Aurifaber (1519–1575), who only asked for the salary of the messenger for sending news so confidential that Aurifaber asked the king to burn his letters to avoid being compromised.[22] This type of news exchange corresponds to the more private and thus more valuable kind of news mentioned by the German jurist Ludewig, which would later take the shape of diplomatic correspondence.

A more publicly available news service began with the selling of printed news sheets about single events of a sensational character. The oldest news sheet in Danish is from 1542 and contains a first-hand account about the destruction caused by a swarm of locusts in the German land of Lausitz.[23] From 1609 and onwards, the first weekly newspapers with several news items began to appear in Germany and the Netherlands. In Denmark, the establishment of a postal service in 1624 furthered the spread of news to a larger public. In 1634, both a bookseller and a book printer in Copenhagen were given the privilege of printing newspapers in Danish and German, but no copies of these have been preserved. A regular production of Danish newspapers did not begin until the 1660s, but printed newspapers from Hamburg continued to dominate the Danish market for printed newspapers until the middle of the eighteenth century.[24] The tone of the first Danish newspapers was official. They consisted of short, factual news reports from abroad and official announcements and propaganda on behalf of the absolutist regime. However, a more personal form of address was used in the Danish and German versions of the weekly newspaper, *Extraordinaire Relation*, published by Joachim Wielandt (1690–1730) and subsequently his widow during the period between 1721 and 1748. Until 1741, each issue opened as though it were a private letter, addressing 'My Lord!' and ending with 'I remain N.N.'[25]

This remediation of the private letter is probably caused by the continued competition from handwritten newsletters. For example, in the letter book of Johan Bartram Ernst (1663–1722), there are some copies of letters with news from Copenhagen, which he wrote in the period from 1699 to 1701. The recipients of his news from Copenhagen were the Danish ambassador in Saxony, a count from Holstein, a Norwegian colonel and a Danish nobleman. Most of Ernst's letters contained private messages, but some consisted of only news items under the headline 'Nouvelles'. Using his connections at the court, Ernst was able to report on sensitive matters, such as a conflict of etiquette between foreign ambassadors at court, the sale of public offices and the conflict with Holstein. This exchange of news was not commercial; rather, it seems to have been a way of networking with possible benefactors. Given the sensibility of his news reports, it is ironic that Ernst would later become censor and author the first ordinance on censorship of the printed newspapers in 1701.[26] From 1697 onwards, a correspondent named Fastenaw published a handwritten newspaper with news from Copenhagen called 'gazette à la main'. The Danish ambassador in Moscow described its content as a mixture of news on what was happening in the capital 'in private circles as well as in public life.'[27]

News from abroad would mostly reach Denmark via the postal offices. In a diary entry from 1677, the later bishop, Jens Bircherod (1658–1708), describes how he as a student went to the postal office in Odense to hear the latest news from the handwritten newspapers sent to the local postmaster.[28] Furthermore, the staff at the Danish post office in Hamburg supplemented their income by writing newspapers based on the latest news from abroad. The later director of the postal services, Christian Erlund (1673–1754), made a fortune from handwritten newsletters during his employment as a postal secretary and controller in Hamburg, 1704–1711. In the last year of his employment, he earned 2,218 rixdollars from this sideline business. He had eighty-six subscribers from the elite, including the Crown Prince, diplomats, members of the nobility and several postmasters, who may have sold copies of Erlunds newsletters.[29]

After his promotion to postal controller in Copenhagen in 1712, and later to director of postal services in 1725, Erlund continued to write newspapers with news from the capital, but now anonymously. He is most likely the author of the handwritten newspaper 'Nouvelles de Copenhague', of which some issues from 1721 have been preserved. In its form, this newspaper is public in the sense that it does not feature the personal opening address and the signature at the end, but some postscripts do contain personal messages. Its contents were in some cases more controversial than that was published in the printed newspapers. For example, in 1727, Erlund was reprimanded after the provincial governor of Aalborg had complained that the Copenhagen newspaper had made it publicly known that the governor had applied for a discharge.[30]

In 1731, the right to publish handwritten newspapers in Copenhagen became a privilege attached to the office of the postal manager and, from 1734, it was subjected to censorship. However, this did not kill off this seemingly more private news service. As we have seen, handwritten newspapers were also the subject of government intervention. Instead, the market for handwritten newspapers appears to have gradually disappeared after 1749, when the Berling newspapers began to publish domestic news which until then had only been available in the handwritten newspapers.[31]

Breaches of privacy

The fact that handwritten newspapers could contain more sensitive information raises the question of whether the postal officers opened private letters to obtain information for their newsletters. If so, this again raises the question of whether newspapers in some cases breached privacy by publishing private letters which had not been intended for publication in the first place. On the other hand, early modern postal services are also known to have opened letters in order to monitor and censor the news flow during times of war. The fact that private letters contradicting the official accounts of the American War of Independence were able to slip through the postal offices in Britain suggests a more liberal postal policy there than in more absolutist regimes such as Austria and Russia. The question is whether this was also the case in the absolutist state of Denmark-Norway.

The extent of postal espionage and censorship during Danish absolutism has previously been investigated by Sune Christian Pedersen. The constitutional principle of privacy of the mails was invented during the French Revolution and was not introduced in Denmark until the Constitution of 1849, which also brought absolutism to an end. However, the international legal literature of the seventeenth and eighteenth centuries operated with an implicit contract of security and confidentiality between the postal services and their customers. Thus, the postal ordinance of 25 December 1694 stated in its ninth section that it was strictly forbidden to remove letters from the mail bags unless the king had specifically ordered this. An instruction for the postmasters from 1705 also states that it was their duty to deliver each letter unopened and unharmed to its proper recipient.[32] Shortly after attaining actual regency in 1784, the crown prince and later king Frederick VI (1768–1839, r. 1808–1839) felt compelled to repeat that the post masters 'should not dare to open or break the letters of anyone'. Only the king, as the absolute ruler, could request the opening of specific letters without a court order. This repetition was, moreover, an expression of the fear that the king and his men could also fall victims to postal espionage. However, Sune Christian Pedersen thinks that the decree of 1784 could also be interpreted as part of the more liberal policy that characterized the early years of the crown prince's new regime.[33]

The monopolization of postal services by the state has in itself been interpreted as a way of enabling postal surveillance.[34] The first known example of Danish postal surveillance occurred shortly after the establishment of a royal postal service, which made the carrying of letters a royal monopoly. In March, 1625, King Christian IV (1577–1648, r. 1596–1648) ordered an English messenger from Hamburg to open and read some diplomatic mail addressed to the English ambassador, revealing a Swedish plan of military attack plan.[35] Other cases of postal surveillance and censorship discussed in Sune Christian Pedersen's study also mostly concern postal espionage in times of war. The case of the postal espionage carried out by Christian Erlund during the Great Northern War, 1701–1721, is of particular interest to the question of private news being leaked in handwritten newspapers written by postal staff. In 1701, Erlund served the king's younger brother as a footman, until he had to flee the country to avoid a death sentence for killing the footman of another prince. Thereafter, he first served in the Danish regiment in the Netherlands, but in 1703, his patrons at court helped him to attain employment at the Danish postal office in Hamburg. He later claimed to have opened many letters there, with information of relevance to the war effort, and to have sent copies of these letters to the Danish king, who in one year should have received as much as 433 copies. He claims to have done so at his own initiative, but according to Pedersen, it is likely that he had been recruited as a spy in return for the pardon he received in 1711. In 1712, Erlund was promoted to a chief position at the main office of the Danish postal services in Copenhagen, where he continued his postal espionage for the King Frederick IV (1671–1730, r. 1699–1730) until the king's death in 1730.[36]

As mentioned earlier, Erlund was also a very successful publisher of handwritten newspapers. His involvement in the systematic opening of letters raises the question of whether the contents of his newspapers were in part based on information in such letters. Sune Christian Pedersen claims that it is unlikely that Erlund would run the risk of openly breaking the law in this way, but does at the same time mention the case of the Hamburg postmaster Johan Heuss (1670–1744) who was later accused of exactly this offense.[37] Heuss was employed as postmaster at the Danish post office in Hamburg in 1712, when Erlund left for Copenhagen. Like Erlund, Heuss began to publish a handwritten newspaper, although he was instructed not to correspond with more than ten or twelve persons outside of the postal services, so as to avoid his work there being hindered by 'private affairs and writings'. To assist him with the newspaper, he enlisted four or five scribes, a composer and four correspondents in the Netherlands. His main competitors on the Danish market for handwritten newsletters were the Danish postal secretary Gangloff, a private correspondent named Barckhausen and a postal secretary at the Prussian post office named Griesch. In 1718, Heuss was accused of opening and copying the newsletters of Barckhausen and Griesch and stealing their content for his own newsletters. His defence strategy was to claim that he received the same news from his correspondents, much as his competitors did from theirs. Referring to some 'curious' letters from Paris in Barckhausen's newsletter, he even claimed that those letters were read aloud in every beer house in Hamburg. 'To avoid several suspicions', he was strictly forbidden to continue publishing his newspaper, but continued nonetheless to do so, now leasing his business to a front man. In 1723, Heuss was denounced by Gangloff for secretly employing a scribe named Hartvig to publish some confidential reports from the Danish ambassador in Moscow, which Hartvig had obtained from a cousin at the court in Petersburg. This time, the Danish resident in Hamburg came to the defence of Heuss and Hartvig promised not to write about Danish ambassadors again.[38] The case of Heuss tells us that a position in the postal services gave ample opportunities to extract information from private letters, but it is difficult to ascertain the extent of this practice.

Masked personalities

According to the royal instruction regarding the censorship of the printed Danish newspapers of 19 March 1701, it was prohibited to publish anything that might threaten the security of the state and the reputation of its officials or that might insult foreign states. The Copenhagen newspapers could only present brief and impartial extracts of the most relevant news from the printed and handwritten newspapers brought in by post. The editors must report only 'what had really happened' and leave out the 'reasonings' and 'useless guesses' of the foreign correspondents.[39]

In other words, news was to be stripped of private opinions. However, as was the case with the news of the Lisbon earthquake in *Kiøbenhavnske Danske Post-Tidender*, most foreign news printed in eighteenth-century newspapers consisted of unedited letters from anonymous correspondents or eyewitnesses. Private letters were not only used to report factual events. From the beginning, Berling's newspaper also printed private letters that contained exactly such political 'reasonings' and 'guesses' that were forbidden in the censorship instruction of 1701. For example, an issue from 1750 contained a letter from a Corsican nobleman to a friend in Livorno with the Corsican's thoughts on a possible union with France. That same year, the newspaper also contained a 'particular' letter sent from Warsaw to 'My lord!' discussing the political situation in Poland.[40] Other private letters contained moral anecdotes such as a letter from Leiden to another lord about a French cavalier who got lured into a correctional prison by a lady whom he had tried to seduce by making indecent advances.[41] Some of the private letters concerned matters of the utmost privacy, such as a vindictive suicide note written by a London gentleman quoted in an issue from 1750:

> My dear wife! This serves you to let you know that you are the cause of this unhappy event. Your conduct towards me has left me out of my mind. We could have lived together in happiness and confidence, if your conduct towards me had matched mine towards you. I hope that the person whose fault it is might reflect upon on this sad and unfortunate incident. The child I leave behind, I leave in the care of God, and I ask him to forgive you for what you have done and hope that he will forgive me, as I have had enough of my life. Your husband, John Bracey.[42]

In this case, the name of the author was mentioned. This was probably done to boost the realistic look of this anecdote with a moral warning against adultery. In most other cases, the private letters were anonymous.

The widespread use of unedited and anonymous private letters in eighteenth-century newspapers can be seen as a strategy of obtaining truth and trust. As mentioned earlier, news in the form of unedited private, non-commercial correspondence between members of the elite would be considered of a higher value than reports written for the public by a paid correspondent.[43] According to William B. Warner, the publishing of unedited letters from abroad was also a way of distributing responsibility for the accuracy of the news. In this way, the responsibility for the truthfulness of a given account shifted from the editor to the newspaper network from which it had been copied.[44]

In the case of the Copenhagen newspapers, most news was copied from the printed and handwritten newspapers of Hamburg. In 1753, Johan Heuss the Younger, who had taken over the newspaper business of his father in Hamburg, was asked by the Danish government to name the author of a certain article. He replied that he did not know the names of his foreign correspondents, and that no one would supply him with news if they could not remain anonymous. He found his suppliers of news through his network of correspondents and diplomats and he communicated with them via middlemen.[45]

The attempt of the Danish government to find the author of a specific article represents a trend that emerges at the end of the eighteenth century to regard texts as the individual expressions of an author. However, in the early modern period and throughout most of the eighteenth century, the norm was to publish anonymously. Censorship laws targeted printers, but neither editors nor authors until the end of the century.[46] In place of the masked author, authenticity and credibility were created by the style of the text and the way the anonymous author addressed the reader.[47] An eloquent, formal style would convince the reader that the author was, in fact, a diplomat or a government official addressing another member of the elite, and this invited the reader into the imagined community of the elite. Such letters dealt with matters of public interests, for instance international politics, but the emotional letters of tragedy and disaster represented a new type of masked personality that had come into fashion in the eighteenth century. In the case of the Lisbon earthquake, the readers would not only be informed of the facts, but also get an insight into the emotional state of mind of the survivors. Even a letter from the Portuguese king to the Spanish king was quoted in the German version of Berling's newspaper to provide insight into the Portuguese king's emotional state of mind: 'I am filled with the most intense pain; the one thing that touches me the most by the sight of my sunken capital, is the destruction of my poor subjects, and I try as best I can to help those, who have survived this disaster.'[48]

The use of letters to express opinions about public matters such as morality was first used in the English weekly magazines *The Tatler* and *The Spectator*, published 1709–1712. This genre soon inspired the emergence of similar magazines across the rest of Europe. In Denmark, a few magazines of this kind appeared in the 1720s and 1730s, but the genre did not really gain ground until the 1740s, with magazines such as *Den danske Spectator* (The Danish Spectator) and *Den patriotiske Tilskuer* (The Patriotic Spectator). Following this, the epistolary form as a medium for debate also entered newspapers and books, as in the moral essays published by enlightenment thinkers such as Ludvig Holberg (1684–1754). It has been assumed that the epistolary essay was used, because a public sphere had not yet come into existence.[49]

However, as argued by Heiko Droste, the early modern press should not be seen as a Habermasian public sphere, but rather as an exclusive medium for the learned elite.[50] According to Tilda Maria Forselius, the authors of private letters in Swedish weekly magazines would mask themselves behind pseudonyms, and the readers would be addressed in second person and even be invited to send in letters to the editors themselves. Forselius interprets the use of the epistolary form as a rhetorical strategy intended to invite the reader into an imagined elite community of shared bourgeois values. Another interesting observation of Forselius is the development of the letters from a classic rhetorical and less personal style in the earliest journals from the 1730s, to letters claimed to be written by a 'real' woman, and with a higher degree of reflection and emotionality, in a women's journal from the 1770s.[51]

The familiar letter

The new genre of the private or familiar letter as a medium to express spontaneous, subjective feelings emerged in the middle of the eighteenth century. The familiar letter was invented as the spontaneous antithesis of the rhetorical letter during Roman antiquity and was revived during the Renaissance, but had its breakthrough in the eighteenth century, where the letter became a more commonly used medium due to more efficient postal services. As mentioned, it was also a literary genre used to create an illusion of subjectivity and immediacy.[52]

The earliest Danish letter manuals of the seventeenth century and early eighteenth century only concerned the rhetorical form of the traditional letter used to network with benefactors. The first Danish manuals on how to write a private or 'natural' letter appeared in the middle of the eighteenth century.[53] The first was *Anmærkninger over den Konst at skrive et godt Brev* (Remarks on the Art of Writing a Good Letter) from 1749 by the Danish author Johan Finkenhagen (1730–1769). In the foreword, Finkenhagen distanced himself from the 'old-fashioned' letter style of 'the polished world', which according to him contained too much 'flattery' and 'affection' and too little 'esprit'. The letter addressing a friend should resemble a natural conversation, but still remain polite and without the digressions of speech. On one hand, you should not be too cautious, writing as if the whole world might read your words. On the other hand, you should not confide too much, because letters might be preserved and used against you, if your friends turned to enemies. In particular, Finkenhagen warned against slandering the honour of a lady or 'swearing like a sailor'.[54] In other words, the fixed nature of writing limited the privacy of communication when it came to socially unacceptable emotions.

An ideal for a more private letter was presented in another manual published by a German author, Christian Fürchtegott Gellert (1715–1769), in 1751, and translated into Danish in 1762. In his foreword, the Danish translator noted that the private letter should resemble a free and innocent conversation, 'where we in a sense open our soul to the person we are speaking to'.[55] Gellert stated in his foreword that the exemplary letters of his manual were, indeed, private letters written to 'real' persons and were never intended for print. This made them livelier, freer and thus more agreeable. In this way, Gellert made a distinction between the authentic private letter and the fake one that appeared in the printed media.[56] According to Gellert, the tasteful emotional letter should be based on the less formal, yet still polished form of conversation practised at the salons of the time, but all the same be free of boring everyday language.[57] Gellert wrote his manual particularly for women whom he believed to be better at writing natural letters because they were more emotional than men, unless they had been raised among people of no taste or had studied too much. The less emotional (man) would write in a blunt and tasteless style that Finkenhagen likewise considered too private for letters.[58] Thus, the private letter of the eighteenth-century should only express an authentic self only insofar as this accorded with the norms of the culture of emotionality which was formed at the end of the century.

Conclusions

This investigation of the private nature of public early modern letters (or lack thereof) began with the question of what was private about the private letters mentioned or quoted as sources for news in the Copenhagen newspapers from the second half of the eighteenth century. The short answer is that 'private' signified that the author was a private merchant or correspondent, not employed by the state.

In the analysis of the use of private letters in the Copenhagen newspapers, I have first shown that they were considered to be more reliable than official communication during times of war, although they could also be suspected of spreading rumours and be subjected to state censorship and manipulation. However, the emotional first-hand accounts from the Lisbon earthquake may also indicate that the private letters were used to convey a sense of authenticity and immediacy to the readers.

Second, I have investigated the qualities of private correspondence as a news source in the printed newspapers and interpreted them as remediations of handwritten newspapers. The manuscript newsletter owed its continued popularity among the elite to its seemingly private character, although this more expensive source of news service was also mass-produced and in fact differed little in content to the more widely available printed newspapers. However, contemporaries such as the author Ludewig thought that the value of news decreased the more public it became, which is why he considered the news in a handwritten newsletter to be more reliable would be more reliable than those in a printed newspaper. This could explain why the first printed newspapers mimicked the form of private letters in terms of subjective and seemingly confidential first-hand accounts from abroad. The reader thus had some sense of being invited into an exclusive community of distinguished readers. However, the case against the director of postal services Erlund, for publishing sensitive information about a civil servant, shows that handwritten newspapers in Denmark were subject to the same censorship as the printed ones.

Thirdly, I have examined the extent to which it was possible to maintain letter privacy during Danish absolutism, when postal officers could open and copy private letters for their manuscript newsletters. Although there was no constitutional right that protected letter privacy during absolutism, the postal ordinances clearly stated that postal officers were not allowed to open letters. Only the king had the right to do so without a court order. Most known cases of systematic postal surveillance stem from times of war, with postal officers such as Erlund seemingly acting on behalf of the king. The proceedings against Heuss show that it was not acceptable for postal officers to use contents from sealed letters in published newsletters, but this happened nevertheless. This case did, however, not concern the privacy of subjects, but rather the theft of state or commercial secrets.

The fourth and last part of the investigation concerned the presence of private or personal opinions and emotions expressed in the private letters published in the newspapers. The censorship ordinance of 1701 ordered the publishers to publish only facts and to edit out the personal reasonings made by the correspondents. As a reaction, however, it became common to print unedited letters so as to distribute responsibility for the content to the news network of correspondents, who were able to hide behind anonymity. Anonymity meant that authenticity and credibility had to be created by means of a particular style. The epistolary form was used, not only to mimic the private newsletter, but also as a platform from which to express private opinions under the mask of anonymity in a pretended dialogue with the reader.

By the middle of the eighteenth century, the ideal of the 'familiar' or 'natural' private letter emerged as the antithesis to both the traditional rhetorical letters as well as the fake personal letters on print. However, the proponents of this new letter style warned against being too candid and open with friends, due to the fixed nature of writing, and instead recommended a relaxed, yet polite form of communication resembling the less formal type of conversation practised at the salons of that time. The amount of privacy in the private letters published in newspapers was therefore limited, given that those letters were indeed authentic private letters and that the authors had the risk of publication in mind. However, I would argue that a positive notion of privacy of correspondence is present in the use of the private letter as a source of information in the Copenhagen newspapers of the late eighteenth century. Although a private letter might just be a letter from a private person of no rank, this type of news source was also associated with positive notions of communicative privacy, such as credibility, authenticity, confidentiality and immediacy.

Notes

1   'Jeg er den eneste af mit Huus, som med Kiolen jeg bær paa Kroppen er undgaaet den skrekkelige Ulykke, som har opslugt Lissabon. Min Lykke, mine Effecter, og alt hvad jeg i denne Verden eyede er begraven under Ruinerne af en Stad, som var bleven mit andet Fæderneland. Jeg er bleven 72 Aar gammel, paa det jeg skulde være et Vidne om den forfærdelige Straf, som Guds Vrede kan lade komme over Menneskene. Fra det Sted paa Marken, hvor jeg var flygtet hen, har jeg seet den store og prægtige Stad at blive ødelagt, og de største Bygninger ved Jordskielvet at blive opløftede og saaledes at kastes frem og tilbage, som de havde været i en Slynge. Dette saa forskrækkelige Syn blev ledsaget med mange tusinde Menneskers ynkelige Jamren og Klagen, som skrege til Himmelen og anraabte Guds Barmhiertighed, hvis strenge Dom de erfore. Hvor jeg seer hen, saa finder jeg hundrede Personer som jeg, der intet har tilbage foruden Erindringen af deres forrige Lykke. Vi ere ulykkelige og vi giøre andre ulykkelige med os. Thi vore Engagementer ere tillige med Staden, i hvilke de vare formerede, og hvoraf de havde deres Bestandighed, gangne til Grunde. Kort, Lissabon er ikke mere til, og skulde den engang blive opbygt igien, hvem torde vove at lade sig ned her', Kiøbenhavnske Danske Post-Tidender (KDP) 15 December 1755, letter from a French merchant to his correspondent in Paris, 5 November.
2   'Jeg skriver dem disse faa Linier til paa aaben Mark, for at give Dem Efterretning om det forskrækkelige Jordskielv, som paakom denne Stad, den 1 hujus om Formiddagen henimod Kl. 10. Alle Huse og Kirker i Staden ere ødelagde, og hvad Jordskielvet har ladet staae, bliver formedelst Ilden som har udbredet sig over den tilbagestaaende Deel af Byen, og som allerede har fortæret Tolhuset og det Indianske Huus med alt dets Varer, forstyrret og lagt øde. Saasnart de Døde, hvis Antal man skatterer paa mange Tusinde, ere begravne, faaer man at see, om endnu noget staaer til at redde. Man formoder, at Kongen lader alt det Gods som bliver berget uddele i lige Deele blant alle. De Vare, som ere opkiøbte for de seglfærdig liggende Floder, kan nu ikke blive betalte, saasom Kiøberne ere omkomne i Ilden. Da alle Møller ere gangne til grunde, saa have vi og her under aaben Himmel Mangel paa Brød, og nyde intet, uden hvad Folk fra Landet af Medlidenhed vil bringe til os', KDP 12 December 1755, excerpt of a letter from Lisbon, 4 November.
3   Kopenhagener Deutsche Post-Zeitungen (CDP) 15 December 1755.
4   Bruhn Jensen 1996, 74–6.
5   De til Forsendelse med Posten allene priviligerede Kiøbenhavnske Tidender (PKT) 7 July 1775.
6   PKT 30 June 1780.
7   PKT 7 and 17 December 1781.
8   'De haabe maaskee, at see vor Handel igien sat i forrige Stand; men de være forsikret, at Ministerium har drevet Sagerne med os saa vidt, at man neppe nogen Tiid skal kunde tænke paa et Forliig. Vi see os nu om efter gode Alliancer, og have i sær vort Øye paa Spanien', PKT 19 July 1776.

9   'I dette Øieblik kommer jeg fra Versailles. Krigen er besluttet; alle Medlemmer
     af Conseilet, den eneste Principalminister undtagen, have givet sin Stemme til
     samme. Til alle Havne er sendt Ordre, at arbeide med største Iver paa vore Skibes
     Udrustning. Man maae forundres over vor Virksomhed, og Verden vil faae at see, at
     Frankrige ikke er saa blottet for hielpekilder, som man troer', PKT 26 October 1787.
10   'Det Tidspunkt, paa hvilken de fleste Nyheds-Elskere lovede os de store Cabinets-
     Hemmeligheder opdagede, synes nu at være temmelig nær, om ikke allerede
     forløben, uden at Publikum endnu har faaet nogen Oplysning om Europas
     hemmelige politiske Forfatning, og om Gienstanden for de saa længe og ivrig
     førte Underhandlinger. Paa en Tiid, da der, saavel efter alle offentlige som private
     Efterretninger, ikke er mere at tvile om den Hollandske Sags mindelige Afgiørelse,
     ophøre dog ikke de Keiserlige Troppers Bevægelser', PKT 2 May 1785.
11   PKT 3 March and 28 November 1777.
12   PKT 14 April 1788.
13   PKT 17 April 1788.
14   PKT 14 May 1787.
15   Forselius 2013, 16–19; Bolter and Gruisin 1999, 21–49.
16   Forselius 2013, 113–30.
17   Darnton 2000.
18   Scarborough 2018.
19   Berndtsson, Fischer, Mattson and Öhrberg 2017, 8–11.
20   Droste 2011 and 2019.
21   Bruhn Jensen 1996, 70–1.
22   Kirchhoff Larsen 1942, 14–17; Stolpe 1878, 104–6.
23   Kirchhoff Larsen 1942, 18; Stolpe 1878, 41.
24   Søllinge and Thomsen 1989, 27. In 1718 the postal service delivered 472 Hamburg
     newspapers in the duchies of Schleswig-Holstein and 355 in the kingdom of
     Denmark.
25   Søllinge and Thomsen 1989, 91–3.
26   Kirchoff Larsen 1942, 114–18; Stolpe, vol. 3, 1879, 295–302; Stolpe, vol. 4, 1882, 27–9.
27   Stolpe, vol. 4, 1882, 29–30.
28   Ibid., 17.
29   Ibid., 40–5.
30   Ibid., 45–52.
31   Ibid., 52–9.
32   Pedersen 2008, 33–6.
33   Ibid., 253–61
34   Ibid., 2008, 25.
35   Madsen 1991, 392.
36   Pedersen 2008, 99–223.
37   Ibid., 108–9.
38   Stolpe 1882, vol. 4, 32–6.
39   Instruction of 19/3 1701, § 3–9, in Stolpe 1879, vol. 2, 352–3. The norm that news
     should contain objective facts and not be mixed with subjective comments is still
     part of the Danish code of press ethics (www.pressenaevnet.dk/god-presseskik).
40   KDP, 27 February and 10 July 1750.
41   KDP, 15 January 1751.
42   'Min kiære Kone! Nærværende tiener eder til Efterretning, at I ere Aarsag i denne
     ulykkelige Tildragelse. Eders Forhold imod mig har giort mig afsindig. Vi kunde

have levet lykkelig og fortrolig med hverandre, dersom eders Opførsel var kommen overens med min. Jeg haaber, at det Menneske, som har med Skyld deri, skal giøre sig nogen Omtanke over denne sørgelige og ulykkelige Tilfælde. Det Barn, som jeg efterlader mig, befaler jeg i Guds Omsorg, og beder ham, at han vil forlade eder, hvad I have giort, og som jeg er mæt og kied af mit Liv, saa haaber jeg, at han skal lade mig vederfares Naade. Eders Mand, John Bracey', KDP, 13 November 1750.

43 Pettegree 2014, 308–25.
44 Warner 2018, 34.
45 Stolpe, vol. 4, 1882, 38–9.
46 Horstbøll 2010.
47 Forselius 2015, 84–6.
48 KDeP, 12/12 1755, a letter from Paris of 25 November with a quote from this letter.
49 Jensen et al. 1983, 225–39.
50 Droste 2019, 35–7.
51 Forselius 2015, 41–50, 131–44, 187–210.
52 Andersen 1999; Anderson and Ehrenpreis 1966.
53 Fjord Jensen et al. 1983, 59–69.
54 Finkenhagen 1749, 1–10, 19–23.
55 Gellert 1762, 3–10. Foreword by the translator Jacob Baden.
56 Ibid., 11–12.
57 Ibid., 30–1.
58 Ibid., 96–9.

Commercial newspaper and public shame pole: Exposure of individuals in the Copenhagen gazette *Adresseavisen* 1759–73

Jesper Jakobsen

The introduction of the commercial newspaper *Kiøbenhavns alene priviligerede Adresse Contoirs Efterretninger* (*Adresseavisen*) in 1759 had a profound impact on how individuals interacted with the public.[1] It was initially intended as a medium for commercial interaction in Copenhagen, but the advertisements and announcements it contained delved ever deeper into the intimate sphere of common Copenhageners, and the paper soon included the deliberate public exposure of individuals, in return for a fixed, modest charge. The eighteenth century was a period of increased local and global commerce, and urban commercial newspapers with a mixed content of advertisements, short essays, sales advertisements, lost and found reports, and local news stories were introduced all over Europe. In Britain and France they were known as *Gazettes*, and in Germany as *Intelligenzblätter*. A variant of this genre, the *Adresseavisen* offered to publish advertisements and announcements to anyone willing to pay. It was not the first newspaper to present sales advertisements and private announcements before the Copenhagen public's eyes. Established newspapers published by the prominent publishing families of Høpfner and Berling also contained advertisement sections. However, the main content of these so-called *politiske tidender* (political newspapers) was foreign news that had mainly been translated from foreign newspapers and printed letters.[2] What was new about the *Adresseavisen* was that it introduced commercial sales advertisements and announcements to the Copenhagen public on an unprecedented scale.

The absolutist kingdom of Denmark-Norway was among the most authoritarian states of eighteenth-century Europe, and control of the flow of information was a cornerstone in its maintenance of political and religious order. For most of the eighteenth century, texts printed in Denmark-Norway were subject to censorship prior to publication by Copenhagen University, the dioceses and other appointed authorities. However, on 14 September 1770, Denmark-Norway introduced a legally guaranteed and wholly unrestricted freedom of print, which resulted in fierce and untamed public debate, until regulation was gradually reintroduced with the Press Laws of 7 October

1771 and 20 October 1773.³ Scholars of eighteenth-century print culture have widely conceived of the public and the private spheres as functionally divided, drawing heavily on Jürgen Habermas's concepts of the emergence of private (bourgeois) spheres within a representative public sphere.⁴ The Norwegian historian Jakob Maliks has stressed that censorship before publication was the state's primary tool for regulating public communication in eighteenth-century Denmark-Norway: 'Within the absolutist body of politics, censorship had the system-specific function of preventing what was private or closed from seeping into the open representative public sphere.'⁵ Within this field of research, scholars have viewed books, learned journals and other periodicals as pivotal in shaping an enlightened public, while *Gazettes*, *Intelligenzblätter* and commercial newspapers, in general, have been neglected because of their often-strictly unpolitical content. Based on a study of late-eighteenth-century North German *Intelligenzblätter*, Ian F. McNeely has stressed that 'censors constrained intelligence gazettes to develop in a circumscribed, ostensibly depoliticised space by distinguishing them from political and deliberative – *räsonnierende* – newspapers in the classic Habarmasian mold'.⁶ However, in recent years the field of research has expanded to include a broader range of texts and genres.⁷

The *Adresseavisen* was inextricably linked to the urban commercial space of Copenhagen and *Kiøbenhavns Adresse-Contoir* (Copenhagen Intelligence Office), which, from 1759, was run by two Copenhagen-based merchants, Hans Holck (1726–83) and Johan Andersen. In the following years, Holck emerged as the driving force behind *Kiøbenhavns Adresse-Contoir*, *Adresseavisen* and a wide range of associated initiatives.⁸ Intelligence Offices were a common feature in commercial hubs all across eighteenth-century Europe. They first appeared in France during the seventeenth century, and quickly spread throughout the rest of Europe. Their primary function was to support trade finance activities in urban commercial centres by facilitating the public's awareness of vacancies, luxury goods, and information about ship arrivals and departures. In this sense, they were a product of the ever-increasing commercial activities and globalizing trade of eighteenth-century Europe.⁹ It was, therefore, no coincidence that the successful introduction of *Kiøbenhavns Adresse-Contoir* coincided with Copenhagen's rise to become a significant northern European centre of international commerce during the 'flourishing period' of the second half of the eighteenth century.¹⁰

Established political newspapers constantly risked exposing sensitive information, but it was a threat well known to the government and one that it regularly dealt with through established regulatory procedures.¹¹ In a classic legal article, Samuel D. Warren and Louis Brandeis defined privacy as the right to be left alone, and this right included the individual's protection from exposure in public newspapers.¹² In the political newspapers, the question of exposure was chiefly a matter of private information that had slipped out into the public sphere. In this case, the private entails sensitive information in general, especially concerning the courts and royal heads-of-state.¹³ However, during the 1750s, the political newspapers were well established, and a well-proven set of procedures dealt effectively with these kinds of slips; in contrast, the *Adresseavisen* posed a hitherto unseen threat whereby everyday people risked public exposure in print.

As a commercial enterprise funded primarily through advertisements, the *Adresseavisen* served as a catalyst for the expanding literary market and the growth of a larger printed public in the mid-eighteenth century. In this article, I aim to show how the introduction of the *Adresseavisen* gave common Copenhageners the opportunity to pay for access to this printed public, and thereby also introduced a conduit through which they could publicly expose and shame others. The period covered in this article starts with the introduction of the newspaper in 1759, and terminates with the passing of the Press Law of 20 October 1773. Like all other printed media in eighteenth-century Denmark-Norway, the paper was subject to constant surveillance and regulation by the authorities. The publishers thus continually negotiated with the authorities over what could be published and how to present information to the public. The *Adresseavisen* had to work primarily with local authorities, such as the Copenhagen chief-of-police and the *Københavns Magistrat*, an assembly of prominent citizens responsible for the administration of the city of Copenhagen, but also, on occasion, the paper had to negotiate with the royal administration, represented by the *Danske Kancelli* (Danish Chancellery).[14]

Private announcements in a public commercial newspaper

Holck and Andersen's initial intentions with *Adresseavisen* were to collate information gathered from both individuals and public sources. This included information about people travelling to and from Copenhagen; recorded deaths, births and marriages; exchange rates; ships arriving; goods for sale; lost and found property; vacancies and travel opportunities.[15] Hans Holck himself summarized the benefit of collating this type of commercial information:

> Skippers may be sought out by merchants who would like to ship goods or by passengers who would travel with them, and the Intelligence Office would guide them to know where the skipper is located. A gentleman can always find a comfortable person for his service, and a servant could find a gentleman who easily could obtain knowledge of previous service, salary and whatever else is required on both sides.[16]

In 1759, the cost for placing advertisements and announcements was calculated by the number of lines, with prices ranging from 6 *skilling* for one to two lines, to 4 *mark* for fifty-one to sixty lines.[17] This means that for a relatively low cost, individuals could buy access to the rapidly expanding printed public of the mid-eighteenth century, and, of course, an essential part of Holck's strategy was to reach out to as many people as possible.[18]

Besides the advertisements and announcements, the *Adresseavisen* included additional content meant to catch the public's attention. The front page often featured essays, treatises and other short texts, which generally satisfied popular demand within the market for printed texts. These items ranged from accounts of the organization of police in China on the one hand, to a printed letter from Provost Lüders to Pastor

Oest about the improvement of agricultural techniques on the other.[19] They were often translated from periodicals, such as the *Schleswig-Holsteinische Anzeigen, Göttingschen gelehrte Anzeigen* or other German journals, which reflects the strong influence of German culture as well as Copenhagen's close connections to the northern German book markets. The short texts featured on the front page were subject to censorship by the university.

Another recurring section that aimed to attract the attention of the Copenhagen public was the news section, *Adskilligt Nyt* (Various News). The *Adresseavisen* was strictly excluded from printing anything about foreign courts, alliances or similar political news, since such content was the privilege of the Høpfner and the Berling families.[20] Instead, the news section presented a mixed bag, ranging from descriptions of the queen and the prince rowing on a lake, to tragic and shocking stories of accidents and murders. It could be tragic reports from Copenhagen, such as that of a three-year-old child who died after falling into a boiling pot of soup, or short foreign notifications, such as that describing a German student who killed his mother and sister with an axe. A shocking description was published in April 1772, recounting how some pigs were seen at the graveyard near Copenhagen Cathedral devouring the corpse of a dead girl that lay hidden beneath the snow.[21] Descriptions such as these mirror the intense public interest in murder ballads and similar depictions of death and execution that formed a substantial part of early modern popular print culture all over Europe.[22] On 3 April 1761, the front page even featured a one-page description of the alleged cruelties of Native Americans towards their prisoners of war:

> Then they knock his toes and fingers between two stones, cut the straps of the skin around the joints, remove the entire strip of meat, and burn it in turn. So they tear the broken and half-fried flesh into pieces and eat it up with greed, and just as they are out of rage by themselves, they smear their whole face with the blood that flows from it.[23]

Of course, this description says more about eighteenth-century Europeans' perception of Native Americans than it does about actual events. But besides being a reminder that death was ever-present in the early modern city, such stories also reflect the broad public interest in these matters, an interest that a commercial enterprise like the *Adresseavisen* could capitalize on. In this respect, a symbiotic commercial correlation existed between the essays, treatises, news and announcements.

The popular texts featured on the front page and in the news section made the paper more attractive for people who wanted to pay for advertisements and announcements. This business plan seems to have been successful because, over the following years, the number of weekly editions increased significantly. The payed-for advertisements and announcements were commercially vital to the business plan and success of the *Adresseavisen*. They appeared in a variety of regular sections, such as those sharing the information of people who were renting out rooms, people who sold goods, public debt claims and calls for runaway servants. Page after page was packed with people selling all sorts of goods, from Chinese soy and Spanish olives, to coaches and surgical instruments, all of which could be bought and retrieved from both shops and private houses. Severin Ferslev announced that he had a small porcelain shop where he sold coffee, 'very good Dutch cheese', Dutch frying pans, sausages from Brunswick and much more.[24] The sales advertisements are great examples of the paper's close connections to urban space, as they served as printed representations of the commercial culture and the spatial characteristics of the city's squares, streets and alleys. The textual representation of the cityscape enabled people to navigate their way to traders' shops or private houses.[25] One citizen announced that he sold tea, Norwegian anchovies and newly arrived English spirits at 'Vorregade, the eighth house on the left hand from Helsingørsgade, next to the butcher'.[26] The sales advertisement enabled common Copenhageners to interact with each other through a printed medium, and thereby gave them a voice in the printed public.

As a medium intended for the exchange of goods and information between individuals, anonymity made no sense in *Adresseavisen*. This differed from the public debates, both before and after the introduction of the Freedom of Print Act on 14 September 1770, where books and pamphlets often were published anonymously or under cover of a pseudonym.[27] The absence of anonymity, within a commercial context, had a profound influence on the connection between individuals and the printed public, and the contents that served as intermediaries in this regard soon progressed beyond the trivial practicalities of the goods-for-sale advertisements.

Public exposure of scandalous rumours

On 10 April 1761, the *Adresseavisen* published a short notification about a woman who gave birth to two children at the Vartov Hospital (a Copenhagen home for the poor): 'At the Vartov Hospital, one of the paupers has given birth to two children, namely one girl and one boy.'[28] As stressed above, the essays and treatises were already subject to the censorship of the university, but following this specific notification, the practice of pre-emptive censorship was extended to all of the paper's contents. Notifications about children born in Copenhagen had frequently appeared in the news section, but birth notifications were presented in completely different ways depending on the status and social class of the parents.

The birth of a child within wealthy and noble families was presented as a joyful event, which offers glimpses of the domestic life of influential Copenhagen families. Often they were just presented as short notifications akin to 'Countess Raben has had a son'.[29] But other times, such notifications were written in a more elaborate manner, as in the following example: 'On the night between the fourth and fifth this month, Chamberlain Count Holstein's wife delivered a perfect young son, to the great joy of the noble family. Yesterday, the wife of legal Councillor Fabricii likewise delivered a young son.'[30] Such statements came out of a long tradition among the royalty, nobility and, increasingly, the bourgeoisie of the public display of their status through their family and domestic life, and it is easily recognized as a popularized reflection of the Habermassian concept of the representational sphere. These notifications of birth are related to other contemporary genres, such as printed memoirs and funeral sermons, which also publicized information that we today consider to be intimate and private.[31]

Of course, the *Adresseavisen* was not as prestigious a marker of status as were expensive and lavish printed books, but the paper undoubtedly reached a much larger public. This suggests that the concept of the public, and how individuals interacted with it, was changing during the 1760s.

Children born into the lower social classes were referred to in the paper in quite a different manner because they were not considered to be of interest in their own right to the Copenhagen public. They only found their way into the *Adresseavisen* when they were the victims of criminal activity, or when they were somehow associated with tragic, sensational or scandalous events. Tragic notifications about dead newborns found around the city recurred throughout the paper's issues, and such stories appeared alongside other sensational news items, such as accounts of artisans falling to their deaths from scaffolding. One specific example from 1760 referred to the finding of a body of a child who had possibly been born out of wedlock, a condition associated with severe social shame: 'This Morning in Lille Kongensgade a newly born baby girl was found completely naked and dead, with the head turned to one side, and whoever put her there has not yet been found.'[32] The births and deaths of poor children were thus negatively charged, and the reporting of such births makes them out to be examples of irresponsibility or of accidents, with clear undertones of horror and scandal. Presumably these stories also sought to arouse readers' curiosity. In 1773, for instance, a sensational bulletin reported that 'a poor woman in this city gave birth to a dead baby girl with two heads, the other limbs were as usual'.[33] The socially stratified notifications about childbirths point towards a duality in how individuals interacted with the Copenhagen public through the commercial context of the *Adresseavisen*: either as a display of status or as a sensational and tragic news item.

The notification published in the *Adresseavisen* on 10 April 1761 about the pauper who gave birth to two children was scandalous, because it insinuated that the children were born out of wedlock. The Vartov Hospital was an institution under the aegis of *Københavns Fattigvæsen* (the Copenhagen Poor Service), which was reserved for worthy citizens from respectable families, and is best described as a combination of nursing home and hospital, primarily for older people. According to a charter of 1607, the Vartov Hospital could only admit 'such persons, who, in truth, by their prosperous times, have made an honest living', and, in particular, those who have contributed to society by paying taxes in Copenhagen.[34] The *Adresseavisen* therefore had not only implied that indecent and scandalous behaviour had taken place at the Vartov Hospital, but also exposed the alleged scandal to the Copenhagen public. The *Københavns Fattigvæsen* reacted promptly by sending a formal complaint directly to Johan Ludvig Holstein (1694–1763), the General Secretary of the *Danske Kancelli*, and a closer examination soon concluded that the woman was in fact a housemaid working at Vartov Hospital, who was lawfully married to a butcher. She had earlier asked the chief of the hospital that she be allowed to deliver her children at the Vartov Hospital; she was allowed this because of the poor condition of her rented apartment.[35] The *Adresseavisen* had publicly exposed the Vartov Hospital by implying indecent and scandalous activities on an entirely false and undocumented basis.

This was not the first time that the *Adresseavisen* had courted troubles with the authorities, but this time it had severe consequences. According to a former associate of the Copenhagen Intelligence Office, Niels Prahl (1724–92), the publishers were repeatedly called 'either to the *Københavns Magistrat* or the chamber of police, following some announcement in the paper, and almost every article that he along the way added to the paper found new opposition'.[36] However, the incidents that Prahl describes were considered to be trivial matters, while the notification about the Vartov Hospital not only involved the royal administration, but also led to the *Adresseavisen* becoming subject to censorship.[37] The notification was recalled on 20 April in the hope that 'the mistake would not offend the simple-minded'.[38]

Nevertheless, the damage had already been done, and the stated reason for subjecting the paper to censorship before publication was that it should no longer be filled with tainted and improper notifications, which were deemed to be offensive to Christians and served no other purpose than to incite public outrage.[39] This was the same rationale that lay behind all of the comprehensive censorship provisions within Denmark-Norway, but the censorship procedures that were henceforth to be applied to the *Adresseavisen* differed substantially from those applied to the publication of books and political newspapers, which tended to be censored by the university and royal administration, respectively. Instead, the responsibility for censoring the *Adresseavisen* was given to the *Københavns Magistrat*, which was an assembly of burgomasters and councillors, comprising merchants, master artisans and other prominent citizens appointed by the king. The newly established censorship in advance of publication was thus placed in the hands of people who themselves were integrated into the commercial space and culture of Copenhagen. This decision reflects a general trend in the years leading up to 1770, whereby the censorship and regulation of printed texts gradually moved away from the jurisdiction of the university and clergy. Instead, trade and economic interests became increasingly important, and the shift away from university and the clergy reflects the growing prominence of economic activity. This trend mirrors ideas found in the German tradition of *Kameralwissenschaft*.[40]

From the spring of 1761, the *Københavns Magistrat* kept a surveillant eye on what was published in the *Adresseavisen*. This proved to be quite the workload for the *Københavns Magistrat* which, in addition to its censoring obligations, still had to perform all its other duties. Six years later, therefore, the magistrate appealed to the king, asking for an exemption from this responsibility. In the supplication to the king, dated 30 September 1767, the *Københavns Magistrat* argued that it had grown to be an impossible task 'to censor all that without the neglect of more important things'.[41] Instead, they pledged that Andersen and Holck should be permitted to publish whatever they found relevant to publish in the *Adresseavisen*, so that Andersen and Holck would be liable for whatever they published. The magistrate was referring to the fact that the owners 'Andersen and Holck claim that they cannot withstand the delays caused by censoring the newspapers'.[42] The *Københavns Magistrat*'s request expresses a profound understanding of the business realities of publishing a commercial newspaper, but the *Danske Kancelli* rejected the magistrate's inquiry on 24 November, stating that the *Adresseavisen* had to be censored and reviewed before being printed and published.[43] This decision is important because it underlines the fact that the *Københavns Magistrat* approved the advertisements and notifications from 1761 until the general abolition of pre-publication censorship on 14 September 1770.

Exposing personal information

In the years between 1759 and 1773, the *Adresseavisen* published numerous announcements that increasingly exposed individuals, and which today would be viewed as defamatory violations of individual privacy. The regular section *Undvigte* (Runaways) requested information about people who had run away from jobs, apprenticeships and other obligations; the people behind these announcements were both authorities and individuals, such as estate owners, burghers, master artisans and officers, each of whom exercised authority over the person who had run away.[44] Besides having their names and physical features described and exposed in the *Adresseavisen*, these people were also publicly accused of running away from their respectable jobs and positions, an accusation that would potentially have had devastating consequences for their lives and honour. In Denmark-Norway, as well as other places in eighteenth-century Europe, individual honour was crucial to the cultural and social status of individuals, so this kind of public exposure potentially had severe consequences for those exposed.[45]

A few examples will illustrate what was made public in the announcements. In 1767, a councillor named Peter Johansen Neergaard (1702–72) published the name and physical features of Jens Mogensen, a peasant enlisted in the local military reserve, who had run away from *Svenstrup Gods* (Svenstrup Estate) near the Zealand town of Ringsted. He was described as well grown with strong limbs and a reddish face, with long, yellowish hair. When Jens ran away, he had been dressed in an old white woollen sweater, a woollen undershirt, canvas trousers, a blue hat and white woollen socks with shoes. He was rumoured to dwell close to Copenhagen, on the island of Amager, and Councillor Neergaard promised a substantial reward of 10 *rigsdaler* (rix dollars, hereafter rdl.) for anyone who provided information that could lead to Jens's seizure.[46] However, Jens Mogensen was just one of hundreds – or perhaps thousands – of individuals who had their names and physical features publicly described and printed in the *Adresseavisen* in its regular section *Undvigte*. A similar announcement was published in 1761, when Christian Fischer, a young apprentice shoemaker, was described as a boy of moderate height with a large head and broad face, wearing a white-grey shirt and a pair of short leather trousers and short socks. The announcement read: 'If anyone should see this boy, then he is asked tenaciously to take him to or let him be taken to Dybensgade up in the corner of the shoemaker Mr Jens Fischer, who offers to pay everyone at his apprehension for the expense.'[47]

The *Undvigte* section also contained numerous appeals for information about soldiers who had deserted. Albrecht Kurz, a musketeer presumed to have deserted from the King's Regiment, was twenty-seven years old and born in Bamberg. He was described as small of stature with blue eyes, a pale face and short curly hair. He had broad shoulders, strong legs and was dressed in a vest, an old green shirt, short leather pants, boots and a hat. It was assumed that he was staying with a Copenhagen shoemaker, since he was a shoemaker himself by profession, and the announcement strictly emphasized that it was punishable to employ him.[48] Today, similar public announcements about people not showing up to their jobs would be unthinkable, but in the mid-eighteenth century, the authorities had no problems with this public naming and shaming of individuals. As demonstrated in the previous section, all content was approved by the *Københavns Magistrat*, and thereby sanctioned by the authorities.

Through the years, people paid for countless similar announcements in the *Adresseavisen*, where individuals' names and physical features were published. The same social stratification that we saw concerning the announcement of childbirths in Copenhagen was also reflected in the announcements in the *Undvigte* section. Again, this mirrors the extreme social hierarchization of eighteenth-century absolutist Denmark-Norway.[49] Until 1788, male peasants up to the age of forty were obligated to stay at the estate where they were born, in order to ensure the recruitment of young men from the peasantry to military service. These peasants were under the jurisdiction of estate owners, and thus Councillor Neergaard exercised authority over Jens Mogensen.[50] Of course, musketeers were subject to harsh military discipline and jurisdiction, but other people behind these announcements, such as master craftsmen, had no direct relationship with the official authorities, so their authority was exercised through their position as the heads of a household.

The people who placed such advertisements generally presented peasants, servants and apprentices almost as objects, with little right to the protection of their privacy. The section *Undvigte* was usually found on the same pages as the section *Bortkomne og bortstiaalne Sager* (Lost and Stolen Property), where calls for information about everything from gold rings to stray dogs were published. It is worth noting how the description of the physical features of runaways from the lower social classes resembles the descriptions of stray dogs. One example comes from Chamberlain Krogh, who on 5 May 1760 described his lost dog as follows: 'A white hunting bitch of medium and thin waist, with short and brown cheeks, which extends over the ears, which are otherwise somewhat speckled, and she has a black spot on the back, all very evenly drawn, and tends to be fearful of strangers.'[51] People of the lower classes were at the greatest risk of public exposure by a mixture of official and unofficial people behind these announcements, which demonstrates the significant reach of the *Adresseavisen* and the influence it had on the Copenhagen public. This is also confirmed by the fact that the royal administration only intervened if the notifications were somehow perceived of as critical of the authorities. The above-mentioned notification published by Councillor Neergaard caused the *General Krigsdirektionen* (War Directorate) to complain to the *Danske Kancelli* because Neergaard had speculated that Mogensen had run away because he was frightened to be included amongst those peasants who 'were to depart for the armed regiments following a most gracious royal decree'.[52] Neergaard's speculation over why Mogensen had absconded spurred the *General Krigsdirektionen* to action, since they considered the speculation to be a public critique of the royal decree. Thus, the *Danske Kancelli* reprimanded the *Københavns Magistrat*, stating that they needed to exercise more caution and ensure that these kinds of 'inappropriate and irrelevant remarks to the public'[53] were henceforth no longer published in the *Adresseavisen*.[54]

Private debt and public shaming

Indeed, the *Adresseavisen* pushed the boundaries concerning what could be communicated in public, and the exposure of individuals became even more pronounced towards the end of the 1760s when announcements of private debt began to appear regularly in the section *Gields fordringer* (Debt Claims). While the authors behind notices in the *Undvigte* section often had a semi-official character, debt claims were entirely a matter between individuals, and here the paper served as an easy and inexpensive means to access the printed public.

The most serious threat to the public exposure of an individual's privacy came in the public debt claims published in the *Adresseavisen*. On 4 October 1771, a creditor announced that he required his debtor to repay 19 rdl., which the debtor had owed since the summer of 1770. The announcement contained an unmistakable threat of public exposure, since the creditor stated that 'the person in question knows himself whom I mean, and so I spare him from publicly announcing his name'.[55] To be exposed in public as untrustworthy – or perhaps unable or unwilling to repay debts – was most probably devastating to an individual's honour and subsequently their business credibility. Again, it was generally people of lower social classes and other marginalized social groups, such as Jewish people, who were at the most significant risk of public exposure in this way.[56]

Public debt claims began to appear in the late 1760s; from the early 1770s, these claims increasingly identified debtors by name, which made them function almost like a printed shame pole. Initially, debt claims generally provided just enough personal details and contextual information for debtors to recognize themselves, without fully exposing their identities to the public. One example is a debt claim announced by J. C. Juncker in the winter of 1770: 'Because a person by the Name of J ** H ** has pledged some clothes at the last Easter's rent, therefore he is warned for the third time.'[57] Indeed, the threat of having one's name and character exposed in print could in itself be a powerful form of pressure. A good demonstration of this comes from 1769, when Friderich Jürgensen, a resident of Store Kongensgade, announced that 'Christian Seyersen Sommer from Jutland is now for the third time summoned to redeem his debt of 35 rdl. that he issued to me four years ago'.[58] This was followed with a threat of exposing his supposedly dubious character and untrustworthiness, 'as the public otherwise shall come to know his true character'.[59] Many claims were published because of unpaid rent for vacated rooms, and the creditors publicly warned that the rent needed to be repaid within a specific time limit, otherwise leftover or mortgaged items would be sold at auction.

During the winter of 1771 to 1772, people increasingly used the *Adresseavisen* as an instrument to expose and shame others publicly and deliberately, and it became normal for creditors to announce both the full names and the professions of their debtors. On 1 February 1772, an announcement was published by a wheelwright named Jens Holgreen, which stated:

> Because sculptor Jens Møller has lived with me and did not appear last Michaelmas Day [29 September] with his rent … This is thus the third time that Mr Jens Møller or another legally entitled person is warned to, within 6 weeks from today's date,

pay me my rent and other expenses; in the event of an absence, the effects will be sold at the expense of the debtor or the person concerned.[60]

Debt claims that publicly exposed and shamed debtors were subject to the exact same publication costs as all other content in the *Adresseavisen*. Sometimes this inspired creative solutions by people. On 1 April 1772, for instance, Jens Sørensen Lystrup published an announcement to all his debtors, reminding them to redeem their pledges within fourteen days, otherwise, he would sell the goods at auction.[61] He also informed them that they could pay him at his address at Teilgaardstrædet, and then added that 'at the same place, grey peas are for sale at a low price'.[62] Lystrup's announcement took up seven lines in *Adresseavisen*, which, according to the applicable price rates, cost him 16 *skilling*, which was equivalent to 1 *mark*. By merging the two announcements, he only had to pay for a single announcement instead of two separate ones. In the spring of 1772, a man named Antonii Børs had fled from a year's rent that amounted to 48 rdl., and this was in addition to other unpaid taxes and costs. Forty-eight rdl. was a significant amount, so in this case, it makes good sense that the creditor paid for a public announcement. However, people were also publicly exposed for much smaller amounts. When the brandy maker Lars Hansen publicly announced that Johan Gotfried Bas owed him money, the announcement took up eight lines, so he was charged one *mark* to demand repayment for money equal to 6 rdl. It seems that for these creditors, debt claims not only concerned the recovery of money, but also presented them with an accessible and affordable way to expose and shame their debtors.

Modest publication fees offered an affordable way to gain access to the world of print, and thereby to Copenhagen's printed public, which in the second half of the eighteenth century saw a rapid expansion in terms of texts, genres and readers.[63] In Copenhagen, this process was also stimulated by the introduction of an unrestricted freedom of print. Following the Freedom of Print Act of 14 September 1770, all censorship prior to publication was abolished, including censorship of the *Adresseavisen* and of the political newspapers. A direct consequence of freedom of print was the remarkable rise of an intense public debate on all kinds of matters, characterized by a previously unseen straightforward, critical and often defamatory quality.[64] In 1772, an author of numerous pamphlets and cheap prints became insultingly exposed by his landlord, a master shoemaker named J. D. Jansen, because of unpaid rent:

Due to the fact that a person named Rosenlund, or the so-called Junior Philopatreias, secretly has removed most of his contents of my house, which he has ascribed to me as security for a year's rent equivalent to 34 rdl. 1 *mark* and 8 *skilling*, and now before the day of the move on 8 May, has sneaked away from the rooms in a deceitful manner, and not even talked to me about it, and has not even handed over to me the little wretched leftover *skramlerie* [small things of little value], which is not insignificant concerning the sums as mentioned earlier, nor has he indicated where he resides, as well as the snatched goods, which I have picked up where they are found and have become known to me, that no host thereby henceforth shall be deceived by him.[65]

As we have seen, debt calls and public exposure because of unpaid rent were not unusual, but this one stands out for being explicitly long, defamatory and confrontational. Søren Rosenlund, who published under the pseudonym Junior Philopatreias, made a name for himself by his harsh critiques of public life, driven by a constant xenophobic tendency to ascribe to foreigners – especially Jewish people – all the calamities falling upon Copenhagen and the rest of the kingdom.[66]

The hardening of direct public exposure and shaming of individuals because of private debt that came to be regularly published in the *Adresseavisen* from the late 1760s was clearly spurred on by the Freedom of Print Act. However, as we have seen, the public exposure and shaming of both runaways and debtors started before the introduction of freedom of print. Regulatory measures were gradually reintroduced from 1771, and the law of 20 October 1773 strictly forbade printing slanderous attacks on individuals, including all kinds of 'fictional narratives containing something insulting, or obscene or similar'.[67] The responsibility to enforce the new regulatory act fell to the chiefs-of-police, who were authorized to impose unappealable fines ranging from 50 to 250 rdl. As we shall see, the new law was enacted a few days after a particular debt claim was published in the *Adresseavisen*.

Unnecessary public exposure

In a written statement of 22 November 1773, chief-of-police in Copenhagen Christian Fædder (1712–93) problematized the basic connection between paid access to the printed public, exposure and public shaming, which had become ever more apparent in the pages of the *Adresseavisen* from its establishment in 1759 up to and including late 1773. The statement was written following a debt claim published only two days after the introduction of the new press law. On 22 October 1773, one Mr H. R. Lange had published yet another debt claim in which the names of the creditors were fully exposed:

> Pauel Jørgensen, Forrester, is now warned to redeem the clothes produced by me within 14 days from the date when it will otherwise be sold for money ... [dated] Copenhagen, 21 October 1773. Former whipmaker Danholm, now living in Fredensborg, is hereby warned to redeem the goods mortgaged with me, within four weeks from today, or it will be sold at auction ... [dated] Friderichssund on 16 October 1773. H.R. Lange.[68]

The debt claim caught the attention of Fædder who considered this specific public debt claim to be unnecessarily defamatory and in breach of the newly issued law of 20 October 1773. Thus, he took the initiative to warn the publishers not to publish similar notifications in the future, i.e. those in which the names of debtors would be exposed. As we have seen, it had become common practice to expose the names of debtors, so the leading board of the Intelligence Office asked the *Danske Kancelli* how they should respond to Fædder's warning.[69] The arguments in favour of and against exposing the names of debtors represent the culmination of developments that had taken place since the *Adresseavisen*'s establishment in 1759, and therefore provide us with an excellent closing case-study.

The board of the Intelligence Office wrote a letter to the *Danske Kancelli*, on 2 November 1773, claiming to be astonished in the wake of the warning they had received. In their opinion, the new law was not in any way compromised, because the *Adresseavisen* never published anything 'against the common good or the private benefits of decent citizens'.[70] Thus, they intended to continue to publish anything which, in their eyes, could in some way contribute to the improvement of people or to the improved production of goods. This included the right 'to announce whatever some private man legally desired to announce',[71] such as and including the debt claim published by Mr Lange. However, the warning by the chief-of-police had made them worry lest this kind of public announcement be considered illegal and thus punishable by fine. So they asked the *Danske Kancelli* whether they correctly understood that the new law merely forbade the printing and publishing of things contrary to religion, good morals and governance, 'or what could separate a private man by his hitherto held honour?'[72] As shown in the previous section, the practice of exposing the full names of debtors was a relatively new one, but even still, the publishers argued that they were merely following established business practice; they had never had evil intentions, because all they wanted was to publish whatever might 'interest or please the Public'.[73]

Before making their decision, the *Danske Kancelli* asked Christian Fædder to explain why he told the *Adresseavisen* to cease publishing debtors' names. Fædder's response was that he considered it entirely unnecessary for Lange to expose the names of Jørgensen and Danholm publicly. On the contrary, he argued that this served the purpose of 'prostituting one's debtor by publicly announcing the name in the papers, rather than to serve to one's advantage'.[74] Thus, according to Fædder, public debt claims had become an easily accessible forum for unnecessary public humiliation, and this was the reason why he had warned the *Adresseavisen* not to expose the names of debtors. He deemed it to be particularly problematic in the case of Jørgensen and Danholm, because the first of these men was a royal official and the second was a creditor and debtor, and both of them resided outside of Copenhagen. As we have seen in the previous sections, neither the *Adresseavisen*, the *Danske Kancelli* nor the chief-of-police expressed any compunction when it came to the deliberate exposure of apprentices, peasants and musketeers in the *Undvigte* section. However, the exposure of the royal official Pauel Jørgensen crossed a line. Finally, Fædder directly addressed the business model of the *Adresseavisen* by stating that 'such warnings may well even with less cost and greater discretion be published in newspapers, which are not acquired and read by everyone'.[75] He therefore concluded that, unless the *Danske Kancelli* provided him with new instructions, he would proceed to hand out fines every time a debt warning was published 'in which the debtors' names are mentioned'.[76]

On this basis, the *Danske Kancelli* authorized Fædder to act the way he had following the Press Law of 20 October 1773. Christian Fædder's warning had an immediate effect on the form and frequency of debt announcements published in the *Adresseavisen*. After his warning, all subsequent announcements concerning debtors either did not mention their names at all, or the debtors were anonymized insofar as only their profession and initials were published. The public announcement of debt henceforth proceeded in this anonymized form.

Concluding remarks

As a printed medium for communication between individuals – mainly artisans, tradespeople and merchants – the *Adresseavisen* became the perfect forum for bringing private matters into the public. The business plan was simple but highly successful. People paid a modest, fixed charge for placing sales advertisements and announcements in the paper, which were printed in combination with local news, essays and other intriguing content. As the number of weekly readers increased, so too did the incentive to place more advertisements. Consequently, the paper soon exercised a significant influence on how individuals interacted with the general public in Copenhagen. This coincided with a general decay of the traditionally strict censorship regulations in the wake of an increasing prioritization of economic and commercial activities. In this respect, the paper reflected the rising market for commercial and popular literature of the mid-eighteenth century, and it became a catalyst for further developments whereby the paper introduced the private into the public amidst the context of print culture and Copenhagen's urban space. The paper offered common Copenhageners access to the printed public, partly as private advertisers and partly as the subjects of news, sensational stories and public exposure.

The exposure of the privacy of the lower social classes, to various degrees, was from early-on established as a recurring feature of the paper, along with sales advertisements and sensational news. This points to a darker side of the interaction between individuals and the printed public, as the paper became a forerunner of the freedom of print debate in terms of public exposure and defamation. During the 1760s, the combination of private commercial interests, sensationalism and the rise of the printed public increasingly led to the exposure and public shaming of named and identifiable persons, as people realized that the comprehensive public outreach of the *Adresseavisen* made it a perfect medium for shaming others for private debt and unpaid goods or rent. Today, the debt enquiries and the searches for runaway peasants would most certainly be considered a violation of individual privacy; but in eighteenth-century Copenhagen, this was generally not perceived to be a problem by the authorities, so long as the public exposure only concerned people of the lower social classes. When the exposure of urban rumours related to the Vartov Hospital in 1761 or a royal official in 1773, then this was deemed problematic, and the publication of such reports had consequences for the *Adresseavisen*. Indeed, the authorities did offer some protection against public exposure, but it was a protection conditioned by honour and social status. This points to a socially stratified protection of privacy: the privacy of prominent people enjoyed greater protection by the authorities than did that of other, lower-status individuals. An individual's exposure in public could have devastating social and financial consequences, and it is striking that at the same time as the Copenhagen courts increasingly dealt with cases of defamation,[77] people could pay a few *skilling* to expose individuals in the *Adresseavisen*.

Notes

1   Research funded by the Danish National Research Foundation (DNRF 138).
2   See Jørgen Mührmann-Lund's chapter in this volume.
3   There is a vast amount of research concerning censorship and the regulation of print culture in eighteenth-century Denmark-Norway that has been written in Danish and Norwegian. Some recent publications are Jakobsen 2011; Rian 2014; Maliks 2014; Jakobsen 2016. A classic study of the Danish freedom-of-print period from 1770 to 1773 is Holm 1885, and recently published in-depth analysis can be found in Horstbøll et al. 2020. A limited number of articles have been published in English; see, for example, Laursen 2002; Maliks 2015; Israel 2015. For a more detailed discussion of censorship in eighteenth-century Denmark, see Jakobsen 2017.
4   For critical discussions of Habermas's theory, see la Vopa 1992; Rospocher 2012, 9–28.
5   Maliks 2015, 135.
6   McNeely 2000, 136. See also McNeely 2003, 225.
7   Both Cowan 2001 and Rospocher 2012 have argued for a more pluralistic approach to eighteenth-century publics. Ian McNeely has shown how German *Intelligenzblätter* gradually developed into a *rässonnierende* genre between the late eighteenth and mid-nineteenth centuries. See McNeely 2003.
8   Recent accounts of the Copenhagen Intelligence Office are Nøding 2013; Horstbøll et al. 2020, 79–89. Some older depictions are also useful, see Davidsen and Gamberg 1884, 180–211; von Westen 1780, 7–80.
9   On Intelligence Offices and *Intelligenzblätter* in German-speaking Europe, see McNeely 2000; McNeely 2003; Blome 2002; Tantner 2016.
10   On the increased global trade and financial activities of eighteenth-century Europe, see Trentmann 2016, 78–118.
11   The political newspapers of Copenhagen were subject to immense regulation, both in terms of who was permitted to print newspapers and in terms of what kind of information that was allowed to be published. A classic study of the history of early modern Danish newspapers is Stolpe 1878–82.
12   Warren and Brandeis 1890.
13   Numerous examples are discussed in Stolpe 1878–82.
14   The unpublished sources are kept at The Danish National Archive (DNA), where they are filed under *Danske Kancelli* (DK). A digitized collection of *Adresseavisen* is now available at http://www2.statsbiblioteket.dk/mediestream/
15   von Westen 1780, 7–27; Søllinge and Thomsen 1989, 108, 110. This specific type of content was also archetypal for German Intelligenzblättern, see McNeely 2000, 136–8; Blome 2002, 196; McNeely 2003, 220–1, 224.
16   'Skippere kan blive opsøgte af Kiøbmænd, som ville have Forsendings-Gods bort, eller som Passagerer, der ville med dem, og disse faae omsonst paa Adresse-Contoiret at viide, hvor Skipperen ligger; at en Herre kan altid finde en beqvem Person til sin

Tieneste, og en Tiener en Herre, samt faae fornøden Kundskab om Fordeelagtighed, Attester, Løn og hvad der paa begge Sider maatte spørges efter', von Westen 1780, 26.

17   Ibid., 28.

18   On the expansion of the eighteenth-century printed public, see Melton 2001, 81–122.

19   *Adresseavisen*, 3 September 1759 and 4 February 1760.

20   On the Copenhagen printing houses and their privileges, see Ilsøe 1992.

21   *Adresseavisen*, 3 July 1761, 1 July 1763 and 1 April 1772.

22   On printed accounts of crime and depictions of executions in early modern Germany, see Wiltenburg 2012, 65–87. On Danish murder ballads and cheap prints about death and executions, see Krogh 2000, 301–18.

23   'Derpaa banker de hans Tæer og Fingre imellem to Stene, skierer Remmer af Huden rundt omkring Ledemødene, borttager hele Strimler Kiød med, og brænder det vexelviis. De river det saaledes sønderknusede og halvstegte Kiød i Stykker af, og spiser det op med Graadighed, og ligesom at de ere uden for sig selv af Raserie, besmører de sig over hele Ansigtet med det Blod, som løber deraf', *Adresseavisen*, 3 April 1761.

24   'Meget god hollandsk ost', *Adresseavise*n, 1 April 1760.

25   Specific places in early modern urban spaces were often infused with symbolic meanings. A study of contemporary Scandinavia is found in Sennefelt 2008, 145–63. Ian McNeely has argued that Gazettes and Intelligenzblätter were outgrowths of the marketplaces in large urban trading centres. See McNeely 2000, 137–8.

26   'I Vorregaden det 8de Huus paa venstre Haand fra Heilsingoersgaden næst ved Slagterens', *Adresseavisen*, 6 June 1760, 304.

27   Horstbøll 2010.

28   'I Wartows Hospital er en af Lemmerne kommet i Barselsseng og faaet 2 Børn, nemlig 1 Pige og 1 Dreng', *Adresseavisen*, 10 April 1761.

29   'Grevinde Raben har faaet en søn', *Adresseavisen*, 3 January 1763.

30   'Natten imellem den 4 og 5 hujus nedkom Hr. Kammerherre Græv Holsteins Frue med en velskabt Søn, til den høye Families store Glæde. Ligeledes blev i Gaar Hr. Justitsraad Fabricii Frue forløst med en ung Søn', *Adresseavisen*, 7 March 1760.

31   On the private and public life of the eighteenth-century home and family, see Farge 1986, 571–607. On printed funeral sermons as representation of individual lives, see Moore 2006.

32   'I Morges blev her i Staden i Lille Kongensgade fundet et nyefødt Pigebarn, gandske nøgen og dødt, samt Hovedet omdreyet til den eene Side, men den, som samme haver henlagt, er endnu ikke opdaget', *Adresseavisen*, 1 February 1760.

33   'I Begyndelsen af denne Uge har en fattig Kone her i Staden født et dødt Pigebarn, som havde tvende hoveder, de øvrige Lemmer vare som sædvanlig', *Adresseavisen*, 2 July 1773.

34   For a general introduction to *Københavns Fattigvæsen*, see Henningsen 2005, 18–56. The quotation from the 1607 charter is translated from p. 41: 'sådanne personer, som man i sandhed ved at have udi deres velmagt ført et ærligt levned'.

35   DNA, DK, Sjællandske Tegnelser 1760–1 (D20-33), no. 335.

36   'Enten for Magistraten eller paa Politiekammeret, i Anledning af en eller anden Indrykkelse i Bladene, og næsten enhver Artikel, som han efterhaanden forøgede Bladet med, fandt en ny Modstand', Prahl 1783, 10.

37   Most of the materials of Copenhagen police were lost to fires in the eighteenth century. Sadly, this includes the protocols of the police court up to 1776.

38   'At Feyltagelsen ikke skulde blive nogen Eenfoldig til Anstød', *Adresseavisen*, 20 April 1761.

39   DNA, DK, Sjællandske Tegnelser 1760–1 (D20-33), no. 335.

40   McNeely 2003, 220–7; Munck 2007; Jakobsen 2017.

41   'At kunde revidere det alt, uden vigtigere tings forsømmelse', DNA, DK, Koncepter og indlæg til Oversekretærens Brevbøger 1767 (D101-80), no. 551, Letter from the *Københavns Magistrat* to the king, 30 September 1767.

42   'Andersen og Agent Holck, foregaver at det ikke kand taale ophold med at lade disse tidender forud revidere', ibid.

43   Ibid. Apparently no records are preserved that shed light on the censorship practice of the Copenhagen Magistrate, but a few incidents concerning censorship reached the *Danske Kancelli*. Without going into too much detail about these episodes, it is clear that the authorities kept a close eye on what was published in the *Adresseavisen*. Jakobsen 2017, 135–143.

44   A general feature of German *Intelligenzblätter* was, that the lines between private and public were rarely clear-cut, as they were often sponsored by the states and used as media for 'policeylicher kommunikation' (police communication). See Schilling 2000; McNeely, 2003, 221. However, as articulated by Astrid Blome, this did not apply to the same extent to the commercial newspapers produced in the state of Hamburg and the German-speaking Danish-Norwegian city of Altona. See Blome 2002, 206.

45   On social hierarchy and honour in eighteenth-century Denmark, see Henningsen 2001.

46   *Adresseavisen*, 11 November 1767.

47   'Dersom nogen skulde antreffe denne Dreng, da ombedes tienstlig at levere eller lade ham levere i Dybensgade oppe i krogen til Skoemageren Sr. Jens Fischer, som tilbyder sig at betale alle paa hans Paagribelse paagaaende Bekostninger', *Adresseavisen*, 3 July 1761.

48   *Adresseavisen*, 4 January 1768.

49   Henningsen 2001.

50   Bregnsbo 1997, 51–8. This also draws attention to the fact that the lines between public and private communication in the *Adresseavisen* were sometimes mixed, not least because the paper was often used as a medium for the proclamation of laws and decrees. There is as yet no comprehensive study of the laws, decrees and official announcements published in Danish eighteenth-century commercial newspapers, but for a study of the German gazettes as a medium for official communication, see Schilling 2000.

51   'En hvid jagt-tæve af middels og spæd Taille, med korte og brune Kind, hvilket for endeel strækker sig over Ørene, som ellers ere noget spættede, og haver hun en sort Plæt bag paa Ryggen, i alt meget jevnt tegnet, og pleyer at være noget frygtsom for Fremmede', *Adresseavisen*, 5 May 1760.

52   'Der af Godset efter Kongel. Allernaadigst Befaling skulde afgaae til de geworbene Regimenter', *Adresseavisen*, 11 November 1767.

53   'Utidige og Publico uvedkommende Anmærkninger', DNA, DK, Oversekretærens Brevbøger 1767 (D99-19), no. 640.

54   Ibid.

55   'Den Vedkommende ved det med sig selv hvem jeg meener, og altsaa forskaaner jeg ham for offentlig at tilkendegive hans Navn', *Adresseavisen*, 4 October 1771.

56   On the significance of honour when thinking of urban life, oral rumours, *Adresseavisen* and pamphleteering in late-eighteenth-century Copenhagen, see

Langen 2014. Examples of individuals explicitly identified as Jewish people can be found in *Adresseavisen*, 4 January 1771 and 18 September 1771.

57 'Da en Person ved Navn J** H** har for sidste Paaske Huusleye sat noget Tøy I Pant, saa advares han derved 3de Gange', *Adresseavisen*, 10 December 1770.

58 'Herved inkaldes 3de Gange i disse Aviser Christian Seyersen Sommer fra Jylland, at indfrie hans til mig for 4 Aar siden udstædte Beviis paa 35 Rdlr', *Adresseavisen*, 1 February 1769.

59 'Da offentligheden hans egentlige Character skal blive bekiendtgiort', *Adresseavisen*, 1 February 1769.

60 'Da Bildthugger Jens Møller har boet hos mig og nu afvigte Michaeli Flyttedag … Saa advares hermed 3de Gange at bemelte Hr. Jens Møller eller hvem anden dertil lovlig findes berettiget, inden 6 Uger fra Dato at betale mig min Leye og øvrig hafte Omkostninger; I udeblivende Tilfælde bliver Effecterne for Debitors eller Vedkommendes Regning', *Adresseavisen*, 1 February 1772.

61 'Inden 14ten Dage at indløse deres Pant, eller setter jeg samme til Auction og giør mig betalt', *Adresseavisen*, 1 April 1772.

62 'Sammested er og graae Ærter til kiøbs for billig Priis', *Adresseavisen*, 1 April 1772.

63 Nyrup 1870; Horstbøll 1999; Dahl 2011.

64 Horstbøll et al. 2020. Sweden introduced a more restricted Freedom of Print Act in 1766, which also led to increased production of printed texts and increased political debate. See Nordin 2020. For a comparison between the Danish and Swedish approaches to freedom-of-press, see Nordin and Laursen 2020.

65 'Da en Person navnlig Rosenlund, eller den saakaldede Junior Philopatreias, af mit Huus hemmelig haver bortpractioceret det meste af sit Boehave, som han mig alt tilskrevet haver til min Securitet for et Aars Huusleye den Summa 34 Rdlr. 1 Mk. 8 S., og nu for Flyttedagen den 8 May paa en bedragerisk Maade bortsneget sig af Værelserne, og ikke engang talt med mig derom, langt mindre overleveret mig det lidet usle efterlatte Skramlerie, som er ikke af nogen Betydenhed imod ermelte Summa, ey heller givet mig tilkiende hvor han sig opholder, tillige med det bortsnegede Gods, som jeg lader afhente hvor det findes og mig bekiendt bliver, paa det ingen Vært derigennem meere skal blive bedraget af ham', *Adresseavisen*, 12 May 1772.

66 Horstbøll et al. 2020, 113–27.

67 'Andre opdigtede Fortællinger, som indeholde noget fornærmeligt, eller uanstændigt, med videre deslige', DNA, DK, Sjællandske Tegnelser 1773–5 (F11-1), no. 559.

68 'Pauel Jørgensen, Skourider, advares herved at indløse det hos mig forfærdigede Tøy inden 14 Dage fra Dato, da ellers samme bliver solgt og giort til Penge … Kiøbenhavn den 21 October 1773. Forrige Piskemester Danholm, nu boende paa Fredensborg, advares herved at indløse det hos mig pantsatte Gods, inden fire uger fra Dato, da ellers samme bliver bortsolgt ved Auction … Friderichssund den 16 October 1773. H.R. Lange', *Adressevisen*, 22 October 1773.

69 The sources are located at DNA, DK, Indlæg til Brevbøger 1773 (F42-8), no. 1258 (hereafter DNA, DK [F42-8], no. 1258).

70 'Som kunde være stridende imod det almindelige Beste, eller enhver god Borgers private fordeel', ibid., 2 November 1773.

71 'At lade bekiendtgiøre det, som én eller anden privat Mand til hans lovlige fordeel, maatte begiære at faae bekiendtgiort', ibid.

72 'Eller hvad som kune skille en Privat Mand ved hans hidtil havte Ære?' Ibid.

73 'Interessere eller fornøye Publikum', ibid.

74 'Prostituere sin Debitor ved bekiendtgiørelse i aviserne end derved at fremme sin
   Tarv', DNA, DK (F42-8), no. 1258, 22 November 1773.
75 'Slige advarsler vel endog med mindre bekostninger og tilforladeligere kune skee end
   udi Aviserne som ikke holdes eller læses af alle', ibid.
76 'Hvorudi Debitorernes Navne nævnes', ibid. For a discussion of this and other
   episodes in relation to the Danish freedom-of-press, see Jakobsen 2017, 179–194.
77 See Camilla Schjerning's chapter in this volume.

Of chamber pots and scorned houses: Exposing hidden bodies and private matters in eighteenth-century Copenhagen

Camilla Schjerning

The flight of the chamber pot

One evening in the winter of 1771 the inhabitants of a house in Borgergade, one of the more common areas of Copenhagen, heard a pot smashing in the central courtyard. It was the chamber pot, which had been sitting – as it quite often did – in the gallery outside the door of Anne Svendsdatter, the wife of able seaman Erichsen. The flight of the pot happened at the hands of ordinary seaman Tobias Schultz, who had been fed up with 'the Spectacle' of the filled pot. He resolutely emptied its contents on Anne's doorstep and threw the pot into the courtyard below.

Unfortunately, a physician paying Anne a visit stepped in the mess as he left her house – causing her 'great Pain and Shame', as she later recounted in court. The following day, she complained to her landlady, who went to reprimand Tobias – and he, in turn, went to Anne in order to settle the matter. Soon a heated discussion erupted between the two in Anne's rooms, during which Tobias asked Anne whether she remembered, 'how last Night Ole the Fiddler lay with [her] in Bed, and that [she] should be careful with her young Lovers in the Door, groping her 10 Cubits up under her Clothes'.[1] Pushing and shoving, the two emerged in the gallery under the loud recital of a common catalogue of insults such as whore, quean, thief and the like. Alerted by the commotion, Tobias's parents came rushing down the stairs and joined the scene – witnessed by curious neighbours peering out of doorways and windows.

The following day, Anne turned to the authorities, penning her grievances to the commander of her husband's naval company. The authorities first tried to settle the dispute between the two parties outside of court, but Anne declined, stating that Tobias, since the initial incident, had repeated his allegations. According to Anne, Tobias had told several of her neighbours that Ole had 'lain in Bed with me in his bare Shirt and I in my bare Smock, which is too intolerable for me to hear and Accusations for which I am now held in low Repute by the People in the House'.[2] In the ensuing court case, presented at the Royal and City Court of Copenhagen, Anne called many of the residents in the house to testify to what had happened, in order to have her honour and good reputation re-established.

While the case of Anne and Tobias may at first sight seem a trivial brawl between neighbours over slanderous remarks and a chamber pot and its contents out of place, the testimonies of this case – and many others like it – open a window onto the everyday construction and contestation of the boundaries between public and private, between hidden and exposed.

Exposing the private

Numerous studies have shown how, in the early modern world, public insults functioned to uphold social order through making illicit and immoral actions publicly known and thus the object of social regulation.[3] In order to serve this function, insults and defamation were by nature staged, and public incidents designed to draw an audience. Thus, witnesses often explained, as in the case of Anne Svendsdatter, how they were drawn to windows and doorways, alerted by loud noises or commotion in the house or the street.[4]

As already mentioned in the introduction to this book, several studies have shown how the early modern home was open, its boundaries porous. Rather than distinguishing between public and private events according to the physical spaces in which they took place, the private or public nature of a matter pertained to the question of its perceived relevance to the community; private matters often took place in public and vice versa. As Mary Thomas Crane has argued, in order to have privacy, understood as freedom from interference, in the early modern town, one would go outside.[5]

But privacy could also be a protective cover for illicit activities that, when brought into the public's attention, had harmful potential to the common good, for instance the 'particular Business' conducted in the bawdy houses of Copenhagen as described by Ulrik Langen or the printed scandals described by Jesper Jakobsen in this book. Private matters thus had the potential to arouse powerful and disorderly emotions such as fear, anger, shame and contempt. The potential danger of private made public was also very real to the individual, for instance as the cause of gut-wrenching shame such as that which Anne may have felt, when her guest stepped in the foul mass on her doorstep. It may also have had very real effects in the shape of marital discord, communal contempt or public punishment, when illicit actions such as sexual transgressions or theft were brought to the attention of spouses, neighbours or authorities.

Robert Shoemaker has argued that public insult as a form of community regulation in the streets of London was in decline throughout the eighteenth century, as a result of a profound shift in the relationship between individual and the community, which in turn caused community regulation to lose its legitimacy. The perceived threat of defamatory words declined and the words themselves were rarely the actual cause of the dispute, but became a strategic weapon, a legitimate reason to pester and pressure one's adversary through litigation. Gradually, insults moved into the secluded space of the house and became less public. Moreover, publicly refuting accusations was no longer the preferred way to obtain respectability for many people, particularly those of higher social status.

Rather, they chose not to air their dirty laundry in public, if possible. According to Shoemaker, this especially applied to women, as it was no longer acceptable to discuss matters of female sexuality in public. Shoemaker refers these changes to the transformation of 'the very nature of public and private life' and the advent of a new individualism, which undermined the collective power of communities – Norbert Elias's famous civilizing process. The gradual progress can, according to Shoemaker, be studied in detail through the lens of defamation and its decline, especially among the urban middle classes.[6] As noted by Katie Barclay, the privacy of the lower orders has been given less attention – Barclay herself offering a discussion of how the Scottish lower orders managed the boundaries between secrecy, privacy and the public.[7]

Cases like the one between Anne Svendsdatter and her neighbour allow us a glimpse into whether similar cultural shifts were at play in the streets and houses of Copenhagen, and how the public staging of insults looked among the lower orders, people far removed from elite's theoretical musings, theoretical musings on public and private spheres. As several articles in this volume demonstrate, the concept of private was rarely used in everyday interactions and even more rarely to describe anything akin to what we today understand as privacy, but rather to describe that which was not the responsibility of neither community nor state.

The cases presented in this article come primarily from the archives of the Royal and City Court (*Hof- og Stadsretten*), a new civic jurisdiction established in 1771 on the initiative of Struensee, whose ambitious reforms are the subject of Langen's chapter in this volume. Its purpose was to end the complex jurisdictional landscape in which every substantial institution sported their separate jurisdiction, making it nearly impossible to pursue cases across social and institutional divides. Cases were led by university-educated procurators, making the litigation more professional, but also more costly. Litigants without means could obtain free process through *beneficium paupertas*, making the court accessible to all, in principle at least – though undoubtedly requiring more effort than the courts of the police, Magistrate or military, from which cases were regularly referred, either because they were not accepted (because they were private quarrels), or could not be settled there. In 1790 a special Commission of Reconciliation (*Forligskommission*) was established in order to keep more interpersonal quarrels out of the court system. Still, a number of civil suits made it to the Royal and City Court unresolved; among them were the cases of defamation and petty violence, which make up the bulk of material for this article.

The court cases, with their detailed depositions and carefully crafted arguments, afford us the opportunity to trace both the spatial practices and communicative strategies that traversed and produced the private–public divide. From words and deeds we may tease out what we analytically understand to be realms of privacy performed and reflected in what was kept secret and hidden, and in particular that which was exposed – the private in the public.

Thus, the following will take a closer look at the communicative and strategic use of private or sensitive information, searching especially the staged public exposures of secret or illicit information, arguing that the perceptions and feelings produced here continuously materialized, pushed and negotiated the boundaries of the private in late-eighteenth-century Copenhagen.

Emotional strategies of exposure

To get at what was concealed and why, we must search out those shameful secrets and instances of exposure which brought the hidden into the public. We must look to the strategies and emotions at play in these practices of exposure and the attempts to 're-cover' intimacies from the public eye and retract them into the safety of the private. Through a closer examination, we can better understand what exposure meant for different people and the feelings it produced, in order to understand how the boundaries between secret, private and public were enacted and materialized in everyday interactions.

This approach draws, among others, on Sara Ahmed's writings on the performativity of emotions. According to Ahmed, while emotions are collective phenomena, they materialize as feelings in the encounters of individual bodies, creating boundaries and situating individual bodies inside or outside the community – thus aligning individual bodies with a collective body. Ahmed argues that situations where feelings are intensified connect these emotions in space and time, thereby producing boundaries between bodies and places. Moreover, the repeated association of specific emotions, such as shame or disgust, to certain bodies or objects makes these emotions 'stick'.[8]

Getting at the individual feelings of people, especially across a divide of almost three centuries, is a task bordering on the impossible. But when dealing with emotions as social and performative, the focus is on how these emotions are put into practice in social interactions – how they do things in the world – rather than what people actually felt in their heart of hearts (supposing that one may distinguish between inner feelings and outer emotions, at all). These emotional practices, a concept coined by Monique Scheer, make use of the body's capacities and embodied social knowledge to elicit effects in the social world – to mobilize, name, communicate and regulate feelings in particular situations.[9] I take a closer look at how people communicate with and about bodies, employing different emotional practices in order to establish, assert or challenge boundaries, whether these be the boundaries of the physical body, home or more intangible matters of secrecy. Also, I analyse which emotional strategies made certain emotions, such as shame, stick to certain people and places.

I approach the question of privacy from the intricately intertwined realms of the body, intimate information, and the physical boundaries of the house and the household within. I will attempt to show how the boundaries of the individual body aligned with the boundaries of household and community, and how these alignments were shaped by intricate social hierarchies of social status and gender.

A matter of shame

Returning now to the scene of the crime of the emptied pot, we may dig deeper into the emotional practices and politics at play. The entire case was brought about by the nuisance of Anne's chamber pot sitting outside her front door in plain view. Even though the presence of body waste and faecal matter was much higher in the city before the advent of the water closet, it was nonetheless a highly unwanted presence, judging from the endless complaints about 'matter out of place'. The old name of its place of production, the privy house, also speaks to the highly private matter of its nature, connected with a great deal of shame – especially because faecal matter was closely associated with corruption and debasement.[10]

Interestingly, Anne did not seem embarrassed by putting it on display, or perhaps she preferred for others to be confronted with it rather than herself. Tobias, though, made his discomfort quite clear, by not only throwing the pot into the courtyard, but also soiling her threshold, thus intensifying Anne's humiliation by not only having her bodily products – her shame – 'displayed' out of place at her front door, but even worse, seeing an esteemed visitor step in it. Before the court she explained how the incident caused her 'Tort and Shame', resulting in 'great Pain' – conjuring up the visceral cringe of shame caused by the disgust we must imagine the guest to have felt and displayed.

More than an interior feeling, shaming was an emotional strategy, a means of exerting social control and establishing hierarchies.[11] The potential of chamber pots and filth in general to make shame and disgust stick, and to function as signifiers of bodily and moral corruption, made it a potent weapon to undermine the dignity and authority of a person.

There are many examples of the pot being used as a weapon. In a complaint from 1791, Sisse Friis, the wife of a naval office clerk, accused Cathrine Hammelev, a seaman's wife, of not only scolding her on a public street, asking how many children she had left at the hospital [The Foundling Institution], but moreover ordering her own children to throw street filth at Sisse.[12] During a brawl between two feuding neighbours (both soldiers' wives) in 1771, Birthe Ortwein flung the fluid contents of a pot out of her window, intended for the displeasure of Dorothea Artmer, who had been gossiping with other neighbours and visitors in the house about Birthe's male acquaintances – unfortunately soiling another woman standing by the front door in the process.[13] Maria Magdalene Stocklisch was also quick to throw her chamber pot, conveniently at hand, in the direction of blacksmith Gottlieb, when he accosted her in the stairway of their shared house in 1799.[14]

The emptying of pots onto the street – and sometimes on 'innocent' passers-by – was a common phenomenon in the early modern city, probably because the content of chamber pots was the most debasing substance and such a powerful elicitor of disgust. The performative power of disgust pertained to not only physical aversions, but also its strong moral component.[15] The chamber pots may sometimes have been a convenient weapon at hand during a conflict, but the disgusting matter, in some instances, appears to have played a symbolic role as a trigger of not only disgust, but also a potential signifier of a person's nature – often the people lowest in the social hierarchy were thought of as the most filthy. Soiling thus made the individual painfully self-aware of being in a body, imagining being seen and judged by others.[16]

A body of shame; displaying immodesty

The case of Anne Svendsdatter's shame sheds light on a different kind of bodily exposure, reflected in Tobias's further testimonies in court. According to Tobias, Anne had let young lovers feel her up under her skirt at the front door – exposing not only her legs, but also her lack of shame. By baring her body, she had revealed her immorality to her neighbours. Moreover, Tobias stated that Anne had lain in bed with another man in her bare smock, essentially claiming that she had been naked. The mere act of being in a bed together was not necessarily a transgression of boundaries – sleeping arrangements often included sharing beds – and Anne was adamant in her claim that her relationship to Ole was strictly 'honourable' (*honnet*).[17] But the claim that the two wore nothing but their bare smock and nightshirt exposed the intimacy of their relation. Whether either of these incidents ever took place is of less importance here. The main issue is how Tobias constructed a narrative of shamelessness, signified by Anne's failure to keep her body covered or hidden from sight and touch.

Space also played an important role in this narrative, as both the doorway and the bed were symbolically laden spaces in terms of the boundaries between private and public. Moreover, space figured in the accusations made by Tobias. Even if a potentially illicit intimacy between Anne and Ole was common knowledge in the house, it was only when Tobias took it out of the realm of secrecy and made it a public matter that it truly became a problem. Even worse, Tobias stated to the neighbours that he had looked Anne 'under the eyes' before the court and repeated his accusations, thus pushing them further into the public eye. Because of this public humiliation, Anne Svendsdatter declared that she could not accept a reconciliation out of court.

By presenting witnesses to support her case and give testimony to her good character, Anne actually succeeded in having Tobias punished for his insulting words, for kicking her and for being the initial cause of conflict. The punishment was a public whipping – a common punishment for military men, while civilians tended to be fined. Whether Anne thus succeeded in (re)obtaining the esteem of her neighbours, we will never know.

The exposure of the female body, voluntary or forced, had clear moral connotations and the failure to keep one's body concealed from others – either due to indifference or direct malice – demonstrated a flaw in one's character, often seen as a sign of insensibility to shame and other 'civilizing' emotions. Being stripped of the socially significant pieces of clothing, intended to determine a person's social standing and create the protective shield of status, was nearly as shameful as being naked.[18]

Nakedness and the shame connected to the female body might conversely be transformed into a weapon in situations of conflict. One afternoon in the summer of 1795, a group of women, mostly wives of Royal Navy seamen, were sitting in the street selling fish. Mounted in front of them on a spike was the head of a lumpsucker – a display which prompted two passing soldiers to stop. An impertinent remark from one of the fishwives soon escalated into a dispute, causing one soldier to lift his cane in a threatening manner, exclaiming that the lot were a group of knacker's whores (Rakkerludere). One of the women stood up, calling him a soldier boy who might discipline only his subordinates, and demonstrated her contempt for him by lifting up her skirts, baring her behind. Through this intentional self-exposure, the potential shame was transformed into a gesture of contempt, meant to elicit embarrassment in onlookers, being confronted with this most private part of a woman's body. The contempt was as evident when, during a dispute, Anna Hansdatter, the wife of a naval quartermaster, bared her behind to her neighbour, exclaiming, 'this is an old Quean, too'.[19] While such self-exposure may have been an efficient weapon, the suspension of the bashfulness attached to the naked body also reflected back on the perception of women who resorted to such tricks.

The image of the shameless fishwife was a well-known trope in the popular wit of many European countries, and late-eighteenth-century Copenhagen was no exception. A number of witty stories in a local newspaper pass on scenes of fishwives baring themselves to customers and passers-by during quarrels. The lack of modesty and shame fit neatly into a narrative of unruly, immoral and grotesque women:

> I could offer my readers a new scene of the Fishwives, how the entire Row, bar a few, was as electrified, how Fists and Foreheads met, Sparks shot from the Eyes, lighting the Locks of these drunken Amazons, where Swearing and Crowing, Storming and Raging was the Tone of the Battle. I could render how intense the Strife was and how it ended, but this would only be to sully my Story and insult every honourable Ear. How can one expect proper behaviour from those, who are not ashamed to publicly be Scum![20]

Thus, the women may have gained the upper hand in a dispute, but also placed themselves outside of a community of respectability – perhaps even humanity proper – and definitely the expected female modesty. Privacy and secrecy were essential to the construction of femininity, making the exposed female body a matter of shame.[21] Precisely because the female body and its sexuality was a potential threat to honour, and therefore something to be hidden and private, it was also 'a public affair, the target of official regulation, informal surveillance, and regular, intimate touch by women and men', as argued by Laura Gowing.[22]

Bounded bodies, bounded houses

One early morning in 1799, the inhabitants of a house on the corner of Prinsensgade awoke to the sound of yelling in the courtyard. Former soldier Peter Groupe, lodging in the back house, rose from his bed at the sound of the disturbance and went down into the courtyard where other inhabitants were already gathering to witness the commotion. From the gallery, shoemaker Fredberg was scolding across the courtyard at Karen Mether, a soldier's wife standing in her window, calling her a 'Whore' and a 'Fuchssvantzer' (someone who sticks their nose in other people's business). Later in court, he stated that he felt entitled to say such things, since Karen had told the landlady and other lodgers what had been spoken between him and his wife. Other witnesses revealed that the initial cause of the quarrel was that Karen had accused Fredberg's wife of soiling the privy house. During the quarrel, Fredberg's wife, carrying a pot in her hand, had told Karen that if she had any honour left in Sweden (where she was from), she should 'sit on this Pot and travel there to fetch it'.[23]

Suspended as it was between public and private, the body – especially the female body – was a very vulnerable and potent object for verbal as well as physical attacks during conflict. Another example demonstrates this as well. In the summer of 1771, Boel Hammerschmidt, a tenant in the house of distiller Rohde, had repeatedly been making comments to her neighbours about a physician, who had visited Rohde's wife to administer an enema, 'because she had a Soreness in her Thing', and similar comments, 'serving to make my House suspicious', as Rohde put it.[24] Merely the act of speaking of and referring to the private parts of his wife was clearly a shameful matter for Rohde, even more so when the remarks suggested the public accessibility of private parts. Even so, the intimate suggestions were brought before court, repeated and scrutinized once again – in order to be re-covered from the realm of suspicion and scandal, and into the private. The elaborate staging of the public exposure and accessibility of the body – even if it was only in words, intensified by the spectacle of shouting and screaming, the gathering of a large crowd in windows, doors and the street – called for 'public' action to reinstate the boundaries of not only the women, but also the household. In this sense, the body exposed – Mrs Rohde's body – was an entire household exposed.

Honour operated not only on an individual but also on a collective household level – guarded by the (mostly male) head of household. According to Elizabeth Cohen and Thomas Cohen, in Renaissance Italy, honour attached to both female bodies and houses – both were vested with the family's honour, and because the house embodied it's owner's honour and shame, its boundaries had to be carefully guarded, both against physical trespassers and against curious neighbours prying out domestic secrets.[25]

Gowing has argued that female virtue in the early modern world was understood spatially and that chastity was to a large extent a question of upholding boundaries. Women were perceived as mostly incapable of upholding these boundaries, because from nature's hand the woman was fluid, leaky and open to her surroundings. It was, therefore, up to men to protect female virtue, by controlling and upholding her physical boundaries.[26] In the absence of a man, the community was to step in and establish or uphold these boundaries.

Perhaps this was what happened when Tobias breached the privacy of the house and brought the sexual immodesty of Anne to the awareness of neighbours. Was this a reflection of an attempt to reinstate the boundaries of Anne's sexuality in the absence of her husband, who was at sea bound for China? Might we even see the flight of the chamber pot and its shameful contents as a symbolic gesture referring to Anne's bodily shame (or rather lack thereof), put on display for her and the neighbours to see? In support of this, it is worth noting how one witness claimed to have heard Tobias shout 'hear how the cat screams', as he threw the chamber pot into the courtyard. As Robert Darnton has noted in his famous description of *The great cat massacre*, cats served as a reference to female sexuality, used as symbols in *Katzenjammer* and *Charivari* rituals, as described, for example, by Natalie Zemon Davis. Noise and symbolic displays drew attention to the breach of moral customs. Davis also points to the fact that it was often young men who were responsible for reprimanding violations to community morals in this manner.[27] It might be no coincidence, then, that the mundane quarrel over a chamber pot turned into a case of slander and accusations of adultery.

The privacy of married life

Other perceived transgressions of the moral order provoked the interest of neighbours as well. This was the case one Saturday morning in 1780, when seaman Smith and his wife, Kirstine, stepped into a coach to go act as godparents for another seaman in the company. Their neighbours, seaman Halvorsen and his wife, were offended because, as they later explained in court, Kirstine Smith was so uppity that she would not greet them. The Halvorsens therefore exclaimed for all in the street to hear 'that it was better if she brought her Bastard with her in the Coach'.²⁸ To defend her good name, Kirstine complained to the Naval Court. She confessed to have given birth to two children before her marriage, but added that since her husband had 'pardoned' her, the neighbours had no business letting her suffer such insults – reflecting a belief that her prior misfortunes were now to be regarded as a private matter. It is noteworthy that Kirstine herself was willing to give up the sensitive details of her past transgressions to exonerate herself. The case also shows how the embarrassing exposure of secrets could be an effective means in status competition, elevating the exposer at the expense of the exposed – meanwhile contributing to continuous negotiation of the boundaries of what was considered secret, private and shameful information.

Past transgressions also came to haunt tripe-maker Thorius in the summer of 1786. In a letter to the chief-of-police, Thorius urged him to put to justice two members of the cavalry regiment, who had gathered a large group of people in front of Thorius's house with 'brutal words and noise-making'. While pointing at Thorius's house, they had called out: 'there lives that Tripe-thing (…), the madame, that sergeant's whore is now finally a wife', referring to Thorius's wife.²⁹ The insults hinted that Thorius and his wife had lived together as husband and wife before they were married, while they shared a house with the two soldiers. When Thorius himself had become a sergeant, he left the military for the tripe-business, probably in order to be able to marry. The court records show that the very public announcement of the Thorius couple's illicit journey into married life was an elaborate revenge on Thorius's wife, who had accused the two men of stealing. The humiliation was intensified by the loud noises and public staging of the allegations, serving to make curious neighbours aware of the juicy gossip.

The notion that dealings between husband and wife were a matter of privacy and not to be meddled in by nosy neighbours can be found in other cases as well. One evening in 1799, upon having undressed himself and made ready to go to bed, hat-maker's apprentice Wilhelm Lohmann heard knocks on his door. When he opened, he was met by the military guard, who took him into custody for being drunk and disorderly in the house. The other inhabitants reported how they had for some time been witnesses to the domestic dealings between Lohmann and his wife, since the thin board walls allowed them to hear everything that went on in the rooms, especially since Lohmann was 'loud of Nature when he has drunk too much'. On occasions he was so rude to his wife that she feared for her life. The neighbours also recounted how Lohmann had threatened to stab the landlord with a knife if he 'came through his Door and tried to make Peace' between Lohmann and his wife, clearly reflecting a notion that the neighbours should stay out of the dealings between husband and wife.

On the night in question, a neighbour had heard Lohmann tell his wife to fetch some candles. After refusing a couple of times, she eventually left. Upon her return, she tried to convince her husband not to get undressed for bed, but without luck. Shortly after, a military guard arrived and took him, first to the Main Guard (*Hovedvagten*) and afterwards the chamber of police.

When presented to the chamber of police on the morning after his arrest, Lohmann was still inebriated, according to the scribe's notes in the protocol. He confessed to, on occasion, having spoken loudly to his wife, but stressed that this had happened only 'in his own Rooms'. Furthermore, he had had good cause, because she had stolen food and other things, and spent all his money with her 'Coffee Sisters'. Now, he claimed, she had colluded with the landlord to have him arrested, upon which they had robbed him down to 'the bare Shirt on his Body'. Lohmann furthermore expressed his regret at not merely being arrested, but being dragged through the streets, stripped of his autonomy and authority. Adding insult to injury, this had happen in a state of undress, without the proper attire to distinguish him from a common criminal and shield him against condemning gazes (it is worth noting, though, that his wife had attempted to spare him from this humiliation by trying to get him to put on his shirt again).

What was primarily at stake for Lohmann in the litigation was neither secrecy, nor the shame of intimate truths being revealed, but rather anger at what Lohmann perceived as transgressions against both his private property and authority as husband and householder – not least the return of the belongings removed by his wife. Nonetheless, that narrative of honour and violation runs through Lohmann's presentation of his misfortune, as well as a clear perception of the boundaries of both private spaces, private matters and spheres of authority.[30]

The boundaries of privacy, or freedom from interference, in the dealings between man and wife were porous and the subject of negotiation. Neighbours listened in on what was going on behind closed doors, carefully asserting when law and custom were being breached, thus transforming otherwise private matters of marriage into a public responsibility.[31]

The right to privacy or secrecy in relations was reserved for married couples. Should others attempt to lock doors or meet in secret, neighbours were likely to expose illicit sex and immorality – whether it be for the enjoyment of curious gossips or benefit of community morals.[32] The neighbours of Anne Marie just did just that: upon seeing her close the shutters shortly after receiving a male visitor in the absence of her husband, they forced their way into her rooms to conduct a house search.[33]

Especially the behaviour of married women alone, in particular military grass widows, was the subject of moral policing. Karen Horslund, the wife of a seaman away on ship, was most definitely the subject of her neighbours' and in particular her landlords' curiosity. On several occasions, the landlord, Jeppe Larsen, and his wife Anne Christina had not only called her out for being an 'Officer's Whore', but also alerted other inhabitants of the house that she was with child, even though her husband had been gone for more than one and a half year. The accusations became impossible to ignore, when one morning in 1771, Karen awoke to find a note nailed to her front door, stating that 'the whoring continues, but the husband is away', written in a hand similar to the landlord's. Upon his return, husband Niels Horslund brought Larsen and his wife before the court, because they had 'in a shameful manner' sought to put his wife in disrepute with their allegations.[34] The materialization of the accusations in writing, posted on the front door, mimicked a strategy of the libel or *pasquille* often used for undermining political adversaries.

In the fall of 1797, readers of the local newspaper, *Adresseavisen*, might have raised an eyebrow or two upon reading a small notice from a young man, Johan Nicolai Gran, relating the sad story of his unfortunate engagement to a Jacobine Jæger. The two had met on the day of his return from the West Indies and became engaged that same night – only for Gran to discover that she was 'prone to Drinking, out of the House on several Nights, and led an indecent Life'. He expressed how he was deeply 'ashamed that my Character has suffered such a great Injury by getting involved with a Woman of this Sort', warning all honest people to avoid consorting with her.[35]

Johan was thus willing to expose himself and swallow his shame in order to publicize the immoral character of his former fiancée for the good of the community – probably also spurred on by a hint of vengefulness. The fact that Jacobine moved from his house to her mother's, which happened to be one of Copenhagen's infamous houses, indicates that there was probably some truth to his story of misfortune. Jacobine immediately reacted to the notice in *Adresseavisen* by litigating Gran for defamation at the Royal and City court. Jacobine refused to enter into marriage, even though Johan declared to be willing to uphold his promise. With no prospects of a happy marriage, Johan in 1799 left Copenhagen and sought his fortunes in Norway.

Ruined houses and the shame within

In 1791, Maria Svendsen, a dancer at the Royal Theatre, turned to the Police Court claiming to have been publicly offended, which neither her 'good Name and Reputation', nor her position at the theatre could bear. It had all started with a fight, with fists and mouths, between Maria and a maidservant by the name of Christiane Lund, in the street in full daylight. In the midst of the dispute, Maria tore the cape from Christiane's head and fled with it, seeking refuge in her lodgings in one of the city's brothels. Christiane called for her to come out, calling her a whore and similar insults. The shouting and commotion soon gathered a crowd, which Christiane used to her advantage by stirring up people, making them cry out and whistle, encouraging them to 'ruin' the house. For fear of the mob's action, the inhabitants ejected Maria back to the street, where she quickly ran away. After the crowd had dispersed, Christiane went home.[36]

Several of the cases presented here mention the strategic use of noise to draw the attention of neighbours to insults. The stirring of the mob and the potential threat of the crowd were ever present in the early modern city. Also the motif of the 'ruined house' was a well-known urban phenomenon with century-old roots. Elizabeth Cohen has described the practice in early modern Rome of attacking a house as a proxy for its owner – a form of ritualized revenge or a moral comment directed at the inhabitants, often on account of sexual impropriety. It regularly began with loud or offensive noises that crossed the threshold into domestic space, and often include the throwing of stones, animal parts and excrement, or the drawing of graffiti.[37]

Although these disturbances were of a haphazard nature, consisting of improvised gatherings of people in the street, they had similarities to other, more organized types of ritualized shaming, such as *Charivari* or 'rough music' intended for making violations of moral codes public. Even with the lack of choreographed rituals, the mob still followed certain unwritten rules of house-scorning. The sounds, attracting attention, were central. Attacks were often directed towards doors and windows, as liminal zones between domestic and public spaces. Moreover, the sound of the breaking window drew the attention of passers-by. These apertures were symbolically linked to the orifices of the human body, and in particular the female body. As Amanda Vickery argues, 'If windows were eyes, the doors represented the mouth, vagina or anus, and the hearth the breast, heart, soul or womb. Apertures symbolized points of human vulnerability. Ink thrown in windows and excrement daubed on the door were visceral attacks on the person, and were read as such'.[38] Making sure that one's house was impenetrable, particularly at night, was thus an important task for the landlord or master of the house, in charge of upholding the morality of the household, symbolically reflected in the locking up for the night.[39]

One August evening in 1790, Birthe Pedersdatter, the wife of hawker Jens Andersen Biering, returned to her home in Tværgade in Copenhagen to find that a crowd had gathered in front of the house. Several windows had already been smashed. Inside her rooms – situated on the ground floor – she found the seamstress Stine lying on a bench, surrounded by a circle of men. Stine was having a seizure (*slag*) after a heated exchange of insults with a seaman's wife, lodging on the top floors. Both had been standing in their respective windows, and their shouting had gathered a crowd in the street below, whereupon the seaman's wife and her daughter had started to encourage people to smash the windows and 'ruin the House'. As Birthe stood by Stine's side, the seaman's wife shouted out the window, 'there she is, that Whore and *Canaille*'. Birthe demanded to know, to whom she was referring, to which the wife replied, 'It is you'. According to Birthe, the crowd replied to the seaman's wife, 'You yourself is a Whore and *Canaille*'. The seaman's wife then threw a bowl of water and some filth (*skarn*) at Birthe. While Birthe sought refuge in the house, some boys in the street started hurling pebbles at the windows. Birthe ran to fetch the military guard. Upon her return, two of her windows had been broken. She lifted the third and last from its latches and carried it to safety. When the guard arrived, the crowd dispersed.

During the subsequent police chamber investigation, Birthe was questioned about the many women who 'strayed' to visit her day and night. She explained that they ate and drank in her rooms, where she kept a tavern, but then went upstairs to visit *Fynske Stine* (Stine from Funen) – she did not know what they did together. Birthe thus drew boundaries of privacy between the households of her house, claiming to have no knowledge of the tenants' private business – in practice insisting that their actions had nothing to do with her as long as they were concealed to her – i.e. kept private.

Several neighbours, though, offered their testimonies to the 'lecherous hospitality' (*liderligt værtsskab*) kept in the house. They also described the incessant skirmishes between the women frequenting the house. One lodger claimed that the seaman's wife had come to his rooms after the incident saying that everything went as it ought to, 'now neither you nor I have to pay Rent' – pointing to pecuniary incentives for stirring up the crowd. When Stine and her husband came to the witness's rooms to light a candle, he pleaded with them, whether it was 'right that proper (*skikkelig*) People should suffer like this for their dishonest way of Life (*Keltringe Levned*)' – at which the seaman's wife shouted down the stairs whether he 'sided with the Whores'.[40] Obviously, the reality of what went on in Stine's rooms was no secret to the neighbours, but it was not talked about or acted upon until a seemingly random dispute offered residents the opportunity to publicly confront the immorality of the household. This opportunity was probably also seized upon by passers-by, who were alerted and inflamed by the insults into taking part in the public staging and shaming, which, at least temporarily, moved and materialized anew the boundaries of privacy within the house.

The incident makes it possible to observe the intricate interplay between different households, owners and individual tenants in one building. The house owners insisted on having no knowledge and part in any illicit encounters taking place in the house, reflecting the notion that tenants had privacy in their own rooms – but just as often, that privacy was refuted, judging from the many clashes between house owners and lodgers.

Moreover, the incident shows the importance of windows, both as semi-public spaces from whence the dispute between the seaman's wife and Stine took off, but also as the main target in the crowd's ensuing attack on the house. Notably, the attack seems to have been directed at the tavern on the ground floor – at least the seaman's wife, living at the top, felt safe to encourage the crowd without fear for her own windows. Even if the disturbance was not a well-planned, intended attack, when the seaman's wife encouraged the destruction, she transformed an interpersonal conflict into a public manifestation or shaming.

Between private conflict and public outrage

Existing studies of riots and mobs in Copenhagen have generally focused on political riots as manifestations of a public sphere, for instance protests directed towards the authorities and their buildings. They have largely excluded smaller cases of disturbances, such as 'private' disputes and skirmishes between drunkards, and outlets for the community's more or less unruly elements, without any obvious political content.[41] While many cases of vandalism against both public and private buildings *may* have been the result of inebriated or restless youth looking for action and outlets of aggression, they also followed certain patterns which made them highly symbolic gestures and performances which had the power to make feelings of shame and suspicions of immorality 'stick' to houses and their inhabitants.

Many of the known cases of house-scorning from Southern Europe were directed at prostitutes or adulterers. Bernard Capp has also noted how the smashing of windows was customary against the houses of prostitutes in early modern England.[42] In Copenhagen, tavern keeper Curtius had trouble with one of his lodgers on a summer night of 1785. The lodger, Simon Rohde, had been drinking next door, when Curtius, as a respectable householder ought to, closed and locked the gate for the night. When in bed, Curtius woke up to insisting knocks and reluctantly, wearing only his nightshirt, went to open the gate. Upon Rohde's entry, Curtius demanded that he be quiet, but he instead began scolding the landlord. Curtius turned out Rohde and slammed the gate. A crowd had begun to gather, which spurred on Rohde to smash a window next to the gate while he persisted in spewing insults such as 'Whore' and 'Procuress', now directed at Curtius' wife, who had come out into the street, attempting to prevent the situation from escalating. The incident then quickly turned into moral arguments directed at the alleged immoral livelihood of the Curtius household.

An incident taking place a decade earlier, in 1772, indicates that the accusations were not farfetched. This unfolded in one of the infamous brothel-streets, just as a police patrol was passing to inquire into the business going on in the houses – precisely the type of house calls addressed by the ordinance from Struensee, which is the subject of Ulrik Langen's chapter. Ane Marie Curtius, who was standing in her front door, informed the officers that they had no need to pay a visit to the house across from hers, as 'the people had already turned in and their door been closed for some time'. This comment spurred on her neighbour, Stine Giermand (coincidentally *Fynske Stine*, from the abovementioned case), to step forward from her doorway and proclaim that Ane Marie was the biggest whore and madam of the street – to which Ane Marie replied that Stine slept with anyone for mere coins, 'while her Husband steadied the folding Screen'. These insults played on the ambiguous and ridiculous character of a husband securing the privacy of his wife in an intimate situation, while neglecting his obligation to protect her honour. The officers restored order by escorting the women to their houses and calming down tempers, especially Stine's, who once again reacted to the stressful situation with a seizure.[43]

The quarrel ended up in court, and to our modern minds, it seems curious that two well-known mistresses of their respective brothels would afford both time and a considerable amount of money pursuing a case in order to clear their names and preserve a secret, which was most likely no secret at all to most people listening in on the dispute. Was it because the accusation that the mistresses themselves were doing the 'dirty work' was an insult to their marriage – and a denial of their social standing and respectability? Or was the charade of the court case a mere display of strength (and wealth, seeing as cases could amount to quite large sums)? Or did their ferocious defences of their good names and reputations reflect an idea that what went on in their respective houses was their private business – and in no way to be perceived as a reflection of their character and the morals of their household?

One evening in the summer of 1772, tavern-keeper Osterbind denied service to some seamen. Shortly after, his house was attacked with stones and chalk, and several windows were smashed. One witness testified that a maid came knocking at her door, asking, 'Does Madame want to see a spectacle, the Tailors Office (*Skræder contoiret*, Osterbind's house in Laxegade) is to be ruined', adding that members of the Royal Navy (*Holmens Folk*) had gone up to her master's workshop, carrying rocks in their pockets.[44]

Another victim of a window-smashing stated to the court that he did 'not run a Tavern, but merely keeps a Girl due to his Wife's weakness' – implying that such attacks usually happened to disorderly houses with a suspiciously high number of servant girls.[45] Yet another case connects the two phenomena, as a landlord described how a young man took a stick, 'smashed a Window in my Rooms and scolded my

Wife as a Whore, and added that I ran a Brothel'.[46] It seems that the action of smashing windows was often related to the accusation of a house being disreputable. The most well-known example of this is a series of events known as *Den store Udfejelsesfest* after the fall of Struensee in 1772, where a mob aimed their anger at the bawdy houses of the city. Both Giermand and Curtius were among the victims of the riot.[47]

For sure, in many cases, smashed windows were most likely a pragmatic choice of destructive behaviour, aimed at harming the inhabitants of the house, seeing as windows were easy targets and expensive to replace. Meanwhile, the broken windows had a strong symbolic effect, due to both the distinctive sound of the smashing and the damage, which even after the incident made it known to passers-by that the community had exposed the inhabitants of the house and their transgressions. Especially after the riots of 1772, broken windows would have carried a strong symbolism. Even though local people might have known very well that a certain tavern housed prostitutes, somehow the action of ruining the house transformed this 'tacit' or hidden knowledge into a public fact. Through the physical attack of the space in which immorality resided and was practised, the community made hidden bodily practices, and the shame connected to them, public.

The facade was the face of the household and the symbolism of the ruined windows was strong. Windows and doors were symbolic of prostitution, because women often courted potential customers from there – or, as we have seen, used them as vantage points for exchanging insults. The case of Anne Svendsdatter, but also other cases involved accusations of women letting men explore the hidden secrets under their skirts in doorways. The fact that they did not even try to cover their sinful bodies and secrets to the community seemingly made it even worse.[48]

In her study of a series of attacks on disreputable houses in early-eighteenth-century Stockholm (a riot similar to the one that took place in Copenhagen in 1772), Karin Sennefelt has argued that the attacks can be perceived as the community's means of exerting patriarchal authority in the homes where the moral control of the husband was absent. The public then acted as the missing – or negligent – (male) householder, who was usually responsible for guarding the morality of a house.[49]

Not all cases of house-scorning were related to whorehouses or women living on their own. One very interesting case reflects a different, but also somehow related, story of the community's preoccupation with what went on in the privacy of the household. One afternoon in the spring of 1772, passers-by in St. Kongensgade heard loud shouting and scuffling from brewer Fischer's house. The noise came from the brewer giving his groom Morten Nielsen a good beating in the courtyard, because Morten had refused to do his chores on the terms offered by the brewer. The groom started calling out 'gewalt', signifying to the surroundings that violence was taking place, urging them to interfere. It did not take long before a large group of people had assembled outside the gate to the house. According to Fischer's testimony in the ensuing court case, the crowd was making a lot of noise. In order to have 'Peace in his Courtyard', he slammed close the inner gate doors. Ironically, the insistence of freedom from interference only caused more people to gather in front of the house – the attempt to keep something secret or concealed awoke public suspicion. People present in the crowd later testified to having heard shouts of 'he is going to kill me, I cannot stand it anymore'. A seaman peered through a crack in the gate, seeing a man flat on the ground, Fischer standing over him, and quickly the rumour spread that the brewer had nearly killed his groom. Suddenly, the gate opened and Fischer faced the crowd, who demanded to know what was going on. The brewer answered that he had merely given the groom a good punch in nose and mouth, to which the crowd responded with flinging street filth at Fischer and the gate. Soon the police appeared to make sure 'that no Harm was done'.[50]

The case shows how the community was quite ready to meddle in what went on in a private courtyard and could be considered a matter of the household between master and groom – demonstrating their perception of Fischer's actions as inappropriate by gathering, shouting and throwing filth. The court agreed with the ruling of the street parliament and found that the brewer with his violent conduct had exceeded the boundaries of 'temperate disciplining', which a head of household was entitled to employ towards disobedient subordinates.

The house-scornings often took their point of departure in 'trivial' conflicts between neighbours or even strangers, but developed along a traditional, ritual 'ruining' of a house, drawing a long tradition of public shaming and communal moral disciplining. The conflicts reflect a particular interest in actions which in different ways constitute trespassing against the boundaries of patriarchal society – either women violating the sacred institution of marriage or husbands neglecting their duties as husbands. But the exposure was also a means for the more powerless members of the early modern city to exert their power and influence towards those who may have been slightly better off, or who were in other aspects of life exerting various types of power over them. In many ways, the power of morality exceeded the limits of gender and/or social status.

Concluding remarks: Making the private public

Approaching secrecy and privacy from its antidote, exposure, has brought us into a world of gossip, slander, social drama and conflict where tempers collide and vengeful remarks turn secrets into potent weapons of defamation. It has taken us into houses, courtyards and back into the streets where crowds gather in front of houses to pass moral judgements on those within – from the interpersonal insults of defamation cases, to the shaming rituals of the crowd. Cases of neighbourly conflicts have let us peer into the 'private' spaces of the homes and the perceptions of their physical and imagined boundaries, as people kept a watchful eye and ear out for the dealings of their neighbours, carefully choosing when knowledge should stay secret or private, and when it was to be public.

The exposure of private in the public as part of everyday conflicts has shed light on how especially the lower orders of late-eighteenth-century Copenhagen perceived the boundaries between public and private, and the feelings they attached to these boundaries as they materialized in everyday negotiations. The incidents presented here show that in late-eighteenth-century Copenhagen people still feared the potential power of insulting words and cared about preserving their good name. To them respectability came from action. They were thus willing to bring slanderers to court in order to 're-cover' delicate or personal information put into public circulation – even if this, according to

Shoemaker, was a phenomenon in decline and mostly in use among the lower orders. Moreover, as the examples given above clearly demonstrate, cases of deformation *were* in fact about much more than words, as they often arose from everyday conflicts over space and/or status in the many crowded houses and tenements of the city. This was an everyday reality, in which insults and the exposure of secret or intimate information became a powerful strategy to undermine, humiliate and shame adversaries.

The emotional strategy of exposure made use of the potentially harmful powers of the private in the public. It therefore opens up a window onto how the boundaries of the private materialized in a continuous negotiation over access to intimate spaces or knowledge. These boundaries were marked by emotional reactions elicited in the exposed or the exposers, such as shame, anger and contempt. Degrading the body through exposing or soiling it served as an efficacious strategy of shaming, underlining verbal insults and making shame or disgust 'stick' to the sinful body. It triggered a heightened awareness of the body and its borders in the individual. The examples given here also show how perceptions of privacy unfolded in relation to different, but intricately related spheres: bodies, spaces and intimate information. Thus the exposure or humiliation of the body served as a symbol of or reference to immodesty, shamelessness and accessibility. The house served as a symbol of the body and the household, reflected in the tainting or violation of a house as a metaphor for the bodies within, and as a way of making legible – and public – the sinful character of a person or an entire household.

Though the many cases of exposure were nearly all brought about, not by a strong moral outrage, but by personal animosities or an urge for revenge, they nonetheless constituted an intentional staging of secret or intimate details in public – stagings that often rehearsed more or less ritualized practices of the public shaming of moral offenders. The intentional shouting and noisemaking, perhaps even clapping and whistling, which signalled that 'public action' was taking place – thus also placed onlookers and potential participants in a specific mindset, and carried the connotation of public disturbance.[51] These ritual markers – rehearsing age-old practices of house-scorning as a symbolic attack on the honour of the house to which they belonged – were part of the emotional practices which marked, challenged and materialized the boundaries between public and private.

Conflicts like the ones presented here however big or small – took place every day in the houses, courtyards and streets of early modern Copenhagen. Most were settled then and there, and the uncomfortable or embarrassing words or things exposed were re-covered and put back under covers or into the closet. But in that fraction of cases, the transgression of boundaries was of such a nature that the secret and the shame stuck – and the exposure made it into the public light of the courts, for the historian to find and ponder the phenomenon of the private in the public.

Notes

1   'Om ieg kunde huske at siste nat at Ole Spillemand laa hos mig i Sengen og ieg skulde kuns passe paa mine Slunker, i gade Døren som ragte mig 10 Alen op under mine Klæder', *Rigsarkivet* (The Danish National Archives, DNA), Hof- og Stadsretten, Pådømte sager, 22 December 1771.

2   'Ole Spillemand havde lagt i Sengen hos mig i sin bare Skjorte og ieg i min bare Særk under Dynen, hvilket er mig alt for utaalelig at høre, og ieg for samme Beskyldninger er anset af Folk i Huset', Ibid.; Letter of complaint from Anne Svendsdatter, 27 January 1772.

3   Important publications in this field are amongst numerous others: Gowing 2003; Capp 2003; Stewart 1994; Sharpe 1980; Ingram 1988.

4   Gowing 1999, 98–9.

5   See Crane 2009 and e.g. Bailey 2006; Longfellow 2006; Gowing 2000; Vickery 2008; Barclay 2021. See introduction for further references.

6   Shoemaker 2000; Elias 1939.

7   Barclay 2021.

8   Ahmed 2004, 2014.

9   Scheer 2012.

10   Bayless 2012; Larrington 2006; Linaa 2016.

11   Kilday and Nash 2010.

12   DNA, Københavns Politiret, Behandlede sager ved 1. protokol, 23 September 1791. Other examples of dirt or filth as weapons include, e.g., DNA, Hof- og Stadsretten, 2. vidnekammer, 28 August 1799; DNA, Københavns Politi, Politiretten, Behandlede sager v. 3. protokol, Letter of 28 March 1789.

13   DNA, Hof- og Stadsretten, Pådømte sager, 14 September 1771. See also DNA, Pådømte sager, 8 February 1773.

14   Ibid., 2. Vidnekammer, 24 August 1799.

15   Bayless 2012; Ahmed 2004, 82–100; Miller 1997; Mary Douglas 1966.

16   On shame see, e.g., Ahmed 2004, 101–21; Sedgwick 2003; Miller 1993.

17   On beds as spaces of sociability see Gowing 2014; Barclay 2017.

18   Reinke-Williams 2011, 82.

19   Ibid., 2. vidnekammer, 5 November 1771.

20   'Jeg kunde fortælle mine Læsere et nyt Optog med Fiskerkiellingerne ved gl. Strand, hvorledes næsten den hele Række paa nogle nær ligesom blev elektrifiseret, og Næver og Pander mødte hverandre, saa Gnisterne fløi af Øinene, og antændte Haarlokkerne paa disse Brændeviinsamazoninder; hvor Banden og Galen, Skielden og Smelden, var Feldtmusikken. Jeg kunde opregne hvor heftig Striden blev, og hvorledes den endte; men det var kun at besudle mine Fortællinger, og fornærme ethvert ærbart Øre. Hvad Skikkelighed skal vi vente af dem, som skamme sig ikke ved offentlig at være Afskum!', *Aftenposten*, no. 77, 29 September 1776.

21   Gowing 1999, chap 3; Gowing 2003, 30–40; Paster 1993; Stallybrass 1986.

22   Gowing 1999, 16.

23   'Har hun nogen Ære i Sverige saa kan hun sætte sig paa denne Bøtte og rejse derover og hente sin Ære', DNA, Hof- og Stadsretten, Pådømte sager, 28 August 1799.

24   'Fordi hun havde Ørme i sin Tingest … brugt saadanne Talemaader, som sigtede til at giøre mit Hus mistænkeligt', DNA, Hof- og Stadsretten, Pådømte sager, 14 September 1771.

25   Cohen and Cohen 2001.

26   Gowing 1999, 55.

27   Davis 1971. See also Darnton 1984, 95. Several studies have looked into these types of shaming rituals, mainly with a focus on the elaborate rituals: Ingram 1994; Underdown and Fletcher 1985. See Kilday and Nash 2010 for an overview.

28   'At det var bedre om hun tog sin Horeunge med sig i Vognen', DNA, Søetaten, den kombinerede ret, Justits- og domprotokol, 27 February 1780.

29 'En del brutale ord og støjen … der bor det Kalluns-stads … Madammen den Sergent
    Hore er nu endelig bleven Kone', DNA, Hof- og Stadsretten, Pådømte sager, 9 January
    1786.

30 Ibid., 9 September 1799. For a more detailed study of the notion of household
    authority in late-eighteenth-century Copenhagen see Schjerning 2019.

31 See, e.g., Amussen 1994; Bailey 2006; Longfellow 2006, Barclay 2021.

32 Gowing 1999, 69–73.

33 DNA, Hof- og Stadsretten, Pådømte sager, 14 October 1799.

34 Ibid., 16 January 1771.

35 'Jeg erfarede snart, at hun var drikfældig, var ude adskillige Nætter af Huset, og førte
    et uanstændigt Levnet … men skammer mig, at min Caracteer har lidet saa stor
    Skaar, ved at indlade mig med et Fruentimmer af denne Klasse', Kiøbenhavns Kgl.
    allene privilegerede Adresse Contoirs Efterretninger, 13, 16, 18 October 1797; DNA,
    Hof- og Stadsretten, Pådømte sager, 10 August 1800.

36 DNA, Københavns Politi, Politiretten, Behandlede sager v. 1. protokol, 31 August
    1791.

37 Cohen 1992. A law from the city of Rome in 1580, with references to a papal edict
    of 1566, punished those who threw 'excrement, or horn, or similar things at the
    thresholds and doorways of houses, and whoever throws rocks or stones at their
    doors, windows, panes, and roofs, to inflict an insult, or befoul the walls'. Cited in
    Dean 2004, 19. No Danish equivalent exists, only a passage in the Danish law on
    Husfred (House Peace) in which it is specified that to hack or slash another man's
    table, walls, doors, windows or other belongings were subject to a heavy fine, but
    there is no mention of symbolic soiling or the like. Danske Lov 1683, 6-9-6. The roots
    of the practice of stoning houses may be traced back to a regulated ritual practice
    of hurling stones at Jewish houses, going back as far as at least 538, possibly with
    reference to a biblical story of the Jews stoning St. Stephen. In particular, in Southern
    Europe, the Jews were considered legitimate targets of public anger within this
    ritualized framework, but the attacks also occurred spontaneously all over Europe
    during the entire early modern period and into the nineteenth century. Jütte 2016;
    Armstrong 2008, chap. 3.

38 Vickery 2008, 153; See also St. George 1998, 128–41.

39 Vickery 2008; Flather 2007, 46–7; Schjerning 2015.

40 'Ret at skikkelig Folk skulle lide saadan for deres Kieltringe Levnet … om de ville
    holde med Horerne'. Københavns Politi, Politiretten, 1. protokol, 27 August 1790.
    See Schjerning 2013 for further discussions of authority within the households of
    eighteenth-century Copenhagen.

41 Blüdnikow 1986; Stevnsborg 1983. Exceptions are, e.g., Langen 2005 and Langen
    2009.

42 Cohen 1992, 610; Capp 2003. The women often sought satisfaction in the courts,
    even though it may have been well known that they were prostitutes.

43 DNA, Hof- og Stadsretten, Pådømte sager, 3 July 1772.

44 'Vil Madamen se Spectacler, Skræder contoiret skal ruineres', Ibid., 22 March 1772.
    The brothels in general were referred to as 'offices'. Curtius's house was called the
    soap-office (*sæbe-contoiret*). See *Grev Struenses mærkværdige Testamente, opsat af
    ham selv og confirmeeret af Lucifer. Kiøbenhavn 1772* (Det Kongelige Bibliotek, Bolle
    Luxdorphs trykkefrihedsskrifter); Stevnsborg 1980, 96.

45 'Da jeg dog ikke holder Værtshus, men alene har en Pige formedelst min Kones
    Svaghed', DNA, Hof- og Stadsretten, Pådømte sager, 19 March 1773.

46   'Slog en Rude itu og skieldte min Kone for en Hore og tillagde at jeg holdt
      Horehus', DNA, Københavns Politi, Politiretten, Behandlede sager ved 1. protokol,
      2 November 1785.
47   See Stjernfelt et al. 2020, chap. 32. See Ulrik Langen's chapter in this volume for a
      description of the riot.
48   DNA, Hof- og Stadsretten, Pådømte sager, 14 September 1771.
49   Sennefelt 2019.
50   DNA, Hof- og Stadsretten, Pådømte sager, 22 March 1773.
51   On the sensuous markers of public disturbance see Langen 2017.

Part Three

Spaces

Spaces for comfort, seclusion and privacy in a Swedish eighteenth-century town

Dag Lindström and Göran Tagesson

Behind the façade of the house at Hunnebergsgatan 30 in Linköping, there is an inner yard and a private garden.[1] This, however, you cannot see from the street; it is all hidden because the house obstructs the view from outside. The house itself was built in 1795 and is today known as *Onkel Adamsgården*, named after a once well-known author who lived there in the nineteenth century. It is a two-storey building with two apartments and a diverse and complex room structure. The two apartments are clearly separated, with front doors, staircases and vestibules, further emphasizing seclusion and regulated entrances to the apartments. The plot itself has a secluded character, as the inner yard is completely closed off from the street space by the residential house.[2]

This arrangement of house and plot is not unique. Similar spatial novelties appeared frequently in eighteenth-century Linköping, especially towards the later part of the century.[3] This development took place, not in a leading European metropolis, but in a small provincial town in Sweden, with only a few thousand inhabitants. Linköping was admittedly an ecclesiastical centre and a central place for the regional nobility, but it was certainly no industrial forerunner or vibrant commercial hub.[4] It was just

Figure 7.1 Onkel Adamsgården. Ortophoto Johan Stenvall, The Archaeologists, Linköping.

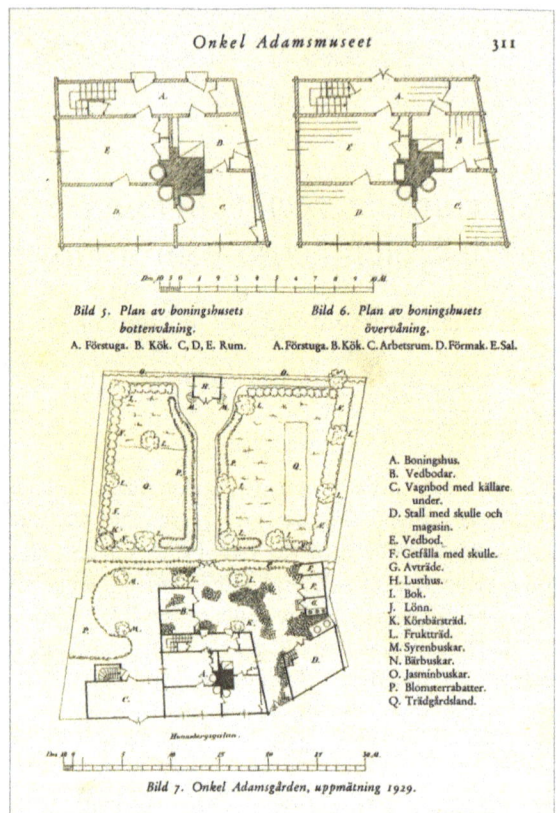

Figure 7.2 Plan of the 1920s of Onkel Adamsgården. After Cnattingius 1929, Archive of Östergötland's museum.

another small and seemingly sleepy provincial town. This, however, does not make the observed changes any less interesting and it raises several questions related to seclusion and privacy.

How do these changes in the spatial organization of houses and urban space relate to seclusion, privacy and intimacy? What specific types of changes in the built urban structures during the eighteenth century may be related to the early emergence of privacy and intimacy? Were these changes in spatial organization restricted to specific social strata, preferably social elites, or can they be detected in various socio-economic contexts?

In this chapter, we will point at some important basic changes in the social organization and the built structures of eighteenth-century Linköping, arguing that specific spatial changes enhanced possible seclusion and privacy. We do not claim that the changes prove the actual emergence of privacy as practice, mentality or ideology.

This is not primarily an analysis of social practice and cultural meaning. What we do claim is that the built urban environment was significantly transformed and that these changes resulted in increased spatial diversity, complexity and seclusion. We also claim that these changes are closely related to changes in the social organization. Our analyses are built primarily on a combination of archaeological documentation, examinations of still standing houses and house documentations from the 1920s to the 1980s. Information about houses and their spatial structures has also been retrieved from contemporary written sources, such as sales documents, probate inventories and inspection documents. For the reconstruction of household structures and cohabitation patterns, various tax records and church records have been used.[5]

Material, social and cultural spaces

Recently, space has emerged as a fundamental dimension of historical analyses and the spatial turn has been added to the many other 'turns' of contemporary social and cultural history. This is particularly evident in urban history.[6] It does not mean that historians previously have completely neglected spatial dimensions. On the contrary, there are numerous examples of space being considered in historical analyses.[7] Rather, the novelty of the spatial turn appears in a more systematic, natural, and theoretically grounded inclusion of space in all kinds of social, cultural and political analyses.

In archaeological analyses, space has long been a prominent dimension. During the twentieth century, many different spatial aspects have been discussed; for example, from a cultural historical tradition, focusing on diffusion and *Kulturkreislehre* vis-à-vis landscape and topography. During the 1960s and 1970s, an influential ecological tradition focused on environmental adaption to the landscape and natural resources. Since the 1980s and onwards, space has been studied from many different aspects; for example, the construction of space, human experience of spatiality, the partialities of power relations, etc. Nowadays, on the other hand, many archaeologists seek to integrate human relations, human agency, and human experiences in a more explicit way in analyses of materiality and spatiality.[8]

Much theoretical inspiration has been drawn from the French Marxist sociologist Henri Lefebvre, discussing the *production of space*, in terms of *spatial practice*, *representation of space* and *representational space*. This triad is meant to cover the interaction between everyday routine practices, conceptualizations of space and experiences of space, as well as to overcome the duality between materiality and ideas, and between space and social interaction.[9] Although Lefebvre points out space as changeable and socially produced, time and historical change are not in the forefront of his arguments. Karl Schlögel, for example, has argued for a more deliberate focus on the linking of space with time and action.[10]

There have been further critical remarks on Lefebvre and some of the research practices associated with the spatial turn. The emphasis on meaning and representation tends to neglect or at least downplay the materiality of space, and several historians have argued for the importance of including physical materiality more directly into the analyses.[11] In addition, while meaning is sometimes ascribed to space itself, others argue strongly against this. Leif Jerram, for example, claims that spaces in themselves never 'possess the quality of being gay, male, or sacred'. These are conclusions based on observations of human actions and thoughts not on analyses of space itself.[12]

These critical remarks are important and should be seriously considered. On the one hand, it is essential that space is never reduced to just a container or a backdrop for human interaction, independent of human relations, actions and thoughts. On the other hand, it is equally important that space is never treated as meaning and interpretation only. It is the combination of materiality, meaning and action that turns space into a powerful analytical dimension. It is important also to consider Lefebvre's basic statements; space is always produced and space has a multitude of dimensions. This is very much in line with Doreen Massey's thoughts about space as produced by (social) relations and interaction, always characterized by heterogeneity, never finished and closed, but always under construction.[13]

Privacy and intimacy

It is not immediately obvious what privacy and intimacy would mean in an eighteenth-century context. There are, however, a number of classical studies in the field. Privacy and the development of a private sphere have been conceptualized in contradistinction to a public sphere and in relation to a changing concept of the public. For Jürgen Habermas, this relates to the development of new forms of communication in the (liberal) public sphere. His main interest is also directed towards the development of the public domain. The new public and the private in many ways appear as two sides of the very same new social and political order. Intimacy developed in contrast to the public sphere and was strongly associated with the emergence of the bourgeois family.[14] Nevertheless, as pointed out by John Brewer, the private often tends to appear as a residual: that which is not public.[15]

In the monumental *A History of Private Life*, edited by Phillippe Ariès and Georges Duby, focus is on privacy rather than the public. According to Ariès, people in late medieval times still did a lot of things in public that would later be restricted to contexts concealed from the public gaze. For Ariès, this is about fundamental changes in the norms of behaviour, and it is related to the emergence of the strong state, growing literacy and new religious practices. Privacy emerged as a new form of sociability, manifested in self-reflecting literature, in the upgrading of personal friendship and in new ways of organizing living spaces.[16]

Christoph Heyl systematically analyses the development of privacy in eighteenth-century London. Although Heyl considers privacy to be basically about mind and human behaviour, he relates the development of privacy closely to spatial and material transformations. New forms of cohabitation were a prerequisite for privacy to become widespread. After the Great Fire in 1666, many houses were built according a new model of inner organization with separately heated rooms, a more specialized room structure and a more distinct separation between different parts of the houses. With this, the relations to neighbours and the concepts of inside and outside of houses changed. A crucial dimension of this change was the creation of specific spaces, from which other people could be kept out, and into which selected individuals could be invited. These were spaces where new forms of social interaction developed. Heyl furthermore distinguishes intimacy from privacy in general terms. Intimacy developed in the core of the private sphere, where relations were based not on, for example, economic relations, but on emotional bonds.[17]

Significant transformations of the residential buildings have also been identified by many other historians and archaeologists. Matthew Johnson points at a transition from 'open' to closed 'houses' in rural England, starting in the sixteenth century. Houses that were dominated by a large central hall with a variety of different functions, which had many openings to the outside and close connections to neighbours, were replaced by houses characterized by a clear spatial division of activities. The creation of a separate kitchen is an important example of this. The creation of different rooms for different tasks and special social activities is interpreted as an expression of developing individualism.[18] Johnson's identification of open house structures carries certain similarities with Joachim Eibach's concept of *das offene Haus* (the open house), which identifies a pre-modern culture of visibility and interaction, where a dichotomy of inside and outside usually is more relevant than a distinction between private and public. Houses were open, activities were visible and rooms were often easily accessible from the outside.[19] Another important innovation in the transition towards modernity is the introduction of organized apartment buildings. This is usually associated with larger cities. In, for example, Vienna, it has been estimated that about 85 per cent of the inner-city population lived in rented accommodations around 1800. This of course meant a fundamental change in the size and the inner spatial organization of houses. Houses were built with distinct apartments, separate kitchens and tiled stoves for heating.[20]

Several historians have focused more explicitly on the development of intimacy and the domestic sphere in early modern Europe. Many studies focus on the large European metropolises like Paris and London, often paying considerable attention to urban elites, and frequently emphasizing material culture and consumption.[21] Analysing everyday objects and the spatial organization of both elegant and humble early modern Parisian homes, Annik Pardailhé-Galabrun concludes that rooms became more diverse and specialized, better heated and better lit, and equipped with more personal objects during the eighteenth century. Greater privacy was gained in this way.[22] According to Rafealla Sarti, the need for privacy in early modern society developed in relation to servants. With increasing physical distance, achieved through the creation of separate areas for servant work, separate sleeping rooms and the introduction of corridors and backstairs, servants became increasingly separated from the family.[23] Amanda Vickery also emphasizes the connections between transformations of the spatial structures of houses, changes in material culture and the advance of privacy in eighteenth-century England. Although Vickery points at the importance of physical separation through corridors, multiple staircases and the introduction of small rooms allowing for solitude, she emphasizes that privacy was not something exclusive and achievable only for the most privileged. Privacy is understood as the possibility of seclusion, withdrawal, refuge and security. It could to some extent be obtained also among servants and lodgers. Vickery uses the portable locking box as an example of a basic privacy achieved with small measures and limited resources.[24]

These spatial tendencies have also been discussed in a Scandinavian setting, e.g. the coming of more advanced apartments and apartment buildings during the nineteenth century, but more from an art historical perspective and related to industrialization after the mid-nineteenth century.[25]

Households and cohabitation

Our primary focus is the built environment, but this needs to be related to the social organization. Household structures and patterns of cohabitation are of particular interest here and it has been established that these underwent important changes in Linköping during the eighteenth century. The time from around 1750 to the 1780s appears as the pivotal period of change. Between 1750 and 1785, the population increased from 1,822 to 2,853 inhabitants, and the number of households indicated in the tax records rose from 340 to 891. These figures represent a sharp decline in the average household size from 5.4 people down to only 3.2 people. The decades after 1785 appear as demographically more stable with just a slight decrease in both the number of inhabitants and the number of households.[26]

An immediate effect of the population growth was a rise in population density, as the built area of the town expanded only slightly over time, from 252 plots in 1754 to 276 plots in 1800. With this, the average number of inhabitants per plot increased from 7.4 people in 1754 to 9.8 people in 1800, and the average number of households per plot increased from 1.6 to 3.1. In other words, more people came to live closer to each other, and often in rather small units.[27]

Average numbers, however, do not tell us the whole story. The diversity in household organization also increased. Small and single-person households gained in prevalence. Already in 1772, no less than 21.5 per cent of all households were singletons, but in 1800, this share had increased even further to 28.7 per cent.[28] Thus, it can be concluded that singles were a significant dimension of late-eighteenth-century households and cohabitation structures in Linköping, and their importance increased over time. This aspect of early modern population structures has until now rarely been considered as an important dimension of social organization and social order.[29] Nonetheless, it is a strong indicator of fundamental changes in the social structure.

The increasing prevalence of single households does not, however, correspond to a declining importance of large households. The share of households with at least eight people admittedly decreased from 9.6 per cent in 1772 to 7.3 per cent in 1800, but the large households still included the same share of the population. In 1772, a total of 583 individuals, or 23.6 per cent of the total population, lived in households with at least eight people. In 1800, these amounted to 642 people or 23.7 per cent of the population. This means that the number of large households on the one hand tended to decline, but that the average size of large households on the other hand increased over time.[30]

Another important change is that the share of households headed by a married couple declined substantially from 60.9 per cent in 1754 to only 46.5 in 1800. At the same time, households headed by single individuals (not married people, widows and widowers) increased from 38.3 per cent to 52.2 per cent. This is another expression of the transformation of household structures and cohabitation patterns in eighteenth-century Linköping. In addition, the increasing population density was not evenly distributed over the town. There was a huge variation in the number of individuals and households residing on the single plots, but generally, the share of plots with very few households declined while those with many households increased. In 1772, 125 town plots (47.2 per cent) housed only one household. By 1800, not more than fifty-five plots (21.4 per cent) held only one household. In 1772, there were forty-eight plots (18.1 per cent) with four or more households. By 1800, there were ninety-one plots (45.5 per cent) housing four or more households.[31]

Increasing complexity of residential buildings

At the same time, the built structures and the housing culture of the town also changed. The internal structure of urban residential buildings became more complex, diverse and heterogeneous. In the seventeenth century, small two- or three-room buildings still dominated. The structure appears as rather simple and homogeneous, including a small vestibule (Sw. *förstuga*), a main room for daily use, heated with a fireplace (Sw. *stuga*), and possibly a third room, not necessarily heated. The rooms were organized in one row, and access was simple, as each room was entered through another room.[32]

The first important indication of a development towards increasing spatial diversity is the introduction of a separate kitchen. This appears to have been a general trend in Swedish towns during the second half of the seventeenth century. In some early modern Swedish towns, like Jönköping and Kalmar, the separation of cooking and food preparation activities into a separate kitchen is possible to observe more closely during that time. In the case of Kalmar, the whole town was moved and rebuilt at a new location around the 1650s and 1660s, and it has recently been stated that separate kitchens were very common in the newly constructed houses, even in more marginal and socially underprivileged parts of the town.[33]

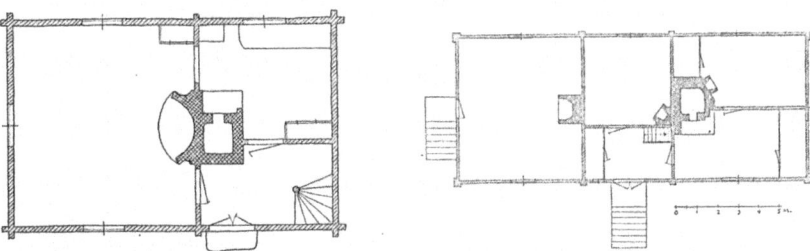

Figure 7.3 Two types of vernacular buildings; a single-room house (Sw. enkelstuga) and a house with two rooms separated by a vestibule (Sw. parstuga), both with separate kitchens. After Hofrén 1937.

Figure 7.4 A house documented in Kalmar, with "stuga" and separate kitchen. After Tagesson & Carelli 2016.

Figure 7.5 A very small house with a single room in Linköping, Hunnebergsgatan 23. Documentation Bengt Cnattingius 1920s, Archive of Östergötland's museum.

Simple house plans were still common in Linköping in the eighteenth century, but there are several examples of increasing complexity and heterogeneity, even in houses that may at first appear as simple and unsophisticated. One of these typically humble and modest buildings still stands on Hunnebergsgatan 7 in Linköping. It looks like a single building completed at one specific time. However, under the surface, and after a meticulous buildings archaeological analysis, this house is revealed to be the result of a series of subsequent building and extension activities. In 1714, this plot was described in terms of 'small houses and a vegetable garden'. The oldest part of the house is a one-room building originally from the early 1630s, or possibly a two-storey building with one room on each floor. Another part, a separate one-room building, is from the mid-1680s. A second floor was added in the early 1780s connecting the two small separate houses. At that time, the total number of rooms was extended from two (or possibly three) to five. The rooms on the second floor were reached by an external, open staircase (Sw. *loftgång*), and seem to represent small, single-room apartments.[34]

This property clearly displays the close connection between the transformation of the physical shape of the house and changes in the housing and cohabitation conditions. In 1771, only one small household inhabited this place: a chamois tanner, his wife and a maid. In 1785, after the completion of the second floor, there were six inhabitants, representing three separate households: a bell-ringer and his wife, a worker and his wife, and a brewer and his wife. Thirteen years later, in 1798, there were thirteen people living in the house, representing seven different households. The house owner, carpenter Magnus Tornstedt, his wife and three children constituted a household of five persons. The six other households were all tenants and lodgers. Four of them were singleton households.[35]

Figure 7.6 Hunnebergsgatan 7 in Linköping, the single and plain facade hides a complex building biography. Photo: Bengt Cnattingius 1920s, Archive of Östergötland's museum.

Figure 7.7 The façade of Hunnebergsgatan 7 in Linköping, documentations from 1970s. Archive of Östergötland's museum.

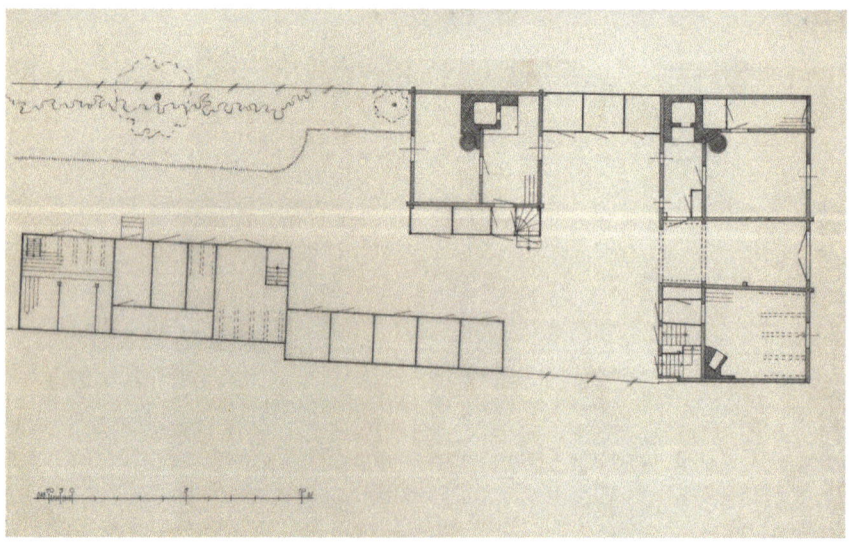

Figure 7.8 The plot of Hunnebergsgatan 7, documented in 1920s, the main building towards the street to the right. Additional residential building with small rooms to let in the middle of the plot. Garden and outbuildings to the left. Archive of Östergötland's museum.

We cannot establish exactly how these households were distributed in the house, but it is quite possible that the carpenter family lived in one room, three elderly women in another, a crippled worker and his wife in a third room, a poor merchant widow and her daughter in a fourth, and an unmarried saltpetre-boiler in a fifth. Although this certainly was a crowded building, it would have been possible, to offer all inhabitants at least a minimum of privacy or seclusion. Several individuals had to share a room, but everyone could close a door, the rooms could not be entered into directly from the outside, and no one had to go through another room to reach their own.

Later, there were further small changes made to this building. An open staircase leading to the second floor was built in. This probably happened in the early nineteenth century; similar rebuilding work has been noticed on several other buildings in Linköping from the same time. In one of the nearby houses in the same street, the construction of two different stairs even created two separate entrances to the second floor. With rather small measures, it was possible to create further potential for separation and seclusion, even in small and over-crowded plots. At Hunnebergsgatan 7, separate kitchens were constructed in some of these narrow and

Figure 7.9 Hunnebergsgatan 7, a small kitchen preserved on the second floor, representing a later addition in the built-in open gallery. Documentation from the 1970s, Archive of Östergötland's museum.

newly built-in spaces, indicating that separate kitchen spaces were coveted even under small circumstances. The small kitchen on the second floor could be used as a closed space, exclusively connected to the inner room, or it could be used as an open space, available for all three rooms on that floor. Many of these secondary modifications (built-in staircase, external vestibules, entrance halls, and separate closets and larders) developed the spatial complexity of the building and increased the depth of the built structures. Rooms and apartments could be reached from the outside only by passing through a sequence of spaces in the house. In the house at Hunnebergsgatan 7, like in many other houses from that period, there are also examples of secondary openings between the rooms, indicating a possible construction of apartments with two or three small rooms. These new entrances between rooms enhanced the inner flexibility of the houses, allowing for both connection and seclusion.[36]

A parallel phenomenon to these changes in the inner building structures is found in the middle of the plots. During the eighteenth century, small residential buildings were added to the inner areas of many plots. One such house with possible residential rooms can be found at Hunnebergsgatan 7. This house was built as early as in the 1750s. There are many other examples from both Linköping and other Swedish towns, indicating that the building of extra houses in the inner yards was rather frequent during the second half of the eighteenth century. In many cases, it can be established that those houses were specifically built for renting out rooms.[37] This adds a further dimension to the development of diversity and separation, when rooms intended for renting were not only separated from the owner's apartment, but also located in a different building.

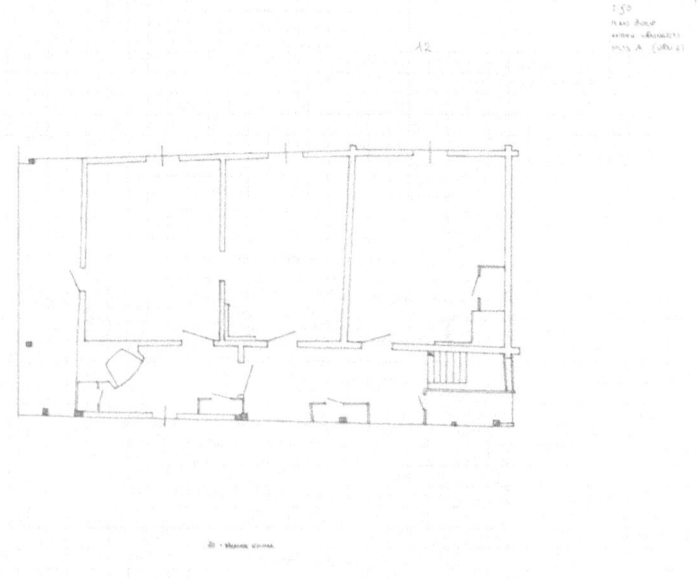

Figure 7.10 Plan of Hunnebergsgatan 7 in Linköping, documentation from 1970's. Notice the difference between the original timber walls, including three separate rooms at the top towards the street, and secondary additions in a lighter construction technique at the bottom, comprising the built-in open gallery and a small kitchen at the bottom left. Archive of Östergötland's museum.

Moreover, the house discussed in the introduction, Hunnebergsgatan 30, represents the development of new inner structures of residential buildings. It was built according to a new type of house plan, with four rooms in two rows. It is a two-storey building with one separate apartment on each floor and an external, open gallery with a staircase, which was later built in. This modification turned the gallery into a small entrance hall for each floor, separating the apartments from the entrance doors of the house. Each apartment is composed of a kitchen and an additional three rooms, with a central chimneystack, providing heating facilities for each room. Later in the nineteenth century, these rooms were specified as a hall or dining room (Sw. *sal*), a bedroom (Sw. *sovrum*) and a drawing room (Sw. *förmak*). This probably also reflects how the rooms were originally used, indicating a diverse and more complex social and residential pattern. The building of this house was commissioned around 1795 by a bookkeeper, Johan Peter Frisk, and it is reasonable to assume that it was meant for housing middle-class families.[38]

The heating facilities were obviously important in the construction of the house at Hunnebergsgatan 30. In Swedish towns, tiled stoves were introduced during the seventeenth and eighteenth centuries. It was a major innovation in heating technology, contributing to a general improvement of indoor comfort. In addition to that, the tiled stove improved the possibilities of individual heating of many separate rooms. In several towns, the use of this heating technique spread during the seventeenth century, but important social and regional differences can be observed. In Linköping, only upper elite houses, like the bishop's residence, provide examples of tiled stoves in the seventeenth century. In Kalmar, on the other hand, tiled stoves appear also in more humble houses in the outskirts of the town even in the second half of the seventeenth century.[39] Here, the introduction of tiled stoves seems to be almost contemporary with the introduction of separate kitchens. In the eighteenth century, the technology was further developed with a front fire opening and a complicated system of heating channels, further facilitating heating for separate rooms. This enabled a more complex and diversified spatial structure. Thus, the development of heating techniques contributed to possible separation and seclusion, and thereby enhanced the potentiality for privacy. This technology eventually spread to all social groups in society.

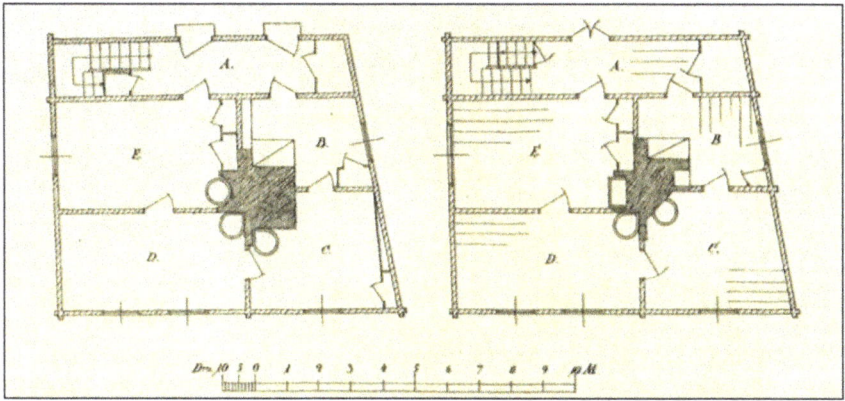

Figure 7.11 Hunnebergsgatan 30, Linköping, the house plan comprising four rooms and a central chimney stack, with heating facilities in each room. After Cnattingius 1929.

Separation between street space and the inner yards

Parallel to the changes in household and cohabitation structures and the development of more complex houses, the structure of town plots and the location of houses on the plots changed as well. According to a reconstruction of the two plots at Ågatan in Linköping from the early seventeenth century, the small two-room dwelling houses stood in an inward-oriented position in the middle of the plot. Various outhouses, stables and storehouses were oriented towards the street, and there were cultivation areas at the rear end of the plots. This type of structure has been documented in many Swedish towns since the Middle Ages, and it was still present in seventeenth-century Linköping.

During the seventeenth and early eighteenth centuries, the pattern changed, and residential buildings became more commonly oriented towards the street. Various examples from both Linköping and other Swedish towns indicate a difference between gable-fronted houses, and a later introduced orientation with the long side of the residential house facing the street. These successive changes brought about a stricter separation of the plot from the street. They created a deeper structure where access to the plots was possible only through a sequence of different steps. These tendencies also appear in the plot boundaries, developing from elusive plot markers, towards more manifest physical barriers.[40]

When houses were relocated from the plot centre towards the street and when houses were built larger, extended and possibly provided with a second floor, a novel type of street space emerged, and a new relation between the streets and the inner yards developed. Figure 7.12 shows Ågatan in Linköping as it was built in

Figure 7.12 Ågatan 7–9, Linköping, with residential buildings along the street, from 18th century. Photo ca 1930, Bengt Cnattingius. Archive of Östergötland's museum.

the early eighteenth century. It is a completely different street space compared to the reconstruction of the plots in 1620.[41] What we meet in the eighteenth century is a closed street space where the inner yard is entirely closed off from the street. The residential building on Hunnebergsgatan 7 (Figures 7.6 and 7.7) exemplifies a similar structure. These tendencies have been discussed as a two-directional movement, constructing a distance between the street and the inner plot, and at the same time transforming the private life to be presented towards the street, and thus made public.[42]

The change was gradual, but in the end quite dramatic. It resulted in a completely transformed urban landscape, from an open to a closed structure. The main residential houses created a barrier between street and inner yards, which were no longer visible from the street. To enter the main residential house, you would usually have to first enter the inner yard through a doorway or a gate. This added to the many passages, such as vestibules, hallways, and staircases, between the outdoor spaces and the residential spaces. In addition, when inside the house, you would no longer enter directly into one main room but encountered a more complicated and diverse set of different rooms and spaces. Again, this does not prove that privacy was practised, perceived or sought for, but these material structures provided physical elements of separation and seclusion. Just as different rooms and apartments inside the houses became more clearly separated and possible to delimit from each other, the streets, the residential houses and the inner yards became more clearly separated and delimited spaces.

Spaces for elite sociability

So far, we have focused on the less conspicuous dwellings of the humbler urban population. During the eighteenth century, new types of houses were introduced also among the urban elite, especially in the town centre. The layout usually included six rooms, distributed in two rows as shown in Figure 7.14, with one large central room (Sw. *sal*) and smaller rooms on the sides. The first known examples are from the late seventeenth century, but after the great fire in 1700 that destroyed a large part of Linköping, several new houses of this type were built there.[43] They represent an architectural innovation and have been interpreted as an example of inspiration from French elite buildings. In Sweden, this style was first introduced in the mid-seventeenth century at the manors of the aristocracy and only slightly later spread to urban contexts.[44]

This type of building allowed for an elaborate distinction between different rooms and spaces with different functions and characters. This also becomes evident in the way the rooms were named. In the centre of the building, there was a larger hall (Sw. *sal*), designed for socialization, for receiving guests and possibly even for public events. There was a vestibule (Sw. *förstuga*), from which the *sal* could be entered, and from which it was possible to enter other rooms as well. There was a kitchen, one or several bedrooms, preferably on one side of the *sal*, and there were other rooms (Sw. *kammare* and *förmak*) preferably on the other side of the *sal*, probably used as parlours and

Figure 7.13 The Barkman house, Apotekaregatan, Linköping, an upper-class building, later converted into a grocer's shop. Photo from the 1920's. Archive of Östergötland's museum.

drawing rooms for more intimate socialization. These more advanced buildings often comprised a file of rooms, mostly interpreted as drawing-room, hall and bedroom, situated in the inner part of the house but oriented towards the street. These rooms for socialization were made public and well apprehended from the street, especially when illuminated for dinners and dances, but at the same time expressing a social distance towards the public street – to be on display but inaccessible for the non-invited.

It can easily be imagined how the spatial structure of these new elite houses corresponded to the specific expectations of polite socialization, but the more elaborate room structure of these larger houses represents more than that. Written sources sometimes provide further insights in the roles of different rooms. A probate inventory from 1820 describes the various rooms in the two-storey house at Storgatan 58, today known as the von Lingen house (Sw. *von Lingens gård*). This house comprises a bedroom but also a special room for the young ladies (sw. *frökenkammare*). The latter could refer to the daughters of the family but could also refer to other unmarried young ladies sometimes present in the household of von Lingen. One room, on the upper floor next to the library, was identified as the Baron's drawing room (Sw. *baronens förmak*). There was also a separate room for the female servants, on the ground floor, and one for male servants, probably located in a separate building.[45] In this way, some of these houses, where large urban elite households resided, also represent a more elaborated separation within the domestic sphere itself and a more manifest spatial dissociation between household members.

These new and more spatially complex houses were primarily built for the urban elite, and they were spatially organized to allow for public sociability. They were also homes providing secluded spaces into which you could *invite* people (preferably into

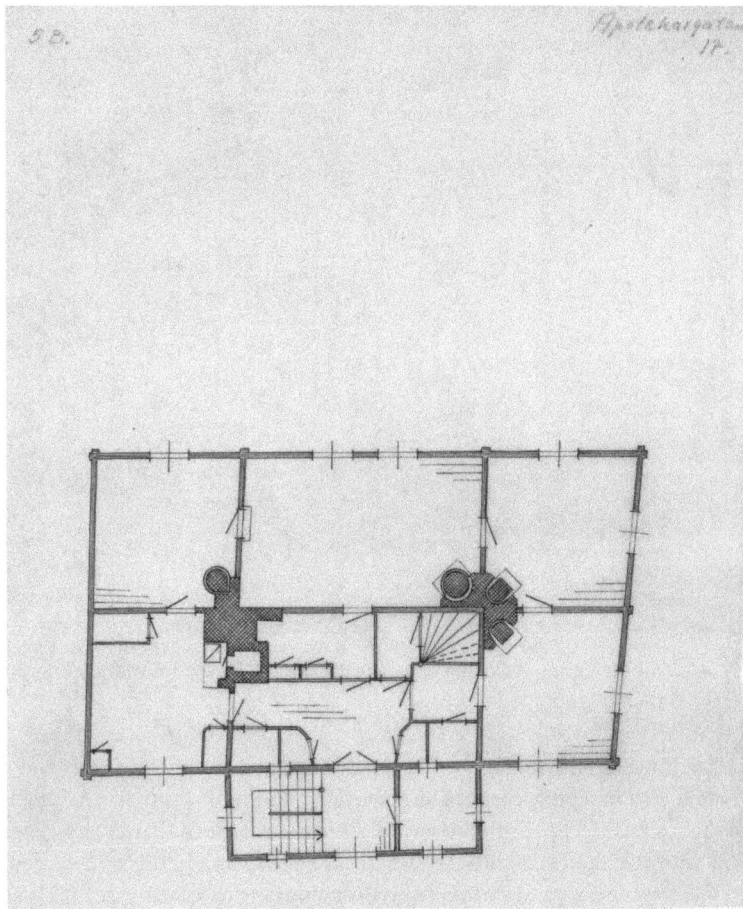

Figure 7.14 The plan of the Barkman house, Apotekaregatan, Linköping, comprising six rooms, with a broader central part including a hall. Documentation in the 1920's. comprising six rooms, with a broader central part including a vestibule and a bigger sal. Archive of Östergötland's museum.

specific rooms) for intimate and secluded sociability. They represent a built structure very different from the kind of spatial and social organization primarily identified by Joachim Eibach as 'the open house' (*das offene Haus*), where privacy was not really a distinct feature or even an option. On the other hand, even this new type of house could in many ways be open. They could be the place of larger social gatherings. One of the buildings in Linköping where we know that larger public events took place was the house at Nygatan 31. A Petter Schenling, a former bookkeeper at the castle, later a merchant and burgomaster, presumably built it. In the late eighteenth and early nineteenth centuries, his two unmarried daughters, Maria and Rebecka Schenling, resided there. They organized various public assemblies, dances and other events, often advertised in the local newspaper. At one time, their garden was even the scene of a balloon ascent.[46]

Figure 7.15 The Linköping Assembly and Theatre House. Photo Bild Linköping, Archive of Östergötland's museum.

In 1806, however, the material and spatial conditions for public events and public socialisation in Linköping changed dramatically. This was when the Assembly and Theatre house (*Assamblé- och spektakelhuset*) was established. It was organized as a company with shareholders (with the bishop as one of them). In this house assemblies, dances, theatre, concerts and various types of entertainment were organized. There was a restaurant and a café, among other things. The organizers explicitly declared that the space was aimed to be a house for 'refined and decent sociability', where all respectable people from different classes, also those of modest circumstances, could take part. And, so they announced, this meant that assemblies and other gatherings could from now on take place in a public building instead of private homes. In the future, no one would have to individually bear the costs for inviting people into their homes, and no one should any longer have to run the risk of being disturbed in their household duties.[47]

Conclusion

The cases presented here exemplify how the built structures and spatial organization of Linköping changed during the eighteenth century. Some processes of change can certainly be traced back to the seventeenth century, but it is during the eighteenth century, and especially towards the second half of that century, that a more general transformation of the built environment becomes evident. This was a time of deep change also in household structures and cohabitation patterns, and there are reasons to believe that these processes were closely related. Houses were built larger, with more rooms and with more complex inner structures. New building practices, room plans and architectural elements accentuated both the separation between the inside and the outside of houses, and the spatial separation between different indoor spaces.

There are many examples illustrating how spatial seclusion was created, often on a small scale and with small measures. In most cases, seclusion was neither complete nor absolute, but seclusion certainly became a more prominent dimension of the built structures. This also applies to the street space and the demarcations between streets, dwelling houses and inner yards. These structures were made deeper, with more manifest material demarcations between different spaces and with more elaborated physical passages between them. In many cases, these changes indicate a substantial step away from an *open house* order towards a new type of closed and partitioned buildings, connected with new cohabitation patterns and potentially also providing spaces for novel social practices. It should, however, be admitted that not all changes necessarily eliminated openness. New modes of openness and possible variations in openness are also part of this transformation.

New types of spaces for both public and more exclusive and intimate socialization developed. This is closely related to the process of increasing specialization and separation between rooms in the dwelling houses: for example, kitchens, bedrooms, entrance halls, parlours and drawing rooms. In addition, rooms could no longer be entered directly from outside and it was possible to close several doors to the outside. Rooms could be entered without going through other rooms. It is important to be aware that even small measures can represent huge steps towards a certain degree of privacy. Consider, for example, the difference between living in a room into which other people would regularly enter or just pass through, and living in a room where you could close a door and where other people may need to ask for permission to enter, even if that room was shared with other people. Many of the observed changes, however, enhanced not only seclusion but also connections and flexibility. Entrance halls, staircases, and the more complicated sequences of doors certainly provided for separation and seclusion. On the other hand, rooms, doors and entrance halls could not only be closed and separated, but they could also be open and connected.

Many of the changes discussed here are more manifest and easily observable in the residential houses of the urban elite, but it is important to notice that these tendencies also appear in more modest houses. It has not been our primary aim to explain systematically the causes behind these changes. There is a multitude of possible reasons for why the built structure of eighteenth-century Linköping was transformed; for example, new building techniques, new aesthetic ideals and population pressure might have influenced the change. Our focus has been on distinct effects of specific modifications of the built material structures: increased spatial separation and enhanced potentialities for seclusion. It is, however, clear that certain conceptualizations of private and public spaces were present in Linköping around 1800, and that at least some individuals took action in order to affect the urban spatial organization according to such perceptions.

As a provincial town in northern Europe, Linköping was by no means a solitaire in the development of increasing spatial separation and seclusion in the eighteenth century. It was not lagging extremely far behind either. Linköping confirms that fundamental spatial transformations of the residential and domestic spheres were not unique to the grand metropolises of Europe. It was not exclusive for the upper classes either. Our observations confirm the importance of including peripheries, small towns and various social classes in analyses of how privacy developed. They also confirm the necessity of close and detailed examinations of specific historical contexts in order to fully grasp the dynamics and variations of these transitions.

Notes

1   This chapter is part of the research project 'House and Household in Early Modern Swedish Towns 1600–1850', generously funded the Berit Wallenberg Foundation and Brandförsäkringsverket's foundation for research into building history. The project has been headed by Göran Tagesson and Dag Lindström, with Per Cornell as scientific advisor.
2   Tagesson and Lindström 2016; Tagesson, Lindström, Hallgren and Linderson 2020b.
3   Lindström and Tagesson (2022) 2021.
4   Lindberg 1946.
5   For a more detailed presentation of sources and methods, see Lindström and Tagesson 2022.
6   E.g. Gunn and Morris 2001; Arnade, Howell and Simons 2002; Stobart, Hann and Morgan 2007; Navickas 2016; Laitinen 2017; van den Heuvel 2019.
7   Rau 2019, 14–28.
8   Hillier and Hanson 1984; Trigger 1989; Parker Pearson and Richards 1994; Tilley 1994; Johnson 2010; Beaudry 2015.
9   Lefebvre 1991. Many of these thoughts have been further developed by the American geographer Edward W. Soja. Soja 1996.
10 Schlögel 2003, 14; Gunn 2001; Stock 2015, 5–10; Kingston 2010; Massey 2015, 9–15.
11 Jerram 2013, 413–18; Stock 2015, 7–8; Laitinen 2017, 24–6.
12 Ibid., 411–12.
13 Massey 2015, 9–15.
14 Habermas 1962. See also Sennett 1977.
15 Brewer 1995, 8–9.
16 Ariès 1989.
17 Heyl 2004, 1, 21, 136, 157–212.
18 Johnson 1993; Johnson 2010, 87–112.
19 Eibach 2011, 646–55.
20 Mitchell 2018.
21 Concerning the interaction between shopping and consumption and the developments of the home, the domestic sphere and personal identity, see, for example, Ponsonby 2006; Stobart, Hann and Morgan 2007; Hussey and Ponsonby 2008.
22 Pardailhé-Galabrun 1991.
23 Sarti 2002, 142–7.
24 Vickery 2008.
25 Gejvall 1988; Paulsson 1972.
26 Lindström 2020, 233–7.

27 Lindström 2020, 239–40.
28 Lindström 2020, 237–9.
29 One of few exceptions is de Groot, Devos and Schmidt 2015.
30 Lindström 2020, 237–9.
31 Ibid., 239–41.
32 Lindström and Tagesson 2022.
33 Tagesson 2016, 174, 176–87, 194–7.
34 Tagesson, Lindström, Linderson and Hallgren 2020a, 88–93.
35 Ibid., 74–7.
36 Ibid., 35–40; Tagesson 2021b, 83–9.
37 Lindström and Tagesson 2016, 220–2; Lindström and Tagesson 2022.
38 Tagesson and Lindström 2016; Tagesson, Lindström, Hallgren and Linderson 2020b; Tagesson 2021b.
39 Tagesson and Jeppsson 2015a; Tagesson and Jeppsson 2015b; Tagesson and Jeppsson 2016.
40 Tagesson and Nordström 2012, 86–90.
41 Tagesson, Lindström, Åkesson, Linderson and Hallgren 2020, 75–9.
42 Thomasson 1997.
43 Tagesson 2021a.
44 Hofrén 1937; Cederlund 1997, 95, 141, 143.
45 Tagesson, Lindström, Hallgren and Linderson 2020c, 67–9.
46 Lindström 2013, 150–1.
47 Lindström 2013; Lindström 2016, 140–7.

In death, nothing is private!:
Public registration of the private home

Pernille Ulla Knudsen

On Saturday, 29 December 1798, the funeral procession for the deceased *gehejmeraadinde*[1] Margrethe Elisabeth Stampe set off. The entourage departed from her mansion in Frederiksholms Canal, Copenhagen, and processed the 700 metres to St Peter's German Church, where the family's burial chapel awaited Margrethe's body.[2] The entourage consisted of seven horse-drawn carriages. The bells of St Peter's Church rang out, and they were likely heard all the way back at the mansion in the icy, snow-covered capital. The funeral cortège was escorted by four police officers who had been seconded from their other duties expressly for this purpose. The procession then slowly passed the shopkeepers who had gathered in the square in front of the town hall.

For four parade days before the procession, Madame Stampe's body rested in a double coffin of oak that had been placed in the large hall of her residence, which was completely covered in black cloth for this occasion. The body of the *gehejmeraadinde* was wrapped in a white shroud with laces and long white gloves. The stairs leading up to the great hall were clad in black. Accounts of the funeral costs mentioned sixty-four boxes of wax candles that were used to illuminate the otherwise carbon-black staircase and parade hall. The accounts also mention the following items: the oilcloth that was placed under her body, the paper shavings and pins that helped maintain the form and shape of the deceased, and the spiced water, spices and spirits intended to purify the air within the covered black hall.

In death, nothing is private. All of the expenses for Madame Stampe's funeral were carefully recorded and accounted for. The price for her funeral totalled an impressive 3,161 *rigsdaler* (rdl.).[3] The entirety of Stampe's funeral ritual well attests to the fact that she was a member of the highest level of the elite in Denmark-Norway. Despite this, Margrethe Stampe has not attracted any significant historical interest. Scholars have been far more interested in her husband, Henrik Stampe, and his public work as a senior official in the absolutist Danish-Norwegian central administration. Nevertheless, it was Margrethe Stampe's private estate that, after her death, made it financially possible for her husband's nephew, Holger Stampe (1754–1827), to enter the nobility as the baron of Stampenborg.

The purpose of this article is to demonstrate how one can use the extant records produced by the public administration of the probate system in order to illuminate aspects of the private household that have traditionally formed a fundamental element in the scholarly articulation of the 'private' during the early modern period. This article, therefore, is a micro-historical study of the division of Margrethe Stampe's estate after her death, and its aim is to examine how far one can reconstruct a specific household. This reconstruction follows the meticulous comparison of the statement of contents for the division of her estate on the one hand, with the property assessments of the deceased's mansion in Frederiksholm Canal, which she acquired in 1792, on the other. We can supplement this source material with other administrative archives, such as auction protocols, wills, marriage contracts, church registers, censuses and guild protocols, as well as with contemporary diaries and newspapers.

The probate records for the *gehejmeraadinde* are found in the Copenhagen Probate Commission's executor cases. These records consist of an execution protocol numbering 188 pages, as well as a myriad of loose appendices and overviews that made up the registration and assessment processes for the estate's significant volume of movables.[4] At the Stampe family's private archive, however, we additionally find an entire archival box with private documents from the estate division after Margrethe Stampe's death, which provides us with a unique opportunity to supplement the public archives.[5]

The Danish archives for probate administration are an important source for biographical, cultural, social and economic history, and probate documents have been instrumental in producing detailed historical studies.[6] However, not all probate proceedings took place in the public probate courts. When, as was the case with Stampe, the couple had made a will, it was the couple themselves who appointed the executors who would take charge of the division of their goods. Only once the division was complete did the probate court need to be informed, whereupon inheritance tax would be paid to the state.[7] The executors of the deceased's estate, who were responsible for seeing through the deceased person's last wishes, generally kept thorough documentation of everything they did. The abundance of such material creates extremely favourable conditions when it comes to conducting micro-historical studies of individual people.

Following one of the main tracks of this present volume, which pursues the private in a spatial context, this article aims to reconstruct the home of the *gehejmeraadinde* as a sort of giant, mental dollhouse. It does so by comparing the two house contents statements of the mansion's furniture – one itemizing what was sold at auction, the other itemizing what the heirs wanted to keep – with the property assessment from the fire insurance policy.[8] Based on these documents, we can prepare a reconstruction of the grounds of the entire property on Frederiksholms Canal, along with floor plans for each of the mansion's three floors (see Figures 2–5).[9]

Margrethe Stampe was one of the wealthiest women in Denmark-Norway, and the layout of her mansion was a clear expression of the interior design preferences of the elite in the late eighteenth century, at a time when those preferences wavered on the edge between rococo and neoclassical styles. Her fortune came from her parents, but she had diligently and competently contributed to the growth of her estate, both while she was married and as a widow. Yet unlike Hampton Court or Soane's house in London, the original interior of the mansion under discussion in this article no longer exists.[10] Fortunately, the interiors of other distinguished Copenhagen mansions from the period still survive, and the studies of these have been invaluable for the present article. These studies have made it possible to compare the unique information contained in the specific probate records with other stately homes of the time, and thus have enabled some more general conclusions.[11] Since the information on the Stampe mansion cannot explicitly be linked to wider European developments in interior design, no attempt has been made to draw comparisons with similar studies of European mansions. However, Amanda Vickery's classic work, *Behind Closed Doors: At Home in Georgian England* (2009), has been a source of inspiration.

A basic precondition to understand a private home is to familiarize one self with its inhabitants. In the case of Margrethe Stampe, this is particularly important because the following case study will challenge the traditional scholarly view of the private home as a private space.

Who was Margrethe Elisabeth Stampe?

Margrethe Elisabeth was born in 1727 as the youngest of three daughters to the silk and cloth merchant, Michael Grøn (1685–1742), and to Elsabe Dorothea Krug (1700–1774). The couple originally came from Lübeck (Germany) and in 1719 they settled in Copenhagen, where Michael Grøn became a member of the Silk and Clothing Traders' Company.[12] In 1726, Michael Grøn bought a large merchant's estate in the centre of Copenhagen that faced the market square, Amagertorv.[13] However, the Grøn family lived in the modern building that faced Østergade; Michael Grøn had this house purpose-built, and it was one of the very few townhouses in Copenhagen that had the honour of being reproduced in Thurah's large, prestigious work, *Den Danske Vitruvius* (1746–9).[14] After Michael Grøn's death in 1742, his wife took over his position in the company, and continued the cloth trade until December 1747.[15]

It was in this environment that Margrethe grew up, alone with an enterprising mother and as a member of the economically elite group of foreigners living in Copenhagen. Such an upbringing no doubt shaped her sense of self-determination, and allowed her to develop the economic and financial skill set that would serve her so well in life. The skills of accountancy and the assessment of value, which were necessary for business success, were widely recognized in the eighteenth century as those that women might acquire.[16] Her mother, in 1750, negotiated the marriage contract between the 23-year-old Margrethe and the 44-year-old secretary of the Danish Foreign Service, Joachim Gustav Klinggraf (1706–60).[17] Their childless marriage lasted ten years until Klinggraf's death.[18] After this, Margrethe took over the joint estate and moved back to her mother's house; as a widow, she gained legal control over her own property. Margrethe was now thirty-three, and could start a new family, perhaps even with a spouse of the same age this time. Gossip about potential suitors can be found in the diary of the high-ranking official, Bolle Willum Luxdorph, one of the key political and personal sources for Copenhagen's history in the second half of the eighteenth century.[19]

Nevertheless, Margrethe lived with her mother until the latter's death in 1774.[20] After that, Margrethe acquired full control as the sole heir over the Grøn family's enormous estate. She chose to remain a widow following her first marriage. It is, therefore, remarkable that Margrethe, in 1776 and at the age of forty-eight, chose to enter into a new marriage with Henrik Stampe, fifteen years her senior; Stampe, like her, had lived alone as a widower for many years after the death in childbirth of his

Figure 8.1 Margrethe Elisabeth Stampe (1727–98). Posthumous pastel painting by the great Danish portrait painter, Jens Juel (1745–1802) as a preliminary study for a later oil painting. Statens Museum for Kunst.

first wife and child in 1761.[21] The son of a rural dean from North Jutland, in 1759 Henrik Stampe received a personal nobility patent after working for many years as a senior lawyer in the Danish-Norwegian central administration. By 1774, he acquired the title of *gehejmeraad,* which placed him among the highest rank of the elite.

The marriage contract between Margrethe and Henrik gave each spouse joint ownership over the family property, and named each party as the other's universal heir. The surviving party thus gained full ownership and disposal of everything that the deceased had left, without risk from any legal claims that may be brought by the deceased party's other heirs.[22] The 1799 division shows that Margrethe and Henrik kept their personal property completely separate during their marriage. Yet, on the other hand, their joint will from 1787 stated that at least 192,000 rdl. of the joint property should subsequently go towards the establishment of the barony of Stampenborg, for Henrik Stampe's oldest nephew.

Margrethe's second marriage attracted public attention. On 1 December 1775, the front page of the newspaper read that their engagement had been declared at the royal court.[23] It was likely something of an upheaval for the clothier's daughter. Nevertheless, after the wedding, the couple rented one of the bigger noble mansions in Copenhagen, Greve Lerche's Mansion, which was close to the royal castle and to Henrik Stampe's workplace in the Danish Chancellery.[24] Margrethe sold the property on Amagertorv in 1780, and the total value of the mortgage bonds in the sale was calculated at 43,625 rdl.[25] The income from the sale went directly into her separate property.

In 1784, Henrik Stampe became prime minister, thereby joining the government of the double monarchy Denmark-Norway. This placed the Stampe couple, who were both of non-noble blood, at the pinnacle of the Danish social elite's ranking system. At the same time, Stampe had his first apoplectic seizure, and he gained no real political influence in government.[26] Henrik Stampe died at the age of 76 in July 1789. On 20 July 1789, he was buried in the Grøn family chapel alongside his long-deceased in-laws, Margrethe's first husband and her two sisters.[27]

Margrethe Stampe once again had full control over her estate, which now also included her deceased husband's private estate, valued at nearly 100,000 rdl.[28] Yet the late Henrik's estate constituted only a fraction of Margrethe's wealth: according to the final estate inventory from 1799, her total wealth at the time of death amounted to 664,381 rdl.[29] It seems like in the years immediately following Henrik Stampe's death, Margrethe disposed of most of his property contents. However, she kept the securities and his extensive collection of medals. Henrik Stampe is largely invisible in the executor's estate after his widow's death in 1798, and there are very few personal traces of him in the contents of the probate case.[30]

On 9 December 1791, at a public auction, the *gehejmeraadinde* bought the baroque mansion in Frederiksholms Canal, with a direct view of the Royal Palace. She paid the cash purchase price of 22,150 rdl.[31] Margrethe Stampe was sixty-four when she moved into her own home in early 1792, and it was here that she lived until her death in 1798.[32] A long-standing chest weakness gave her time to get her business in order; the last testamentary changes to hers and Henrik's common will from 1787 are dated only three weeks before her death.

Margrethe's mansion

The estate that Margrethe Stampe bought comprised several buildings. The actual mansion itself consisted of a building that measured 34 metres by 11.5 metres. Three separate floors had a total area of 1,129 square metres; these floors consisted of a high basement (mezzanine) with windows facing the street, and the first and second floors each had eleven large bays for windows. A 4-metre-wide gate led into the courtyard, and it bisected the two lower floors into two separate sections. In the courtyard, two large side-buildings formed an extension from the main building, with each of these wings having a total area of nearly 500 metres². The large garden, which had a fountain and a pavilion, stretched 100 metres back into the estate, and its 2,400 square metres formed a significant proportion of the total estate size of roughly 3,800 metres². Finally, two minor properties with an entrance through the street Ny Vestergade also belonged to the estate. One was used as stable for six horses and three carriages (no. 319), and the other was used as a warehouse (no. 321).

We know of these details because of the property's fire insurance policy, which provides a highly descriptive account of the estate.[33] *Kiøbenhavns Brandforsikring* (Copenhagen Fire Insurance) was Denmark's first insurance company. It was established in 1731 following a big 1728 fire in Copenhagen that destroyed more than 30 per cent of the city's houses.[34] According to the insurance company's instructions, two building experts carried out the valuation under the supervision of a member of the insurance company's board.[35] It seems likely, therefore, that the opposing interests between the customer purchasing the insurance and the company providing it created a good basis for a balanced assessment.[36]

These records also contain information that is relevant when studying the physical frameworks in which concepts of privacy might have developed – and this is true regardless of whether those records describe room decoration within large mansions or that of the many single-room apartments located in the city's slums. Otherwise, one tends only to catch glimpses of these places when the private home has been exposed to public scrutiny following some disturbance, such as in court cases. But when one looks at private life or privacy based on descriptions and testimonies of court cases, one is left with a conflict-orientated view of private life in the past, and our impression of the past becomes too skewed towards issues about the violation of privacy. Take, for example, Amanda Vickery's interesting study of Old Bailey procedures from the principal criminal court in London. She uses court records 'to open the door of the London house to consider how internal

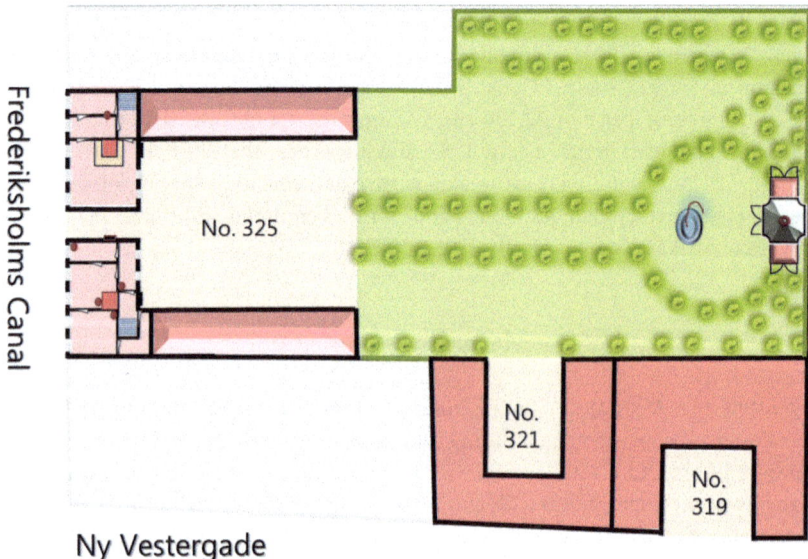

Figure 8.2 Layout of the entire property, with the main building (lower floor) facing Frederiksholms Canal. Towards the courtyard we find the two independent side buildings, which were rented out. Behind was the large private garden with a pavilion and a fountain. The planting is 'freely' reproduced according to J. H. Rawert's cadastral map of Copenhagen from 1800. The two properties in Ny Vestergade contained the stable (no. 319) and a warehouse (no. 321). The model is drawn on the basis of the information provided in the property valuation in Københavns Brandforsikringsselskab. Knudsen 2020.

space was conceptualized, demarcated and policed'.[37] In cases of breaking and entering, she illustrates the inviolability of the domestic threshold and efforts to protect private property, as well as highlighting the major role that locks seem to have played in defining the private home.[38] However, in cases concerning property crimes it is important to clarify under what conditions the stolen goods had been taken from their owner if one is to determine the nature of the crime. Breaking and entering, for instance, is a more serious crime than simple theft. The issue of locking doors, therefore, has a specific, forensic purpose within a court record, making it uncertain how far locks (or not) can be considered as essential when defining the thresholds of the private home. On the other hand, in reading within the insurance policy for the Stampe mansion, for example, that all the doors in the home had locks, one acquires factual information about the actual physical ability to create potentially private spaces within the 1,129 square metres of the main building.[39]

The basement

The property valuation worked from the ground-up, beginning with the basement. The basement had two large rooms and two smaller ones, all with tiled stoves. It also had plank floors, plastered ceilings and windows that faced on to both the street and the courtyard. A covered staircase descending from the courtyard led to an entrance hall, which granted access to the basement's storeroom, and also had a staircase leading up to the first floor.

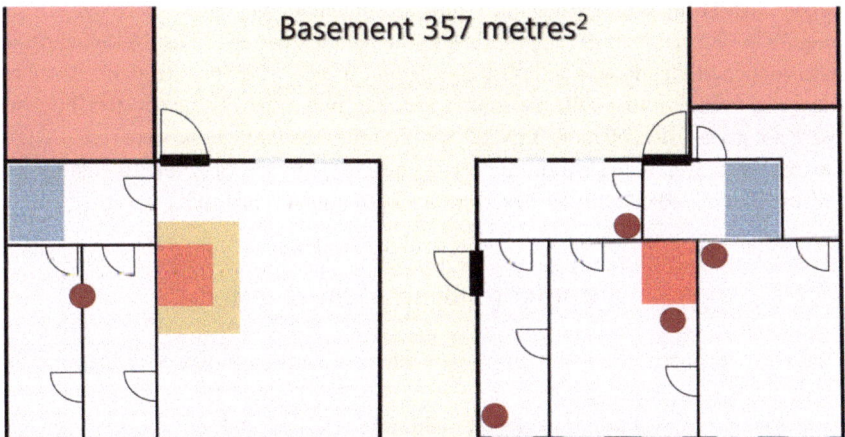

Figure 8.3 Floor plan of the two basements divided by the gate-room that ran through the main building. The right basement was used as a residence for the servants. Descent into the left basement was possible from the courtyard, and led directly into the 100 metres2 large kitchen. Behind the kitchen was access to a distribution room that led into two chambers, and to the only through-going staircase in the mansion. The red circles indicate the location of tile-stoves, while the red squares represent the chimneys. The model is drawn on basis of the information in the property valuation in Københavns Brandforsikringsselskab. Knudsen 2020.

The storeroom housed the stocked furniture. All this furniture – chests of drawers, tables, mirrors and chairs – was described as 'old'.[40] But because there was so much 'old furniture', one must assume that these items had been collected in this part of the basement for the express purpose of registering them for the subsequent public auction. The storage of old furniture in this basement means it is impossible to form an impression of what the original decor in this part of the mansion would have looked like. On the other hand, all this old furniture suggests that the rest of the *gehejmeraadinde's* home was decorated in line with the latest fashions, and that she had probably acquired numerous items of new furniture when decorating the mansion. Thus, even though the basement furniture was described as old, this need not necessarily mean that it was worn. The change between the rococo and neoclassical styles was so radical that all Danish interior design prior to 1790 could be described as old by 1799. A mansion's interior design was primarily meant to display the owner's wealth, and it was thus largely intended to impress guests, rather than to satisfy the mistress's personal tastes.[41]

The following is based on Thomas Lyngby's definition of the three types of quarters (*lejlighedstyper*) that can be found in Danish stately homes from the middle of the eighteenth century. I shall briefly describe the three types here, which can subsequently be used when referring to different sections of the mansion. The first type consisted of the *paradelejlighed* (parade quarters), which from the 1750s onward was designed to demonstrate the owner's economic and cultural prestige.[42] The second type was comprised of the *selskabelige lejlighed* (quarters for entertainment), which flourished during the second half of the eighteenth century, and constituted an alternative space that did not require the formal manners appropriate to the parade quarters.[43] Finally, the mansions also contained the master's and mistress's *personlige lejligheder* (private quarters), where they could retire from 'public life' activities in their mansions. Private quarters, however, were not necessarily any more 'private' than the other sections: guests were received here as well. Moreover, it was within the private quarters, in particular, that the master and mistress depended on intimate help from their servants several times a day.[44]

The other residents of the mansion

The right section of the basement most likely formed the residence for the servants. The narrow room facing the gate – and with its own exit – must have housed the porter, who was also accessible to outsiders at night, when the large oak gate had been securely closed. Beyond the porter, the staff comprised ten people: a postilion, a groom and two servants, a cook, a housemaid, a chambermaid, the married couple Poul Gundestrup and Louise Berg – a servant and chambermaid respectively, who, after the death of the Margrethe Stampe, served as housekeepers with responsibility for the other staff – and a coachman. The household also included the coachman's wife, and the couple must have lived in the building on Ny Vestergade, where the stable was located.

The large rooms in the right basement facing the street may have been used by the four male servants. The last, somewhat smaller space that faced the courtyard was probably used by the couple of Gundestrup and Berg. Usually, servants left their employment once they married. Their continued employment at the mansion must have been by special agreement with the *gehejmeraadinde*. Two canopied beds with a green damask curtain were in the basement.[45] These were the most expensive beds listed in the inventory.[46] Maybe Margrethe Stampe had left her old marriage beds to the couple? It is at least a nice thought that the expensive beds ended up in the servants' quarters!

In the first preserved Danish census from 1787, we find the names of the residents of Lerche's mansion, where the Stampe couple had lived. In addition to the Stampe couple, thirteen servants lived there.[47] Most of these servants were still in the service of Margrethe Stampe at the time of her death. Some of them may even have gone back to her childhood home. They had experienced the changes in Margrethe Stampe's life as members of her household for many years. The *gehejmeraadinde* thus did not live alone in the mansion. In addition to managing her own economic business, she had the day-to-day responsibilities over her eleven employees. She had also rented out the two large side houses in the courtyard behind the mansion. One was rented to the couple Antoinette and Peter Uldall – Peter was one of Henrik Stampe's old colleagues from the Supreme Court, and Antoinette grew up within the same social circles as Margrethe Stampe. This couple perhaps also made use of the private garden and socialized with Margrethe. At any rate, there was a financial relationship between Margrethe and Mrs Uldahl's family, who were among Margrethe's business associates.[48]

Margrethe's servants continued to be employed by their late mistress's two principal heirs until May 1799 – i.e. for some five months after Margrethe's funeral – in order to prepare the house for its sale and for the liquidation of its contents. On the day that the servants left the mansion, the heirs paid all of them a double wage.[49] Three weeks before her death, Margrethe Stampe had also supplemented her earlier will from 1787. Among the persons she considered in her revised will were her servants, all of whom were granted a lifelong pension, roughly equivalent to the annual salary that they had received while in her employment.[50] Two of the servants were over fifty, and the coachman was seventy-one, though he died before the division of the estate was finally settled. The heirs therefore allowed his widow to take over the pension.[51] Costs of medicine from during the coachman's illness also appeared in the heirs' bills, showing something of the obligation they felt towards Margrethe Stampe's staff.[52] The employees were not just anonymous, easily interchangeable servants.

The kitchen region

In the left basement, a covered staircase from the courtyard led directly into the 100 square metres kitchen, which ran all the way from the front to the back of the house, and was the second largest room in the mansion. The same phenomenon can be observed in another of Copenhagen's large mansions, Gyldenløve's Palace, which was built in the same period.[53] The Stampe mansion's kitchen was fully equipped. The chimney wall was dominated by the large fireplace with a built-in oven, eight stoves and a built-in cauldron. An open-brick chimney shaft hung over the fireplace, and the kitchen equipment recorded in the inventory shows that the fireplace also could prepare a whole roasted pig on a skewer. Kitchen stoves only became common in Copenhagen during the nineteenth century, and thus the Stampe mansion kitchen was a modern one for the standards of the time. The kitchen's interior went back to the previous owner, and had been installed before 1779.[54]

The kitchen region was the mansion's largest workplace. The inventory lists contain a wealth of information about the kitchen's interiors, which well attests to the fact that most of the housework took place here. There were several washbasins, kettles, tubs, a stool for beating washing, a linen and tablecloth mangle, a napkin press and an iron. The napkin press and iron had certainly been used diligently if the 207 tablecloths and 2,418 napkins registered in the inventories are anything to go by. It was also possible to brew beer, distil alcohol and knead dough in this space, and there were several worktables and kitchen cabinets, in addition to the many shelves and permanent-mounted cabinets mentioned in the property valuation.[55]

The varied metal and wooden kitchenware provides insight into the elegant cuisine on offer at the Stampe mansion. There were moulds for soufflé, terrine, pâté, sugar bread and pudding; there were kettles for broth, pickled pork and fish; other implements such as skewers, baking-trays, carving knives, a coffee roaster, ice-moulds and waffle irons were also mentioned.[56] The annual bill from the royal court confectioner, Michael Aagaard, which is found in the probate records, can be used as a supplementary source. This bill shows that regular supplies of fresh lemons, Spanish wine, sugar bread, macaroon cake, almond cake, vanilla ice cream, macaroni, olive oil and parmesan cheese were all delivered to the mansion.[57] The library contained cookbooks, household books and gardening books, although this hardly meant that Margrethe Stampe herself was responsible for any of these activities.[58]

There were two rooms behind the kitchen, each over 20 square metres, which were used as a larder and as a room for the maids, respectively. At least two beds with fabric curtains were found in the kitchen region; and in the fire insurance assessment from 1779, one of these chambers was referred to as the maids' room.[59] A single bed may have been shared by the two maids, and the other bed may have been used by the cook. A common tiled stove was installed in a partition between the two chambers, which provided heat to both rooms. Finally, another room behind the kitchen contained the single staircase that led to the other floors of the mansion. This staircase formed the main conduit between the kitchen and the rest of the house.

The inventory lists for the kitchen region provide other examples of the kinds of work done in the household. There were two spinning wheels, which indicates that yarn was spun in the mansion. There does not seem to have been a significant level of in-house production, however; the enormous quantities of upscale textiles in the mansion suggest that there was no need for home production. It seems likely, instead, that the spinning wheels were used by the house's servants, who may have spun yarn for their own use. Mentions of a wheelbarrow, a woodcutter's axe, a sawbuck, nail baskets and stepladders also demonstrate that chopping firewood, gardening and other general maintenance activities were included in the normal work routines at the mansion.

First floor

The gatehouse led to the entrance of the two separate sections of the mansion's first floor. On either side of the gate, three stone steps led to a set of double doors with large glass panes. On the right side, the door led into a vestibule that provided access to the other three rooms, as well as a staircase leading up to the second floor.

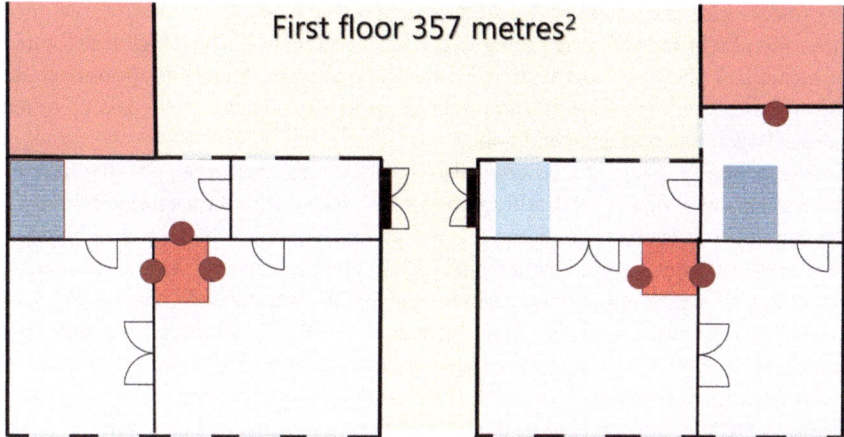

Figure 8.4 Floor plan of the two sections on the first floor. As in the basement, the first floor was bisected into two by the gateway. This floor has both the quarters for entertainment and the gehejmeraadinde's private quarters. The model is drawn on basis of the information in the property valuation in Københavns Brandforsikringsselskab. Knudsen 2020.

The two sections of the first floor were divided into a 'front', consisting of the large halls that faced the street, and some smaller rooms facing the courtyard that formed a kind of 'back' to the large, en suite living rooms. Here, the decor distinguished between what Thomas Lyngby has called 'the essentially different types of social scenes' provided for by the layout of eighteenth-century mansions.[60] By dividing the rooms in this way, 'corridors' were established whereby the servants could work and move around the house without disturbing the mistress or her guests. Similarly, the back rooms created another exit so that people did not need to use the large, en suite rooms as passageways. When combined with the entrance halls, the division of space within the mansion points towards a greater design emphasis on the functionality of different rooms. This represents a key difference separating the decor of baroque mansions from their rococo counterparts. The mansion in Frederiksholms Canal was originally built in the baroque style, but the smaller cabinet rooms that faced the courtyard were added sometime later. The many 'secret' stairways that made it possible to move relatively unseen throughout a rococo mansion cannot be found in other houses on Frederiksholms Canal.[61] Yet the Stampe mansion's first floor, which served as the middle floor, had three separate staircases, two of which in the right-hand section were located very close to each other. The large main staircase that led up from the vestibule to the distinguished second floor of the mansion was reserved for the mistress and her house guests. The back set of stairs connected the first floor of the right section to the basement, and allowed the servants to move back and forth for work, without having to use the main staircase.

Each of the three rooms located in the right-hand section had a large, porcelain-covered tiled stove placed in walled niches, right up against the chimney. To the left of the gate, the first floor consisted of an entrance hall leading to the other rooms of the floor, which mirrored the right-hand section that faced the street. A large, tiled stove was also installed in every room in this left-hand section. The stoves were located in niches and placed on marble tiles. Facing the courtyard, there was a room behind the entrance hall; here, a set of stairs went down to the kitchen regions and up to the house's largest hall on the second floor.

The property valuation records also contain information about the interior decoration and design of the first-floor rooms. Consistent with the fashions of the time, the two upper floors had panels on the lower part of the walls, while the walls between the windows were covered with panels from floor-to-ceiling[62] Above the dados, according to eighteenth-century fashion, the walls were divided into independent panels, each framed by mouldings and friezes. It left the visual impression that each independent panel constituted a separately framed painting. These panels consisted of a canvas-covered frame that provided the foundation for the many different types of wall decoration that competed in the late eighteenth century, and of which the Royal Palace's decor offered such an excellent example.[63]

Wallpaper had been known for a long time, but its use increased exponentially in the latter part of the eighteenth century.[64] This was an international development, so it is unsurprising that one of the highest fashions of the time also influenced Danish interior design. Wallpaper covered the walls on the mansion's first floor: the wallpaper in all the living rooms in the right-hand section was framed by mouldings and friezes, and those located close to the vestibule were even gilded. Various paintings hung above the double doors located between the three rooms on the right-hand side.

The walls of the living rooms in the left wing, on the other hand, were painted. In the largest living room on this side – the one with three window bays – the walls were covered with canvases painted with foliage. In the second living room facing the street, the walls had painted borders. Both these styles of decoration were neoclassical, which became common from the last decade of the eighteenth century.[65]

During the eighteenth century, the salons located within a house's entertainment quarters had become the primary centres for the social activities that went on inside a mansion. These rooms, unsurprisingly, fostered the development of a salon culture. The idea of a 'salon culture' plays a major role in research about the private and the public, and was key in Jürgen Habermas's influential work, *Structural Transformation of the Public Sphere* (1962). This culture developed in the private households of distinguished mansions after the French model. It was often the mistress of the house who acted as the hostess and centre of attention for the societies forming around the salons. In contrast to the parade halls located on a mansion's upper floors, the salons were more accessible for people, mirroring the fact that social conventions in the salons were more intimate and contributed to a sense of equality for its participants.[66] In this context, salon culture should be seen in a much more nuanced light when thinking about discourses of the private home versus the public and political on the one hand, and when thinking about the roles of men and women on the other. In Frederiksholms Canal, the *gehejmeraadinde* was the undisputed hostess. Therefore, it is also interesting to see how she followed the latest and highest fashions in interior design, decorating her first-floor salons with light fabrics.[67]

The two salons were decorated with white and yellow furniture, respectively. The large white living room furniture consisted of a sofa and eight armchairs with white embroidered upholstery, and six further armchairs with embroidered upholstery in a different fabric. Faience plates rested on tray tables, which were probably placed under mirrors between the windows. An alabaster vase stood atop a corner console table, and on the walls hung six bracket lamps in white lacquered frames. The mirror frames and the mouldings framing the wallpapered panels on the walls were gilded. The white salon was also equipped with two harpsichords, making it possible for the mistress and her guests to play duets.

The slightly smaller yellow salon was furnished with four chairs that had open back-rests, and a further six armchairs in a yellow damask fabric. There were also several smaller tables, either painted in yellow or gilded. The three tea tables in the yellow salon give some indication as to the uses of this particular salon. Lighting for the room was provided by a four-armed chandelier that hung from the ceiling, along with the six brass bracket lamps. Together with the gilded mirror frame between the salon's windows – a very yellow impression!

A systematic analysis of the insurance policy and the executor's inventory lists makes it possible to recreate the interior design choices made for the individual rooms. We start to form an image of the salon culture of the time when we can place these many comfortable pieces of furniture, upholstered in their bright, costly fabrics, alongside various musical instruments within a concrete space. The development of a salon culture first took place in the stately homes of the elite, and it was not until the next century that this style of furnishing spread to the homes of the bourgeoisie, where the comforts of the living room made it the standard space for a bourgeois family's salon in the nineteenth-century Victorian house.[68] These bourgeois houses, which in the late 1800s and early 1900s set the norms for ideas about the nuclear family and for ideas about private life within the home, still shape the physical and mental frameworks by which we today understand the concepts of privacy, the private home and the household.

The salons in Margrethe Stampe's first-floor 'entertainment quarters' were arranged according to the new fashion, but these two living rooms cannot be considered as a part of her private life. They were only arranged to receive and entertain guests, and she probably only used them when she had visitors. It is, for instance, clear from the inventories that the mansion's furniture was also equipped with extra canvas covers, which would have protected the furniture when not in use.

On the other, left-hand side of the entrance gate, we find Margrethe Stampe's bedroom, befitted with a throne bed that had an exclusive, red chintz curtain, lined with yellow-patterned silk taffeta. There was also a myriad of storage furniture, which of course included the very large wardrobe of the *gehejmeraadinde* that was registered in the heirs' inventory list. Among other things, seventy-two dresses were mentioned in the inventory, including the forty 'old' and 'useless' silk dresses, valued at only 1–3 rdl. per dress. However, we should probably not take these sums at face value. The low valuation of these dresses likely reflected the efforts taken to avoid paying the full inheritance tax of 4 per cent on what was, in fact, quite a valuable part of the inheritance. Undeniably, dress fashion had changed radically in the 1790s, but even in her old age, the wardrobe of the daughter of a silk and cloth merchant was probably anything but 'old' and 'useless'. While the wages paid to seamstresses to update the many changing tastes in fashion would have been rather insignificant, the dress fabric itself would literally have been worth a fortune. The interest shown by the heirs to the *gehejmeraadinde*'s clothing, however, may also reflect their desire for these items not to be disposed of at a public auction for everyone to buy.

The many pieces of furniture in Margrethe Stampe's private quarters do indicate, not surprisingly, that the rooms may have been used during the day. In the bedroom and the main hall facing the street, which was furnished as a living room, we find the following: an ottoman and twelve chairs, as well as an armchair with red damask covers; ten chairs and two armchairs with red silk cushions; a canapé, four chairs and two stools with red plush covers; and an oak bureau with a cabinet, which was presumably Margrethe Stampe's personal desk. Additionally, there were several small tables, including a card-table and a tea-table fitted with a brass tray and a brass tea box. Gilded mirrors and bracket lamps, in combination with the red furniture, would have given the 67 square metres room a personal look. The volume of furniture indicates that the *gehejmeraadinde* also received visits in her private quarters, but, contrary to earlier traditions, she did not receive visitors in the actual bedchamber, which was a custom no longer considered to be proper behaviour.

Margrethe Stampe's private rooms also housed the cabinet containing her husband's medal collection. At the auction, these were sold for a total sum of 2,269 rdl.; by keeping such costly items within a cupboard in her private room, we may appreciate something of the care that the *gehejmeraadinde* gave to her valuables.[69]

But in thinking about Margrethe's private quarters, it is the red furniture that especially attracts our attention. This furniture was of the comfortable kind, just as in the white and yellow salons, with numerous plush and silk cushions. In considering the mansion as a whole, there were no fewer than eighty pieces of red furniture, which corresponds to nearly 25 per cent of the total volume of furniture. I would suggest that the red furniture should be seen as an expression of Margrethe Stampe's personal taste. However, it should also be noted that a 1777 book about Copenhagen design tastes mentioned red as a fashionable colour for furniture fabrics, and also emphasized that red silk cushions and gilded furniture were in vogue.[70] Earlier in the century, for example, red damask had been very popular, and it was said that within Count Moltke's large rococo mansion, whose interior was completed in 1754, the countess's visiting room was almost entirely decorated in red damask – the walls, the curtains and the furniture.[71] Whereas the yellow and white salons in the right wing of Margrethe Stampe's mansion displayed the latest neoclassical trends in home decor, the red living rooms in her personal quarters can be considered as a more traditional – or even private – choice.

We also learn of another item of furniture that was located in Margrethe's personal quarters: a wicker cot. Such a bed may have been placed in Margrethe's bedroom, or in the room with the staircase that faced the courtyard; its presence could suggest that Margrethe Stampe's chambermaid slept close to her mistress, as opposed to sleeping with the other women behind the kitchen. This may even have been a permanent arrangement, since it had been normal in earlier times. With the rococo mansions, however, it became common for servants to sleep in basements. The apparent arrangement between Margrethe and her chambermaid may, therefore, have been something specific for the last period of Margrethe's life, when she needed constant care.

Toilet facilities were left unmentioned in the insurance valuation, and this was probably because none were installed. The decor of rococo mansions had encouraged the creation of spaces for small retreat rooms. By the late eighteenth century, Renaissance ideas about the symbolic significance of faeces had long since been complemented by the great medical interest in the various functions of the human body.[72] The Copenhagen fashion book from 1777 instructed that 'although a toilet might be necessary in cases of illness, ordinarily, the daily considerations of health, cleanliness and the sensitivities of the senses should take precedence over convenience, unless one could have an enclosure that was tight enough so as not to spread the toilet's unpleasant atmosphere'.[73]

If, conversely, one looks at the insurance valuation of the courtyards off Ny Vestergade, one finds outdoor privy sheds in both of them. These were probably used by the mansion's servants, while Margrethe herself used a chamber pot which was then carried down the kitchen stairs.[74] Yet evidence for items related to this particular bodily function was not entirely omitted from the inventory lists (as opposed to the insurance valuation). Thus, included in the list of tin wares was an enema syringe in a holster.[75] One wonders, further, if the toilet furniture with two drawers, located in Margrethe's bed chamber, had been arranged in a practical way so that the lower drawer also contained a cupboard for a chamber pot with lid.[76] Such furniture is known from this period.[77] Regardless, one thing is for sure, Margrethe Stampe's chamber pot did not cause the same trouble as the chamber pots we encounter in Camilla Schjerning's chapter in this volume.

The inventory also shows that the windows were covered with curtains, according to the fashions of the time. Blinds, which were primarily intended to protect the furniture from sunlight, also hung from the windows. It was not to avoid curious glances of passers-by that led the *gehejmeraadinde* to install fixed blinds in all her windows, because no one would be able to look through her windows anyway. When the inventories were completed in early 1799, only the blinds were left hanging; the other two sets of curtains had been taken down and placed with the rest of the mansion's linen. The inner curtains were made of a thin cotton fabric that could be pulled up and down.[78] In the late eighteenth century, this type of cotton fabric, made in Asia, was an extremely expensive luxury item.[79] The outer layer of curtains was solely meant for decoration. As was in vogue at the time, these curtains had to be long, they had to be draped around the curtain rods with ribbons and rosettes, and they had to fall obliquely down each side of the window sills.[80] Here the decor once again shows that

Margrethe Stampe followed the latest fashions, going from the heavier, more elegant curtain fabrics to the lighter cotton fabrics, which were available in both embroidered and striped variants throughout the mansion.[81]

All the mansion's windows had English frames and were made of white glass, which meant that the window panes were larger than they would have been in older, metal frames.[82] With only the low wall encircling the Royal Palace's riding arena on the other side of Frederiksholms Canal, the south-east-facing mansion would have had plenty of light in the living rooms – especially in the high-ceilinged second floor, to which we now turn.

Second floor

The second floor was the mansion's *bel étage*, which formed the heart of the display quarters in large mansions. Here, the doorways between the rooms were placed in a line in order to emphasize the splendour of the mansion – the so-called enfilade.[83] The floor-to-ceiling height was 4.4 metres, and the ceilings were decorated with stucco.

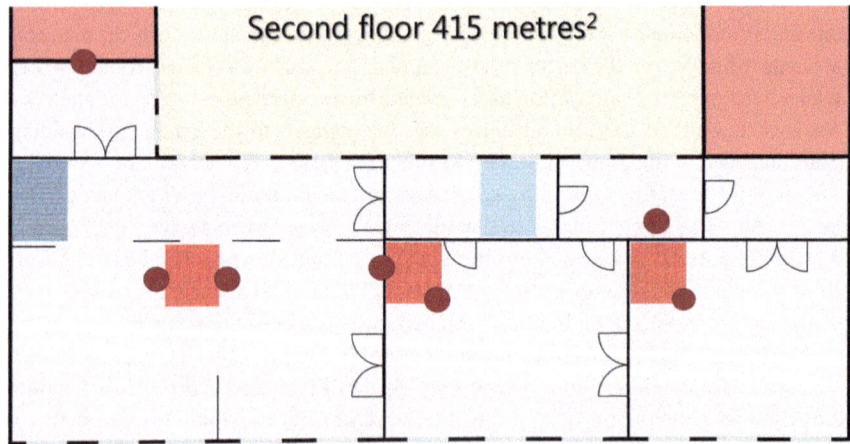

Second floor 415 metres²

Frederiksholms Canal

Figure 8.5 Floor plan of the second floor. The upper floor constituted the most distinguished part of the mansion, with three en suite halls, the largest of which was more than 170 metres2. This hall, however, had smaller room dividers that created the illusion of a section facing the courtyard, which lined up with the vestibule, and the two en suite cabinet rooms to the right of the main staircase. Behind the large hall, by the stairs leading to the basement, was a cabinet room that extended into the left side building. The model is drawn on basis of the information in the property valuation in Københavns Brandforsikringsselskab. Knudsen 2020.

On the street-facing part of the floor, there were en suite halls that ran the entire length of the main building. The two halls on the right-hand side each consisted of three window bays. One of these halls was upholstered in silk damask, which clearly demonstrates that the silk and cloth merchant's daughter found this type of wall decoration to be better suited to add distinction to the hall, compared to the modern wallpapers that were used in the first-floor halls.[84] In the first hall, the walls were covered with painted canvas. Unlike the painted walls with borders and foliage in the *gehejmeraadinde*'s private room, there were no motifs here. Coloured wall panels reflected the neoclassical fashion of the 1790s, where colour choices and motifs drew inspiration from Antiquity.[85]

Above the double doors between each of these two halls on the right-side of the house hung four paintings in carved, gilded frames. The floors in one of the halls were made of walnut, while those of the other hall were made of oak planks, dating back to the previous owner. Both halls were equipped with large, three-tier stoves placed in walled niches on marble tiles.

These two halls also housed the rest of Margrethe Stampe's red furniture. The first hall was furnished with an ottoman, two armchairs and twelve chairs with red damask covers, while the second hall had twelve gilded chairs with red damask covers. Both halls had large glass chandeliers hanging from the ceiling. There is, therefore, a clear difference between the furniture in the first-floor salons, which included many comfortable reading chairs, on the one hand, and the more limited furnishings in the second-floor halls, where the chairs were most likely arranged along the walls, as was the general custom for parade quarters.[86]

The first hall had a wool carpet. Carpets are only seldom found in Danish decor during this period, and only in the wealthiest circles. This carpet, together with the damask wallpaper and the red chairs, leads one to think that red was the favourite colour of the *gehejmeraadinde*. There is reason to believe that this first 'red' hall was Margrethe Stampe's preferred place to receive distinguished visitors, and that it served as a pleasant alternative choice to the mansion's huge hall, which took up almost half of the entire second floor.

The twelve gilded, high-backed chairs, which usually stayed in the adjoining hall and were arranged along the walls, probably constituted the dining-room furniture, along with the folding-table in the adjacent cabinet room, whenever Margrethe Stampe invited guests to a banquet and displayed her sumptuous collection of table linen, porcelain and silverware.[87]

Yet there was an object located in the first 'red' parade hall that complicates our formal impression of the space: an exercise machine, which was unfortunately not described in greater detail. What was an exercise machine doing in one of the mansion's most elegant rooms? Exercise machines are, of course, known from the period. For instance, one such machine was mentioned in the estate inventory of the late Johan Leonhard Fix, who died in his house in Amaliegade in 1807. But in Fix's case, the exercise machine was located in his bedroom.[88] Further, exercise machines also appear in several newspaper advertisements from the time. For example, locksmith Lars Bagsværd's advertisement from 1779 reads, 'Since I for some gentle persons have made several steel springs for exercise chairs and wagon seats of all kinds and shapes'; he thus announced to the paper's readership that he made steel springs on demand for a range of uses.[89] Moreover, in 1787, the owner of a shooting range in Sølvgade announced that he offered potential clients shooting practice and 'good and unadulterated milk … for those who use a milk cure', and to this he added that he had also set up exercise machines.[90]

Although it is not possible to describe these specific devices, we are left with the impression that exercise machines – and probably also diets – seem to have attracted the interest of the elite. In the closing decades of the eighteenth century, the leading circles in Copenhagen are known to have been preoccupied with natural bodily ideals and with health, in accordance with Enlightenment ideals.[91] An active communicator of health information was the doctor Professor Johan Clemens Tode (1736–1806), who contributed to the wider view that the body was central to understand the individual. Lifestyle and health were no longer subject to God, but became an individual matter.[92] Tode's *Health Journal* (*Sundhedsjournal*), moreover, was included among Margrethe Stampe's book collection.[93] The *gehejmeraadinde* was thus also caught up in these health trends, and it is probably in this light that we should understand why the exercise machine was located in the middle of the display quarters. Conversely, the placement of the machine suggests that Margrethe Stampe mainly used it for display purposes.[94]

Behind the first 'red' hall – the one with the exercise machine and carpet – there were two smaller cabinet rooms that faced the courtyard, following the same room division as on the first floor. In the first cabinet room stood a canapé and eight armchairs in blue damask covers. The furniture immediately makes us think of the more comfortable decor found in the salons downstairs. In the 'blue' cabinet room, Margrethe could invite her guests to a more informal gathering space, while still making use of the splendour of the parade quarters. The second cabinet room contained six small tables, of which half were gilded, in addition to the folding-table that was mentioned earlier. This cabinet room was used for storing the furniture that served the halls. The tables would only have been brought out when needed.[95] Additionally, this cabinet room also contained a so-called 'Polish' bed (or polonaise) with modern, striped-cotton curtains and six cane chairs with red damask seats, as well as two bureaus.

The executor's protocol specifically mentioned the two bureaus. According to the protocol, the heirs and the executor opened the two bureaus together, and extracted from them the wills and the many financial securities that constituted the largest part of the wealth of the *geheimeraadinde*'s estate. One of the bureaus also contained a large cash holding, which was immediately handed over to the future Baron Holger Stampe; Holger was then responsible for the funeral and for the payment of any receivables owed to any of Margrethe's creditors.[96] The accounts concerning this bit of the probate case are, perhaps unsurprisingly, located in the Stampe family's private archive.

One wonders if the inner cabinet room functioned as Margrethe Stampe's 'official' office, where she received her business contacts. The modern Polish bed may indicate that this cabinet room could also be used as a guest suite, together with the blue cabinet room.[97] Alternatively, Margrethe Stampe may have used the bed to receive visitors during her illness at the end of her life, or used it simply to retire when she had guests in the two 'red' halls.

The great hall

On the left side of the second floor was the mansion's largest and most distinguished hall, which encompassed five window bays across the entire width of the building, and corresponded to an area of just over 170 square metres. This hall was equipped with two, three-tier stoves that were placed in walled niches, as well as an additional faience stove used to help heat this huge room. The walls of the great hall were decorated with painted canvas.

Placed between the windows, according to the latest fashions, were the many mirrors that formed an integral part of Copenhagen mansions. The inventory list itemizes twenty-six mirrors in gilded frames. Such mirrors (in their gilded frames) were mounted on all the walls between the street-facing windows on both floors, and the windows in the large hall and in the cabinet room facing the courtyard also had mounted mirrors in gilded frames. The mirrors, in part, had an aesthetic function; but they also had a practical purpose in that they helped make the rooms seem larger and helped reflect the light emanating from the glass chandeliers and the many gilded bracket lamps mounted to the walls. The mirrors also had an important social function, letting one view others – and be viewed by others – unbeknownst to the person being watched. Mirrors exercised a major influence upon how the people acted and interacted within these halls.[98] The mirrors on both sides of Margrethe's great hall meant that her guests would have behaved as though they were participants in a public event, in view for all to see.[99]

It should now be obvious that what was by far the largest part of Margrethe's mansion had nothing to do with the type of privacy that is associated with private homes in the twentieth and twenty-first centuries. This statement applies to the mistress and to her servants alike. Perhaps it was the porter, in fact, with his own room located in the basement and with direct access to the entrance gate, who came the closest to having something vaguely resembling modern privacy.

After her death, Margrethe's coffin rested on a *lit de parade* placed in the great hall, where it remained for the four days prior to the funeral. Her rank and status as a *gehejmeraadinde* had a decisive importance in this regard because only the two upper ranks of the nobility were allowed to display the coffin on a *lit de parade*. Margrethe's coffin was covered with black cloth, and a canopy had been placed above it.[100]

Three six-armed chandeliers hung in the hall. In the official inventory list we find the console tables that stood under the mirrors, as well as a host of small tables, barometers, thermometers and plaster figures that were found in rich quantities throughout all three of the parade quarters' halls. None of the great hall furniture, however, was listed in the inventories with the other items to be auctioned off. Initially, the hall must have been emptied in preparation for the *lit de parade*. Nevertheless, in the inventory of the goods that the heirs kept for themselves, we find descriptions of the hall's furniture. This comprised a sofa and six chairs with embroidered upholstery; eighteen chairs with open backs; twenty-four gold-plated chairs, upholstered in a gold-plated leather;

and ten mahogany tables that were of the highest fashion. The items that the heirs kept also included twelve pairs of silk curtains, and six sections of red damask curtains that hung in the two 'red' halls. The heirs may thus have chosen to hold on to the *gehejmeraadinde*'s absolute finest, most expensive and most modern furnishings.

Behind the staircase leading to the kitchen region was the last cabinet room on the floor. Here, the walls were of painted canvas, framed within friezes. Over the doors hung three paintings in gilded, sculpted frames. This cabinet room presumably served as Margrethe Stampe's audience room, and was reserved for particularly distinguished visitors. It must be here that the canapé, the twelve armchairs in green damask and the two mahogany chests of drawers were placed. Upscale audience rooms such as this can also be found at other Copenhagen mansions. Those who wanted an audience with Margrethe thus had to ascend the main stairs, progress through the two 'red halls' and the large hall, all the while seeing a display of the *gehejmeraadinde*'s impressive wealth.[101]

Margrethe Stampe's business associates, however, must have come more frequently to the mansion. For this purpose, direct access to Margrethe's office in the cabinet room with the two bureaus was provided from the vestibule. She could, therefore, receive her business contacts without requiring them to be invited into the parade quarters. It would seem, accordingly, that business and social gatherings could be kept separate, if desired. From the many financial securities that Margrethe had, we know of the identities of her business connections, who came from both the nobility and the bourgeoisie. It is with these connections that all the traditional notions of the private home as the framework for women's life fall apart: even though the *gehejmeraadinde* did not continue her mother's work in the public clothing store, she nevertheless had just as much business activity, if not more, than did her mother.

Margrethe Stampe enjoyed eight productive years in the mansion, during which her wealth grew considerably. She subscribed to the monthly official releases of *Statstidende*, *Kollegietidende* and the published decisions of the local court. Since she speculated in securities and shares, she needed the most up-to-date information provided in the two daily Copenhagen newspapers. She also managed to become the first female member of the newly founded Natural History Society,[102] which was located in the neighbouring Palace of the Crown Prince.[103]

The garden pavilion

Finally, we come to the garden pavilion that Margrethe Stampe had built at the far end of the large private garden. A 40-metres-long tree-lined path led from the courtyard towards an open, tree-lined circular area with a fountain in the middle. On the edge of the circular area, opposite the path, we find the stone-built pavilion of 34 square metres, consisting of two smaller side rooms and a hall in the middle, upon which rose an octagonal dome. The walls inside the pavilion were marbled.[104] The panels and the inside of the dome were painted with images of foliage and sparrows, and the entrance to the pavilion, in the middle of the hall, consisted of a double door with twenty-four glass panes. At the age of sixty-four, Margrethe Stampe had decided to construct her very own pavilion, a decision which fit perfectly into the styles and tastes of the time. Very few Danish pavilions from the eighteenth century have survived, nor are there many examples of stone-built pavilions within Copenhagen's private gardens in this period. The inspiration for the octagonal dome perhaps came from one of the finest pavilions in the period, namely *The Great Garden House* in the park at the royal summer residence at Hirschholm Castle, north of Copenhagen. *The Great Garden House* also had an octagonal dome over the middle hall, along with two separate wings.[105] The architectural drawing of the royal pavilion was included in Thurah's *Den Danske Vitruvius*, the publication which also reproduced images of Margrethe's childhood home.[106] The pavilion in Margrethe's private garden seems to have been an adapted miniature of the royal one.

A concluding perspective on public and private

With this, our reconstruction of Margrethe Stampe's residence is now complete.

Margrethe Stampe was almost invisible in public life. Nevertheless, a considerable number of exceptional public records end up providing us with much information about her and her life. These sources include the records from St Peter's German Church, where the family's private burial chapel still survives to this day, and whose congregation served as the primary network that formed the basis of Margrethe's social life. We also find traces of her life in the royal resolutions from the Danish Chancellery, whereby she and her husband secured permission for their legal arrangements over matters of family and property. Likewise, the protocols from the Copenhagen Silk and Clothing Traders' Company help us uncover her background and social status, and this company constituted the second main network that framed her life. Then there is the official auction protocol and the register of mortgage, both of which document all of Margrethe's property holdings. Further, from the first preserved census in Copenhagen, dating from 1787, along with the information provided in the execution protocol, we can glean that Margrethe knew how to keep hold of her servants. And last but not least, the property valuation of her estate and her fire insurance policy let us step into her mansion, which was anything but private. All of these *public* records, produced by various administrative processes of the state, end up showing us the frameworks of *private* law that structured Margrethe's life and her socio-economic horizons.

Margrethe Stampe can also be found in the pages of the Copenhagen newspapers. Although the papers were, *sensu stricto*, privately created source material, they nevertheless conveyed information to the public sphere. This same observation goes for the few contemporary private records that mentioned Margrethe, and which contain information about the people with whom she socialized. Such records help us reconstruct the third network that shaped the framework of her life: namely, her husband's social circle.

Mentioning the various networks that framed Margrethe's life is necessary in order to draw attention to the fact that the various financial dispositions she made as a private person took place within a social framework that was limited neither to her marriage nor to her private household. Margrethe Stampe's most important network was comprised of her business connections, and it was these connections that formed the entire financial prerequisite for her various private opportunities.

The paradox here is that the public records help us uncover the size of the private space present in and around Margrethe's life, whereas the privately produced source material, on the other hand, reveals something of Margrethe's public life. It shows how open-minded the researcher must be if s/he is to penetrate the private during this period. In the vast majority of cases, only public records accord insight into the private. This methodological paradox underlines the fact that we very often are looking for the private in the past though the lens of public administration – thus we see the private not as a reflection in a mirror but more as the 'refraction' of light through a glass of water. The public administration will always constitute a disruption of the private, and one should, in general, be extremely careful when articulating the conceptual dichotomy between the private and the public.

Research into the private sphere has often been based on Aristotle's division between the private sphere or the *oikos* (the household) on the one hand, and the public sphere or the *polis* (society) on the other, with the *oikos* serving as the conceptual foundation for our understanding of the private. Aristotle, in particular, was constantly reinterpreted by political philosophers during the early modern period – not least in the context of Lutheran moral theology.[107] Aristotle's views of the *oikos* have also served as the basis for sociologists, such as Hannah Arendt and very likely Jürgen Habermas, for whom the *oikos* was a sort of Weberian 'ideal type', providing an explanation for the basis of modernity.[108] But it is often overlooked that Aristotle's model lost its relevance during the eighteenth century, when theories of state-formation were integrated into the modern natural law ideas about sovereignty and the social contract. Henceforth, the moral–theological Lutheran idea of the household lost steam when it was confronted with Enlightenment thought.[109]

The study of Margrethe Stampe's private home paves the way for an understanding that challenges the traditional distinctions articulated to explain the relationship between women and men, and how they interacted in private and public spaces.[110] The household in the eighteenth century was not the type of private home that we would later associate with private life and privacy, or with the relationship between men and women as economic agents.[111] The micro-historical approach allows us to see the details that nuance our understanding of these issues. Margrethe Elisabeth Stampe's economic situation was a unique. During this study, however, I have incidentally come across two other women within Margrethe's social network who also managed their own large fortunes.[112] Neither Margrethe nor these women are included in Carol Gold's recent study of women in business in early Modern Copenhagen 1740–1835 – a point that also applies to Margrethe's mother, Dorothea Elsabe Grøn. So maybe the *gehejmeraadinde* wasn't that unique after all. Yet the liquid capital that a woman like Margrethe Stampe made available for the Copenhagen credit market – together with other rich women who speculated in financial securities – was so large that it must have had a significant influence on the economic system within the city.

Margrethe Stampe conducted her business from her mansion, and this changes our understanding of the function of her household completely. As has often been pointed out in research looking at the private in the early modern period, households actually allowed for very little privacy. Family, tenants and servants all tended to live under the same roof.[113] Margrethe had 1,129 square metres at her disposal, and presumably she could have established some form of privacy; but the private households of the elite were, in fact, more about reflecting the economic and social status of their occupants to the wider public.[114] Amanda Vickery has wittily called the visitors to elite households in this period 'hyperactive', and she mentions the example of Lady Mary Coke, who easily made eighteen visits a day to other households in May 1767.[115] The visitors to these houses could also be described as 'hypersocial', to use another modern term. This same phenomenon can be observed in Danish diaries surviving from the period. The designation of being socially hyperactive would certainly apply to the civil servant Bolle Luxdorph or to Anna Christine Becker, the wife of a pharmacist, both of whom moved in the same circles as Margrethe Stampe.[116] Both of them, like Margrethe, had a busy working life; nevertheless, their respective diaries are filled with mentions of social activities that would have taken place in homes such as Margrethe Stampe's. This was a home that, in many ways, was designed more for her guests than it was for herself.[117]

Just like people today display a selective vision of their lives on social media with little regard for personal privacy or concern over who may be watching, so too did Margrethe Stampe decorate her private home in the same way as all other mansion owners: in order for it to be seen.

Notes

1 The title *gehejmeraadinde* refers to the fact that Margrethe Stampe was the widow of Privy Councilor Henrik Stampe, member of the kings Privy Counsel (*Gehejmerådet*). Women used their husbands' titles also after the husbands' death. The title Widow was never used in higher social circles. *Gehejmeraadinde*, however, cannot be translated into English – the Danish term will therefore be used throughout this article.
2 Steenberg 1945–58, 387.
3 Private Archive B2.
4 Eks.bo 13 14.
5 See note 3.
6 Jørgensen 1968, 49.
7 Schous forordninger, forordning af 5. April 1754 anl. stifteforvalteres salær, § 5, and Nørregaard 1791, vol. 1, § 233. Fire insurance policies and probates have previously been included in building history studies, e.g. Tønnesen 1981, but they have not been used to study the 'private' household.
8 Københavns Brandforsikring, vurderingsforretninger over ejendomme, mat. no. 239–243B, Vester Kvarter. Police no. 3473 (1779/1797). (Hereafter Police no. 3473).
9 The reconstruction is in addition based on Police no. 3473 (1779/1797), *Geddes matrikelkort* (1757) and *J.H. Rawerts matrikelkort* (1800) of Vester Kvarter in Copenhagen, both of which are digitized on the Copenhagen City Archive's website: Kbharkiv.dk.
10 Today, the mansion has been rebuilt to such an extent that only some of the exterior remains.

11   Of recent Danish works that have contributed to this study, see Clemmensen and
     Raabyemagle 1996; Lyngby 2007–2008 and 2015; Bregnhøi 2010; Pedersen 2013;
     Skak-Nielsen 2017.
12   Københavns Stadsarkiv: Silke-, ulden- og lærredskræmmerlavet: Lavsprotokol
     (hereafter Lavsprotokol) 1718–39.
13   Københavns Byret: Tinglysningsafdeling, Pante- og brevskriverkontorets 1. Afdeling:
     Realregister: Øster kvarter 1759–1818, matrikelnummer 36.
14   Thurah 1746, vol. I, table 119. This work was a royally commissioned work meant to
     present monumental Danish architecture to an international audience.
15   Lavsprotokol 1739–70. December 1742 to December 1747.
16   Shepard 2015, 66.
17   Danske Kancelli: Sjællandske Registre 1749–50. The marriage contract was
     confirmed by the king on 3 April 1750.
18   Sankt Petri Tyske Kirke: Enesteministerielbogen 1728–67 (death). (Hereafter St.
     Peter).
19   Nystrøm 1930, vol. 1, 2–8 January 1770.
20   St. Peter: Enesteministerielbogen 1767–83, (death), 7 June 1774.
21   Ibid., 1728–67 (death) buried on 20 October 1761.
22   Danske Kancelli: Sjællandske Registre 1776–7, no. 4.
23   Adresseavisen, 1 December 1775.
24   Folketælling 1787, København, Strandens Kvarter, Bag børsen 96.
25   See note 13.
26   Deutzner 1891, 77.
27   St. Peter: Enesteministerielbogen 1783–1813 (death).
28   Private Archive B2: The statements concerning Henrik Stampe's estate were written
     by Stampe himself.
29   Eks.bo 13 14: Recapitulation attachments, which contain a complete overview of the
     estate's accounts.
30   Henrik Stampe's nephews must have received the property that is still in the
     family's possession today after his death but before Margrethe died, since it did not
     appear in the contents listed in the executor's statement following the death of the
     gehejmeraadinde.
31   Eks.bo 13 14, 9 December 1791.
32   *Kiøbenhavnske Danske Post-Tidender*, 17 December 1798.
33   Police no. 3473 (1797).
34   Knudsen 1945, 200–11.
35   Schous Forordninger, kongelig anordning ang. Brandforsikringen for Staden
     Kjøbenhavn af 17 July 1795, § 8 and § 10.
36   When Margrethe Stampe's home was put up for auction after her death, potential
     buyers were also directed to the valuation by the fire insurance company done in
     1797.
37   Vickery 2009, 28.
38   Ibid., 31–4.
39   Police no. 3473 (1797).
40   *Gamle.* Eks.bo 13 14, inventory lists, XI furniture, 50.
41   See Vickery 2009, 18–20 for the importance of personal taste.
42   Lyngby 2015, 162–4. Lyngby uses the term 'apartments'. For the sake of clarity, and so
     that the word 'apartment' is not misunderstood to mean a 'separate apartment', I have
     used the word 'quarters' instead.

43   Ibid., 169–71.
44   Ibid., 173–5.
45   Eks.bo 13 14, inventory lists, XI furniture
46   Clemmensen 1996, 198.
47   Folketælling 1787, København, Strandens Kvarter, Bag børsen 96.
48   Eks.bo 13 14, 9.
49   Ibid., 3.
50   Ibid., Copies of the wills are placed first in the probate.
51   Ibid., 26.
52   Private Archive B2, appendix 47.
53   Lyngby 2015, 137.
54   Police no. 3473 (1779).
55   Eks.bo 13 14, inventory list, XI furniture and XIII linen. Private Archive B2, III linen.
56   Eks.bo 13 14, inventory lists, IV–IX.
57   Private Archive B2, appendix no. 55.
58   Eks.bo13 14, inventory lists, books.
59   Clemmensen and Raabyemagle 1996, 146.
60   Lyngby 2007–2008, 83: 'De væsensforskellige typer af sociale scener'.
61   Ibid., 74–5.
62   Alstrup 2019, 72.
63   Skak-Nielsen 2017, 97.
64   Vickery 2009, 167–8.
65   Skak-Nielsen 2017, 94–5.
66   Lyngby 2015, 169–75.
67   Clemmensen 1996, 122–25 and Bregnhøi 2010, 103.
68   Lyngby 2015, 218–19.
69   Eks.bo 13 14, inventory lists, medals and coins.
70   Anonymous 1777, 51–2.
71   Skak-Nielsen 2017, 79.
72   Lyngby 2015, 180, 255.
73   Bode 1796, 72. In J.H. Rawert's cadastral map (1800), which plots out water pumps and buildings, and their corresponding number of 'privies', only the houses on Ny Vestergade have privies.
74   Police no. 3473 (1779).
75   Eks.bo 13 14, inventory lists, IV tin.
76   Ibid., III silver.
77   Clemmensen and Raabyemagle 1996, figure 155.
78   Skak-Nielsen 2017, 98.
79   Pedersen 2013, 12.
80   Anonymous 1777, 49.
81   Eks.bo 13 14, inventory lists, XII linen.
82   Clemmesen and Raabyemagle 1996, 124.
83   Lyngby 2007–8, 74.
84   Skak-Nielsen 2017, 55.
85   Bregnhøi 2010, 17–8.
86   Anonymous 1777, 50.
87   Eks.bo 13 14, inventory lists, III silver, IX porcelain og XII linen.
88   Tønnesen 1981, 50.

89   'Da jeg for nogle høje herskaber har forfærdiget adskillige stålfjedre til motionsstole og vognsæder af alle slags facon', *Adresseavisen*, 17 November 1779.
90   'God og uforfalsket mælk ... for dem som bruger mælkekur', *Adresseavisen*, 20 April 1787. Ibid., 25 July 1788, 14 July 1792 and 8 November 1799.
91   Nielsen 2003, 47–8.
92   Mellemgaard 1995, 6–7.
93   Eks.bo 13 14, inventory lists, books, no. 849.
94   In the early 1800s, there are several examples of English advertisements with pictures for exercise machines (*gymnasticons*). Unfortunately, it has not been possible to discover if these were the same types of machine in Denmark. See also Kennaway and Knoeff 2020, 127–33.
95   Lyngby 2015, 174.
96   Eks.bo 13 14, 1.
97   Clemmensen 1996, 162.
98   Lyngby 2007–8, 84–5.
99   Clemmesen 1984, 32–3.
100 Schous Forordninger, sørgeforordningen af 14 April 1752, § 12.
101 Lyngby 2007–8, 76.
102 *Adresseavisen*, 23 October 1789.
103 Strøm 2006, 10.
104 Bregnhøi 2010, 145.
105 Hein 2016, 42–3.
106 Thurah 1746, vol. II, table 31.
107 Becker 2013, 136–7.
108 Becker 2017, 847.
109 See the chapter of Pernille Ulla Knudsen, in this volume.
110 Gold 2015, 70.
111 Shepard 2015, 73–4 and Gold 2018, 14–6.
112 Antoinette Uldall (1741–1804) and Caroline von Hoppe (1732–1819). Both women were a part of social circles.
113 Vincent 2016, 40–1.
114 McKeon 2005, 246–52.
115 Vickery 2009, 294.
116 Boritz 2000, 251.
117 Nystrøm (Luxdorph) 1930 and Becker 1870.

Public order and the experiment of implementing privacy in eighteenth-century Copenhagen

Ulrik Langen

On the night of 17 January 1772 Cabinet Minister Johann Friedrich Struensee (1737–1772) was arrested after attending a masquerade at the royal castle in Copenhagen. Over the past two years Struensee had – in the capacity of royal physician – gradually gained nearly absolute power in the kingdom of Denmark-Norway by way of his personal influence on the mentally ill king Christian VII and through his love affair with Queen Caroline Matilda (1751–75, r. 1766–72). The Struensee reign lasted sixteen months during which a considerable number of reforms were launched.

The Struensee reign had a profound influence on the city of Copenhagen and its population. Everything from taxation to funeral practices were turned upside down by public reorganization and administrative reform. While the freedom of the press introduced in September 1770 literally created a new public sphere, a string of initiatives, on the other hand, dealt with the boundaries between the private and the public.

The first taste of a new policy regarding public/private matters was a cabinet order of 31 December 1770 in which the king prohibited any domiciliary visits when the customs authorities searched for contraband goods. But the major turning point came when the municipal council was dismissed in the beginning of April 1771 and a new lord mayor of Copenhagen was appointed. On 3 April 1771, the new lord mayor count Ulrich Adolph Holstein (1731–89) – one of Struensee's carefully chosen administrators – dispatched a bill proclaiming the composition of a new city council. Furthermore, the bill presented five articles by which the terms of reference for the new council were presented. Two articles concerned the elections of the citizens' representatives, while the following three dealt with more basic conditions of the social life of the city.

One article had specific importance regarding privacy concerns. In article 2 it was stated that 'anyone has the right to enjoy absolute liberty in one's own house without being prevented – neither day nor night – by the police from doing private business (*particulaires Forretninger*)'.[1] This was a significant break from the police's license – which had been codified in 1684 – to examine private houses if any activity going against good moral conduct was suspected.[2]

The meaning of the phrase 'private business' in article 2 of the Bill of 3 April was open to extensive interpretation, but it seems apparent that one purpose of the article was to establish more firm boundaries between private and public by introducing limitations on the public control and interference with what were considered belonging to the private sphere.[3] In the same way as Struensee had created a new public sphere by introducing freedom of the press, one could argue that he wanted to outline a private sphere, which was to be fundamentally inaccessible to the public, as long no illegal activities were taking place.

After the fall of Struensee in January 1772 this policy was heavily criticized by prominent civil servants and public intellectuals – especially article 2 which was intensely proclaimed to be the root of the trouble. In this article, I will demonstrate how the critics – the chief of police, the Danish Chancellery and public intellectual Peter Frederik Suhm (1728–98) – managed to evoke a narrative of social disorder and create an argument, that made the extended privacy introduced during the Struensee reign proportionate to the (in their eyes) increasing depravity among Copenhageners, and ultimately, how the policy of privacy was staged as a reflection of the immoral conduct at court represented by Struensee and Queen Caroline Matilda.

The Bill of 3 April 1771

The regulation of urban public space was of great concern to the Danish government as well as to the municipal authorities, and since mid-eighteenth century the idea of 'good police' had dominated the ongoing discussions on the maintenance of security and order in the urban environment.[4] The emergence of *Polizeiwissenschaft* was a major contribution to this debate on civic order and urban development, but public order and urban stability were not solely matters of law and regulation. Throughout Western Europe, negotiations between city authorities and town dwellers played a prominent role in the attempt to regulate urban public space.[5]

It is not clear where the inspiration to article 2 of the Bill of 3 April came from. After the fall of Struensee, Holstein specifically maintained, regarding the passage about the police visitations, that it was delivered to him by Struensee as a verbal order.[6] In more general terms, he explained that the main goal was to provide the Copenhageners with as much personal freedom and as many commercial opportunities as possible.[7] This ambition becomes even more clear when studying an aide-memoire written by U. A. Holstein in April 1771 to follow up on the Bill, in which the concept of 'private business' (*particulaires Forretninger*) came closer to a definition. It is not clear from the aide-memoire who the specifically intended receiver was; the contained instructions were directed to the chief of police, but he was mentioned in third person throughout the document. I will carefully go through the relevant parts of the document in order to determine the key ideas behind article 2.

In the aide-memoire the new lord mayor particularly forbade the chief of police to initiate any investigation into activities taking place within 'the houses'. The aide-memoire was written in German, and Holstein used the phrase 'was in den Häusern geschieht oder nicht geschieht' (what happens and what does not happen in the houses).

It is not clear if the term 'den Häusern' refers to the buildings in which people live as well as the confinement of private homes – and in this regard, did the phrase 'one's own house' (as stated in article 2) apply to tenants as well as house owners? It is also worth noting the ambiguity of the phrase 'what happens or does not happen'. This hazy wording probably referred to concurrent views on activities, which were considered being inconsistent with moral and social norms or judgements on the one hand as well as what was considered proper and expected homely conduct within the household on the other. But the bottom line was that houses (or homes) would from now on be protected against random police investigation, and it was – once more and verbatim to article 2 – clearly highlighted in the aide-memoire that 'anyone has the right to enjoy full liberty' in one's own house. The question is *whose* privacy this measure was aimed at. Did it really concern anyone without considering, for instance, gender or social class? What did 'absolute liberty' mean?

Holstein indicated in more detail that the chief of police was not to worry about any trade taking place in the private houses, nor was he – and this was more controversial – to be concerned if 'a woman lived independently or not'. This was a clear break with common attitudes towards Lutheran household regulations, and moreover, it ran contrary to the prevailing idea that a woman living on her own was to be regarded as a vagrant (*løsgænger*) – if not a prostitute – if she was not tied to either her father, a householder or a husband.[8] This part of the aide-memoire specifically aimed at protecting independent and self-supporting women against social stigmatization and unwarranted interference from public authorities.

Furthermore, directions in the aide-memoire specified that it was to be of no concern to the police what went on in the houses on Sundays and holidays; consequently, the observance of the third commandment was openly disregarded. This decision was clearly at odds with the laws on sacrilege. Finally, it was declared that it was to be of no concern to the police if drinking and gambling took place in public houses during night time.[9] In this way, the lord mayor indicated that no distinction should be made between night and day, which was a break from the traditional distinction between night and day in early modern cities and the social code that belonged to this distinction. The difference between day and night marked not only a transition between work and leisure, but also between the orderly practices of everyday life and the more disordered nocturnal life outside the searchlight of the authorities and the social control of the surroundings. Therefore, during the second half of the seventeenth century, a strong demand arose among the inhabitants in the cities for – as mentioned before – *god politi* (good police), i.e. law, order and decent behaviour. The hiring of police officers in the market towns originated from this demand for supervision of *nattesæde* (illegal night-time serving of costumers), which was considered to be sacrilegious, especially if it happened on Sundays and public holidays. For the same reason, the first local police officers hired in the towns were paid from the funds of the church. The church bell's evening ring marked the transition to the night – 'police night' (*politinat*), as it was sometimes called – with strict rules for orderly behaviour. However, it was rarely a particularly easy task for the officers to get citizens to abide by the rules.[10]

To sum up, the house or the home was inviolable according to the Holstein aide-memoire. Gambling, drinking, retail business, (suspension of) Sunday observance and *nattesæde* were to be regarded as private matters as long as they took place within the confines of private houses or – as in the case of drinking, gambling and *nattesæde* – in the liminal zones of the public houses (alehouses, taverns, etc.).

Two questions remain unanswered from reading the Holstein aide-memoire: Did house mean home – and did home mean private? There is general agreement that such distinctions easily become anachronistic if applied too rigorously to eighteenth-century urban life.[11] In the aide-memoire Holstein focused on a set of practices rather than a spatial definition of house and home. The activities taking place within the private houses were not necessarily private as opposed to public – or rather; home did not necessarily mean private as the home was frequently used for commercial purposes. To many craftsmen, home and workshop were not spatially separated, as well as trading or serving alcohol would take place within what we in modern terms would understand as 'homes'. The spatial division between private and public, between home and commercial premises was more likely to be established by mental line-drawing than by precise physical boundaries.

In some ways, Holstein's aide-memoire seems to represent an initial example of the early-nineteenth-century idea – originating from the so-called *Rechtsstaat* ideology – that the state should refrain from intervening in the private sphere of its citizens, while the traditional jurisdictional powers of the police were to be limited and transferred to common criminal code and regular courts.[12] The legal reform introduced by Struensee in June 1771 – when a new court (*Hof- og Stadsretten*) was established to replace the entanglement of several local courts in Copenhagen – points in the same direction.

Reactions

Before the fall of Struensee in January 1772, the 'privacy article' was left more or less uncommented in public. But as soon as the cabinet minister was imprisoned, the critics surfaced. In the eyes of the critics, the initiatives of the Struensee-appointed Holstein had created unwanted dislocations in the social geography of the city. The initiatives were furthermore perceived as promoting a morally unacceptable license regarding sexual conduct, as well as encouraging popular insubordination and unruliness which challenged the social order of the city.

This interpretation was heavily influenced by the dismay caused by the violent riot, which took place in Copenhagen during the night of 17 January 1772, following the imprisonment of Struensee. The popular celebration of Struensee's downfall in the streets of Copenhagen had turned into a riot during which more than 70 'disreputable houses' (suspected brothels) around the city were attacked by the crowd and property was demolished. Doors and windows were smashed, followed by the destruction of furniture and equipment thrown into the streets. Tapestries were torn down from walls, fixed panels were broken down, floors were forced up, stoves were wrecked, and household effects were stolen and sold on the black market. Even more serious were the physical abuses experienced by the women who the attackers regarded as prostitutes. The incidence can be added to a line of eighteenth-century European 'pulling down' of brothels, for example in Brussels 1718 and London 1749.[13]

A significant feature of the numerous broadsides, penny-prints and pamphlets, which were published shortly after the incidence, was the number of detailed narratives (often in the form of ballads) unfolding the determined vandalism and the destruction of the contents of the houses. The violent event became known as 'The Great Clean-Up Party' by the sympathizers of the mayhem – implying that the Copenhageners were cleaning up after the immoral regime of Struensee. Despite the few critical voices, the wrecking and the plundering seem to have been regarded as acceptable to most pamphleteers.[14] One author stated that it was alright for the plunderers to sell the stolen furniture because it was 'unlawful goods' – meaning that the brothel keepers had purchased the goods with money unlawfully earned in a time of high prices and financial decline. Furthermore, the pamphlets made a considerable effort to justify the trespassing and vandalism of the rioters by describing (and assigning) the house as belonging to a liminal zone between public and private.[15]

Just a few days after the coup, the first criticism of the Bill of 3 April 1771 was put forward. On 20 January the government demanded – with reference to 'The Great Clean-Up Party' – an explanation from the chief of police for the reasons why the police were unable to 'maintain public order' in the city. Four days later the chief of police, Vilhelm Bornemann (1731–1801), sent his report to the government.[16]

There was no doubt in Bornemann's mind that article 2 of the Bill of 3 April 1771 was the sole reason for the disorder, and he was convinced that public stability would instantly be re-established the moment the article was revoked. The article had deprived the police 'the authority to keep an eye on the morals and manners of the common man in the houses and regarding his household, which previously had procured the Police the confidence and respect with the crowd, which in case of disturbance had an unfailing effect. Because of this, the city has been filled with prostitutes, lewd people and vagrants'.[17] According to Bornemann, the Copenhageners did whatever they wanted to do in the houses without restraint, but still worse, they 'forage a supply of impudence, obstinacy, and contempt for every kind of order, and brutish manners and habits of taking the law into their own hands which inevitably will lead to severe violence, when they discover that they are the strongest'.[18] Indeed, it was a grave scenario, which the chief of police evoked in his report.

Bornemann was convinced that the 'privacy-article' had to be revoked and the domiciliary searches 'in bad and suspicious houses' once again allowed. Furthermore, many of the previous regulations – generated by many years of experience, as Bornemann solemnly emphasized – against 'hobos, prostitutes, *Nattesæde*, amok-running, crowding in the streets' and everything running contrary to decency and good moral ought to be put back in force.[19] It was impossible to maintain public order as long as article 2 was in force.

Moreover, the chief of police suggested that all the alehouse keepers and publicans in the city were to be counted and registered in order for the municipal authorities to have complete overview of the situation and – not least – reduce their number. There were too many of them and they had become 'a sort of privileged vagrants' who made the common man accustomed to 'very harmful idleness and lewdness'. This comment pointed directly to the pervasive practice – made possible by the 'privacy article' and Holsteins orders – of using the private houses for serving alcohol to customers after closing time.

The report was processed in the Danish Chancellery (*Danske Kancelli*) in order to present the case as well as a possible solution to the king. The members of the Chancellery were all in agreement about the benefits of revoking the privacy article. On the question of reducing the number of pubs and alehouses, the opinions were divided. Some of the members argued that no obstacles should be made to trade and industry, while one member highlighted that the considerable number of public houses had disadvantageous effects on trade as well as morals. The alehouse keepers were 'living on top of each other' in Copenhagen and the large number resulted in very little income for most of them, 'which make them urge not only grown-ups but also boys, even women, to drunkenness, night-crowding and other disorderliness'.[20] This particular member of the Chancellery knew of several cases of young boys being led astray by beguiling alehouse keepers. Furthermore, he was generally worried about the public houses being a seedbed for pimping and prostitution. Another member argued that it could be dangerous in the present situation to reduce the number of alehouses because it would cause disturbance and bustle 'because it is exactly this mean class of citizens who are instigators of most conspiracies'.[21] In the heated days after the fall of Struensee, any measure that potentially could cause any disturbance of public order was to be avoided – and in the opinion of this particular civil servant, introducing restrictions on alehouses had the potential of generating severe popular dissatisfaction.

Following the debate in the Chancellery, article 2 of the Bill of 3 April 1771 was revoked on the 6 February 1772 by a royal resolution, which staged the article as nothing less than 'the source to all the disorder which rules the city'.[22] The article had deprived the police of its authority and its means to monitor the common people's 'lifestyle and manners in the houses', leading them to 'commit all kinds of lewdness and depravity with impunity'.[23] In this way, the resolution paraphrased the report from the chief of police. The suggestion on reducing the number of public houses was passed over in silence in the royal resolution.

On 27 January 1772, it was communicated in the newspapers that the prohibition against *nattesæde* was restored and that a decree dating back from 1701 was reintroduced. This decree stated that no one was allowed to be present in alehouses after 10 pm and that the chief of police was to make sure that no indecent behaviour was going on. In a police bill (*politiplakat*), Bornemann communicated the royal decision on revoking article 2. Seemingly, to prevent any misreading of the royal decision, i.e. to avoid any popular discontent with this new imposition of restrictions on urban social life, he added an explanation on how to interpret of the revocation of article 2. The chief of police emphasized that 'the appropriate freedom which everyone always had enjoyed when conducting lawful and honest business' would in no way expire or be reduced.[24] The purpose of the re-introduction of the police's license to conduct house searches was to observe the maintenance of order, good practice, modesty, decency and good moral character. In the future, the house searches would be carried out to make sure that no sacrilege was committed (for instance, serving alcohol or engaging in unnecessary work or commercial activities during service time) or that no illegal gambling or *nattesæde* was taking place in the alehouses. Furthermore, the police would examine the houses to see if the number of servant girls employed was disproportionate to the size of the household; this explanation was evidently directed at houses suspected of procuring. Last, but not least, the police would use the house searches to make sure that no 'loose and unattached persons' were living independently but were going into service unless they could prove that they were making an honest living.[25]

The re-introduction of the house searches was conveyed as a means to fight illegal nightly conduct, gambling and prostitution. The message was that anyone who lived according to moral standards and traditional Lutheran household practice had nothing to fear ('the appropriate freedom which everyone always had enjoyed when conduction lawful and honest business', as mentioned above), while any inclination towards the idea of privacy inherent in article 2 of the Bill of 3 April was considered morally unacceptable and a danger to public order.

The immoral court

U. H. Holstein was dismissed 18 January 1772, the day after the fall of Struensee. It has been argued that the reason for his removal was directly connected to the disturbances of the 17 January. To calm down the Copenhageners, the government considered it to be necessary to remove the person who was generally regarded as the author of the prohibition against police interference with whatever activities taking place in the houses.[26] There are some indications that Holstein's innovative and wide-ranging urban reforms were overshadowed by the banning of the domiciliary visits and that he – quite unfairly – came to be viewed as the incarnation of all trouble and public disorder in Copenhagen during the nine months he was active as lord mayor.

In his diary, historian and public intellectual Peter Frederik Suhm was quite explicit when characterizing U. H. Holstein. Back in April 1771, when Holstein had been appointed lord mayor of Copenhagen, Suhm wrote that Holstein 'was unfit for office, and furthermore lecherous'; he was rumoured to be running about whorehouses and 'gathering thoughts and ideas on ordinances and new arrangements from prostitutes and pimps'. Specifically regarding article 2, Suhm wrote in his diary how the police no longer was allowed to do domiciliary visit. According to Suhm, the sole purpose of this measure was to protect the prostitutes.[27]

After the fall of Struensee and the dismissal of Holstein, Gothard Albert Braem (1710–88) was appointed new lord mayor of Copenhagen. He was an ardent enemy of the Struensee regime, a sentiment that was quite explicitly communicated in a longer account on the state of Copenhagen he sent to the king in June 1772. After painting a very dark picture of the fatal economic and commercial conditions in the Capital, he mentions the Bill of 3 April 1770. In his opinion, article 2 had made the number of 'lecherous houses and loose women' increase dramatically and the number of people infected with venereal diseases was so large that the hospitals were heavily burdened.[28] In this narrative, the 'privacy article' was solely tied to moral decay and lechery. This view was common in many of the pamphlets published after the downfall of Struensee; the main purpose of the 'privacy article' was said to have been to protect brothels from inquisition and prostitutes from indictment. This went hand in hand with the idea of the depraved policy of the fallen cabinet minister; the rationale being that because Struensee was an immoral man, he wanted to care for the safety of prostitutes, and article 2 was the instrument to accomplish this protection. To the new regime, this was a convenient interpretation because it moved the attention away from the political aspects of Struensee's measures by insisting on a moral and religious judgement of the Struensee reign.[29]

The before-mentioned Suhm expanded this view in an anonymous pamphlet entitled 'To my countrymen and fellow citizens: Danes, Norwegians and Holsteiners' ('Til mine Landsmænd og Medborgere: De Danske, Norske og Holstenere') in which he examined the state of affairs during the Struensee reign. Among a long line of offences, he highlighted article 2 of the Bill of 3 April 1771 and elaborated a theory of political deviousness and moral decay at court.[30] He claimed that the purpose of article 2 was to pacify the Copenhageners. The Struensee government had reasoned that man loves freedom and wilfulness and is by nature inclined to pleasure, which makes him immoral and indulgent towards petty crimes. By introducing article 2, the government hoped to obtain support of the crowd and thereby remove popular attention from the government's undertakings in general. The government aimed at lulling the crowd to sleep by providing entertainment, freedom of the press, distribution of free wine and bread, spectacles, etc. According to this interpretation, article 2 was regarded as a part of a political strategy of concealment.

Furthermore, Struensee and his associates – including Queen Caroline Matilda – provided this 'illegal freedom' in order to justify and legalize their own deeds. If we are to believe Suhm, everyone shivered when thinking of the conduct at court during the Struensee reign; the realm was disgraced, the people were despised and virtue was ridiculed. Suhm's argument gained a strong gender dimension, as he highlighted how 'shameless women' in this period were preferred to other ladies at court. Thus, the privacy aspect of the article 2 was elevated to be a reflection of the immoral behaviour at court.

Conclusion

When Holstein wrote his aide-memoire in an attempt to elaborate on the use of article 2 of the Bill of 3 April 1771, he presented a string of restrictions regarding the monitoring of the urban population. In short, Holstein demanded restraint from the police officers and referred to 'the houses' as places fundamentally off-limits unless any citizen required the presence of the police. Holstein did not say much about the desired effects of these new rules for police conduct. But article 2 and the aide-memoire can – in a favourable light – be viewed among other things as an attempt to stimulate private business and economic activity by relieving small businesses (like serving on the premises) from any non-mercantile restrictions, i.e. religious rules and moral claims. It can also be seen as a progressive initiative to encourage independent and self-supporting women, as well as a quite radical introduction of privacy as a certain domain free from random police interference.

This did not necessarily mean that the private domain was synonymous with private life and homely confinement. The private domain was just as much a place for commercial leisurely activities, such as drinking and gambling. In this way there was some kind of performative quality attributed to the private domain of the city houses – privacy could be acted out. According to the chief of police and the members of the Chancellery, the performance of this privacy resulted in popular insubordination and moral decay – ultimately in a threatening public disorder. The 'mean class of citizens' – as a member of the Chancellery put it – could not be trusted the right to privacy, i.e. the right to avoid random house searches. P. F. Suhm took the argument to the next level by integrating the privacy indicated by article 2 in a line of initiatives with which the Struensee government attempted to cover up their activities by giving the people a false feeling of freedom along with *panem et circenses*. To Suhm, the privacy stipulated by article 2 was nothing but a phantom invented to anesthetize the people.

From a perspective of public order, the opponents of article 2 were focused on the morality and mores of the inhabitants, which was why they persistently opposed what they considered to be attempts to destabilize religious practices, whereas Holstein seems to have been much more attentive to stimulating trade and manufacturing – which would have a positive impact on public revenues – by limiting police interference. While Holstein regarded privacy as a means to further economic growth and the welfare of the urban population (even if it encouraged morally dubious activities as gambling and *nattesæde* – and even prostitution), his opponents were convinced that privacy, in the form represented in article 2, was undermining public order and 'good police'.

Notes

1 'Skal enhver i sit Huus nyde fuldkommen Frihed uden at blive forhindrede af Politiet Dag eller Nat i deres particulaires Forretninger'.

2 *Schous forordninger*, 29 April 1684, 409, specified by an instruction of 24 March 1741 and an ordinance of 19 April 1743, see Kolderup Rosenvinge 1828, 21 and Koch 1982, 46.

3 On the Bill of 3 April 1771, see also Stevnsborg 1998, 247–56.

4 On 'good police', see Munck 2007. Jørgen Mührmann-Lund has convincingly argued that even in absolutist Denmark, 'good police' was not 'social disciplining' meaning an authoritarian policy to change society, but rather a conservative policy demanded by the subjects. The unintended effects of the absolutist reforms of police enforcement on traditional social order were also minimal and due to resistance adapted to the changing demands of the subjects during the eighteenth century, which meant a greater emphasis on criminal investigation, which had not been a police task in the beginning of the century. Mührmann-Lund 2011, 359–60 (English summary) and Mührmann-Lund 2016.

5 On the relationship between negotiating and regulating the urban public space, see, for example, Rau 2007 and Sennefelt 2008.

6 'daß was den Passum betrift, daß, um allen Anstoß zu vermeiden, die Polizey-Bediente nicht wie gewonhnlich in den Häusern visitiren dürfen, auf mündlichen Befehl des Grafen Struensee mit eingerück ist', Hansen 1916–23, 586.

7 Trier 1916, 135. It is very likely that Holstein was inspired by German *Polizeiwissenschaft*, which seems to have been a concern in his administrative

practice as county governor (*amtmand*) in the town of Tønder in the years before he became lord mayor of Copenhagen.

8   On vagrancy and households, see Koefoed 2017; Jacobsen 2008; Henningsen and Langen 2010, 61–2.

9   'Er [the Chief of Police] hat sich übrigens mit dem jenigen auf keine Weise zu bemängen was in den Häusern geschiehet oder nicht geschiehet, sondern einem jeden hierin alle Freiheit zu lassen, auch nicht nur das Gewerbe dieser oder jenen zu bekümmern, oder ab eine Persohn auf ihre eigene Hand sitzet oder nicht, ob in den Wirtshäusern des Nachts getrunken oder gespielt wird, oder was an Festtagen in den Häusern passiret oder nicht passiret, kundschaft einzuziehen, solange man seine Beystand nicht verlanget', Copenhagen City Archives: Magistratens almindelige øvrighedsforretninger, Struensees kabinetsordrer m.v. 1770–2, memorandum written by Holstein (undated).

10   Regarding *nattesæde*, see Mührmann-Lund 2015. On the early modern night, see Ekirch 2005 and Koslofsky 2011.

11   See, for instance, Klein 1995 and Shoemaker 2003. For an interesting summary and new perspectives on the debate on gender and early modern public/private distinctions in the historiography of the last decades, see Heuvel 2019.

12   Kotkas 2013, 190.

13   Stevnsborg 1980, 570–99. On physical abuses during the riot, see Horstbøll, Langen and Stjernfelt 2020, 237–58.

14   Langen 2020.

15   As George Rudé and numerous other scholars have pointed out, mob aggression in this period was predominantly directed towards material property rather than turning into physical abuse of fellow city dwellers. Although in this case, many women were brutally victimized by raging intruders. Rudé 1971, 17–34.

16   Bornemann's report: Danish National Archive (DNA), Danish Chancellery, 'Koncepter og indlæg til 1. departements missiver 6 Februar 1772', no. 71.

17   'Derved er Politiet sat ud af den Myndighed at have øye med meeninge Mands Sæder og Levemaade i Husene; og af den Forbindelse med hans Huusholdning, der (…) tilforn forskaffede Politiet den Fortroelighed og Ærbødighed hos Pøbelen, som i Tilfælde af Sammenløb havde en ufeylbar Virkning. Derved er paa den anden Side Byen bleven opofyldt med Skiøger, liderlige Mennesker og Løsgiængere', DNA, Danish Chancellery, 'Koncepter og indlæg til 1. departements missiver 6 Februar 1772', no. 71: Bornemann to the King, 22 January 1772.

18   'samler sig en Forraad af Frækhed, Selvraadighed, Foragt for alle Befalinger, fæiske Sæder, og Vane at tage sig selv til rette, der nødvendigvis maae bryde ud til de største Voldsomheder, naar de seer at de ere de stærkeste', DNA, Danish Chancellery, 'Koncepter og indlæg til 1. departements missiver 6 Februar 1772', no. 71: Bornemann to the King, 22 January 1772.

19   'Løgiængere, Skiøger, Nattesæde, Grassategang og Stimen paa Gaderne. Ibid.

20   ' ey alene Voxne men Drænge, ja Qvindfolk med til Drukkenskab, Nattestiimen og andre uordentligheder', DNA, Danish Chancellery, 'Koncepter og indlæg til 1. departements missiver 6 Februar 1772', no. 71: written deliberations of the chancellery members (undated).

21   'thi det er just denne nedrige Classe af Borgere som ere Ophavsmænd til de fleste Sammenrottelser', ibid.

22   'Kilden til den Uorden, som nu hersker her i Staden', DNA, Danish Chancellery, 'Koncepter og indlæg til 1. departements missiver 6 Februar 1772', no. 71: royal resolution 6 February 1772.

23 'ustraffet kand begaae alle Liderligheder og Laster'. Ibid.
24 'den tilbørlige Friehed, som enhver stedse har havt udi sine lovlige og ærlige Forretninger'. Public notice (*Politiplakat*) of 10 February 1772, *Kiøbenhavns Politiske Veyviser* 1773, 84.
25 'løse og ledisge Personer'. Ibid., 83–4.
26 Trier 1916, 163–4.
27 Suhm 1918, 56.
28 Trier 1905, 12–13. The entire account is printed in Trier 1905, 9–32.
29 See, for instance, Anonymous *Sandfærdig Beskrivelse over De betydelige Forandringer og mærkværdige Tildragelser i Kiøbenhavn Fredagen den 17 Jan. 1772*, (no year of publication).
30 Suhm 1772, 6–7.

Murder at the threshold: Private and public in an early modern peasant rebellion

Sari Nauman

On 1 March 1710, the Swedish king Charles XII summoned the peasants of the hundred of Vadsbo for a meeting at Binneberg, their usual gathering place at the heart of the hundred.[1] Sweden was at the time at war with Russia and Denmark, and Danish troops had recently broken into Scania, the southernmost part of Sweden, and were threatening to march north. The peasants of Vadsbo, situated in western Sweden, and the surrounding hundreds were therefore called upon to go '*man ur huse*' – meaning all men to arms, but literally translating as 'all men out of their homes' – to march south against the Danes.

Numerous peasants showed up at Binneberg, several of whom were prepared to march. Not towards Scania, however; they refused to march farther than their forefathers had done, which was as far as the previous border to Denmark-Norway, marked in the landscape by the river Göta. In the midst of negotiations, old grudges resurfaced as the peasants met Johan Warenberg, bailiff in the hundred and one of the officers in charge of the enrolment procedure. At the end of the meeting, Warenberg was violently murdered, and a group of peasants threatened to slay whomsoever marched south as well.[2]

The rebellion lasted only for a couple of days, but it involved several hundred peasants. At its core were issues of thresholds: thresholds between the community and outsiders, old borders and new, and, most notably, spatial thresholds in the locality. Whereas urban thresholds have been well studied, the relationship of rural thresholds to issues of the private and public remains rather unexplored. In this article, I investigate how the rebels of Binneberg used the spaces of courthouse, courtyard and road to further their case against the bailiff. Particular attention is given to how notions of private and public influenced which actions were deemed proper for certain spaces, and how the rebels, through their actions, partook in shaping the nature of these spaces altogether.

The source material for this event consists mainly of records from the commission that was sent out by the Crown to investigate. The commission not only insisted on written statements from several of the witnesses, but also thoroughly interrogated those peasants who had attended the meeting. Combined with letters from various office holders, plea letters from the accused, court protocols and sentences, the material amounts to over 400 handwritten pages, giving a detailed account of what transpired during this exceptionally short, but nevertheless brutal, rebellion. All statements were made before the authorities, giving reason to suspect that the peasants carefully considered how to present their cases. Still, the many different testimonies are generally consistent, at least when it comes to spatial details. Together, the sources point to the dynamics of public and private space in an early modern rural society.

The implications of public and private spaces have long been in focus for researchers of the early modern period. Previously, scholars tended to identify the boundaries between these two spheres as more or less clear-cut. While women have been studied indoors, in what has been characterized as the private spaces of households and bedchambers, men's actions have been analysed in the urban outdoors, in public squares, coffeehouses and political buildings.[3] More recently, new evidence has been brought to the fore, revealing that the dichotomy of public and private was less clear-cut than this separation of spheres suggests. This was for three main reasons. First, the boundaries between public and private spaces were porous. Women not only dwelled indoors but were frequently present outdoors as well, taking up public space. Moreover, indoors could also be a public space, one that was open for visitors.[4] Secondly, private and public spaces were overlapping: while spaces could be coded as more or less public or private, private actions could also be carried out in public, and vice versa.[5] Thirdly, spaces were not clearly distinct in and of themselves; instead, they were characterized by movement. Continuous movements between and within different spaces imply that the factors that characterized any given space as public or private were situational, meaning that the public and the private had an ephemeral, fleeting quality.[6]

Private and public spaces were thus porous, overlapping and fleeting. Acknowledging these aspects of what otherwise risk appearing to us as clear-cut concepts, scholars today investigate how early modern people acted on and thought of liminal spaces, such as doors, windows and thresholds. Boundaries have of course always been an integral part of human societies, differentiating between inside and outside, between us and them. The early modern period was teeming with rituals and beliefs regarding boundaries, intensified by the state-formation process and its attention to frontiers.[7] A common denominator among scholars of liminality is that they tend to highlight the ambiguous nature of boundaries, which both separate and unite. Private and public merged in these sites, a feature that does not seem to have bothered the people navigating them. In discussing early modern boundaries and thresholds, Robert Scribner claims that one of the challenges facing researchers today is how to acknowledge 'the looseness of structure of daily life and the free-floating manner in which such symbols seem to operate'.[8] Other scholars, recognizing the ambiguous nature of thresholds in art, literature and everyday life, support Scribner's claim.[9]

Still, however fruitful liminality has proven to be, it has one disadvantage: it is an essentially spatial concept. If we recognize that private and public spaces were porous, overlapping and fleeting, we also need to recognize that they were not simply defined spatially, but that they were also temporally defined. They had a transitory character; private and public was something people did, not distinct spheres into which they entered. In discussing how privacy is enacted, Beate Roessler defines it as 'a protective shield that we always carry with us, regardless of where we are'.[10] While Roessler claims that we always carry our privacy with us, she also acknowledges that it needs protection, as it can be, and in effect constantly is, challenged and attacked – and, thus, lost.[11] I therefore argue that privacy, but also publicness, is in fact *not* always with us, but *potentially* so. The incessant potential for privacy or publicness cuts across both time and space. It pinpoints how these spheres could be temporarily amalgamated, that is combined and fused, sometimes with the result of creating a sphere that was neither private nor public, although simultaneously both. At the same time, it acknowledges that a situation or space could lose its private or public quality as a result of actions or events.

I use the concept of thresholds to capture this potential for privacy and publicness. Besides having strong undertones of liminality, thresholds also carry connotations of movement; as Aleida Assman and Jan Assman put it, they are there to be crossed over.[12] As they separate inside from outside, they also bridge these two worlds, not only spatially but temporally, carrying the possibility of travelling from one to the other.[13] Thresholds will thus be used as an analytical concept, but I will also analyse the use of physical thresholds, since crossing the spatial threshold of the courthouse was a central feature in the murder of Warenberg. During the first day of the rebellion, peasants followed the bailiff in and out of official buildings, and their actions shifted accordingly. During the second day, they dragged him over the threshold of the courthouse into the courtyard and back again, repeatedly. In a final act of defiance, they dragged his body out in the road, leaving his corpse there as a statement. In the following pages, I will trace these actions and analyse the ways in which they were informed by notions of private and public.

First, I give a short account of the rebellion, placing the event within its context. Thereafter, I focus the discussion on the spaces where the rebellion took place – the Binneberg courthouse, courtyard and road, respectively – and examine how these spaces interacted with the accusations made against the bailiff. In the conclusions, I summarize my findings and zoom back out, discussing their implications for how we can understand privacy and publicness in rural areas during the early modern period.

The rebellion

Despite its involvement in many wars, early modern Sweden was a supposedly peaceful country internally. Open rebellions against the royal power have long been considered practically non-existent, thereby distinguishing Sweden from other European countries where rebellions were more common. The lack of Swedish rebellions has led scholars to argue for the long historical roots of a specific Swedish political culture, one directed towards dialogue and negotiation.[14] Critics have claimed the opposite, suggesting that royal power's monopoly on violence and harsh control kept people at bay.[15] During the past couple of decades, most scholars have come to agree that the achievements of the Swedish state depended on both negotiation and control.[16]

At the beginning of the eighteenth century, however, commotion was starting to rise across the Swedish realm. In 1700, the Great Northern War began, and Sweden fought against Russia and Denmark-Norway to keep possession of its domains around the Baltic Sea. In June 1709, the Swedish army lost the decisive battle of Poltava. Russian armies conquered the Baltic provinces, and then marched north to occupy Finland. At the same time, Danish troops entered Scania. Attacked on several fronts, the Swedish Crown imposed unprecedented drafts upon its populace. According to the military system at hand, Swedish peasants were collectively in charge of appointing soldiers amongst themselves and of maintaining them. As a result of this system, Sweden kept an army which, in proportion to its population, was unparalleled in other European countries, enabling its previous successes in warfare. In 1710, however, the extra drafts befell an already heavily burdened peasantry. Furthermore, the prospects of surviving a war were slim at best; if not killed by the enemy, one risked succumbing to the countless illnesses spreading in the camps.[17]

Danish troops entered Scania in December 1709, and in the early months of the following year they threatened to march farther north. The king and the Royal Council of Sweden, therefore, sent orders that all able men in the hundred of Vadsbo were to drive the enemy off and defend the country's borders. Early on the morning of Tuesday, 1 March 1710, the people of the hundred were to gather at Binneberg, where they held their judicial hearings three times a year. There, they were to be counted and noted, and that same day march together, first towards Timmele, 86 kilometres to the south, and then onwards to Scania.[18]

In order to be present in the early morning of 1 March, peasants who lived far away from Binneberg started to arrive in the vicinity during the afternoon of Monday, 28 February. Some of them went straight to the inn, located in the same building as the courthouse but with a separate door, for something to drink. Across the road, they could see the church, and the parish priest lived within eyesight. Several parishes had brought what was required of them: clothes and arms, as well as food for a six-week journey. Others, however, had only brought their weapons.[19]

Already upon their arrival, the mood among the peasants was agitated. The peasants of the Väring parish later testified in court: 'As the evening approached, more people arrived from faraway parishes, causing too much noise and commotion for one to be able to achieve anything.'[20] When the governor of Skaraborg, Carl Gustaf Soop, arrived on Monday afternoon, his efforts to appease the congregation were drowned out in the turmoil. He quickly fled the scene.[21] Shortly thereafter, at around four o'clock, Bailiff Johan Warenberg arrived at Binneberg, whereupon he was immediately surrounded by an angry crowd. He managed to reach his night quarters just north of the courthouse, where three other office holders had also sought shelter. At first, the crowd followed him, but he temporarily succeeded in calming them down, and went to sleep.[22]

On Tuesday morning, Warenberg went to the courthouse to meet with the district judge, Jonas Aurell, who was also his brother-in-law. At the same time, one of the peasants, Jon Andersson, came walking along the road, saying, 'Yesterday I loaded my gun with three bullets, but now I shall load it with sixteen, and they are all for the bailiff.'[23] Before long, Andersson had entered the courthouse, and demanded that Warenberg repay him 8 *caroliner*,[24] which Warenberg had received as a bribe to refrain from enlisting Andersson's farmhands as soldiers a few years earlier. Since all able men were now nonetheless enlisted, Andersson and several with him thought it only fair that the bailiff repaid their bribes. Others had bribed the bailiff in other matters, and likewise demanded their money back.[25] By now, the peasants displayed quite a bit of hostility towards the bailiff. According to the testimonies, the courthouse was packed with peasants standing on benches and tables, shouting at and threatening Warenberg.[26]

In the meantime, District Judge Aurell was outside with two priests, who were holding an outdoor service in an attempt to calm the peasants. Their efforts were futile. Sometime before noon, the peasants dragged the bailiff out of the courthouse, feet first, and hurled him down in the courtyard. They attacked him with spears and guns, and he received a severe beating. After that, Warenberg was hauled back inside, to one of the chambers of the courthouse, where the peasants again started to demand money, and insult and threaten him. He was subsequently dragged back and forth between the courthouse and the courtyard no less than six times. After the fourth haul, he yielded and started to hand out all the money that he had. His attempt at restitution was, however, insufficient, because far too many peasants demanded their money back.[27] After the sixth and final dragging, and after repeated attacks with fists, spears and guns, Warenberg died in the courtyard. Witnesses and surgeons performing the autopsy claimed that by the time of his death, he had been so abused that there was not one part of his body left unharmed.[28] Finally, the peasants dragged the bailiff's body out on the road, and left it there.[29]

During the beating of the bailiff, District Judge Aurell and other officials had fled to the nearby village of Horn. When they heard about the murder of Warenberg, they decided to bring the matter to the attention of higher authorities, and visited Governor Carl Gustav Soop in Skövde. Soop recounted the events in a letter to the Royal Council on 3 March, and shortly thereafter, the Royal Council appointed a commission and assigned a regiment of soldiers to protect it. In this form, the authorities returned to Binneberg at the end of April, and the trial commenced shortly after.[30] In the middle of June, sentence was passed on the rebels. Five of them, recognized as the leaders, were sentenced to death, and thirty-eight others received harsh corporal punishments in the form of running the gauntlet or prison sentences. Due to the miserable conditions in jail, seven of them either died beforehand or were too sick to receive their punishments. The other peasants, who could not be proven to have taken part of the rebellion but who nevertheless had failed to intercede, were sentenced to pay heavy fines for failing in their duty to obey their king.[31]

The official building

The courthouse was an official building, with an official purpose: the peasants of the hundred met there at least three times a year for hearings and trials. The sessions were traditionally directed towards conflict resolution, and the peasants themselves generally instigated the cases.[32] However, the transition to a more formal court had started during the early eighteenth century: greater emphasis was placed on educated judges instead of laymen, and court protocols were sent to courts of appeal for scrutiny. The building was thus an extension of the royal power into the local community, representing the crown. As such, it was a protected space. Any crimes committed inside a courthouse were punishable as *edsöresbrott*, crimes committed against the king's oath, meaning that the culprit risked becoming an outlaw; anyone could kill or harm him or her without punishment.[33]

Still, the courthouse also had an important communal role, and most peasants visited it as plaintiff, defendant or spectator repeatedly during a lifetime. The matters solved within this space did not only pertain to crimes against the crown, but also included minor disputes among the peasantry.[34] Its position in Binneberg close to the parish church enhanced the space's public function: it was a place where people from the hundred met to solve issues of greater or lesser importance, and where they interacted with spiritual and secular authorities, as well as with each other. Furthermore, at the inn, they could get something to eat or drink, and mix business with pleasure.

The courthouse thus had both an official and a public function, and these functions were sometimes hard to distinguish from one another. Nonetheless, considering the events that took place there during the rebellion, the peasants and authorities seem to have disagreed over which function the courthouse served first. A closer look at the rebels' actions reveals that they treated it as a space for the presentation of their grievances and as a space to argue their cases, much as they were accustomed to do under more normal circumstances. First, they forced the bailiff to sit down at the court table. They then placed themselves around him and demanded to be repaid for the inducements he had previously received. Compared with regular hearings in the courthouse, the peasants' actions this time were undoubtedly infused with violence: some of them were standing on benches or even atop the table, and, to keep the bailiff seated, they stuck their spears into the wall above his head. A few peasants even fired their guns.[35] The threat of violence was, however, not realized within this space. The shooters aimed above Warenberg's head rather than directly at him, nor did they punch or hurt him physically in any way.[36] They seem to have restrained themselves, using the courthouse as a public space for conflict resolution.

Their restraint, however, was considered to be insufficient by the commission. During the trial, and in accordance with the law, the commissioners argued that the fact that some of the rebels' actions had taken place within the courthouse aggravated their crime. They asserted that the courthouse was a 'privileged room'. The bailiff had sought refuge there, and in attacking him within the courthouse, the peasants transgressed the boundary of this protected space, thereby warranting harsher punishments.[37] Moreover, the rebels' crime was not only committed against the bailiff; by their actions, they had attacked the courthouse itself. Mayor Svante Segervald argued that the rebels had 'destroyed that same public house with every kind of deed, and turned it into a den of thieves'.[38] Testimonies asserting that some of the peasants had stood on the court table, broken it, or entered the area behind the bar with drawn weapons were remarked upon sternly by the commissioners in their sentences.[39] To them, the courthouse was primarily an official building, and actions taken against it and its contents were taken as acts against the royal power itself.

Since the rebels were convicted for their actions, the commissioners' opinion prevailed. Still, the events also tell us that the peasants assigned a public function to the courthouse, and, notably, knew how to use this function when protesting against the bailiff's wrongs. They did not need the authorities to present their case; they used this public space as if it were their own.

The public outdoors

Outside, a severe beating took place, however. Lying in the courtyard, the bailiff endured hits and kicks, and was struck with spikes and hammers. According to numerous testimonies, the assaulters were furious. The autopsy protocol supports these findings; according to the performing surgeons, several of the blows he received had been fatal in themselves. Both of Warenberg's arms and hands were severely injured, and the surgeons concluded: 'Taking everything into consideration, no one can count all of the deceased man's little wounds, cuts, and injuries, as he was not treated as a human being, but without mercy.'[40]

Thus, whereas the inside space was reserved for arguing their case and threating the bailiff to give in, the rebels used the outdoor space, in contrast, for public retaliation and punishment. According to the testimonies, a 'large bunch of people' stood around Warenberg as he was beaten.[41] Many of them partook in the beating, and several peasants testified that the leaders had urged others on, or even forced them to hit the bailiff. The rebels further drew attention to the act by yelling, screaming, and cursing, shouting insults to the bailiff and entreating others to join in. They drew attention to themselves, urging everyone to bear witness to their actions.[42] That the peasants reserved the aggressive acts of violence for outside, and tried to draw as much attention as possible, suggests that, even though the courthouse was a public building, the courtyard itself potentially carried an even higher degree of publicness. In this space, it was possible to address the community as a whole.

In early modern Scandinavia, as in early modern Europe, hidden actions were considered suspicious and possibly dishonest, whereas the open carried connotations of honesty.[43] By conducting their deed in the open, the rebels made the claim that their actions were not to be hidden, implying that they were legitimate and honest. Several of the testimonies support this interpretation. During and after the murder, the rebels boasted of their deeds, saying, 'It was right that shame was slain.'[44] They claimed that the beating was 'just' (*rättmätigt*),[45] 'right' (*rätt*)[46] and 'a good deed' (*en god gärning*),[47] and that the bailiff had been a 'rascal' (*skälm*),[48] 'devil' (*fan*)[49] or 'sheriff's cunt' (*länsmansfitta*).[50] When leaving the bailiff to die on the road, one of the rebels said, 'The bailiff should not die in an honest man's farm, but as he has been the king's thief, he shall die on the king's road.'[51] It is unclear whether they meant that the bailiff was stealing on behalf of the king, or that he stole from the king by keeping their taxes for himself. There is some evidence to suggest that the former was more to the point. Some of the rebels told one of the priests, 'Thus we shall treat all of the king's thieves,' which the priest interpreted as a threat.[52] Also, when asked if they were going to follow the king's command and march south, a few of the rebels answered that they had no king, suggesting that they did not consider King Charles XII to be their king anymore. This might have insinuated that they thought that the king had failed in his obligation to protect them and thereby lost his right to reign over them.[53]

In accordance with this, the rebels lashed out at those who did not participate.[54] They quickly challenged anyone who acted disapprovingly. For example, they asked a man who was bringing Warenberg water if 'you, you rascal, agree with this rascal bailiff?'[55] One of the rebels asked the bystanders 'if they did not want to be men and stand their ground', goading them to join in.[56] Others were threatened with spears and guns, and forced to take part.[57] Several testimonies indicate that some of the peasants thought that the murder would only be punishable with fines, saying that if all partook, 'we will not get any more wergild than 1 *öre silvermynt* per man.'[58] The attempts to persuade all to participate might have been motivated by economic considerations, but the rebels' shouts and insults indicate instead that it was an attempt to promote the honesty of their actions.

Kimmo Katajala has previously shown that rebellious peasants in the Swedish realm frequently presented rebellions as communal activities. They argued that they had taken all decisions together and were thus collectively responsible for those decisions. According to Katajala, this points to communalistic horizontal structures among the peasantry, and he contrasts this notion with the fact that the authorities nevertheless tried each peasant separately, thus insisting on facing them as individuals.[59] The events in Binneberg show us what happened if the peasants did *not* agree on a rebellion. The rebels argued that all should stand united, but several parishes had withdrawn when the beating started. Others claimed to have been forced to participate upon fear of death, and others still made efforts to assist the bailiff.[60] Yet their actions were insufficient in the eyes of the authorities, who maintained that they should have put up a united front against the rebellious parties:

> The reported rebellious instigators of this uprising were a limited few, to stand against the manifold and large gathering of the peasantry of Vadsbo hundred ... so that the rebellious bunch should not have been able to prevent them from continuing this march ... had their determination and love for their noble king and dear fatherland been steadfast and persistent.[61]

In this rebellion as well, the peasants were tried and received their sentences one by one, but the quote suggests that the authorities also held that the peasants should have been able to resist the rebels had they stood united. The publicness of the event, with many peasants gathered at one place and at one time, should have made resistance possible. Instead, the publicness seems to have worked to the rebels' advantage. It guaranteed them an audience, in front of which they could claim that their actions were honest. They did this through their public beating of the bailiff, but also by their boasting and insults.

Several studies have shown how people in urban settings used public, open spaces for solving conflicts, whether with violence or words. Both men and women took part in upholding order in the streets, and they did this in front of each other.[62] At Binneberg, the courtyard functioned in the same way as urban streets; it served as a public space where conflicts were enacted and resolved, and where order was restored. Furthermore, this public function spilled over into the surrounding peasants' homes, as the rebels went to their night quarters in the evening after the murder. Due to the many peasants gathered at Binneberg, the inn had quickly filled, leaving several peasants to sleep at other peasants' homes. On their way to and then within these homes, the rebels continued in their boasting, praising themselves for having 'put the bailiff to sleep',[63] and saying that 'it was right that shame was slain'.[64] In so doing, the public act of declaring their actions to be honest crossed another threshold, converting the peasants' homes into semi-public spaces.

When passing the threshold from the courthouse to the courtyard, the rebels moved from an official space to a public one. They demonstrated that the bailiff was not under the crown's authority anymore, but subjected to a social order communally upheld by the peasants. The courtyard was *their* space. At the same time, they might have been trying to escape the authorities' control: by conducting the murder outside, they might have believed that they would escape the harsher punishments of an *edsöresbrott*. As they repeatedly dragged the bailiff first outside, then inside, they paraded their control over the threshold, as well as their power to decide which kind of public the bailiff would face. The threshold made it possible to separate their actions and to carry out both trial and punishment.

The open road

This brings us to the role of the road at Binneberg. Read closely, the testimonies of those involved show why this was the space chosen by the peasants as the final resting place for Warenberg. After the bailiff had died, the peasants dragged him onto the road, claiming that he was not honest enough to lie in the courtyard. The act indicates that the peasants attached certain values to the courthouse and courtyard as spaces of justice and honour, and that the presence of Warenberg's body risked contaminating those spaces. Such a view resonates with how authorities treated criminals, such as murderers, who were not allowed to be buried in cemeteries after execution. While the cemetery was a hallowed space, the courtyard was here claimed as a public and honest space, one from which the bailiff was expelled.

According to the sources, the road carried contradictory connotations. First, it was supposed to be a space of free movement. After the murder, two priests came riding along the road with a mission from District Judge Aurell to try and gather information concerning the events at Binneberg. Some peasants blocked their way, asking them about their intentions. The priests replied: 'It is an open King's road, where people are allowed to travel, even if the peasantry is gathered'.[65] After noting that the travellers were a couple of priests, the peasants reluctantly escorted them through the crowd. There is a certain discrepancy here: while the priests argued that it was the king's road, the peasants had clearly taken it over and claimed command of it as their own. The road at Binneberg was a space of movement, but no longer free for all.

Secondly, the road was simultaneously recognized as beyond the peasants' – or anyone else's – area of control. After the priests had been led past the crowd, they insisted on being shown the bailiff's body, which was by then lying on the road. They later returned to Aurell and recounted what they had seen. Aurell was terrified, and demanded that someone should collect the body from the road, 'so that he must not lay there [exposed to] dog and claw, or to be hurt and eaten by brutish animals.'[66] Two men did as he asked and tried to move the body, but the peasants stopped them, saying that '[Warenberg] was not worthy of anything else, than to lie where he [is], and be eaten.'[67] The rural road was thus framed as an unprotected space, where dangerous, wild animals roamed. To leave the bailiff's body in such a place must be interpreted as a final act of insult. It indicated that the rebels would allow the bailiff's body to be eaten, thus refusing him the possibility of ever being buried in a cemetery, which would have enabled him to enter God's kingdom.[68] Furthermore, it echoed the treatment of outlaws, who could be killed but not sacrificed, and who stood outside of the protection of justice.[69]

The rebellion was carried out in three different locations, but they were all connected to each other and gained their respective significance partly through these connections. The courthouse was both an official and a public building, and was used by the rebels for public complaints during the rebellion. Their defiling of an official space condemned them to harsh punishments. The courtyard was a public space, and was used for public revenge on the bailiff. The road, finally, was a space beyond order and control, characterized instead by movement and unruliness. The peasants used it to demonstrate that the bailiff was no longer included in their community – human and Christian. They expelled him, both in this life and the next, echoing the punishment of the *edsöresbrott* and marking the bailiff as an outlaw.

A private man, a public official

So far, I have shown how the peasants drew on notions of official and public spaces to inform their actions in attacking Bailiff Warenberg. In this section, I shall take a closer look at the accusations made against the bailiff – namely that he had taken bribes – and argue that the peasants' actions and choice of venues should be read with this in mind. First, the accusations need to be put into perspective. During the early eighteenth century, private individuals often compensated state servants in money or in kind for fulfilling certain tasks. These tasks were not necessarily considered to be outside of the duties of their offices, but nor were they indubitably within them; rather, they were tasks that the officeholder had the ability perform, but that the state did not pay him to perform. Such tasks could include the writing of supplications for individuals asking for help, the procurement of passports for those wishing to travel, or acting as a middleman in various conflicts or disagreements. Performing such tasks was a much-needed way for the state servant to earn some extra money; the wage received by the state was rarely enough for his subsistence.[70]

Such payments are not to be confused with bribes, although the line between the two was not always clear. Taking a bribe for performing (or not performing) a task was not looked kindly upon by the authorities, since it implied that their orders would not be followed, and that money that might otherwise have ended up with the state went instead into the state servant's pocket. Battling corruption was thus high on the early modern state's agenda, and the Swedish state was no exception. People around the country were encouraged to inform their closest authorities of any transgressions of bailiffs or other state servants in rural areas.[71]

As Magnus Linnarsson and Mats Hallenberg have shown, the danger of public officials taking bribes was repeatedly evoked during parliamentary debates in early modern Sweden. A solution was to have private companies or individuals operate public services, and several experiments were conducted within such diverse areas as tax farming, street cleaning, transportation and waste management. However, a private organization was not without its faults: by gaining profit, a private organization could enrich itself at the public's expense. This argument was consistently brought forward during parliamentary discussions on the topic, as Linnarsson has shown.[72]

The public official thus had to find a balance between receiving money for private tasks executed within his profession, and staying clear of accusations that he was gaining private profit, namely by taking bribes and enrichments that his supervisors might consider to be unlawful. The bailiffs, hardly adulated by their communities, were in an especially exposed position, also risking accusations from affronted peasants. Still, accusations of bribery against bailiffs seldom reached the top, either because such behaviour was infrequent, or because local societies had much to gain from a bailiff that could be bought.[73]

The allegations against Bailiff Warenberg thus stand out during this period. According to several letters of accusation, Warenberg repeatedly took money for small services, and most of the accusations concerned conscription. During the Great Northern War, Sweden used an allotment system in which peasants were divided into *rote* (units), each of which was responsible for procuring a certain number of soldiers for the army. If a man was appointed as a soldier, he was generally not allowed to pay the authorities to be released from service, but it was possible to pay another man to take one's place. Nevertheless, the peasants accused Warenberg of having accepted bribes; for example, Håkan from Önnerud claimed to have given Warenberg 8 *caroliner* to exempt two farmhands from military service.[74] In paying the bailiff to be released from service, it was implied that Warenberg would be responsible for finding another recruit – otherwise, such a bribe would only amount to the *rote* having to find another soldier. Still, the bailiff sometimes failed to do this; Anders Svensson accused Warenberg of accepting 9 *daler* to exempt his son from service, but because Warenberg failed to replace his son, Anders ended up having to enlist himself.[75]

Another example indicates that Warenberg not only took money to exempt certain peasants from service, but also manipulated and tricked peasants into paying him several times over. Lars Bengtsson and his neighbours had recently recruited a man as their soldier for 100 *daler*, only to have Warenberg assign that same man to another *rote* and instead conscript Lars. Lars's father paid Warenberg some silver to exempt the son from service, but instead Warenberg conscripted their farmhand. The farmhand also paid Warenberg to be exempted, after which the *rote* had to recruit and pay for yet another replacement. Then Warenberg drafted Lars's brother for another *rote*, forcing their father to give him even more silver.[76] Similar accusations were made by the peasants in Delsbäck *rote*.[77]

Having to pay to keep sons and workers from harm's way repeatedly during a period with recurrent recruitments must have been trying for the peasants. Still, several of the accusations, including Lars's and the one from Delsbäck, indicate that it was not the payment itself that frustrated them. Rather, it was the failure of Warenberg to honour his agreements. In 1710, one third of all men in Vadsbo had been drafted, and due to the state's continuous demand for soldiers, it must have become difficult for Warenberg to exempt peasants from service. However, he failed in other tasks as well. Seeking to retrieve her deceased husband's pay, Annika Persdotter gave Warenberg a set of plaited leather reins and some birch bark to sort the matter out. This sort of payment might fall under the category of fair compensation for services procured, and the main accusation in Annika's letter was not that Warenberg had collected payment, but rather that he had failed to follow through with his promise. When she confronted him, he rebuffed her 'with curses and harsh words', with the result that she did not dare raise the issue again.[78] Warenberg was thus accused of failing in his duties. He took payment without giving anything back, he cursed and behaved as a commoner; where he should have behaved as a public official, he acted as a private man – a dishonest one, at that.

Early modern Sweden was strictly hierarchical. A public servant had the right to expect a certain amount of respect, especially from those below him. The peasants' reaction to Warenberg's habit of acting contrary to his position was to treat him accordingly; the beating he received reflected a degradation of Warenberg's person. By calling Warenberg foul names and beating him publicly, the crowd stripped from him his public role, and labelled him as their peer, or rather, as their inferior. That the peasants thought that they would only be penalized with fines for the murder of Warenberg further supports this interpretation: they treated him as any other man, not as a public official. That Warenberg should have behaved better most likely only exacerbated their animosity towards him.

The commission disagreed. According to them, Bailiff Warenberg's position as a state servant warranted him extra protection. The crime against him was thus not primarily a crime against Warenberg's private person, but a crime against the state, the king, and even against God's creation, as was made overtly clear in the sentence:

> The peasants of Vadsbo hundred have ... indefensibly forsaken their loyalty, against the First Epistle of Peter, 2nd chapter – which bids and commands to fear God and honour the King, and that whoever defies his authorities defies God's creation, as there is no authority but that which is given by God – the Epistle of the Romans [chapter] 13, and against the 2nd and 5th chapter 3§ in the King's law, when they in Binneberg dreadfully tortured and murdered the office holder of the crown, Johan Olofsson Warenberg ... having thus committed *Crimen parricidii, periurii, proditionis, et falsi*; whereby they have abandoned their subordinate devotion and obligation to their most gracious King, and forsaken it as treacherous subjects.[79]

According to the commission, Warenberg was not a private man, but a public official. Furthermore, he was murdered while conducting his public duty of summoning the peasants to march against the enemy.[80] The peasants' failure to appreciate this, together with the fact that their refusal to march against Scania had endangered the whole country, warranted the harshest punishment.

From the written testimonies, the extent of Warenberg's corruption seems to have been evident. Still, during the trial, and following explicit questioning from the commission, the peasants collectively recanted their stories, and claimed to know nothing about any supposed corruption. Village after village, community after community, agreed: 'The late bailiff had never done them any wrong, instead he only did good, and they have no reason to bring up the least reproach against any royal servant.'[81] The trial thus ended up reinstating Warenberg's reputation as a public official, marking the peasants' attack on his body as all the more appalling and unforgivable.

Moving between spaces

In medieval and early modern imagery, the threshold stood for ambiguity. It conveyed change, of being inside and outside and of moving in between, and it indicated the passage between this life and the next.[82] In the rebellion at Binneberg 1710, these meanings were concretized through the rebels' actions. Passing over the thresholds – from the courthouse, to the courtyard, to the road – signified going from an official space, to a public space, to an open space, and the peasants changed their actions accordingly. Moreover, their movements and actions reflected the accusations they made against the bailiff; they spatially enacted notions of private and public.

A main conclusion of this study is that the peasants who gathered at Binneberg differentiated between two kinds of public. Being inside an official building – a public where the peasants met their authorities – led the rebels to exercise restraint with regard to their violence. They used the courthouse for the official part of the rebellion, which centred on presenting their grievances: they declared that the bailiff had transgressed his authority, and demanded repayment for the money that they had paid him. While the peasants did violate the rules of the building according to the authorities, thereby warranting harsh punishments, the testimonies all suggest that they showed some restraint since they chose to reserve their most violent acts for outside.

The main attack on the bailiff took place outside the courthouse, where the second kind of public actions was carried through. Apart from the gruesome violence that ultimately left the bailiff slain, the peasants used this space to yell insults and to degrade their victim. They urged others to participate in the beating, with the explicit aim of making the rebellion a joint action against the authorities. They used their audience, drawing people close to bear witness to their actions, turning the beating into a public event. Publicness was thus not only dependent on space, but also on actions; the rebels created a public atmosphere. They evoked the potentiality for publicness in a way that indicates that they experienced a need for it; publicness seems to have served their purposes. Scholars have previously found that urban open and public spaces were often used for violent acts, turning a physical attack into an attack on the victim's honour as well. My investigation shows that this kind of public display was important in rural societies as well. Violent acts took place outside, so that everyone could see what happened, as public display implied that the perpetrators had nothing of which to be ashamed.

The treatment of the bailiff at Binneberg in fact mimicked the treatment of criminals in early modern Sweden. They were accused and sentenced within the courthouse, but corporal punishments were performed outside, in the open, before a public. Even in the slaying of Warenberg, the rebels mirrored the punishments they themselves risked, if found guilty for the *edsöre* crime: by casting him out in the road, they expelled him from the community, and refused him the right of a Christian burial. The dependence on a public to do this is evident from the sources; the rebels insisted on witnesses. The witnesses, however, did not witness what the rebels had intended. Instead of testifying to the wrongdoings of the bailiff, they testified to the crimes of the rebels. The public in this respect was thus both a promise and a threat; it could easily turn on those who called for it.

Furthermore, the investigation identifies how the private interacted with the public when it came to the accusations brought against Bailiff Warenberg. The bailiff was accused of taking private profit and acting as a private man, thus not fulfilling his public duties. The privateness of Warenberg's business was flaunted publicly, the accusations made for anyone to hear, and the beating itself can be read as a display of how the peasants exposed Warenberg's descent into a private man to a wider audience. In a way, it was Warenberg's persona as private or public that was at trial at Binneberg. According to the commission, Warenberg's position as a bailiff accorded him the respect due to a public official. According to the peasants, however, Warenberg had shown in his actions and words that he was not a true servant to the king, and thus not worthy of their respect. To them, he had failed as a public official: as an inferior private man, he was brutally punished.

Notes

1   This research was funded by a generous grant from *Vetenskapsrådet* (*The Swedish Research Council*), no. 2018–06596.

2   The main source material for this meeting and the ensuing rebellion is kept in the Swedish National Archive (SNA), Äldre kommittéer ([Older Committees], ÄK) vol. 44. Findings have been corroborated in SNA, Skrivelser till Kungl. Maj:t, Landshövdingen i Skaraborgs län, vol. 20 (1709–11).

3   See the excellent research overview in van den Heuvel 2019, 695–6.

4   Cohen 2008, 311–12; van den Heuvel 2019, 697; Laitinen 2017, 142; Ågren 2006, 24–5.

5   Gowing 2000, 133; Muurling and Pluskota 2017, 158–9.

6   Nussdorfer 1997, 169–70.

7   Scribner 1992, 823.

8   Ibid., 840.

9   See, for example, Jacobs 2018, 3–15; Bawden 2014, 20–32; Justitz 2002, 631–2; Jütte 2015, 11–13; Williamson 2015, 173–6.

10   Roessler 2016, 243.

11   Ibid., 251–4. See also Roessler and Mokrosinska 2013.

12   'Schwellen sind dazu da, überschritten zu warden', Assman and Assman 1997, 8.

13   Cf. Simmel [1909] 1994.

14   The main proponents are Aronsson 1992; Österberg 1989.

15   The main proponents are Nilsson 1990; Lindegren 1992.

16   See, for example, Katajala 2004, 263–9; Kepsu 2017.

17   See, for example, Villstrand 1992.

18   Stille 1903, 204–21.

19 See, for example, Protocol 7 May 1710, 194–5; 9 May 1710, 133; 16 May 1710, 173–6, 180, all in SNA ÄK 44.

20 'Ju längre det led mot aftonen ju mera folk stötte till från de långväga församlingarna, så att det blev allt för mycket sorl och buller att man intet kunde uträtta', Letter from Väring parish, no date, SNA ÄK 44. Translations are mine throughout this chapter.

21 Johan Ek's testimony, no date, SNA ÄK 44.

22 Gabriel Andersson's testimony 5 May 1710; Johan Ek's testimony, no date, both in SNA ÄK 44.

23 'Igår laddade jag med 3 styckor förr, men nu skall jag det göra med 16, och dem skall fogden få smaka på', Bengt Larsson's testimony 15 March 1710; Protocol 13 May 1710, 140, both in SNA ÄK 44.

24 8 *caroliner* equalled about 15 *daler kopparmynt*, roughly a half year's pay for a farm hand, see Lindström and Mispelaere 2015; Edvinsson and Söderberg 2011.

25 Protocol 13 May 1710, 139–42. For other examples, see Protocol 7 May 1710, 86; 16 May 1710, 166; 17 May 1710, 187–8, all in SNA ÄK 44.

26 See, for example, Gabriel Andersson's testimony 5 May 1710, SNA ÄK 44.

27 Bengt Larsson's testimony 15 March 1710, SNA ÄK 44.

28 Letter from the surgeons 26 May 1710, SNA ÄK 44.

29 Bengt Larsson's testimony 15 March 1710, SNA ÄK 44.

30 Soop to the Royal Council 3 and 8 March 1710, in Letters from the governor of Skaraborg to the Royal Majesty, vol. 20, SNA Skrivelser till Kungl. Maj:t. See also Ericsson 2013, 263–4.

31 Sentences, SNA ÄK 44.

32 This was generally the case in Europe during this period; see, for example, van der Heijden and Muurling 2018, 700–1.

33 *Christopher of Bavaria's Law of the Realm*, Edsöresbalken Ch XIII–XV. Even the road to and from court was protected by this law.

34 Sundin 1992, 5–11.

35 See, for example, Protocol 4 May 1710, 48; 7 May 1710, 85, 13 May 1710, 140–2, all in SNA ÄK 44.

36 Protocol 14 May 1710, 150; 17 May 1710, 186; Sentences: 23, 44, all in SNA ÄK 44.

37 The sentence of Lars Collin against Hova gäld, and Fägre gäld; Sentences: 5, both in SNA ÄK 44.

38 'Med varjehanda åtgärd samma publika hus fördärvat, och likt en rövarkula gjort', Svante Segervald to the Commission 25 May 1710, SNA ÄK 44. On references to the courthouse as a 'privileged room', see Lars Collin's sentence on Hova and Fägre gäld; Sentences: 5, 23, all in SNA ÄK 44.

39 See, for example, Bengt Larsson's testimony 15 March 1710; Håkan Larsson's testimony 30 April 1710, both in SNA ÄK 44. See also Sentences: 17, 33, SNA ÄK 44.

40 'Uti en summa alla den sal[iga] mannens små sår, blemma och blodviten, kan ingen räkna, ty han var icke hanterad som en mänsk [människa], utan obarmhärtl[igen]', Autopsy protocol 26 May 1710, SNA ÄK 44.

41 'En stor hop allmoge', Protocol 2 May 1710, 9, SNA ÄK 44.

42 Bengt Larsson's testimony 15 March 1710; Protocol 10 May 1710, 97–104, both in SNA ÄK 44.

43 See, for example, Shapin 1994, 9–15.

44 'Det var rätt att skam blev ihjälslagen', Protocol 6 May 1710, 70, SNA ÄK 44.

45 Bengt Larsson's testimony 15 March 1710, SNA ÄK 44.

46 Erik Lundgren's testimony 14 May 1710; Johan Ek's testimony, no date; Protocol 6 May 1710, 90, all in SNA ÄK 44.
47 Protocol 2 May 1710, 21, SNA ÄK 44.
48 Protocol 14 May 1710, 121, 157, 187, SNA ÄK 44.
49 Protocol 13 May 1710, 137–8, SNA ÄK 44.
50 Protocol 12 May 1710, 125, SNA ÄK 44.
51 'Fogden ej skulle dö på en ärlig mans gård, utan som han skall varit kungens tjuv, så skulle han dö på kungens landsväg', Protocol 2 May 1710, 21, SNA ÄK 44. See also Protocol 2 May 1710, 22, SNA ÄK 44.
52 '[Så s]kola vi hantera alla kungens tjuvar', Johan Ek's testimony, no date, SNA ÄK 44. See also Protocol 7 May 1710, 90, and Sentences: 38, both in SNA ÄK 44.
53 Protocol 17 May 1710, 195, SNA ÄK 44. On the bailiff as the king's thief, see also Bengt Larsson's testimony 15 March 1710; Protocol 6 May 1710, 90, both in SNA ÄK 44.
54 Protocol 2 May 1710, 17, SNA ÄK 44.
55 'Håller icke du skälmer med den här skälmsfogden', Bengt Elg's testimony, no date, SNA ÄK 44. See also Protocol 6 May 1710, 85, SNA ÄK 44.
56 'Om de icke ville vara karlar och stå på sig', Protocol 4 May 1710, 45, SNA ÄK 44.
57 Protocol 12 May 1710, 124–6, SNA ÄK 44.
58 'Lärandes [vi] intet mer löpa i mansbot, än 1 öre Smt till mans', Sven Nilsson of Tattartorpet, quoted in Protocol 10 May 1710, 104, SNA ÄK 44. See also Protocol 2 May 1710, 21; 4 May 1710, 46, SNA ÄK 44. Murder was punishable by death.
59 Katajala 2009, 177–8.
60 See, for example, Protocol 3 May 1710, 31–2, 35–6; 4 May 1710, 44–51; 6 May 1710, 71–2; 10 May 1710, 97–104; 12 May 1710, 123–6, all in SNA ÄK 44.
61 'Såsom de till detta oväsendet angivna upproriska upphovsmän, voro fast få och ringa, att räkna, emot den mångdubbla och stora myckenhet … så att den upproriska hopen ingalunda kunnat hindra, dem ifrån denna marschens fortsättande … där viljan och kärleken för dess allranådigste konung och kära fädernesland varit beständig och trofast', Sentence 23 June 1710, 5–6, SNA ÄK 44.
62 Lipscomb 2011, 411–13; Laitinen and Lindström 2008, 287; van der Heijden and Muurling 2018, 707–8. See also Ågren 2006, 31–2, 43.
63 '[De har] sövt fogden', Protocol 17 May 1710, 191, SNA ÄK 44.
64 'Det var rätt att skam blev ihjälslagen', Protocol 6 May 1710, 70. See also Bengt Larsson's testimony 15 March 1710; Johan Ek's testimony, no date, all in SNA ÄK 44.
65 'Det var en öppen kungsväg, den folk får resa, fast allmogen är församlad', Johan Ek's testimony, no date, SNA ÄK 44.
66 'Att han icke må ligga där för hund och ram, eller och oskäliga kreatur skadas och uppätas', Erik Lundgren's testimony 14 May 1710, SNA ÄK 44.
67 '[Warenberg] intet annat vara värd, än där som han låg, ligga och uppätas', Erik Lundgren's testimony 14 May 1710, SNA ÄK 44.
68 On the importance of being buried in a cemetery, see Engström 2019, 167–70.
69 Agamben 1998.
70 Cavallin 2003, 55–65; Frohnert 1993, 74–5.
71 Lennersand 1999, 308–13. On corruption in early modern Europe, see, for example, Durand 2017; Knights 2017; Frisk Jensen 2017.
72 Linnarsson 2018; Hallenberg and Linnarsson 2016; Linnarsson 2017, 238–44.
73 Haikari 2017.
74 Håkan Larsson's testimony 30 April 1710, SNA ÄK 44.
75 Anders Svensson's testimony, no date, SNA ÄK 44.

76 Lars and Nils Bengtsson's testimony, no date, SNA ÄK 44.
77 Letter from Delsbäck *rote* 2 June 1710, SNA ÄK 44.
78 'Med bannor och hårda ord', letter from Annika Persdotter, no date, SNA ÄK 44. See also letter from Per Larsson, no date, SNA ÄK 44.
79 'Men däremot sin trohetsplikt oförsvarligen eftersatt, emot den 1 Pet[rus] epist[el] 2:dra kap[itlet], som bjuder och befaller, att frukta Gud och ära konungen, och den som sätter sig emot överheten, han sätter sig emot Guds skickelse, efter ingen överhet är utan av Gudi, Rom[arbrevet] 13 lika så emot det 2:dra och 5:te kapitlen 3 § konungsb[a]l[ke]n l[ands]l[agen], utan i Binneberg, kronans befallningsman Johan Olofsson Warenberg jämmerligen pinat och mördat ... och således skolat commiterat och begått *Crimen parricidij, perjurij, proditionis, et falsi*; varmed de sin underdånigaste devotion och skyldighet, emot sin allranådigaste konung, och kära fädernesland avklätt, och som genstörtiga undersåtar åsidosatt', Sentence 23 June 1710, SNA ÄK 44.
80 See, for example, the first letter from Svante Segervald, no date, SNA ÄK 44.
81 'Att sal[ige] befallningsmannen aldrig dem någon orätt tillfogat, utan allt gott gjort, ej heller de hava orsak över någon annan kronobetjänt det ringaste besvär anföra', Horns *gäld*, Protocol 6 May 1710, 79, SNA ÄK 44. For other communities, see, for example, Protocol 4 May 1710, 60–1; 7 May 1710, 93; 9 May 1710, 96; 10 May 1710, 106–7; 11 May 1710, 115, all in SNA ÄK 44.
82 Bawden 2014, 21–32, 384–9; Jacobs 2018, 6–8; Jütte 2015, 11–13.

Bibliography

Introduction

Ågren, M. (2013), 'Emissaries, Allies, Accomplices and Enemies: Married Women's Work in Eighteenth-century Urban Sweden', *Urban History*, 41 (3): 394–414.

Ågren, M., ed. (2016), Making a Living, *Making a Difference: Gender and Work in Early Modern European Society*, New York: Oxford University Press.

Ågren, M. (2017), *The State as Master: Gender, State Formation and Commercialisation in Urban Sweden, 1650–1780*, Manchester: Manchester University Press.

Ågren, M. (2018), 'Providing Security for Others: Swedish Women in Early Modern Credit Networks', in E.M. Dermineur (ed.), *Women and Credit in Pre-industrial Europe*, 121–42, Turnhout: Brepols.

Aminoff-Winberg, J. (2007), *På flykt i eget land: Internflyktingar i Sverige under stora nordiska kriget*, Åbo: Åbo Akademis förlag.

Ariès, P. (1986), 'Introduction', in P. Ariès and G. Duby (eds), *Histoire de la vie privée T. 3: De la Renaissance aux Lumières*, 1–11, Paris: Seuil.

Barker, H. and E. Chalus (1995), 'Introduction', in H. Barker and E. Chalus (eds), *Gender in Eighteenth-Century England: Roles, Representations and Responsibilities*, 1–28, London/New York: Routledge.

Bay, C.F. (1798), *Fuldstændigt Dansk og Engelsk Haandleksikon udarbejdet efter de bedste og nyeste Ordbøger*, Copenhagen: Gyldendal.

Bodensten, E. (2016), *Politikens drivfjäder: Frihetstidens partiberättelser och den moralpolitiska logiken*, Lund: Lund University.

Brilkman, K. (2016), 'Konfessionalisering, konfessionskonflikt och konfessionskultur under tidigmodern tid', *Scandia*, 82 (1): 93–106.

Christiansen, P.O. (1995), 'Culture and Contrasts in a Northern European Village: Lifestyles among Manorial Peasants in 18th-century Denmark', *Journal of Social History*, 29 (2): 275–94.

Cohen, E.S. (2008), 'To Pray, to Work, to Hear, to Speak: Women in Roman Streets c. 1600', *Journal of Early Modern History*, 12: 289–311.

Cott, N.F. (1977), *The Bonds of Womanhood: 'Woman's Sphere' in New England, 1780–1835*, New Haven/London: Yale University Press.

Cowan, B. (2013), 'English Coffeehouses and French Salons: Rethinking Habermas, Gender and Sociability in Early Modern French and British Historiography', in J.P. Ward and A. Vanhaelen (eds), *Making Space Public in Early Modern Europe: Performance, Geography, Privacy*, 41–53, New York: Routledge.

Crane, M.T. (2009), 'Illicit Privacy and Outdoor Spaces in Early Modern England', *The Journal of Early Modern Cultural Studies*, 9 (1): 4–22.

Crowley, J.E. (1999), 'The Sensibility of Comfort', *The American Historical Review*, 104 (3): 749–82.

Davidoff, L. and C. Hall ([1987] 2019), *Family Fortunes: Men and Women of the English Middle Class 1780–1850*, London: Routledge.

Eibach, J. (2011), 'Das offene Haus: Kommunikative Praxis im sozialen Nahraum der europäischen Frühen Neuzeit', *Zeitschrift für Historische Forschung*, 38 (4): 621–64.

Engelhardt, J. (2006), 'Borgerskab og fællesskab: De patriotiske selskaber i den danske helstat 1769–1814', *Historiske Tidsskrift*, 106 (1): 33–63.

Feldbæk, O. (1993), *Danmarks økonomiske historie 1500–1840*, Copenhagen: Systime.

Feldbæk, O. (1997), *Dansk søfarts historie, vol. 3, Storhandelens tid 1720–1814*, Copenhagen: Gyldendal.

Glete, J. (2002), *War and the State in Early Modern Europe: Spain, the Dutch Republic and Sweden as Fiscal-military States, 1500–1600*, London: Routledge.

Goodman, D. (1992), 'Public Sphere and Private Life: Toward a Synthesis of Current Historiographical Approaches to the Old Regime', *History and Theory*, 31 (1): 1–20.

Gowing, L. (2000), '"The Freedom of the Streets": Women and Social Space, 1560–1640', in P. Griffiths and M.S.R. Jenner (eds), *Londinopolis: Essays in the Cultural and Social History of Early Modern London*, 130–52, Manchester: Manchester University Press.

Gowing, L. (2014), 'The Twinkling of a Bedstaff: Recovering the Social Life of English Beds 1500–1700', *Home Cultures*, 11 (3): 275–304.

Habermas, J. ([1962] 2001), *Strukturwandel der Öffentlichkeit: Untersuchungen zu einer Kategorie der bürgerlichen Gesellschaft*, Frankfurt am Main: Suhrkamp.

Habermas, J. (1989), *The Structural Transformation of the Public Sphere: An Inquiry into a Category of Bourgeois Society*, trans. T. Burger and F. Lawrence, Cambridge, MA: MIT Press.

Hallenberg, M. (2008), *Statsmakt till salu: Arrendesystemet och privatiseringen av skatteuppbörden i det svenska riket 1618–1635*, Lund: Nordic Academic Press.

Hallenberg, M., J. Holm and D. Johansson (2008), 'Organization, Legitimation, Participation: State Formation as a Dynamic Process – the Swedish Example, c. 1523–1680', *Scandinavian Journal of History*, 33 (3): 247–68.

Harvey, K. (2001), 'Gender, Space and Modernity in Eighteenth-century England: A Place Called Sex', *History Workshop Journal*, 51: 158–79.

Hassan Jansson, K. (2017), 'Haus und Haushalt im frühneuzeitlichen Schweden: Geschictswissenschaftliche Trends und neue Zugänge', in J. Eibach and I. Schmidt-Voges (eds), *Das Haus in der Geschichte Europas: Ein Handbuch*, 113–29, Berlin/Boston: de Gruyter.

Hoff, A. (2015), *Den danske kaffehistorie*, Højbjerg: Wormianum.

Holvast, J. (2009), 'History of Privacy', in Vashek Matyáš et al. (eds), *The Future of Identity in the Information Society*, 13–42, Berlin: Springer.

Horstbøll, H. (1989), 'Cosmology and Economics', *Scandinavian Economic History Review*, 37 (2): 26–50.

Ilmakunnas, J. (2019), 'Aristocratic Townhouse as Urban Space: The Fersen Palace in Eighteenth-century Stockholm', in E. Chalus and M. Kaartinen (eds), *Gendering Spaces in European Towns, 1500–1914*, 15–31, New York/London: Routledge.

Johansson, E. (2002), 'Kyrkan och undervisningen', in I. Montgomery (ed.), *Sveriges kyrkohistoria del 4: Enhetskyrkans tid*, 248–58, Stockholm: Verbum.

Justitz, G. (2002), 'Reforming Space, Reordering Reality: Naumburg's Herren Gasse in the 1540s', *The Sixteenth Century Journal*, 33 (3): 625–48.

Jütte, D. (2015), *The Strait Gate: Thresholds and Power in Western History*, New Haven: Yale University Press.

Jütte, D. (2016), '"They Shall not Keep Their Doors or Windows Open": Urban Space and the Dynamics of Conflict and Contact in Premodern Jewish-Christian Relations', *European History Quarterly*, 46 (2): 209–37.

Koefoed, N.J. (2018), 'The Lutheran Household as Part of Danish Confessional Culture', in B.K. Holm and N.J. Koefoed (eds), *Lutheran Theology and the Shaping of Society: The Danish Monarchy as Example*, 321–40, Göttingen: Vandenhoeck & Ruprecht.

Koops, B.-J., et al. (2017), 'A Typology of Privacy', *University of Pennsylvania Journal of International Law*, 38 (2): 483–575.

Korpiola, M. and H. Pihlajamäki (2021), 'Introduction: Reformation and Early Modern Times', in K.Å. Modéer and H. Vogt (eds), *Law and the Christian Tradition in Scandinavia: The Writings of Great Nordic Jurists*, 59–67, New York: Routledge.

Koselleck, R. (1973), *Kritik und Krise: Eine Studie zur Pathogenese der bürgerlichen Welt*, Frankfurt am Main: Suhrkamp-Taschenbuch-Verl.

Koselleck, R. (1988), *Critique and Crisis: Enlightenment and the Pathogenesis of Modern Society*, Cambridge, MA: MIT Press.

Laitinen, R. (2017a), *Order, Materiality and Urban Space in the Early Modern Kingdom of Sweden*, Amsterdam: Amsterdam University Press.

Laitinen, R. (2017b), 'Home, Urban Space and Gendered Practices in Mid-seventeenth-century Turku', in D. Simonton (ed.), *The Routledge History Handbook of Gender and the Urban Experience*, 142–52, New York: Routledge.

Larsen, J., ed. (1984), *Bidrag til den danske skoles historie: Bd 1: 1536–1784*, Copenhagen: Unge Pædagoger.

Lawton, R. and R.W. Lee (2002), *Population and Society in Western European Port Cities, c.1650–1939*, Liverpool: Liverpool University Press.

Linnarsson, M. (2014), '"Ett wist bequämligitt rum": Byråkratin som platsskapare i 1600-talets Sverige', in M. Hallenberg and M. Linnarsson (eds), *Politiska rum: Kontroll, konflikt och rörelse i det förmoderna Sverige 1300–1850*, 215–34, Lund: Nordic Academic Press.

Linnarsson, M. (2017), *Problemet med vinster: Riksdagsdebatter om privat och offentlig drift under 400 år*, Lund: Nordic Academic Press.

Linnarsson, M. (2018), 'Farming Out State Revenue: The Debate about the General Customs Lease Company in Sweden, 1723–65', *Parliaments, Estates and Representations*, 38 (2): 175–91.

Longfellow, E. (2006), 'Public, Private, and the Household in Early Seventeenth-century England', *Journal of British studies*, 45 (2): 313–34.

Lyngby, T. (2015), *Måder at bo på: Indretning, liv, stemninger og bevidsthedsformer i danske overklasseboliger i byen 1570–1870*, Frederiksborg: Det Nationalhistoriske Museum på Frederiksborg.

Moth, M. (c. 1700), *Moths ordbog*, Copenhagen. Available online: https://mothsordbog.dk/kort-om-moth-og-hans-ordbog (visited 22 March 2021).

Müller, L. (2013), 'Sweden's Neutrality and the Eighteenth-century Inter-state System', in G. Rydén (ed.), *Sweden in the Eighteenth-century World: Provincial Cosmopolitans*, 203–21, Farnham: Ashgate.

Müller, L. (2019), *Neutrality in World History*, New York: Routledge.

Munck, T. (1979), *The Peasantry and the Early Absolute Monarchy in Denmark 1660–1708*, Copenhagen: Landbohistorisk Selskab.

Munck, T. (1998), 'Absolute Monarchy in Later 18th-century Denmark: Centralized Reform, Public Expectations, and the Copenhagen Press', *Historical Journal*, 41 (1): 201–24.

Muurling, S. and M. Pluskota (2017), 'The Gendered Geography of Violence in Bologna, Seventeenth to Nineteenth Centuries', in D. Simonton (ed.), *The Routledge History Handbook of Gender and the Urban Experience*, 153–63, New York: Routledge.

Nauman, S. (2017), *Ordens kraft: Politiska eder i Sverige 1520–1718*, Lund: Nordic Academic Press.

Nauman, S. (2019), 'Flyktingmottagandet i Uppsala domkapitel 1710–1719', *Upplands fornminnesförenings årsbok*: 49–65.

Nielsen, B.K. (2000), *Engelsk-Dansk Ordbog. Gyldendals store røde ordbøger*, Copenhagen: Gyldendal.

Nilsson, K. (2017), *The Money of Monarchs: The Importance of Non-tax Revenue for Autocratic Rule in Early Modern Sweden*, Lund: Department of Political Science, Lund University.

Nordin, J. and J.C. Laursen (2020), 'Northern Declarations of Freedom of the Press: The Relative Importance of Philosophical Ideas and of Local Politics', *Journal of the History of Ideas*, 81 (2): 217–37.

Norrhem, S. (2007), *Kvinnor vid maktens sida 1632–1772*, Lund: Nordic Academic Press.

Orlin, L.C. (2007), *Locating Privacy in Tudor London*, Oxford: Oxford University Press.

Pleijel, H. (1970), *Hustavlans värld: Kyrkligt folkliv i äldre tiders Sverige*, Stockholm: Verbum.

Rahikainen, M. (2019), 'Marriage Markets for Elite Women: Imperial St Petersburg and Helsinki', in E. Chalus and M. Kaartinen (eds), *Gendering Spaces in European Towns, 1500–1914*, 95–113, New York: Routledge.

Reimann, C. and M. Öhman (2021), 'Introduction', in C. Reimann and M. Öhman (eds), *Migrants and the Making of the Urban-maritime World: Agency and Mobility in Port Cities, c. 1570–1940*, 1–16, New York/London: Routledge.

Runefelt, L. (2015), *Att hasta mot undergången: Anspråk, flyktighet, förställning i debatten om konsumtion i Sverige 1730–1830*, Lund: Nordic Academic Press.

Ryan, M.P. (1981), *Cradle of the Middle Class: The Family in Oneida County, New York, 1790–1865*, Cambridge: Cambridge University Press.

Sahlstedt, A. (1773), *Dictionarium Svecium cum interpretatione Latina: Svensk ordbok, med latinsk uttolkning*, Stockholm: C. Stolpe.

Schjerning, C. (2019), 'Behind Thin Walls: Contested Spaces and Spheres of Authority in Late Eighteenth-century Copenhagen', in E. Chalus and M. Kaartinen (eds), *Gendering Spaces in European Towns, 1500–1914*, 184–99, New York/London: Routledge.

Schou, J.H. (1777), *Chronologisk Register over de Kongelige Forordninger og Aabne Breve samt andre trykte Anordninger som fra aar 1670 ere udkomne […]: Deel 1-2*, Copenhagen: Gyldendalsk Boghandlings Forlag.

Sennefelt, K. (2011), *Politikens hjärta: Medborgarskap, manlighet och plats i frihetstidens Stockholm*, Stockholm: Stockholmia.

Sennefelt, K. (2014), 'Wine, Corruption, and the Politics of Intoxication in Eighteenth-century Stockholm', *Past & Present*, 222 (9): 277–95.

Simonton, D. (2019), '"For the Gentlemen of the Town to Walk on by Way of Exchange": Gender, Space and Commerce in the Eighteenth-century Town', in E. Chalus and M. Kaartinen (eds), *Gendering Space in European Towns, 1500–1914*, 46–74, New York/London: Routledge.

Skuncke, M.-C. and H. Tandefelt (2003), *Riksdag, kaffehus och predikstol: Frihetstidens politiska kultur, 1766–1772*, Stockholm/Helsingfors: Atlantis/Svenska litteratursällskapet i Finland.

Spegel, H. (1712), *Glossarium-sveo-gothicum eller Swensk ordabook*, Lund: Abraham Habereger.

Stobart, J. (1998), 'Shopping Streets as Social Space: Leisure, Consumerism and Improvement in an Eighteenth-century County Town', *Urban History*, 25 (1): 3–21.

Swedberg, J. [1714] (2009), *Swensk ordabok*, Värnamo: Stiftelsen för utgivande av Skaramissalet.

Svenska akademiens ordbok (SAOB) (1949) 'Lund: Svenska akademien'. Available online: www.saob.se (visited 30 September 2020).

Svenska akademiens ordbok (SAOB) (1954), 'Lund: Svenska akademien'. Available online: www.saob.se (visited 30 September 2020).

Taussi Sjöberg, M. (2009), *Släkten, pengarna och Caroline Gother: En grosshandlarsläkt i Stockholm under tre generationer 1740–1836*, Stockholm: Atlantis.

Thomson, J.J. (1984), 'The Right to Privacy', in F. Schoeman (ed.), *Philosophical Dimensions of Privacy and Anthology*, 272–89, Cambridge: Cambridge University Press.

Ulväng, G. (2004), *Hus och gård i förändring: Uppländska herrgårdar, boställen och bondgårdar under 1700- och 1800-talens agrara revolution*, Södertälje: Gidlunds förlag.

van den Heuvel, D. (2019), 'Gender in the Streets of the Premodern City', *Journal of Urban History*, 45 (4): 693–710.

van der Heijden, M. (2013), 'Women, Violence and Urban Justice in Holland c. 1600–1838', *Crime, Histoire & Sociétés/ Crime, History & Societies*, 17 (2): 71–100.

van der Heijden, M. and S. Muurling (2018), 'Violence and Gender in Eighteenth-century Bologna and Rotterdam', *Journal of Social History*, 51 (4): 695–716.

Vickery, A. (1993), 'Golden Age to Separate Spheres? A Review of the Categories and Chronology of English Women's History', *The Historical Journal*, 36 (2): 393–414.

Vickery, A. (2008), 'An Englisman's Home Is His Castle? Thresholds, Boundaries and Privacies in the Eighteenth-century London House', *Past and Present*, 199 (1): 147–73.

Villstrand, N.E. (2011), 'Kungen, onden och skriften 1500–1800', *Kungl. Vitterhets historie och antikvitets akademien*, 215–23.

Warrend, S.D. and L.D. Brandeis (1890), 'The Right to Privacy', *Harvard Law Review*, IV (5): 193–220.

Westin, A.F. (1967), *Privacy and Freedom*, New York: Athenum.

Whyman, S.E. (2009), 'Sharing Public Spaces', in C. Brant and S.E. Whyman (eds), *Walking the Streets of Eighteenth-century London: John Gay's Trivia (1716)*, 43–57, Oxford: Oxford University Press.

Williamson, F. (2015), 'Space and the City: Gender Identities in the Seventeenth Century', *Cultural and Social History*, 9 (2): 169–85.

Internet sources

https://danmarkshistorien.dk/leksikon-og-kilder/vis/materiale/danmarks-befolkningsudvikling/ (visited 22 March 2021).

https://mothsordbog.dk/ (visited 22 March 2021).

https://www.carlsbergfondet.dk/da/Nyheder/Nyt-fra-fondet/Nyheder/Trykkefrihed-og-tilblivelsen-af-en-ny-offentlighed (visited 22 March 2021).

https://www.scb.se/hitta-statistik/artiklar/2015/Urbanisering–fran-land-till-stad/ (visited 22 March 2021).

Chapter 1

Ariès, P. and G. Duby, eds (1986), *Histoire de la vie privée*, vol. 3, *De la Renaissance aux Lumières*, Paris: Seuil.

Berger, A. (1953), *Encyclopedic Dictionary of Roman Law* (*Transactions of The American Philosophical Society*, vol. 43:2), Philadelphia: American Philosophical Society.

Brewer, J. (1995), 'This, That and the Other: Public, Social and Private in the Seventeenth and Eighteenth Centuries', in D. Castiglione and L. Sharpe (eds), *Shifting the*

Boundaries: Transformation of the Languages of Public and Private in the Eighteenth Century, 1–21, Exeter: University of Exeter Press.

Chartier, R. (1986), 'Introduction', in P. Ariès and G. Duby (eds), *Histoire de la vie privée*, vol. 3, *De la Renaissance aux Lumières*, Paris: Seuil.

Condren, C. (2009), 'Public, Private and the Idea of the "Public Sphere" in Early-Modern England', *Intellectual History Review*, 19 (1): 15–28.

Förhammar, S. (2011), 'Det offentliga tryckets framväxt', in S. Förhammar, J. Harvard and D. Lindström (eds), *Dolt i offentligheten. Nya perspektiv på traditionellt källmaterial*, 19–24, Lund: Sekel Bokförlag.

Goodman, D. (1992), 'Public Sphere and Private Life: Toward a Synthesis of Current Historiographical Approaches to the Old Regime', *History and Theory*, 31 (1): 1–20.

Habermas, J. (1962), *Strukturwandel der Öffentlichkeit: Untersuchungen zu einer Kategorie der bürgerlichen Gesellschaft*, Neuwied: H. Lucherland.

Horn, E. (2011), 'Logics of Political Secrecy', *Theory, Culture & Society*, 28 (7–8): 103–22.

Ihalainen, P. and K. Palonen (2009), 'Parliamentary Sources in the Comparative Study of Conceptual History: Methodological Aspects and Illustrations of a Research Proposal', *Parliaments, Estates & Representation*, 29 (1): 17–34.

Koselleck, R. (1972), 'Einleitung', in O. Brunner, W. Conze and R. Koselleck (eds), *Geschichtliche Grundbegriffe: Historisches Lexicon zur politisch-sozialen Sprache in Deutschland*, vol. 1 (A–D), Stuttgart: Ernst Klett Verlag.

Koselleck, R. (1973), *Kritik und Krise: Eine Studie zur Pathogenesis der bürgerlichen Welt*, Frankfurt am Main: Suhrkampf-Taschembuch-Verlag.

Landahl, S., ed. *Bondeståndets riksdagsprotokoll*, vol. 1–13 (1720–79), Stockholm 1939–1986.

Landahl, S., ed. *Borgarståndets riksdagsprotokoll före frihetstiden*, Stockholm 1933.

Landahl, S., ed. *Borgarståndets riksdagsprotokoll från frihetstidens början*, vol. 1–10 (1719–1752), Stockholm 1945–2008.

Lindberg, B. (2006), *Den antika skevheten. Politiska ord och begrepp i det tidigmoderna Sverige*, Stockholm: Kungl. Vitterhets historie och antikvitets akademin.

Lindberg, B. (2014), 'Den förmoderna offentligheten. En begreppshistorisk exposé', in L. Runefelt and O. Sjöström (eds), *Förmoderna offentligheter: Arenor och uttryck för politisk debatt 1550–1830*, 21–38, Lund: Nordic Academic Press.

Lindström, D. (2011), 'Om dyrhet och brist: Saltfrågan debatterad vid svenska riksdagar 1650–1741', in S. Förhammar, J. Harvard and D. Lindström (eds), *Dolt i offentligheten. Nya perspektiv på traditionellt källmaterial*, 61–80, Lund: Sekel Bokförlag.

Linnarsson, M- (2017), *Problemet med vinster. Riksdagdebatter om privat och offentlig drift under 400 år*, Lund: Nordic Academic Press.

Ljungberg, J. (2017), *Toleransens gränser. Religionspolitiska dilemman i det tidiga 1700-talets Sverige och Europa*, Lund: Media-Tryck, Lund University.

Longfellow, E. (2006), 'Public, Private, and the Household in Early Seventeenth-Century England', *Journal of British Studies*, 45 (2): 313–34.

Melkersson, M. (1997), *Staten, ordningen och friheten. En studie av den styrande elitens syn på statens roll mellan stormaktstiden och 1800-talet*, Uppsala: Acta Universitatis Upsaliensis.

Nauman, S. (2017), *Ordens kraft: politiska eder i Sverige 1520–1718*, Lund: Nordic Academic Press.

Nordbäck, C. (2004), *Samvetets röst. Om mötet mellan luthersk ortodoxi och konservativ pietism i 1720-talets Sverige*, Umeå: Institutionen för historiska studier.

Petri, J. (1640), *Dictionarium Latino-Sveco-Germanicum*, Linköping: Christ. Günther.

Thanner, L., ed. *Prästeståndets riksdagsprotokoll*, vol. 1–13 (1642–1752), Stockholm 1921–2007.

Runefelt, L. (2001), *Hushållningens dygder. Affektlära, hushållningslära och ekonomiskt tänkande under svensk stormaktstid*, Stockholm: Almqvist & Wiksell International.

Rystad, G. (1992), 'Stormaktstidens riksdag', in N. Stjernquist (ed.), *Riksdagen genom tiderna*, 67–123, Stockholm: Sveriges riksdag.

Schück, H. (1992), 'Riksdagens framväxt. Tiden intill 1611', in N. Stjernquist (ed.), *Riksdagen genom tiderna*, 11–66, Stockholm: Sveriges riksdag.

Spegel, H. (1712), *Glossarium-Sveo-Gothicum Eller Swensk-Ordabook, Inrättat Them til en wällmeent Anledning, som om thet härliga Språket willia begynna någon kunskap inhämta; Utgifven af Haq: Spegel*, Lund: Abrah. Habereger.

Stiernman, A.A.v. (1728–1733), *Alla riksdagars och mötens besluth, samt arfföreningar, regementsformer, försäkringar och bewillningar, som på allmenna riksdagar och möten, ifrån år 1521 intill år 1731 giorde, stadgade och bewiljade äro; med the för hwart och ett stånd utfärdade allmenna resolutioner*, vol. 1–3, Stockholm: Joh. H. Werner.

Stiernman, A.A.v. (1743), *Bihang utaf Åtskillige allmenna Handlingar Ifrån år 1529 intil år 1698. Hörande til the förr i tre serskilte delar utgifne riksdagars och mötens beslut, arfföreningar, regements-former, försäkringar, bewillningar och the för hwart stånd utfärdade allmenna resolutioner*, Stockholm: Lars Salvius.

Swedberg, J. (2009), *Swensk Ordabok: Jesper Swedberg: Svensk ordabok: Utgiven efter Uppsala-handskriften, med tillägg och rättelser ur övriga handskrifter*, ed. L. Holm, Järpås: Stiftelsen för utgivande av Skaramissalet.

Svenska riksdagsakter jämte andra handlingar som höra till statsförvaltningens historia. Ser. 1, Tidehvarfvet 1521–1718, Avd. 1, 1521–1611, vol. 1–4 (1521–1598) (1887–1938), Stockholm: P. A. Norstedt & söner.

Svenska riksdagsakter jämte andra handlingar som höra till statsförvaltningens historia. Ser. 1, Tidehvarfvet 1521–1718, Avd. 2, Tiden från 1611, vol. 1–2 (1611–1617) (1931–1943), Stockholm: Riksarkivet.

Svenska riksdagsakter jämte andra handlingar som höra till statsförvaltningens historia. Ser. 2 Tidehvarfvet 1719–1800, vol. 1–3 (1719–1734) (1909–1922), Stockholm: Riksarkivet.

Sveriges ridderskaps och adels riksdagsprotokoll, vol. 1–17 (1627–1697) (1855–1910), Stockholm.

Sveriges ridderskaps och adels riksdagsprotokoll från och med 1719, vol. 1–32 (1719–1779) (1875–1982), Stockholm: P. A. Norstedt & söner.

Chapter 2

Ancher, P.K. (1759), 'Om handelens Nytte for Borgerlige Stater', in M. Melon (ed.), *Forsøg til en politisk afhandling om handel*, Copenhagen: Nicolaus Møller.

Andersen, D.H. and J.C.V. Johansen (2016), 'Economy and Social Conditions' in E.I. Kouri and J.E. Olesen (eds), *The Cambridge History of Scandinavia*, vol. 2: 1520–1870, 454–508, Cambridge: Cambridge University Press.

Astorri, P. (2020), 'Grotius's Contract Theory in the Works of His German Commentators: First Explorations', *Grotiana*, 41: 88–107.

Becker, A. (2004), 'Jean Bodin on Oeconomic and Politics', *History of European Ideas*, 40 (2): 135–54.

Benn, S.I. and G.F. Gaus, eds (1983), *Public and Private in Social Life*, New York: St. Martin's Press.

Bisset, S. (2015), 'Jean Barbeyrac's Theory of Permissive Natural Law and the Foundation of Property Rights', *Journal of the History of Ideas*, 76 (4): 541–62.

Bregnsbo, M. (1997), *Folk skriver til kongen: Supplikkerne og deres funktion i den dansk-norske enevælde i 1700-tallet: Et kildestudie i Danske Kancellis supplikprotokoller*, Copenhagen: Selskabet for Udgivelse af Kilder til Dansk Historie.

Buckle, S. (1993), *Natural Law and the Theory of Property*, Oxford: Oxford University Press.

Darwall, S. (2000), 'Norm and Normativity', in K. Haakonssen (ed.), *The Cambridge History of Eighteenth-Century Philosophy*, 987–1025, Cambridge: Cambridge University Press.

Dybdahl, V., ed. (1968), *For fædrelandets bedre flor: Bidrag til Det Kgl. Danske Landhusholdningsselskabs historie 1769-1969*, Copenhagen: Det Kgl. Danske Landhusholdningsselskab.

Gaus, G.F. (1983), 'Public and Private Interests in Liberal Political Economy, Old and New', in S.I. Benn and G.F. Gaus (eds), *Public and Private in Social Life*, 183–222, New York: St. Martin's Press.

Grotius, H. (1525), *The Rights of War and Peace I–III*, Richard Tuck (ed.), Carmel, IN: from the Jean Barbeyrac Liberty Fund edition.

Haakonssen, K. and Michael J. Seidler, 'Natural Law: Law, Rights and Duties', in R. Whatmore and B. Young (eds), *A Companion to Intellectual History*, 377–401, Malden: John Wiley & Sons.

Haara, H. (2018), *Pufendorf's Theory of Sociability. Passions, Habits and Social Order*, Cham: Springer.

Haara, H. and A. Lahdenranta, 'Smithian Sentimentalism Anticipated: Pufendorf on the Desire for Esteem and Moral Conduct', *Journal of Scottish Philosophy*, 16 (1): 19–37.

Habermas, J. ([1962] 1991), *The Structural Transformation and the Public Sphere*, Massachusetts: MIT Press.

Hertel, H. (1919–1921), *Det kgl. danske Landhusholdningsselskabs Historie*, 2 vols, Copenhagen: Det kgl. danske Landhusholdningsselskab.

Hobbes, T. ([1651] 1985), *Leviathan*, C.B. Macherson (ed.), London: Andrew Crooke.

Hochstrasser, T.J. (2009), *Natural Law Theories in the Early Enlightenment*, Cambridge: Cambridge University Press.

Horstbøll, H. (1987), *Natural Jurisprudence, Discourses of Improvement and the Absolutist State. The Formation of Modern Economic and Historical Thought in Eighteenth-century Denmark. Revised paper from the Seventh International Congress on Enlightenment*, Budapest: Århus University.

Horstbøll, H. (1989), 'Cosmology and Economics', *Scandinavian Economic History Review*, 37 (2): 26–50.

Härter, K. and M. Stolleis, eds (1996), *Repertorium der Policeyordnungen der frühen Neuzeit*, vol. 1, Frankfurt am Main: Henrik Halbleib und Inke Worgitzki.

Härter, K. (2010), 'Security and "Gute Policey" in Early modern Europe: Concepts, Law and Instruments', *Historical Social Research*, 35: 41–65.

Jespersen, L. (2016), 'Fiscal and Military Developments' in E.I. Kouri and J.E. Olesen (eds), *The Cambridge History of Scandinavia,* Vol. 2: 1520–1870, 362–342, Cambridge: Cambridge University Press.

Keulen, S. and R. Kroeze (2018), 'Privacy from a Historical Perspective', in B.v.d. Sloot and A.d. Groot (eds), *The Handbook of Privacy Studies,* 21–56, Amsterdam: Amsterdam University Press.

Knudsen, P.U. (2001), *Lovkyndighed & vederhæftighed Sjællandske byfogeder 1682–1801,* Copenhagen: DJØF.

Lindgreen, E.R. (2018), 'Privacy from an Economic Perspective', in B.v.d. Sloot and A.d. Groot (eds), *The Handbook of Privacy Studies,* 181–207, Amsterdam: Amsterdam University Press.

Locke, J. (1690), *Second Treatise of Government.* Available online The Gutenberg Project 2012: https://english.hku.hk/staff/kjohnson/PDF/LockeJohnSECONDTREATISE1690.pdf (visited 1 October 2020).

McKeon, M. (2006), *The Secret History of Domesticity, Public, Private, and the Division of Knowledge,* Charles Village: John Hopkins University Press.

Modéer, K.Å. (2001), 'Samuel Pufendorf och "De mänskliga och medborgerliga plikterna": En inledning', in S. Pufendorf, *Om de mänskliga och medborgerliga plikterna enligt naturrätten i två böcker,* B. Bergh trans. 11–23, Lund: Stiftelsen City-universitetet.

Mührmann-Lund, J. (2019), *Borgerligt regimente: Politiforvaltningen i købstæderne og på landet under den danske enevælde,* Copenhagen: Museum Tusculanum.

Posner, R.A. (1984), 'An Economic Theory of Privacy', in F. Schoeman (ed.) *Philosophical Dimensions of Privacy: An Anthology,* 334–45, Cambridge: Cambridge University Press.

Puffendorfii, S. (1673), *De Officio Hominis et Civis juxta Legem Naturalem Libri Duo,* Lund.

Pufendorf, S. (1718), *Les devoirs de l'homme et du citoyen* I–II, J. Barbeyrac trans. 4. ed., Amsterdam.

Puffendorf, S. ([1673] 1742), *Et Menneskes og en Borgers Pligter efter Naturens Lov,* C.H. Brugman trans. from French, Copenhagen: Kgl. Vaisenhus' Borgtrykkeri.

Pufendorf, S. ([1673] 1991), *On the Duty of Man and Citizen According to Natural Law,* J. Tully (ed.), M. Silverthore trans. Cambridge: Cambridge University Press.

Pufendorf, S. ([1673] 2001), *Om de mänskliga och medborgerliga plikterna enligt naturrätten i två böcker,* B. Bergh trans. Lund: Stiftelsen City-universitetet.

Pufendorf, S. ([1698] 2002), *Of the Nature and Qualification of Religion in Reference to Civil Society,* J. Crull (ed.), Carmel, IN: Liberty Fund.

Roessler, B. and D. Mokrosinska, eds (2015), *Social Dimensions of Privacy Interdisciplinary Perspectives,* Cambridge: Cambridge University Press.

Rosenblatt, H. (2018), *The Lost History of Liberalism: From Ancient Rome to the Twenty-First Century,* Princeton: Princeton University Press.

Rosello, D. (2012), 'Hobbes and the Wolf-man: Melancholy and Animality in Modern Sovereignty', *New Literary History,* 43 (2): 255–79.

Saastamoinen, K. (2010), 'Pufendorf on Natural Equality, Human Dignity, and Self-Esteem', *Journal of History of Ideas,* 71 (1): 39–62.

Saastamoinen, K. (2019), 'Pufendorf on the Law of Sociality and the Law of Nations', in K. Haakonssen (ed.), *Early Modern Natural Law,* 107–31, Leiden/Boston: Brill.

Saunders, D. (2003), 'The Natural Jurisprudence of Jean Barbeyrac: Translation as an Art of Political Adjustment', *Eighteenth-Century Studies,* 36 (4): 473–90.

Scattola, M. (2009), 'Scientia iuris and ius naturae: The Jurisprudence of the Holy Roman Empire in the Seventeenth and Eighteenth Centuries', in D. Canale (ed.), *A Treatise of*

Legal Philosophy and General Jurisprudence, vol. 9, A History of the Philosophy of Law in the Civil Law World, *1600-1900*, 1–41, Dordrecht: Springer.

Scoeman, F. (1984), 'Privacy and Intimate Information', in Fredinand Schoeman (ed.), *Philosophical Dimensions of Privacy an Anthology*, 403–24, Cambridge: Cambridge University Press.

Simonton, D. and A. Montenach, eds (2013), *Female Agency in the Urban Economy Gender in European Towns, 1640-1830*, London/New York: Routledge.

Sloot, B.v.d. (2018), 'Privacy from a Legal Perspective', in B.v.d. Sloot and A.d. Groot (eds), *The Handbook of Privacy Studies*, 63–136, Amsterdam: Amsterdam University Press.

Smith, A. (1779–1780), *Undersøgelse om National-Velstands Natur og Aarsag*, F. Dræbye trans. vol. 2., Copenhagen: Gyldendal.

Søllinge, J.D. and N. Thomsen (1987), *De Danske Aviser 1634–1989, vol. 1 1634–1847*, Odense: Odense Universitetsforlag.

Stuat-Buttle, T. and H. Heikki (2019), 'Beyond Justice: Pufendorf and Locke on the Desire for Esteem', *Political Theory*, 47 (5): 699–723.

Sunde, J.Ø. (2007), *'Fornuft og Erfarenhed': Framveksten av metodisk medvit i dansknorsk rett på 1700-talet*, Bergen: Det juridiske fakultet.

Sæther, A. (2017), *Natural Law and the Origin of Political Economy, Samuel Pufendorf and the History of Economics*, London/New York: Routledge.

Thomson, J.J. (1984), 'The Right to Privacy', in F. Schoeman (ed.), *Philosophical Dimensions of Privacy. An Anthology*, 272–89, Cambridge: Cambridge University Press.

Vogt, H. (2007), 'Den juridiske undervisning på det andet ridderlige akademi i Sorø', *Tidsskrift for Rettsvitenskap*, 120: 579–613.

Walton, A.S. (1983), 'Public and Private Interests. Hegel on Civil Society and the State', in S.I. Benn and G.F. Gaus (eds), *Public and Private in Social Life*, 249–66, New York: St. Martin's Press.

Westen, P.v. (1780), *Adresse-Contoirers Natur, Oprindelse og Rettigheder*, Odense.

Zimmermann, R. (1996), *The Law of Obligations: Roman Foundation of the Civilian Tradition*, Oxford: Oxford University Press.

Zuruchen, S. (2000), 'Religion and Society', in K. Haakonssen (ed.), *The Cambridge History of Eighteenth-Century Philosophy*, 779–814, Cambridge: Cambridge University Press.

Zuruchen, S. (2002), 'Introduction', in *Samuel Pufendorf: Of the Nature and Qualification of Religion in Reference to Civil Society*, J. Crull trans. Indianapolis: Liberty Fund, ix–xix.

Chapter 3

1686 års kyrkolag, utgiven av Samfundet Pro fide et christianismo; med inledning av Gabriel Thulin (1936), Stockholm: Svenska kyrkans diakonistyrelse.

Adam, W., ed. (1997), *Geselligkeit und Gesellschaft im Barockzeitalter*, Wiesbaden: Harrassowitz Verlag.

Ågren, M. (2006), 'Hemligt eller offentligt? Om kön, egendom och offentlighet i 1700-talets Sverige', *Historisk tidskrift*, 126 (1): 23–45.

Ariès, P. (1977), *L'homme devant la mort*, Paris: Seuil.

Ariès, P. (1986), 'Pour une histoire de la privée', in P. Ariès and G. Duby (eds), *Histoire de la vie privée, T. 3 De la Renaissance aux Lumières*, 7–20, Paris: Seuil.

Arnold, A. (2016), 'Raum für Unterhaltung(en): Der frühneuzeitliche Salon', *Daphnis*, 44 (3): 340–59.

Bardsley, S. (2006), *Venomous Tongues: Speech and Gender in Late Medieval England*, Philadelphia: University of Pennsylvania Press.

Bellingradt, D. (2012), 'The Early Modern City as a Box: Media, Public Opinion, and the Urban Space of the Holy Roman Empire, Cologne and Hamburg ca. 1700', *Journal of Early Modern History*, 16 (3): 201–40.

Bishop, J. (2017), 'Speech and Sociability: The Regulation of Language in the Livery Companies of Early Modern London', in J. Colson and A. Van Steensel (eds), *Cities and Solidarities: Urban Communities in Pre-Modern Europe*, 208–20, New York: Routledge.

Bourdieu, P. ([1980] 1990), *The Logic of Practice*, Stanford: Stanford University Press.

Brecht, M. (1997), 'Pietismus als alternative GeselligkeitResonating', in W. Adam (ed.), *Geselligkeit und Gesellschaft im Barockzeitalter* vol. 1, 261–74, Wiesbaden: Harrassowitz Verlag.

Burke, P. (1993), *The Art of Conversation*, Cambridge: Polity.

Claesson, U. (2015), *Kris och kristnande: Olof Ekmans kamp för kristendomens återupprättande vid Stora Kopparberget 1689–1713: Pietism, program och praktik*, Göteborg: Makadam.

Collstedt, C. (2007), *Duellanten och rättvisan: Duellbrott och synen på manlighet i stormaktsväldets slutskede*, Lund: Sekel.

Cohen, E.S. (2012), 'She Said, He Said: Situated Oralities in Judicial Records from Early Modern Rome', *Journal of Early Modern History*, 16 (4–5): 403–30.

Cohen, T. V. and E.S. Cohen (1993), *Words and Deeds in Renaissance Rome: Trials before the Papal Magistrates*, Toronto: University of Toronto Press.

Cressy, D. (2010), *Dangerous Talk: Scandalous, Seditious, and Treasonable Speech in Pre-Modern England*, Oxford: Oxford University Press.

Fauster, M. (1991), *Das Gespräch im 18. Jahrhundert: Rhetorik und Geselligkeit in Deutschland*, Stuttgart: M & P Verlag.

Forselius, T.M. (2015), *God dag min läsare! Bland berättare, brevskrivare, boktryckare och andra bidragsgivare i tidig svensk veckopress 1730–1773*, Lund: Ellerströms.

Freise, F. (2004), 'Einleitung', in C. Emmelius, F. Freise, R.v. Mallinckrodt, P. Paschinger, C. Sittig and R. Töpfer (eds), *Offen und Verborgen: Vorstellungen und Praktiken des Öffentlichen und Privaten in Mittelalter und Früher Neuzeit*, 9–32, Göttingen: Wallstein Verlag.

Fry, T., ed. (1865), *The Rule of St. Benedict in English*, Collegeville: The Liturgical Press.

Gierl, M. (2014), 'Pietism, Enlightenment, and Modernity', in Douglas H. Schantz (ed.), *A Companion to German Pietism, 1660–1800*, 348–92, Leiden: Brill.

Gleixner, Ulrike (2014), 'Pietism and Gender: Self-modelling and Agency', in D.H. Schantz (ed.), *A Companion to German Pietism, 1660–1800*, 423–71, Leiden: Brill.

Habermas, J. ([1961] 1990), *Strukturwandel der Öffentlichkeit: Untersuchungen zu einer Kategori der bürgerlichen Gesellschaft*, Frankfurt am Main: Suhrkamp Verlag.

Halsey, K. and J. Slinn (2008), *The Concept and Practice of Conversation in the Long Eighteenth Century, 1688–1848*, Newcastle: Cambridge Scholars Publishing.

Hanneken, P.L. (1723), *Twänne bref om winckel-predikanter och olofliga sammankomster, af doct. Martin Luther och doct. Phil. L. Hannekio skrefne samt efter mångas åstundan på vårt modersmål översatte*, Stockholm: Johan Henr. Werner.

Hansen, A. (2006), *Ordnade hushåll: Genus och kontroll i Jämtland under 1600-talet*, Uppsala: Acta Universitatis Upsaliensis (Studia historica Upsaliensia 224).

Horodowich, E. (2008), *Language and Statecraft in Early Modern Venice*, Cambridge: Cambridge University Press.

Horodowich, E. (2012), 'Introduction: Speech and Oral Culture in Early Modern Europe and Beyond', *Journal of Early Modern History*, 16 (4–5): 301–13.

Inness, J.C. (1992), *Privacy, Intimacy, and Isolation*, New York: Oxford University Press.

Jakobsen, J. (2011), 'Omorganiseringen af den teologiske censur: Generalkirkeinspektionskollegiets censurvirksomhed 1737–1747', *Historisk Tidsskrift* 111 (1): 1–36.

Jakubowski-Tiessen, M. (1995), 'Der Pietismus in Dänemark und Schleswig-Holstein', in M. Brecht and K. Deppermann (eds), *Geschichte des Pietismus*, vol. 2, 446–71, Göttingen: Vandenhoeck & Ruprecht, Göttingen.

Juster, S. (2014), 'Heretics, Blasphemers, and Sabbath Breakers: The Prosecution of Religious Crime in Early America', in C. Beneke and C.S. Grenda (eds), *The First Prejudice: Religious Tolerance and Intolerance in Early America*, 123–42, Philadelphia: University of Pennsylvania Press.

Kermode, J. and G. Walker (1994), *Women, Crime and the Courts in Early Modern England*, Chapel Hill: University of North Carolina Press.

Kilian, T. (1998), 'Public and Private, Power and Space', in A. Light and J. Smith (eds), *The Production of Public Space*, 115–34, Lanham: Rowman & Littlefield.

Lehmann, H. (2017), 'Philipp Jakob Spener's Pia Desideria: A Small Book with a Far-Reaching Effect', in D. Gudmundsson, A. Maurits and M. Nykvist (eds), *Classics in Northern European Church History over 500 Years: Essays in Honour of Anders Jarlert*, 41–60, Frankfurt am Main: Peter Lang.

Lenhammar, H. (2000), *Sveriges kyrkohistoria 5 Individualismens och upplysningens tid*, Stockholm: Verbum.

Lennersand, M. (1999), *Rättvisans och allmogens beskyddare: Den absoluta staten, kommissionerna och tjänstemännen*, Uppsala: Acta Universitatis Upsaliensis (Studia historica Upsaliensia 224).

Lindberg, B.H. (1992), *Praemia et poenae: Etik och straffrätt i Sverige i tidig ny tid*, vol. 2, Uppsala: Uppsala University.

Lindstedt Cronberg, M. (1997), *Synd och skam: ogifta mödrar på svensk landsbygd 1680–1880*, Lund: Studentlitteratur.

Ljungberg, J. (forthcoming), 'Threatening Piety: Perceptions and Interpretations of Pietist Activities during the Early Phase of Sweden's Age of Liberty, 1719–1726', *Pietismus und Neuzeit* (forthcoming).

Ljungberg, J. (2017), *Toleransens gränser: Religionspolitiska dilemman i det tidiga 1700-talets Sverige och Europa*, Lund: Lund University.

Malmstedt, G. (2012), 'De fruktansvärda ederna: Om kampen mot eder och svordomar i Sverige under 1500- och 1600-talen', in E. Nydahl and M. Perlestam (eds), *Från legofolk till stadsfolk: Festskrift till Börje Harnesk*, 67–78, Härnösand: Mittuniversitetet.

Matthias, M. (2015). 'Pietism and Protestant Orthodoxy', in D.H. Schantz (ed.), *A Companion to German Pietism, 1660–1800*, 17–49, Leiden: Brill.

Meyer Spacks, P. (2003), *Privacy: Concealing the Eighteenth-Century Self*, Chicago: University of Chicago Press.

Montgomery, I. (1995), 'Der Pietismus in Schweden im 18. Jahrhundert', in M. Brecht and K. Deppermann (eds), *Geschichte des Pietismus (Bd 2)*, 490–665, Göttingen: Vandenhoeck & Ruprecht.

Moore, jr., B. (1983), *Privacy: Studies in Social and Cultural History*, Armonk: M. E. Sharpe.

Mori, R. (2014), 'The Conventicle Piety of the Radicals', in D.H. Schantz (ed.), *A Companion to German Pietism, 1660–1800*, 201–24, Leiden: Brill.

Naess, H.E. and E. Österberg (2000), 'Sanctions, Agreements, Sufferings', in E. Österberg and S.B. Sogner (eds), *People Meet the Law: Control and Conflict-handling in the Court: The Nordic Countries in the Post-Reformation and Pre-industrial Period*, 140–66, Oslo: Universitetsforlaget.

Nilzén, G. (1971), *Studier i 1730-talets partväsen*, Stockholm: Faibo graf.

Nissenbaum, H. (2010), *Privacy in Context: Technology, Policy, and the Integrity of Social Life*, Stanford: Stanford Law Books.

Norberg, A., ed. (1982), *Prästeståndets riksdagsprotokoll 1723*, Stockholm: Norstedts.

Nordbäck, C. (2004), *Samvetets röst: Om mötet mellan luthersk ortodoxi och konservativ pietism i 1720-talets Sverige*, Umeå: Umeå universitet.

Nordbäck, C. (2006), 'The Conservative Pietism and the Swedish Confessional State', in F.v. Lieburg (ed.), *Confessionalism and Pietism: Religious Reform in Early Modern Europe*, 213–29, Mainz: von Zabern.

Nordstrandh, O. (1951), *Den äldre svenska pietismens litteratur*, Stockholm: Svenska kyrkans diakonistyrelse.

Öhrberg, A. (2011), '"A Threat to Civic Coexistence": Forbidden Religious Literature and Censorship in Eighteenth-Century Sweden', in C. Appel and M. Fink-Jensen (eds), *Religious Reading in the Lutheran North: Studies in Early Modern Scandinavian Book Culture*, 112–32, Newcastle: Cambridge Scholars.

Oja, L. (2000), 'God, enighet, sämja och kärlek uti landet: Den religiösa lagstiftningen och ambitionen att göra goda kristna av stormaktstidens svenskar', in Torkel Jansson and Torbjörn Eng (eds), *Stat – kyrka – samhälle: Den stormaktstida samhällsordningen i Sverige och Östersjöprovinserna*, 17–85, Stockholm: Almqvist & Wiksell.

Österberg, E. and E. Sandmo (2000), 'Introduction', in E. Österberg and S.B. Sogner (eds), *People Meet the Law: Control and Conflict-handling in the Court: The Nordic Countries in the Post-Reformation and Pre-industrial Period*, 9–26, Oslo: Universitetsforlaget.

Rau, S. (2004), 'Das Wirtshaus: Zur Konstitution eines öffentlichen Raumes', in C. Emmelius, F. Freise, R.v. Mallinckrodt, P. Paschinger, C. Sittig and R. Töpfer (eds), *Offen und Verborgen: Vorstellungen und Praktiken des Öffentlichen und Privaten in Mittelalter und Früher Neuzeit*, 211–27, Göttingen: Wallstein Verlag.

Rössler, B. ([2001] 2005), *The Value of Privacy*, Cambridge: Polity.

Sandmo, E. (1999), *Voldssamfunnets undergang: Om disciplineringen av Norge på 1600-talet*, Oslo: Universitetsforl. cop.

Scudéry, M.d. (1682), *Les conversations sur divers sujets par mademoiselle De Scudery*, Amsterdam: Daniel Du Fresne.

Snyder, J.R. (2009), *Dissimulation and the Culture of Secrecy in Early Modern Europe*, Berkeley: University of California Press.

Solove, D.J. (2008), *Understanding Privacy*, Cambridge, MA: Harvard University Press.

Spegel, H. ([1713] 1728), 'Sal. Herr archie-biskopens i Upsala, dr. Haqvini Spegels korta doch mogna betenckande om privatis conventiulis eller enskylta sammankomster; upsatt i Stockholm åhr 1713', in G.A. Humble (ed.), *Novator ataktos, eller, om några nygirigas oordenteliga privata conventicler och enskylta sammankomster*, 443–8, Stockholm: J.L. Horrn.

Swedberg, J. (1960), *Levernesbeskrivning: Urval och inledning av Inge Jonsson*, Stockholm: Natur & Kultur.

van der Geest, S. (2018), 'Privacy from an Anthropological Perspective', in B. Van Der Sloot and A. Groot (eds), *The Handbook of Privacy Studies. An Interdisciplinary Introduction*, 413–41, Amsterdam: Amsterdam University Press.

Van Horn Melton, J. (2001), 'Pietism, Politics and the Public Sphere in Germany', in J.E. Bradley and D.K.V. Kley (eds), *Religion and Politics in Enlightenment Europe*, 294–333, Notre Dame: University of Notre Dame Press.

Van Kley, D. (1996), *The Religious Origins of the French Revolution: From Calvin to the Civil Constitution, 1560–1791*, New Haven: Yale University Press.

Vincent, D. (2016), *Privacy: A Short History*, Cambridge: Polity Press.
Wallmann, J. (2005), *Der Pietismus* 2nd edn., Göttingen: Vandenhoeck & Ruprecht.
Warren, S.D. and L. Brandeis (1890), 'The Right to Privacy', *Harvard Law Review* 4 (5): 193–220.
Westin, A. (1967), *Privacy and Freedom*, New York: Atheneum.
Yligangas, H., J.C.V. Johansen, K. Johansson and H.E. Naess (2000), 'Family, State, and Patterns of Criminality: Major Tendencies in the Work of the Courts, 1550–1850', in E. Österberg and S.B. Sogner (eds), *People Meet the Law: Control and Conflict-handling in the Court: The Nordic Countries in the Post-reformation and Pre-industrial Period*, 57–139, Oslo: Universitetsforlaget.
Zemon Davis, N. (1987), *Fiction in the Archives: Pardon Tales and Their Tellers in Sixteenth-century France*, Stanford: Stanford University Press.

Dictionaries

Cambridge Dictionary https://dictionary.cambridge.org/dictionary/english/conversation (visited 22 March 2021)

The Swedish National Archive (SNA)

Äldre kommittéer (ÄK), vol. 189: Kommission ang oväsendet i Umeå församling [prosten Nils Grubb] (1723), 3 volumes.
Äldre kommittéer (ÄK), vol. 190: Kommission ang religiösa sammankomster i Sickla (1723), 2 volumes.
Äldre kommittéer (ÄK), vol. 191: Kommission ang kyrkoherden Erik Tolstadius såsom anhängare av Dippels lära (1729), 4 volumes.
Kanslikollegium (1411), Inkomna handlingar (E), Skrivelser i kyrko- och undervisningsärenden (XII), vol. 30 (1722–1800).
Riksrådet, K 23:1138: Handlingar rörande conventikelplakatet (1725).

Chapter 4

Andersen, O.B. (1999), '1700-tallets brevkultur og romanen', in F. Andersen, O. Birklund and P. Dahl (eds), *1700-tallets litterære kultur*, 80–96, Aarhus: Aarhus Universitetsforlag.
Anderson, H. and I. Ehrenpreis (1966), 'The Familiar Letter in the Eighteenth-century: Some Generalizations', in H. Anderson, P.B. Daghlian and I. Ehrenpreis (eds), *The Familiar Letter in the Eighteenth-century*, Lawrence: University Press of Kansas.
Berndtson, T., O. Fischer, A. Mattson and A. Öhrberg (2017), 'Inledning: 1700-talets handskriftskulturer', *Sjuttonhundratal: Nordic Yearbook for Eighteenth-Century Studies*, 14: 8–16.
Bolter, J. D. and R. Gruisin (1999), *Remediation: Understanding New Media*, Cambridge, MA: The MIT Press.
Bruhn Jensen, K., ed. (1996), *Dansk mediehistorie 1: Mediernes forhistorie og 1840–1880*, København: Samlerens Forlag.
De til Forsendelse med Posten allene priviligerede Kiøbenhavnske Tidender (PKT), 1762–1808. Available online: http://www2.statsbiblioteket.dk/mediestream/avis (accessed 23 October 2020).

Darnton, R. (2000), 'An Early Information Society. News and the Media in Eighteenth-Century Paris', *The American Historical Review*, 105 (1): 1–35.

Droste, H. (2011), 'Degrees of Publicity. Handwritten Newspapers in the Seventeenth and Eighteenth Centuries', *LIR.journal* 1: 67–83.

Droste, H. (2019), 'How Public Was the News in Early Modern Times?' in H. Droste and K. Salmi-Niklander (eds), *Handwritten Newspapers: An Alternate Medium during Early Modern and Modern Periods*, 29–44, Helsinki: Suomalaisen Kirjallisuuden Seura.

Finkenhagen, J. (1749), *Anmerkninger over den Kunst at skrive et godt Brev*, Copenhagen: Ernst Heinrich Berling.

Forselius, T.M. (2015), *God dag, min läsare! Bland berättare, brevskrivare, boktryckare och andre bidragsgivare i tidig svensk veckopress 1730–1773*, Lund: Ellerströms Förlag.

Gellert, C.F. ([1751] 1762), *Breve, tilligemed en praktisk Afhandling om den gode Smag i Breve*, Copenhagen: Nicolaus Møller.

Horstbøll, H. (2010), 'Anonymsiteten, trykkefriheden og forfatterrollens forandring i 1700-tallets Danmark', *Lychnos. Årsbok for idé- og lärdomshistorie*, 147–61.

Jensen, J.F., M. Møller, T. Nielsen and J. Stiegel (1983), *Dansk litteraturhistorie 4. Patriotismens tid 1746–1807*, Copenhagen: Gyldendal.

Kiøbenhavnske Danske Post-Tidender (KDP) (1749–1762). Available online: http://www2.statsbiblioteket.dk/mediestream/avis (accessed 23 October 2020).

Kirchhoff-Larsen, C. (1942), *Den danske Presses Historie*, vol. 1, Copenhagen: Munksgaard.

Kopenhagener Deutsche Post-Zeitungen (KDeP) (1749–1767). Available online: http://www2.statsbiblioteket.dk/mediestream/avis (accessed 23 October 2020).

Madsen, O. (1991), *Et nyttigt og gavnligt Postværk. P&Ts historie til 1711*, Copenhagen: Generaldirektoratet for Post- og Telegrafvæsenet.

Pedersen, S.C. (2008), *Brudte segl. Spionage og censur i enevældens Danmark*, Copenhagen: Post & Tele Museum.

Pettegree, A. (2014), *The Invention of News: How the World Came to Know about Itself*, New Haven: Yale University Press.

Scarborough, R. (2018), 'All the News That's Fit to Write: The Eighteenth-Century Manuscript Newsletter', in S.G. Brandtzæg, P. Goring and C. Watson (eds), *Travelling Chronicles. News and Newspapers from the Early Modern Period to the Eighteenth-century*, 95–118, Leiden: Brill.

Stolpe, P. M. (1878–82), *Dagspressen i Danmark, dens Vilkaar og Personer indtil Midten af det attende Aarhundrede*, vol. 1–4, Copenhagen: Samfundet til den Danske Litteraturs Fremme.

Søllinge, J.D. and N. Thomsen (1991), *De danske aviser 1634–1989*, vol. 1, Odense: Odense Universitetsforlag.

Warner, W. B. (2018), 'Truth and Trust and the Eighteenth-century Anglophone Newspaper', in S. G. Brandtzæg, P. Goring and C. Watson (eds), *Travelling Chronicles. News and Newspapers from the Early Modern Period to the Eighteenth-century*, 27–48, Leiden: Brill.

Chapter 5

Adresseavisen (Kiøbenhavns Kongelig alene priviligerede Adresse-Contoirs Efterretninger) (1759–1854). Available online: *http://www2.statsbiblioteket.dk/mediestream/avis/list/doms_newspaperAuthority%3Auuid%3A39fa5737-c2a9-4d5a-988e-c260f24cd76b* (visited 31 March 2021).

Blome, A. (2002), 'Das Intelligenzwesen in Hamburg und Altona', in S. Doering-Manteuffel, J. Mancal and W. Wüst (eds), *Pressewesen der Aufklärung: Periodische Schriften im Alten Reich*, 183–207, Berlin: De Gruyter.

Bregnsbo, M. (1997), *Folk skriver til kongen: Supplikkerne og deres funktion i den dank-norske enevælde i 1700-tallet*, Copenhagen: Selskabet for Udgivelse af Kilder til Dansk Historie.

Cowan, B. (2001), 'What Was Masculine about the Public Sphere? Gender and the Coffeehouse Milieu in Post-Restoration England', *History Workshop Journal*, 51: 127–57.

Dahl, G. (2011), *Books in Early Modern Norway*, Leiden/Boston: Brill.

Davidsen, J. and K. Gamberg (1884), *Fra vore Fædres Tid*, Copenhagen: Gyldendal.

Farge, A. (1986), 'The Honor and Secrecy of Families', in R. Chartier (ed.), *A History of the Private Life, vol. III: Passions of the Renaissance*, 571–607, Cambridge, MA: The Bellknap Press of Harvard Univeristy Press.

Henningsen, P. (2001), 'Den bestandige maskerade: Standssamfund, rangsamfund og det 18. århundredes Honnette kultur', *Historisk Tidsskrift*, 101 (2): 313–44.

Henningsen, P. (2005), 'Misericordia: Tiggere, husarme og andre fattige i København, 1500–1800', *Historiske meddelelser om København*, 98: 18–56.

Holm, E. (1885), *Nogle hovedtræk af trykkefrihedstidens historie*, Copenhagen: Schultz.

Horstbøll, H. (1999), *Menigmands medie: Det folkelige bogtryk i Danmark 1500–1840*, Copenhagen: Museum Tusculanum.

Horstbøll, H. (2010), 'Anonymiteten, trykkefriheden og forfatterrollens forandring i 1700-tallets Danmark', *Lychnos: Årsbok för idé- och lärdomshistoria*, 147–61.

Horstbøll, H., U. Langen and F. Stjernfelt (2020), *Grov Konfekt: Tre vilde år med trykkefrihed 1770-73*, Copenhagen: Gyldendal.

Israel, J. (2015), 'Northern Varieties: Contrasting the Dano-Norwegian and the Swedish-Finnish Enlightenments', in E. Krefting, A. Nøding and M. Ringvej (eds), *Eighteenth-Century Periodicals as Agents of Change*, 17–45, Leiden/Boston: Brill.

Ilsøe, H. (1992), *Bogtrykkerne i København 1600–1810*, Copenhagen: Museum Tusculanum.

Jakobsen, J. (2011), 'Omorganiseringen af den teologiske censur', *Historisk Tidsskrift*, 111 (1): 1–36.

Jakobsen, J. (2017), *Uanstændige, utilladelige og unyttige skrifte:. En undersøgelse af censuren i praksis 1746–1773*, Unpublished PhD dissertation, University of Copehagen.

Jakobsen, J. (2016), '"… At I for saadant Eders u-tilladelige forhold skal vorde anseet og straffet … ": Bogtrykkeren Johan Jørgen Høpfner mellem politimyndighed og akademisk censur i 1740'ernes København', in S.L. Bak et al. (eds), *'Kildekunst' Historiske og kulturhistoriske studier: Festskrift til John. T. Lauridsen*, 165–83, Copenhagen: Museum Tusculanum.

Krogh, T. (2000), *Oplysningstiden og det magiske: Henrettelser og korporlige straffe i 1700-tallets første halvdel*, Copenhagen: Samleren.

Langen, U. (2014), 'Defending Citizenship, Defining Citizenship: Rumours, Pamphleteering and the General Public in Late Eighteenth Century Copenhagen', in K. Cowman (ed.), *Gender in Urban Europe: Sites of Political Activity and Citizenship, 1750–1900*, 42–57, New York: Routledge.

Laursen, J.C. (2002), 'Luxdorph's Press Freedom Writings: Before the Fall of Struensee in Early 1770s Denmark-Norway', *The European Legacy: Toward New Padigms*, 7 (1): 61–77.

Maliks, J. (2014), 'Imprimatur i provinsen: Sensuren av det trykte ord utenfor København 1737–1770', in E. Tjønneland (ed.), *Kritikk før 1814*, 78–102, Oslo: Dreyers forlag.

Maliks, J. (2015), 'To Rule is to Communicate: The Absolutist System of Political Communication in Denmark-Norway, 1660–1750', in E. Krefting, A. Nøding and

M. Ringvej (eds), *Eighteenth-Century Periodicals as Agents of Change: Perspectives on Northern Enlightenment*, 134–52, Leiden/Boston: Brill.

McNeely, I.F. (2000), 'The Intelligence Gazette (Intelligenzblatt) as a Road Map to Civil Society', in F. Trentmann and C. Maier (eds), *Paradoxes of Civil Society*, 135–56, New York: Berghahn Books.

McNeely, I.F. (2003), *The Emancipation of Writing: German Civil Society in the Making, 1790s–1820s*, Berkeley, Los Angeles/London: University of California Press.

Melton, J.v.H. (2001), *The Rise of the Public in Enlightenment Europe*, Cambridge: Cambridge University Press.

Moore, C.N. (2006), *Patterned Lives: The Lutheran Funeral Biography in Early Modern Germany*, Weisbaden: Harrassowitz Verlag.

Munck, T. (2007), 'Keeping the Peace: Good Police and Civic Order in 18th-century Copenhagen', *Scandinavian Journal of History*, 32 (1): 38–62.

Nordin, J. (2020), 'En revolution i tryck: Tryckfrihet och tryckproduktion i Sverige 1766–1772 och däromkring', in D. Möller (ed.), *Vetenskapssocieteten i Lund. Årsbok 2020*, 87–112, Lund: Vetenskapssocieteten i Lund.

Nordin, J. and J.C. Laursen (2020), 'Northern Declarations of Freedom of the Press: The Relative Importance of Philosophical Ideas and of Local Politics', *Journal of the History of Ideas*, 81 (2): 217–37.

Nøding, A. (2013), 'Københavns adressekontor: Mediehus og litterær aktør', in J.K. Smidt, T. Vold and K. Oterholm (eds), *Litteratursocialogiske perspektiv*, 118–40, Oslo: Universitetsforlaget.

Nyrup, C. (1870), *Bidrag til den danske boghandels historie*, vol. 1, Copenhagen: Gyldendal.

Prahl, N. (1783), *Herr Agent Hans Holcks Levnetsløb, i korthed*, Copenhagen: C.L. Buch.

Rian, Ø. (2014), *Sensuren i Danmark-Norge*, Oslo: Universitetsforlaget.

Rospocher, M., ed. (2012), *Beyond the Public Sphere: Opinions, Publics, Spaces in Early Modern Europe*, Bologna: Il Mulino.

Schilling, L. (2000), 'Policey und Druckmedien im 18. Jahrhundert: Das Intelligenzblatt als Medium policeylicher Kommunikation', in K. Härter (ed.), *Policey und frühneuzeitliche Gesellschaft*, 413–52, Frankfurt am Main: Vittorio Klostermann.

Sennefelt, K. (2008), 'Citizenship and the Political Landscape of Libelling in Stockholm, c. 1720–70', *Social History*, 33 (2): 145–63.

Stolpe, P.M. (1878–1882), *Dagspressen i Danmark*, 4 vols., Copenhagen: Rosenkilde og Bagger.

Søllinge, J.D. and N. Thomsen (1989), *De danske aviser 1634–1989*, vol. 1, Odense: Odense Universitetsforlag.

Tantner, A. (2016), 'The Intelligence Offices in the Habsburg Monarchy', in J. Raymond and N. Moxham (eds), *News Networks in Early Modern Europe*, 443–64, Leiden/Boston: Brill.

Trentmann, F. (2016), *Empire of Things*, London: Penguin.

La Vopa, A.J. (1992), 'Conceiving a Public: Ideas and Society in Eighteenth-Century Europe', *The Journal of Modern History*, 64 (1): 79–116.

Warren, S.D. and L. Brandeis (1890), 'The Right to Privacy', *Harvard Law Review*, 4 (5): 193–220.

von Westen, P. (1780), *Adresse-Contoirers Natur, Oprindelse og Rettigheder*, Odense: Det Kongelige Priviligerede Adresse-Contoirs Bogtrykkerie.

Wiltenburg, J. (2012), *Crime and Culture in Early Modern Germany*, Charlottesville: University of Virginia Press.

The Danish National Archive (DNA)

Danske Kancelli, Indlæg til Brevbøger (F42)
Danske Kancelli, Koncepter og indlæg til Oversekretærens brevbøger (D101)
Danske Kancelli, Oversekretærens Brevbøger (D99)
Danske Kancelli, Sjællandske Tegnelser (F11)
Danske Kancelli (DK), Sjællandske Tegnelser (D20)

Chapter 6

Ahmed, S. (2004), 'Collective Feelings: Or, the Impressions Left by Others', *Theory, Culture & Society*, 21 (2): 25–42.
Ahmed, S. (2014), *The Cultural Politics of Emotion*, Edinburgh: Edinburgh University Press.
Amussen, S. (1994), '"Being Stirred to Much Unquietness": Violence and Domestic Violence in Early Modern England', *Journal of Women's History*, 6 (2): 70–89.
Armstrong, I. (2008), *Victorian Glassworlds: Glass Culture and the Imagination, 1830–1880*, Oxford: Oxford University Press.
Bailey, J. (2006), '"I dye [sic] by Inches": Locating Wife Beating in the Concept of a Privatization of Marriage and Violence in Eighteenth-century England', *Social History*, 31 (3): 273–94.
Barclay, K. (2017), 'Intimacy, Community and Power: Bedding Rituals in Eighteenth-Century Scotland', in K. Barclay and M. Bailey (eds), *Emotion, Ritual and Power in Europe, 1200–1920*, 43–61, Cham: Springer.
Barclay, K. (2021), *Caritas: Neighbourly Love and the Early Modern Self*, Oxford: Oxford University Press.
Bayless, M. (2012), *Sin and Filth in Medieval Culture: The Devil in the Latrine*, New York: Routledge.
Blüdnikow, B. (1986), 'Folkelig uro i København 1789–1820', *Fortid og Nutid*, 33: 1–54.
Capp, B. (2003), *When Gossips Meet. Women, Family, and Neighbourhood in Early Modern England*, Oxford: Oxford University Press.
Cohen, E. (1992), 'Honor and Gender in the Streets of Early Modern Rome', *The Journal of Interdisciplinary History*, 22 (4): 597–625.
Cohen, T. and E. Cohen (2001), 'Open and Shut: The Social Meanings of the Cinquecento Roman House', *Studies in the Decorative Arts*, 9 (1): 61–84.
Crane, M. (2009), 'Illicit Privacy and Outdoor Spaces in Early Modern England', *Journal for Early Modern Cultural Studies*, 9 (1): 4–22.
Darnton, R. (1984), *The Great Cat Massacre and Other Episodes in French Cultural History*, New York: Basic Books.
Davis, N. Z. (1971), 'The Reasons of Misrule: Youth Groups and Charivaris in 16th-Century France', *Past & Present*, 50 (1): 41–75.
Davis, N.Z. (1984), 'Charivari, Honor, and Community in Seventeenth-Century Lyon and Geneva', in J.A. MacAloon (ed.), *Rite, Drama, Festival, Spectacle: Rehearsals toward a Theory of Cultural Performance*, 42–57, Philadelphia: Ishe Press.
Dean, T. (2004), 'Gender and Insult in an Italian City: Bologna in the Later Middle Ages', *Social History*, 29: 217–31.
Douglas, M. (1966), *Purity and Danger: An Analysis of the Concepts of Pollution and Taboo*. London: Routledge.

Elias, N. ([1939] 1978), *The Civilizing Process: The History of Manners*, Oxford: Blackwell.

Flather, A. (2007), *Gender and Space in Early Modern England*, Woodbridge: Royal Historical Society/Boydell Press.

Gowing, L. (1999), *Domestic Dangers: Women, Words, and Sex in Early Modern London*, Oxford: Clarendon.

Gowing, L. (2000), 'The Freedom of the Streets: Women and Social Space in London, 1560–1640', in *Griffiths, and Jenner Londinopolis: Essays in the Cultural and Social History of Early Modern London*, 130–51, Manchester: Manchester University Press.

Gowing, L. (2003), *Common Bodies. Women, Touch and Power in Seventeenth-century England*, New Haven and London: Yale University Press.

Gowing, L. (2014), 'The Twinkling of a Bedstaff: Recovering the Social Life of English Beds 1500–1700', *Home Cultures* 11 (3): 275–304.

Ingram, M. (1988), *Church Courts, Sex and Marriage in England, 1570–1640*, Cambridge: Cambridge University Press.

Ingram, M. (1994), '"Scolding Women Cucked or Washed"': A Crisis in Gender Relations in Early Modern England? in J. Kermode and G. Walker (eds), *Women, Crime and the Courts in Early Modern England*, 48–80. London: Routledge.

Jütte, D. (2016), '"They Shall Not Keep Their Doors or Windows Open": Urban Space and the Dynamics of Conflict and Contact in Premodern Jewish-Christian Relations', *European History Quarterly*, 46 (2): 209–37.

Kilday, A. and D. Nash (2010), *Exploring Crime and Morality in Britain 1600–1900*, Chippenham: Palgrave MacMillan.

Langen, U. (2005), 'Taskenspilleren og den danske nation. Historien om et slagsmål og et parti billard, der aldrig blev spillet', *Fortid og Nutid*, 4: 243–60.

Langen, U. (2009), 'Den æreløse ordensmagt: Kampen om byrummet mellem vægtere, gardere og pøbel i 1700-tallets København', *Fortid og Nutid*, 2: 83–105.

Langen, U. (2017), 'The Post Office Feud: Sensing Urban Disturbance in Late Eighteenth-century Copenhagen', *The Senses and Society*, 12 (2): 132–46.

Larrington, C. (2006), 'Diet, Defecation and the Devil: Disgust and the Pagan Past', in N. McDonald (ed.) *Medieval Obscenities*, 138–55, Woodbridge: York Medieval Press.

Linaa, J. (2016), 'Den monstrøse materialitet. Om placeringen af 16 middelalderlige latriner fra Aarhus', *Kulturstudier*, 7 (2): 23–40.

Miller, W. I. (1993), *Humiliation: And Other Essays on Honor, Social Discomfort, and Violence*. Ithaca, NY: Cornell University Press.

Miller, W. I. (1997), *The Anatomy of Disgust*, Cambridge: Harvard University Press.

Paster, G. K. (1993), *The Body Embarrassed: Drama and the Disciplines of Shame in Early Modern England*. Ithaca, NY: Cornell University Press.

Reinke-Williams, T. (2011), 'Women's Clothes and Female Honour in Early Modern London', *Continuity and Change*, 26 (1): 69–88.

Scheer, M. (2012), 'Are Emotions a Kind of Practice (and Is That What Makes Them Have a History)? A Bourdieuian Approach to Understanding Emotion', *History and Theory* 51 (2): 193–220.

Schjerning, C. (2013), *Moralske følelser og sociale relationer i København 1771–1800*, Unpublished PhD dissertaion, University of Copenhagen.

Schjerning, C. (2015), 'Følelsesgeografier og fællesskaber i København 1771–1800', *Temp – Tidsskrift for Historie*, 6 (11): 26–49.

Schjerning, C. (2019), 'Behind Thin Walls. Private Spaces and Spheres of Authority in Late Eighteenth-Century Copenhagen', in E. Chalus and M. Kaartinen (eds), *Conceived, Constructed & Contested Spaces: Gender in the European Town, c.1500–1914*, 184–99, New York: Routledge.

Sedgwick, E. K. (2003), *Touching Feeling: Affect, Pedagogy, Performativity*. Durham: Duke University Press.

Sharpe, J.A. (1980), *Defamation and Sexual Slander in Early Modern England: The Church Courts at York*, York: Borthwick Institute for Archives York.

Shoemaker, R. (2000), 'The Decline of Public Insult in London 1660-1800', *Past & Present*, 169 (1): 97-131.

Sennefelt, K. (2019). 'Absent Men and Tainted Houses: Gender, Place and Self in Stockholm in 1719', in E. Chalus and M. Kaartinen (eds), *Conceived, Constructed & Contested Spaces: Gender in the European* Town, *c.1500-1914*, 168-83, New York: Routledge.

St. George, R.B. (1998), *Conversing by Signs: Poetics of Implication in Colonial New England Culture*, Chapel Hill: University of North Carolina Press.

Stallybrass, P. (1986), 'Patriarchal Territories: The Body Enclosed', in M. Ferguson, M. Quilligan N. and Vickers (eds) *Rewriting the Renaissance: The Discourses of Sexual Difference in Early Modern Europe*, 123-42, Chicago-London: University of Chicago Press.

Stevnsborg, H. (1983), '"Opløb" og "Oprør" i 17- og 1800-tallets København', *Den jyske historiker*, 25: 39-61.

Stevnsborg, H. (1980), 'Fra Den store Udfejelsesfest til Tømrerstrejken. Om førindustriel, folkelig protest i København i sidste halvdel af det 18. århundrede', *Fortid og Nutid*, 28: 570-99.

Stewart, F. H. (1994), *Honor*. Chicago: University of Chicago Press.

Stjernfelt, F, U. Langen and H. Horstbøll (2020), Grov *Konfækt: Tre vilde år med trykkefrihed - 1770-73*, Copenhagen: Gyldendal.

Underdown, D. and A. Fletcher (1985), 'The Taming of the Scold: The Enforcement of Patriarchal Authority in Early Modern England', in A. Fletcher and J. Stevenson (eds), *Order and Disorder in Early Modern England*, 116-36, Cambridge: Cambridge University Press.

Vickery, A. (2008), 'An Englisman's Home Is His Castle? Thresholds, Boundaries and Privacies in the Eighteenth-century London House', *Past & Present* 199 (1): 147-73.

Chapter 7

Ariès, P. (1989), 'Introduction', in P. Ariès and G. Duby (eds), *A History of Private Life. Volume 3*: R. Chartier (ed.), *Passions of the Renaissance*, 1-12, Cambridge, MA: Belknap Press of Harvard University.

Arnade, P., M.C. Howell and W. Simons (2002), 'Fertile Spaces: The Productivity of Urban Space in Northern Europe', *Journal of Interdisciplinary History* 32 (4): 515-48.

Beaudry, M.C. (2015), 'Households Beyond the House: On the Archaeology and Materiality of Historical Households', in K.R. Fogle, J.A. Nyman and M.C. Beaudry (eds), *Beyond the Walls: New Perspectives on the Archaeology of Historical Households*, 1-22, Gainesville, FL: University Press of Florida.

Brewer, J. (1995), 'This, That and the Other: Public, Social and Private in the Seventeenth and Eighteenth Centuries', in D. Castignole and L. Sharpe (eds), *Shifting the Boundaries: Transformation of the Language of Public and Private in the Eighteenth Century*, 1-21, Exeter: University of Exeter Press.

Cederlund, J. (1997), 'Arkitekturen 1690-1730', in G. Alm (ed.), *Signums svenska konsthistoria*, 105-58, Lund: Signum.

Cnattingius, B. (1929), 'Onkel Adamshuset i Linköping', in S. Erixon and S. Wallin (eds), *Svenska kulturbilder 1*, 303–20, Stockholm: Skoglund.

De Groot, J., I. Devos and A. Schmidt, eds (2015), *Single Life and the City, 1200–1900*, Houndmills: Palgrave Macmillan.

Dobres, M.-A. and J.E. Robb (2000), 'Agency in Archaeology. Paradigm or Platitude?' in M.-A. Dobres and J.E. Robb (eds), *Agency in Archaeology*, 3–17, London: Routledge.

Eibach, J. (2011), 'Das offene Haus: Kommunikative Praxis im sozialen Nahraum der europäischen Frühen Neuzeit', *Zeitschrift für Historische Forschung*, 38 (4): 621–64.

Gejvall, B. (1988), *1800-talets stockholmsbostad. En studie över den borgerliga bostadens planlösning i bostadshusen*, Stockholm: Stockholmia.

Gunn, S. (2001), 'The Spatial Turn: Changing Histories of Space and Place', in S. Gunn and R.J. Morris (eds), *Identities in Space: Contested Terrains in the Western City Since 1850*, 1–14, Aldershot: Ashgate.

Gunn, S. and R.J. Morris, eds (2001), *Identities in Space: Contested Terrains in the Western City Since 1850*, Aldershot: Ashgate.

Habermas, J. (1962), *Struktuirwandel der Öffentlichkeit. Untersuchungen zu einer Kategorie der bürgerlichen Gesellschaft*, Neuwied: Luchterhand.

Heyl, C. (2004), *A Passion for Privacy: Untersuchungen zur Genese der bürgerlichen Privatsphäre in London, 1660–1800*, München: Oldenbourg.

Hillier, B. and J. Hanson (1984), *The Social Logic of Space*, Cambridge: Cambridge University Press.

Hofrén, M. (1937), *Herrgårdar och boställen: En översikt över byggnadskultur och heminredning å Kalmar läns herrgårdar 1650–1850*, Stockholm: Nordiska Museet.

Hussey, D. and M. Ponsonby, eds (2008), *Buying for the Home: Shopping for the Domestic from the Seventeenth Century to the Present*, Burlington: Ashgate.

Jerram, L. (2013), 'Space: A Useless Category for Historical Analysis?' *History and Theory* 52 (3): 400–19.

Johnson, M. (1993), *Housing Culture: Traditional Architecture in an English Landscape*, London: UCL Press.

Johnson, M. (2010), *English Houses, 1300–1800: Vernacular Architecture, Social Life*, Harlow: Pearson Longman.

Kingston, R. (2010). 'Mind over Matter? History and the Spatial Turn', *Cultural and Social History*, 7 (1): 111–21.

Laitinen, R. (2017), *Order, Materiality, and Urban Space in the Early Modern Kingdom of Sweden*, Amsterdam: Amsterdam University Press.

Lefebvre, H. (1991), *The Production of Space*, trans. D. Nicholson-Smith, Oxford: Basil Blackwell.

Lindberg, F. (1946), *Linköpings historia 2: 1567–1862*, Uppsala: Almqvist & Wiksell.

Lindström, D. (2013), 'Bland lindansare, oskyldiga nöjen och offentliga bakverk: Assemblé- och spektakelhuset i Linköping', in H. Edgren, et al. (eds), *Nationen så in i Norden: En festskrift till Torkel Jansson*, 143–56, Skellefteå: Artos & Norma.

Lindström, D. (2016), 'Leisure Culture, Entrepreneurs and Urban Space: Swedish Towns in a European Perspective, Eighteenth–Nineteenth Centuries', in Peter B. and J.H. Furnée (eds), *Leisure Cultures in Urban Europe, c. 1700–1870: A Transnational Perspective*, 140–60, Manchester: Manchester University Press.

Lindström, D. (2020), 'Families and Households, Tenants and Lodgers: Cohabitation in an Early Modern Swedish Town, Linköping 1750–1800', *Journal of Family History*, 45 (2): 228–49.

Lindström, D. and G. Tagesson (2015), 'On Spatializing History – the Household as Spatial Unit in Early Modern Swedish Towns', *META Historisk-arkeologisk tidskrift*: 47–60.

Lindström, D. and G. Tagesson (2016), 'Ägande, boende och hushåll på Kvarnholmen under1700-talet', in G. Tagesson and P. Carelli (eds), *Kalmar mellan dröm och verklighet. Konstruktionen av den tidigmoderna staden*, Linköping: Arkeologerna, Statens historiska museer.

Lindström, D. and G. Tagesson (forthcoming, 2022). *Houses, Families, and Cohabitation in Eighteenth-Century Swedish Towns*, London/New York: Routledge.

Massey, D. (2015), *For Space*, London: SAGE.

Mitchell, P. (2018), 'The Development of the Apartment Building in 18th Century Vienna', in L. Thomas and J. Campbell (eds), *Buildings in Society: International Studies in the Historic Era*, 95–111, Oxford: Archaeopress, 2018.

Navickas, K. (2016), *Protest and the Politics of Space and Place, 1789-1848*, Manchester: Manchester University Press.

Pardailhé-Galabrun, A. (1991), *The Birth of Intimacy: Privacy and Domestic Life in Early Modern Paris*, trans. J. Phelps, Cambridge: Polity Press.

Parker Pearson, M. and C. Richards, eds (1994), *Architecture and Order: Approaches to Social Space*, London/New York: Routledge.

Paulsson, G. (1972), *Svensk stad*, Lund: Studentlitteratur.

Ponsonby, M. (2006), *Stories from Home: English Domestic Interiors, 1750-1850*, Burlington: Ashgate.

Rau, S. (2019), *History, Space, and Place*, trans. Michael Thomas Taylor, London/New York: Routledge.

Sarti, R. (2002), *Europe at Home: Family and Material Culture, 1500-1800*, trans. A. Cameron, New Haven/London: Yale University Press,

Schlögel, K. (2003). *Im Raume lesen wir die Zeit: Über Zivilisationsgeschichte und Geopolitik*, Munich/Vienna: Carl Hanser Verlag.

Sennett, R. (1977), *The Fall of Public Man*, Cambridge: Cambridge University Press.

Soja, E.W. (1996), *Thirdspace: Journeys to Los Angeles and Other Real-and-Imagined Places*, Oxford: Basil Blackwell.

Stobart, J., A. Hann and V. Morgan (2007), *Spaces of Consumption: Leisure and Shopping in the English Town, c. 1680-1830*, London/New York: Routledge.

Stock, P. (2015), 'History and the Uses of Space', in P. Stock (ed.), *The Uses of Space in Early Modern History*, 1–18, New York: Palgrave Macmillan.

Tageson, G. (2016), 'Hus, tomt och gård', in G. Tagesson and P. Carelli (eds), *Kalmar mellan dröm och verklighet. Konstruktionen av den tidigmoderna staden*, 162–201, Linköping: Arkeologerna, Statens historiska museer.

Tagesson, G. (2021a), (In print) *Äldre trähus i Linköping: En byggnadshistorisk inventering.* (Hus och hushåll i svenska städer 1600-1850. Rapport 3.), Linköping: Arkeologerna, Statens historiska museer.

Tagesson, G. (2021b), 'The Brilliant Idea of the Bookkeeper Johan Peter Frisk – a Micro-Historical Study', in A. Clemente, D. Lindström and J. Stobart (eds), *Micro-geographies of the Western City, c.1750-1900*, London/New York: Routledge.

Tagesson, G. and A. Nordström (2012), *Kvarteret Mästaren, Kalmar stad och kommun: särskild arkeologisk undersökning 2009*, Rapport 2012: 104, Linköping: Riksantikvarieämbetet, arkeologiska uppdragsverksamheten, UV Öst.

Tagesson, G. and A. Jeppsson (2015a), *Kakel och kakelugnar i fyra tidigmoderna städer: Rapport från ett forskningsprojekt 2012-2014*. Available online: https://www.academia.edu/12625052 (visited 31 March 2021).

Tagesson, G. and A. Jeppsson (2015b), 'Varmt och skönt – och iögonfallande modernt: Kakelugnar som social konsumtion i det tidigmoderna Sverige', *Fornvännen,* 110 (2): 111–25.

Tagesson, G. and A. Jeppsson (2016), 'Varm och skönt och iögonenfallande modernt', in G. Tagesson and P. Carelli (eds), *Kalmar mellan dröm och verklighet. Konstruktionen av den tidigmoderna staden,* 224–39, Linköping: Arkeologerna, Statens historiska museer.

Tagesson, G. and D. Lindström (2016), 'Onkel Adamsgården: Hus och miljö i förändring', in G. Mörkfors and A.L. Ek (eds), *Onkel Adam: Författaren och gården,* 135–55, Linköping: Östergötlands Museum.

Tagesson, G., D. Lindström, H. Linderson and M. Hallgren (2020a), *Hunnebergsgatan 5-7-9. En byggnadshistorisk studie,* (Hus och hushåll i svenska städer 1600–1850. Rapport 1), Linköping: Arkeologerna, Statens historiska museer. Available online: https://www.academia.edu/44510794 (visited 31 March 2021).

Tagesson, G., D. Lindström, M. Hallgren and H. Linderson (2020b), *Onkel Adamsgården. Hunnebergsgatan 30, Linköping: En byggnadshistorisk studie* (Hus och hushåll i svenska städer 1600–1850. Rapport 2), Linköping: Arkeologerna, Statens historiska museer. Available online: https://www.academia.edu/44510917 (visited 31 March 2021).

Tagesson, G., D. Lindström, M. Hallgren and H. Linderson (2020c), *Äldre trähus i friluftsmuseet Gamla Linköping. En byggnadshistorisk undersökning* (Hus och hushåll i svenska städer 1600–1850. Rapport 5), Linköping: Arkeologerna, Statens historiska museer. Available online: https://www.academia.edu/44510983 (visited 31 March 2021).

Tagesson, G., D. Lindström, J. Åkeson, H. Linderson and M. Hallgren (2020), *Fröken Löfgrens gård: En byggnadshistorisk undersökning* (Hus och hushåll i svenska städer 1600–1850. Rapport 4), Linköping: Arkeologerna, Statens historiska museer. Available online: https://www.academia.edu/44510956 (visited 31 March 2021).

Tilley, C. (1994), *A Phenomenology of Landscape: Places, Paths and Monuments,* Oxford: Berg.

Thomasson, J. (1997), 'Private Life Made Public. One Aspect of the Emergence of the Burghers in Medieval Denmark', in H. Andersson, P. Carelli and L. Ersgård (eds), *Visions of the Past: Trends and Tradition in Swedish Medieval Archaeology,* Stockholm: Riksantikvarieämbetet.

Trigger, B. (1989), *A History of Archaeological Thought,* Cambridge: Cambridge University Press.

van den Heuvel, D. (2019), 'Gender in the Streets of the Pre-Modern City', *Journal of Urban History,* 45 (4): 693–710.

Vickery, A. (2008), *Behind Closed Doors: At Home in Georgian England,* New Haven/ London: Yale University Press.

Chapter 8

Adresseavisen (Kiøbenhavns Kongelig alene priviligerede Adresse-Contoirs Efterretninger) (1759–1789). Available online: http://www2.statsbiblioteket.dk/ mediestream/ (accessed 23 October 2020).

Alstrup, K. (2019), 'Ligning med ubekendte, Det 1. Christiansborg og dets interiørers plads i stiludvikling og indretning 1740-94', *1700-tal,* 16: 44–78.

Becker, A. (2014), 'Jean Bodin on Oeconomics and Politics', *History of European Ideas,* 40 (2): 135–54.

Becker, A. (2017), 'Gender in Political Thought', *The Historical Journal*, 60 (4): 843–63.

Becker, J.G.B., ed. (1870), *Anna Christine Beckers Dagbog*, Copenhagen: E.C. Løsers Bog og Nodetrykkeri.

Bode, A.M. (1796), *Den erfarne rådgiverinde for huslige fruentimmere eller anvisning til vigtige kundskaber og fordele i husholdningen*, Copenhagen: A. Goldins Forlag hos Zacharigs Breum.

Boritz, M. (2000), 'Anne Christine Beckers dagbog 1787–1790: Ideal og praksis i borgerskabskvindernes liv', *Fortid og Nutid*, 4: 251–70.

Bregnhøi, L. (2010), *Det malede Rum: Materialer, teknikker og dekoration 1790–1900*, Copenhagen: Historismus.

Clemmesen, T. (1984), *Skæbner og Interiører: Danske tegninger fra barok til klunketid*, Copenhagen: Nationalmuseet.

Clemmensen, T. and H. Raabyemagle (1996), *Brede Hovedbygning 1795–1806*, Copenhagen: Nationalmuseet.

Deutzner, J.H. (1891), *Henrik Stampe: Meddelelser om hans Liv og hans Virksomhed*, Copenhagen: Københavns Universitet.

Gold, C. (2015), 'Women in Business in the Late Eighteenth-Century-Copenhagen Luxury Trades', in D. Simonton, M. Kaartinen and A. Montenach (eds), *Luxury and Gender in European Towns 1700–1914*, 57–73, Oxford: Routledge.

Gold, C. (2018), *Women in Business in Early Modern Copenhagen 1740–1835*, Copenhagen: Museum Tusculanum.

Habermas, J. (1991), *The Structural Transformation and the Public Sphere*, Cambridge, MA: MIT Press.

Hein, L. (2016), 'Det store Havehus ved Hirschholm Slot', in *Alle tideres Nordsjælland*, 35–50, Hillerød: Museum Nordsjællands årbog.

Jørgensen, J. (1968), *Skifter og testamenter*, Copenhagen: Dansk historisk Fællesforenings Håndbøger.

Kennaway, J. and R. Knoeff, eds (2020), 'For It Is the Debilitating Fibres That Exercise Restores ': Movement, Morality and Moderation in Eighteenth-century Medical Advice Literature', in *Lifestyle and Medicine in the Enlightenment the Six Non-naturals in the Long Eighteenth Century*, 111–38, New York: Routledge.

Kiøbenhavnske Danske Post-Tidender (1749–1762). Available online: http://www2. statsbibliotekct.dk/mediestream/ (accessed 23 October 2020).

Knudsen, H. (1945), 'Bygningshistoriske Brandforsikringsarkivalier', *Fortid og Nutid*, Ser 1, 16: 201–11.

Lyngby, T. (2007–8), ' Decorum og Commodité: Aristokratiets fornemme boliger I 1700-årenes København', in P. Henningsen (ed.), *Miraklernes tid og andre fortællinger om livet i 1700-tallets København*, 63–94, Copenhagen: Københavnsk Stadsarkiv.

Lyngby, T. (2015), *Måder at bo på: Indretning, liv, stemninger og bevidsthedsformer i danske overklasseboliger i byen 1570–1870*, vol. 1. Hillerød: Studier fra Det Nationalhistoriske Museum på Frederiksborg.

Mckeon, M. (2005), *The Secret History of Domensticity: Public, Private and Division of Knowledge*, Baltimore: The Johns Hopkins University Press.

Mellemgaard, S. (1995), 'Den daglige fare', *Folk og Kultur, årbog for Dansk Etnologi Og Folkemindevidenskab*, 24 (1): 5–21.

Anonym (1777), *Moderne i København for begge køn og værelsers møblering efter moden for året 1777*, Copenhagen: August Friderich Stein.

Nielsen, N.K. (2003), 'Nationalisme, disciplin og folkelighed i 1800-tallets Danmark', *Grundtvig-Studier*, 54 (1): 45–64.

Nystrøm, E. (publ.) (1930), *Bolle Willum Luxdorphs dagbøger bind 1–2*, Copenhagen: Gad.
Nørregaard, L. (1791), *Forelæsninger over den danske og norske Privatret*, vol. 1, Copenhagen: Gyldendal.
Pedersen, M.V. (2013), *Luksus. Forbrug og kolonier I Danmark i det 18. århundrede*, Copenhagen: Museum Tusculanum.
Schou, J. (1777–1825), *Chronologisk Register over de Kongelige Forordninger og Aabne Breve samt andre trykte Anordninger, som fra Aar 1670 ere udkomne*, København: Gyldendal.
Shepard, A. (2015), 'Minding Their Own Business: Married Women and Credit in Early Eighteenth-century London', *Royal Historical Society*, 25: 53–74.
Skak-Nielsen, L. (2017), *Det påklædte hjem: Tekstiler og boligkultur i Danmark gennem 300 år*, Copenhagen: Historismus.
Steenberg, J. (1945), 'Sankt Petri Kirke', *Danmarks Kirker I*, Copenhagen: Nationalmuseet.
Strøm, E. (2006), *Naturhistorie-Selskabet i København 1789–1804*, Oslo: Universitetet i Oslo.
Thurah, L. de (1746), *Den danske Vitruvius*, vol. I, tab. CXIX, Copenhagen:Ernst Henrich Berlings bogtrykkeri.
Tønnesen, A. (1981), 'Et hus I Amaliegade', *Historiske meddelelser om København*, 35–83.
Vickery, A. (2009), *Behind Closed Doors: At Home in Georgian England*, New Hampshire: Yale University Press.
Vincent, D. (2016), Privacy a Short History, Cambridge: Polity Press.

The Danish National Archive (DNA)

Københavns Stadsarkiv
Danske Kancelli (1749–1750), *Sjællandske Registre*.
Københavns Brandforsikring, vurderingsforretninger over ejendomme, mat. no. 239–243B, Vester Kvarter. Police no. 3473 (1779/1797). (Police no. 3473)
Københavns Byret (1759–1818), *Tinglysningsafdeling, Pante- og brevskriverkontorets 1. Afdeling, Realregister, Øster kvarter matrikelnummer 36.*
Landsover- samt Hof- og Stadsretten (1790–1979), *Københavns Skiftekommission, Eksekutorboer, nr. 13 14 (Eks.bo 13 14).*
Rentekammeret (1787), *Folketælling, København, Strandens Kvarter, Bag børsen 96.*Sankt Petri Tyske Kirke (1728–1799), *Enesteministerielbøger.*
Stampe-familiens privatarkiv (1742–1804), *B2, Dokumenter vedr. eksekutorskiftet (Private Archive B2).*
Silke-, ulden- og lærredskræmmerlavet (1718–1739), *Lavsprotokol.*

Chapter 9

Ekirch, A.R. (2005), *At Day's Close: A History of Nighttime*, London: Phoenix.
Hansen, H. (1916–23), *Kabinetsstyrelsen i Danmark 1768–1772: Aktstykker og Oplysninger*, II, Copenhagen: Rigsarkivet.
Henningsen, P and U. Langen (2010), *Hundemordet i Vimmelskaftet – og andre fortællinger fra 1700-tallets København*, Copenhagen: Politikens Forlag.
Heuvel, D.v.d. (2019), 'Gender in the Streets of the Premodern City', *Journal of Urban History*, 45 (4): 693–710.

Horstbøll, H., U. Langen and F. Stjernfelt (2020), *Grov konfækt: Tre vilde år med trykkefrihed 1770–1773*, II, Copenhagen: Gyldendal.

Jacobsen, A.F. (2008), *Husbondret: Rettighedskulturer i Danmark 1750–1920*, Copenhagen: Museum Tusculanum Press.

Kiøbenhavns Politiske Veyviser (1773), København: Adressekontoret.

Klein, L.E. (1995), 'Gender and the Public/Private Distinction in the Eighteenth Century: Some Questions about Evidence and Analytic Procedure', *Eighteenth-Century Studies*, 29 (1): 97–109.

Koch, H. (1982), 'Politimyndighedens oprindelse (1681–1684): Organisation og beføjelser', *Historisk Tidsskrift*, 82 (1): 27–56.

Koefoed, N.J. (2017), 'Regulating Eighteenth Century Households: Offences against the Fourth and the Six Commandments as Criminal Behaviour', in T. Krogh, L.N. Kallestrup and C.B. Christensen (eds), *Cultural Histories of Crime in Denmark, 1500–2000*, 57–74, London: Routledge.

Kolderup Rosenvinge, J.L.A. (1828), *Grundrids af den danske Politiret*, Copenhagen: Gyldendal.

Koslofsky, C. (2011), *Evening's Empire: A History of the Night in Early Modern Europe*, Cambridge: Cambridge University Press.

Kotkas, T. (2013), *Royal Police Ordinances in Early Modern Sweden: The Emergence of Voluntaristic Understanding of Law*, Leiden: Brill.

Langen, U. (2020) 'Representing a Disreputable House', in D. Linström and J. Stobart (eds), *Micro-geographies of the Western City, c. 1750–1900*, London: Routledge.

Munck, T. (2007), 'Keeping the Peace: "Good Police" and the Civic Order in 18th-century Copenhagen', *Scandinavian Journal of History*, 32 (1): 38–62.

Mührmann-Lund, J. (2011), *Borgerligt regimente*, unpublished PhD Thesis, Aarhus.

Mührmann-Lund, J. (2015), 'Politinatten', in P. Duedahl and U. Langen (eds), *Nattens gerninger*, Copenhagen: Gads Forlag.

Mührmann-Lund, J. (2016), 'Good Order and Police: Policing in the Towns and the Countryside during Danish Absolutism (1660–1800)', *Scandinavian Journal of History*, 41 (1): 70–90.

Rau, S. (2007), 'Public Order in Public Space: Tavern Conflict in Early Modern Lyon', *Urban History*, 34 (1): 102–13.

Rudé, G. (1971), *Paris and London in the Eighteenth Century: Studies in Popular Protest*, New York: The Viking Press.

Sandfærdig Beskrivelse over De betydelige Forandringer og mærkværdige Ttildragelser i Kiøbenhavn Fredagen den 17 Jan. 1772 (no year of publication).

Sennefelt, K. (2008), 'Social and Political Thresholds in Stockholm, c. 1720–1770', *Urban History*, 35 (2): 185–201.

Stevnsborg, H. (1980), 'Fra Den store Udfejelsesfest til Tømrerstrejken: Om før-industriel, folkelig protest i København i sidste halvdel af det 18. århundrede', *Fortid og Nutid – tidsskrift for kulturhistorie og lokalhistorie*, 28: 570–99.

Stevnsborg, H. (1998), 'Medicinen, der var værre end sygdommen: Om boligens ikrænkelighed 1771–1772', in J. Vestergaard, F. Balvig and V. Greve (eds), *Med lov … : Retsvidenskabelige betragtninger i anledning af professor Vagn Greves 60 års fødselsdag*, 247–56, Copenhagen: Jurist- og Økonomforbundet.

Shoemaker, R.B. (2003), 'Public Spaces, Public Dispute? Fights and Insults on London's Streets 1660–1800', in T. Hitchcock and H. Shore (eds), *The Streets of London: From the Great Fire to the Great Stink*, 54–68, London: Rivers Oram Press.

Suhm, P.F. (1918), *Hemmelige Efterretninger om de danske Konger efter Souverainiteten*, Copenhagen: H. Hagerups Forlag.
Suhm, P.F. (1772), *Til mine Landsmænd og Medborgere. De Danske, Norske og Holstenere*, Copenhagen: Stein.
Trier, C.A. (1916), *Ulrik Adolf Holstein (1731–1789): Studier over den oplyste Enevældes første Dage i Danmark*, Copenhagen: Reitzel.
Trier, H. (1905), *Revolutionen i Raadstuen april 1771: Aktstykker fra Struensee-Tiden vedrørende Staden Københavns Styrelse*, Copenhagen: Schultz.

Chapter 10

Agamben, G. (1998), *Homo Sacer: Sovereign Power and Bare Life*, Stanford: Stanford University Press.
Ågren, M. (2006), 'Hemligt eller offentligt? Om kön, egendom och offentlighet i 1700-talets Sverige', *Historisk tidskrift*, 126 (1): 23–45.
Aronsson, P. (1992), *Bönder gör politik: Det lokala självstyret som social arena i tre Smålandssocknar, 1680–1850*, Lund: Lund University Press.
Assman, A. and J. Assman (1997), 'Das Geheimnis und die Archäologie der literarischen Kommunikation: Einführende Bemerkungen', in A. Assman and J. Assman (eds), *Schleier und Schwelle: Band 1 Geheimnis und Öffentlichkeit*, 7–16, München: Wilhelm Fink Verlag.
Bawden, T. (2014), *Die Schwelle im Mittelalter: Bildmotiv und Bildort*, Köln: Böhlau Verlag.
Cavallin, M. (2003), *I kungens och folkets tjänst: Synen på den svenske ämbetsmannen 1750–1780*, Gothenburg: Department of Historical Studies, University of Gothenburg.
Christopher of Bavaria's Law of the Realm, in C. J. Schlyter (eds) (1869), *Corpus iuris sueo-gotorum antiqui: Samling av Sweriges gamla lagar, vol. 12*, Lund: Berlingska boktryckeriet.
Cohen, E. S. (2008), 'To Pray, to Work, to Hear, to Speak: Women in Roman Streets c. 1600', *Journal of Early Modern History*, 12 (3–4): 289–311.
Durand, S. (2017), 'Corruption and Anticorruption in France between the 1670s and the 1780s', in R. Kroeze, A. Vitória and G. Geltner (eds), *Anti-Corruption in History: From Antiquity to the Modern Era*, 153–64, Oxford: Oxford University Press.
Edvinsson, R. and J. Söderberg (2011), 'A Consumer Price Index for Sweden, 1290–2008', *Review of Income and Wealth*, 57 (2): 270–92.
Engström, A. (2019), *Olikhetens praktiker: Adlig begravningskultur i Sverige ca 1630–1680*, Uppsala: Department of Historical Studies, Uppsala University.
Ericsson, P. (2013), 'Mordet på fogden Warenberg: Våldsam interaktion mellan stat och lokalsamhälle i Karl XII:s Sverige', in P. Ericsson, F. Thisner, P. Winton and A. Åkerlund (eds), *Allt på ett bräde: Stat, ekonomi och bondeoffer*, 257–69, Uppsala: Department of Historical Studies, Uppsala University.
Frisk Jensen, M. (2017), 'Statebuilding, Establishing Rule of Law and Fighting Corruption in Denmark, 1660–1900', in R. Kroeze, A. Vitória and G. Geltner (eds), *Anti-Corruption in History: From Antiquity to the Modern Era*, 197–210, Oxford: Oxford University Press.
Frohnert, P. (1993), *Kronans skatter och bondens bröd: Den lokala förvaltningen och bönderna i Sverige 1719–1775*, Lund: Nerenius & Santérus Förlag.
Gowing, L. (2000), '"The Freedom of the Streets": Women and Social Space, 1560–1640', in P. Griffiths and M. S. R. Jenner (eds), *Londinopolis: Essays in the Cultural and Social History of Early Modern London*, 130–52, Manchester: Manchester University Press.

Haikari, J. (2017), 'The Bailiff: Between a Rock and a Hard Place (1600–1690)?' in P. Karonen and M. Hakanen (eds), *Personal Agency at the Swedish Age of Greatness 1560–1720*, 165–90, Helsinki: The Finnish Literature Society.

Hallenberg, M. and M. Linnarsson (2016), 'Vem tar bäst hand om det allmänna? Politiska konflikter om privata och offentliga utövare 1720–1860', *Historisk tidskrift*, 136 (1): 32–63.

van der Heijden, M. and S. Muurling (2018), ' Violence and Gender in Eighteenth-Century Bologna and Rotterdam', *Journal of Social History*, 51 (4): 695–716.

van den Heuvel, D. (2019), 'Gender in the Streets of the Premodern City', *Journal of Urban History*, 45 (4): 693–710.

Jacobs, L. F. (2018), *Thresholds and Boundaries: Liminality in Netherlandish Art (1385–1530)*, New York: Routledge.

Justitz, G. (2002), 'Reforming Space, Reordering Reality: Naumburg's Herren Gasse in the 1540s', *The Sixteenth Century Journal*, 33 (3): 625–48.

Jütte, D. (2015), *The Strait Gate: Thresholds and Power in Western History*, New Haven: Yale University Press.

Katajala, K. (2004), 'Conclusions: Peasant Unrest and Political Culture', in K. Katajala (ed), *Northern Revolts: Medieval and Early Modern Peasant Unrest in the Nordic Countries*, 258–69, Helsinki: Finnish Literature Society.

Katajala, K. (2009), 'En för alla, alla för en: Upproret i Tohmajärvi 1679', *Karolinska förbundets årsbok*: 163–91.

Kepsu, K. (2017), 'The Unruly Buffer Zone: The Swedish Province of Ingria in the Late 17th Century', *Scandinavian Journal of History*, 42 (4): 414–38.

Knights, M. (2017), 'Anticorruption in Seventeenth- and Eighteenth-century Britain', in R. Kroeze, A. Vitória and G. Geltner (eds), *Anti-Corruption in History: From Antiquity to the Modern Era*, 181–96, Oxford: Oxford University Press.

Laitinen, R. (2017), 'Home, Urban Space and Gendered Practices in Mid-Seventeenth-Century Turku', in D. Simonton (ed.), *The Routledge History Handbook of Gender and the Urban Experience*, 142–52, New York: Routledge.

Laitinen, R. and D. Lindström (2008), 'Urban Order and Street Regulation in Seventeenth-Century Sweden', *Journal of Early Modern History*, 12 (3–4): 257–87.

Lennersand, M. (1999), *Rättvisans och allmogens beskyddare: Den absoluta staten, kommissionerna och tjänstemännen, ca. 1680–1730*, Uppsala: Acta Universitatis Upsaliensis.

Lindegren, J. (1992), 'Ökade ekonomiska krav och offentliga bördor 1550–1750', in H. Winge (ed.), *Lokalsamfunn og øvrighet i Norden ca. 1550–1750*, 189–202, Oslo: Norsk lokalhistorisk institutt.

Lindström, J. and J. Mispelaere (2015), 'Vad fick 1600-talets arbetare i lön?' *Historisk tidskrift*, 135 (3): 432–63.

Linnarsson, M. (2017), *Problemet med vinster: Riksdagsdebatter om privat och offentlig drift under 400 år*, Lund: Nordic Academic Press.

Linnarsson, M. (2017), 'Farming Out State Revenue: The Debate about the General Customs Lease Company in Sweden, 1723–65', *Parliaments, Estates and Representations*, 38 (2): 175–91.

Lipscomb, S. (2011), 'Crossing Boundaries: Women's Gossip, Insults and Violence in Sixteenth-Century France', *French History*, 25 (4): 408–26.

Muurling, S. and M. Pluskota (2017), 'The Gendered Geography of Violence in Bologna, Seventeenth to Nineteenth Centuries', in D. Simonton (ed.), *The Routledge History Handbook of Gender and the Urban Experience*, 153–63, New York: Routledge.

Nilsson, S. A. (1990), *De stora krigens tid: Om Sverige som militärstat och bondesamhälle*, Uppsala: Department of Historical Studies, Uppsala University.

Nussdorfer, L. (1997), 'The Politics of Space in Early Modern Rome', *Memoirs of the American Academy in Rome*, 42: 161–86.

Roessler, B. (2016), 'Privacy and/in the Public Sphere', *Yearbook for Eastern and Western Philosophy*, 1: 243–56.

Roessler, B. and D. Mokrosinska (2013), 'Privacy and Social Interaction', *Philosophy and Social Criticism*, 39 (8): 771–91.

Scribner, R. (1992), 'Symbolising Boundaries: Defining Social Space in the Daily Life of Early Modern Germany', in G. Blaschitz (ed.), *Symbole des Alltags, Alltag der Symbole: Festschrift für Harry Kühnel zum 65. Geburtstag*, 821–41, Graz: Akademisxhe Druck.

Shapin, S. (1994), *A Social History of Truth: Civility and Science in Seventeenth-Century England*, Chicago: The University of Chicago Press.

Simmel, G. ([1909] 1994), 'Bridge and Door', *Theory, Culture & Society*, 11: 5–10.

Snyder, J. R. (2009), *Dissimulation and the Culture of Secrecy in Early Modern Europe*, Berkeley, CA: University of California Press.

Stille, A. (1903), *Kriget i Skåne 1709–1710*, Stockholm: Militärlitteraturföreningens förlag.

Sundin, J. (1992), *För Gud, staten och folket: Brott och rättskipning i Sverige 1600–1840*, Stockholm: Institutet för rättshistorisk forskning.

Williamson, F. (2015), 'Space and the City: Gender Identities in the Seventeenth Century', *Cultural and Social History*, 9 (2): 169–85.

Villstrand, N. E. (1992), *Anpassning eller protest: Lokalsamhället inför utskrivningarna av fotfolk till den svenska krigsmakten 1620–1679*, Åbo: Åbo akademi.

Österberg, E. (1989), 'Bönder och centralmakt i det tidigmoderna Sverige: Konflikt – kompromiss – politisk kultur', *Scandia*, 55 (1): 73–95.

The Swedish National Archive (SNA)

- Skrivelser till Kungl. Maj:t, Landshövdingen i Skaraborgs län, vol. 20 (1709–1711)
- Äldre kommittéer (ÄK) ('Older Commissions') vol. 44.

Index